Euclid's Elements of Geometry...

1871
P871E
Bks 1-6
OTC

THE SCHOOL EDITION.

EUCLID'S ELEMENTS OF GEOMETRY,

THE FIRST SIX BOOKS,

CHIEFLY FROM THE TEXT OF DR. SIMSON,

WITH

EXPLANATORY NOTES;

A Series of Questions on each Book;

AND

A SELECTION OF GEOMETRICAL EXERCISES FROM THE SENATE-HOUSE AND COLLEGE EXAMINATION PAPERS;
WITH HINTS, ETC.

DESIGNED FOR THE USE OF THE JUNIOR CLASSES IN PUBLIC AND PRIVATE SCHOOLS.

BY

ROBERT POTTS, M.A.,

TRINITY COLLEGE.

CORRECTED AND IMPROVED.

NEW YORK:
JOHN F. TROW, PRINTER, 50 GREENE STREET.
1871.

CONTENTS.

PREFACE to the Third Edition...................................	iii
First Book of the Elements..	1
Notes to the First Book..	42
Questions on the First Book......................................	59
On the Ancient Geometrical Analysis.........................	64
Geometrical Exercises on Book I................................	69
Second Book of the Elements....................................	85
Notes to the Second Book...	99
Note on the Algebraical Symbols and Abbreviations used in Geometry.	109
Questions on the Second Book..................................	110
Geometrical Exercises on Book II..............................	113
Third Book of the Elements......................................	120
Notes to the Third Book...	153
Questions on the Third Book....................................	157
Geometrical Exercises on Book III.............................	160
Fourth Book of the Elements.....................................	175
Notes to the Fourth Book..	190
Questions on the Fourth Book...................................	193
Geometrical Exercises on Book IV..............................	196
Fifth Book of the Elements..	204
Notes to the Fifth Book..	235
Questions on the Fifth Book......................................	257
Sixth Book of the Elements.......................................	259
Notes to the Sixth Book..	294
Questions on the Sixth Book.....................................	299
Geometrical Exercises on Book VI.............................	302
Solutions, Hints, &c. on Book I..................................	313
" " " II...	323
" " " III..	326
" " " IV..	338
" " " VI..	345
Index to the Geometrical Exercises............................	356

PREFACE TO THE THIRD EDITION.

Some time after the publication of an Octavo Edition of Euclid's Elements with Geometrical Exercises, &c., designed for the use of Academical Students, at the request of some schoolmasters of eminence, a duodecimo Edition of the Six Books was put forth on the same plan for the use of Schools. Soon after its appearance, Professor Christie, the Secretary of the Royal Society, in the Preface to his Treatise on Descriptive Geometry for the use of the Royal Military Academy, was pleased to notice these works in the following terms:—"When the greater Portion of this Part of the Course was printed, and had for some time been in use in the Academy, a new Edition of Euclid's Elements, by Mr Robert Potts, M. A., of Trinity College, Cambridge, which is likely to supersede most others, to the extent, at least, of the Six Books, was published. From the manner of arranging the Demonstrations, this edition has the advantages of the symbolical form, and it is at the same time free from the manifold objections to which that form is open. The duodecimo edition of this Work, comprising only the first Six Books of Euclid, with Deductions from them, having been introduced at this Institution as a text book, now renders any other Treatise on Plane Geometry unnecessary in our course of Mathematics."

For the very favourable reception which both Editions have met with, the Editor's grateful acknowledgements are due. It has been his desire in putting forth a revised Edition of the School Euclid, to render the work in some degree more worthy of the favour which the former editions have received. In the present Edition several errors and oversights have been corrected, and some additions made to the notes the questions on each book have been considerably augmented and a better arrangement of the Geometrical Exercises has been attempted: and lastly, some hints and remarks on them have been given to assist the learner. The additions made to the present Edition amount to more than fifty pages, and it is hoped that they will render the work more useful to the learner.

And here an occasion may be taken to quote the opinions of some able men respecting the use and importance of the Mathematical Sciences.

On the subject of Education in its most extensive sense, an ancient writer "directs the aspirant after excellence to commence with the Science of Moral Culture, to proceed next to Logic; next to Mathematics; next to Physics; and lastly, to Theology." Another writer on Education would place Mathematics before Logic, which (he remarks) "seems the preferable course: for by practising itself in the former, the mind becomes stored with distinctions; the faculties of constancy and firmness are established; and its rule is always to distinguish between cavilling and investigation—between *close reasoning* and *cross reasoning;* for the contrary of all which habits, those are for the most part noted, who apply themselves to Logic without studying in some department of Mathematics; taking noise and wrangling for proficiency, and thinking refutation accomplished by the instancing of a doubt. This will explain the inscription placed by Plato over the door of his house: 'Whoso knows not Geometry, let him not enter here.' On the precedence of Moral Culture, however, to all the other Sciences, the acknowledgement is general, and the agreement entire." The same writer recommends the study of the Mathematics, for the cure of "compound ignorance." "Of this," he proceeds to say, "the essence is opinion not agreeable to fact; and it necessarily involves another opinion, namely, that we are already possessed of knowledge. So that besides not knowing, we know not that we know not; and hence its designation of compound ignorance. In like manner, as of many chronic complaints, and established maladies, no cure can be effected by physicians of the body: of this, no cure can be effected by physicians of the mind: for with a pre-supposal of knowledge in our own regard, the pursuit and acquirement of further knowledge is not to be looked for. The approximate cure, and one from which in the main much benefit may be anticipated, is to engage the patient in the study of measures (Geometry, computation, &c.); for in such pursuits the true and the false are separated by the clearest interval, and no room is left for the intrusions of fancy. From these the mind may discover the delight of certainty; and when, on returning to his own opinions, it finds in them no such sort of repose and gratification, it may discover their erroneous character, its ignorance may become simple, and a capacity for the acquirement of truth and virtue be obtained."

Lord Bacon, the founder of Inductive Philosophy, was not insensible of the high importance of the Mathematical Sciences, as appears in the following passage from his work on "The Advancement of Learning."

"The Mathematics are either pure or mixed. To the pure Mathematics are those sciences belonging which handle quantity determinate, merely severed from any axioms of natural philosophy; and these are two, Geometry, and Arithmetic; the one handling quantity continued, and the other dissevered. Mixed hath for subject some axioms or parts of natural philosophy, and considereth quantity determined, as it is auxiliary and incident unto them. For many parts of nature can neither be invented with sufficient subtlety, nor demonstrated with sufficient perspicuity, nor accommodated unto use with sufficient dexterity, without the aid and intervening of the Mathematics; of which sort are perspective, music, astronomy, cosmography, architecture, enginery, and divers others.

"In the Mathematics I can report no deficience, except it be that men do not sufficiently understand the excellent use of the pure Mathematics, in that they do remedy and cure many defects in the wit and faculties intellectual. For, if the wit be dull, they sharpen it, if too wandering, they fix it; if too inherent in the sense, they abstract it. So that as tennis is a game of no use in itself, but of great use in respect that it maketh a quick eye, and a body ready to put itself into all postures; so in the Mathematics, that use which is collateral and intervenient, is no less worthy than that which is principal and intended. And as for the mixed Mathematics, I may only make this prediction, that there cannot fail to be more kinds of them, as nature grows further disclosed."

How truly has this prediction been fulfilled in the subsequent advancement of the Mixed Sciences, and in the applications of the pure Mathematics to Natural Philosophy!

Dr. Whewell, in his "Thoughts on the Study of Mathematics," has maintained, that mathematical studies judiciously pursued, form one of the most effective means of developing and cultivating the reason: and that "the object of a *liberal education* is to develope the whole mental system of man,—to make his speculative inferences coincide with his practical convictions;—to enable him to render a reason for the belief that is in him, and not to leave him in the condition of Solomon's sluggard, who is wiser in his own conceit than seven men that *can* render a reason." And in his more recent work entitled, "Of a Liberal Education, &c." he has more fully shewn the importance of Geometry as one of the most effectual instruments of intellectual education. In page 55 he thus proceeds —"But besides the value of Mathematical Studies in Education, as a perfect example and complete exercise of demonstrative reasoning; Mathematical Truths have this additional recommendation, that they have always been referred to, by each successive generation of thoughtful and cultivated men, as examples of truth and of demonstration; and have thus become standard points of reference, among cultivated men, whenever they speak of truth, knowledge, or proof. Thus Mathematics has not only a disciplinal but an historical interest. This is peculiarly the case with those portions of Mathematics which we have mentioned. We find geometrical proof adduced in illustration of the nature of reasoning, in the earliest speculations on this subject, the Dialogues of Plato; we find geometrical proof one of the main subjects of discussion in some of the most recent of such speculations, as those of Dugald Stewart and his contemporaries. The recollection of the truths of Elementary Geometry has, in all ages, given a meaning and a reality to the best attempts to explain man's power of arriving at truth. Other branches of Mathematics have, in like manner, become recognized examples, among educated men, of man's powers of attaining truth."

Dr Pemberton, in the preface to his view of Sir Isaac Newton's Discoveries, makes mention of the circumstance, "that Newton used to speak with regret of his mistake, at the beginning of his Mathematical Studies, in having applied himself to the works of Descartes and other Algebraical writers, before he had considered the Elements of Euclid with the attention they deserve."

To these we may subjoin the opinion of Mr. John Stuart Mill, which he has recorded in his invaluable System of Logic, (Vol. II. p. 180,) in the following terms:—"The value of Mathematical instruction as a preparation for those more difficult investigations, (physiology, society, government, &c.,) consists in the applicability not of its doctrines, but of its method. Mathematics will ever remain the most perfect type of the Deductive Method in general; and the applications of Mathematics to the simpler branches of physics, furnish the only school in which philosophers can effectually learn the most difficult and important portion of their art, the employment of the laws of simpler phenomena for explaining and predicting those of the more complex. These grounds are quite sufficient for deeming mathematical training an indispensable basis of real scientific education, and regarding, with Plato, one who is ἀγεωμέτρητος, as wanting in one of the most essential qualifications for the successful cultivation of the higher branches of philosophy."

In addition to these authorities it may be remarked, that the new Regulations which were confirmed by a Grace of the Senate on the 11th of May, 1846, assign to Geometry and to Geometrical methods, a more important place in the Examinations both for Honors and for the Ordinary Degree in this University.

TRINITY COLLEGE, R. P.
March 1, 1850.

This Edition (the fifth) has been augmented by about fifty pages of additional Notes, Questions, and Geometrical Exercises.

TRINITY COLLEGE, R. P.
November 5, 1859.

EUCLID'S
ELEMENTS OF GEOMETRY.

BOOK I.

DEFINITIONS.

I.
A POINT is that which has no parts, or which has no magnitude.

II.
A line is length without breadth.

III.
The extremities of a line are points.

IV.
A straight line is that which lies evenly between its extreme points.

V.
A superficies is that which has only length and breadth.

VI.
The extremities of a superficies are lines.

VII.
A plane superficies is that in which any two points being taken, the straight line between them lies wholly in that superficies.

VIII.
A plane angle is the inclination of two lines to each other in a plane, which meet together, but are not in the same straight line.

IX.
A plane rectilineal angle is the inclination of two straight lines to one another, which meet together, but are not in the same straight line.

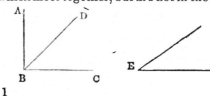

N.B. If there be only one angle at a point, it may be expressed by a letter placed at that point, as the angle at E: but when several angles are at one point B, either of them is expressed by three letters, of which the letter that is at the vertex of the angle, that is, at the point in which the straight lines that contain the angle meet one another, is put between the other two letters, and one of these two is somewhere upon one of these straight lines, and the other upon the other line. Thus the angle which is contained by the straight lines AB, CB, is named the angle ABC, or CBA; that which is contained by AB, DB, is named the angle ABD, or DBA; and that which is contained by DB, CB, is called the angle DBC, or CBD.

X.

When a straight line standing on another straight line, makes the adjacent angles equal to one another, each of these angles is called a right angle; and the straight line which stands on the other is called a perpendicular to it.

XI.

An obtuse angle is that which is greater than a right angle.

XII.

An acute angle is that which is less than a right angle.

XIII.

A term or boundary is the extremity of any thing.

XIV.

A figure is that which is enclosed by one or more boundaries

XV.

A circle is a plane figure contained by one line, which is called the circumference, and is such that all straight lines drawn from a certain point within the figure to the circumference, are equal to one another.

XVI.

And this point is called the center of the circle.

XVII.

A diameter of a circle is a straight line drawn through the center, and terminated both ways by the circumference.

XVIII.

A semicircle is the figure contained by a diameter and the part of the circumference cut off by the diameter.

XIX.

The center of a semicircle is the same with that of the circle.

XX.

Rectilineal figures are those which are contained by straight lines.

XXI.

Trilateral figures, or triangles, by three straight lines.

XXII.

Quadrilateral, by four straight lines.

XXIII.

Multilateral figures, or polygons, by more than four straight lines.

XXIV.

Of three-sided figures, an equilateral triangle is that which has three equal sides.

XXV.

An isosceles triangle is that which has two sides equal.

XXVI.

A scalene triangle is that which has three unequal sides.

XXVII.

A right-angled triangle is that which has a right angle.

XXVIII.

An obtuse-angled triangle is that which has an obtuse angle.

XXIX.

An acute-angled triangle is that which has three acute angles.

XXX.

Of quadrilateral or four-sided figures, a square has all its sides equal and all its angles right angles.

DEFINITIONS.

XXXI.

An oblong is that which has all its angles right angles, but has not all its sides equal.

XXXII.

A rhombus has all its sides equal, but its angles are not right angles.

XXXIII.

A rhomboid has its opposite sides equal to each other, but all its sides are not equal, nor its angles right angles.

XXXIV.

All other four-sided figures besides these, are called Trapeziums.

XXXV.

Parallel straight lines are such as are in the same plane, and which being produced ever so far both ways, do not meet.

A.

A parallelogram is a four-sided figure, of which the opposite sides are parallel: and the diameter, or the diagonal is the straight line joining two of its opposite angles.

POSTULATES.

I.

Let it be granted that a straight line may be drawn from any one point to any other point.

II.

That a terminated straight line may be produced to any length in a straight line.

III.

And that a circle may be described from any center, at any distance from that center.

AXIOMS.

I.
Things which are equal to the same thing are equal to one another.

II.
If equals be added to equals, the wholes are equal.

III.
If equals be taken from equals, the remainders are equal.

IV.
If equals be added to unequals, the wholes are unequal.

V.
If equals be taken from unequals, the remainders are unequal.

VI.
Things which are double of the same, are equal to one another.

VII.
Things which are halves of the same, are equal to one another.

VIII.
Magnitudes which coincide with one another, that is, which exactly fill the same space, are equal to one another.

IX.
The whole is greater than its part.

X.
Two straight lines cannot enclose a space.

XI.
All right angles are equal to one another.

XII.
If a straight line meets two straight lines, so as to make the two interior angles on the same side of it taken together less than two right angles, these straight lines being continually produced, shall at length meet upon that side on which are the angles which are less than two right angles.

PROPOSITION I. PROBLEM.

To describe an equilateral triangle upon a given finite straight line.

Let AB be the given straight line.
It is required to describe an equilateral triangle upon AB.

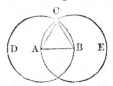

From the center A, at the distance AB, describe the circle BCD; (post. 3.)
from the center B, at the distance BA, describe the circle ACE;
and from C, one of the points in which the circles cut one another, draw the straight lines CA, CB to the points A, B. (post. 1.)
Then ABC shall be an equilateral triangle.
Because the point A is the center of the circle BCD,
therefore AC is equal to AB; (def. 15.)
and because the point B is the center of the circle ACE,
therefore BC is equal to AB;
but it has been proved that AC is equal to AB;
therefore AC, BC are each of them equal to AB;
but things which are equal to the same thing are equal to one another;
therefore AC is equal to BC; (ax. 1.)
wherefore AB, BC, CA are equal to one another:
and the triangle ABC is therefore equilateral,
and it is described upon the given straight line AB.
Which was required to be done.

PROPOSITION II. PROBLEM.

From a given point, to draw a straight line equal to a given straight line.

Let A be the given point, and BC the given straight line.
It is required to draw from the point A, a straight line equal to BC.

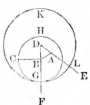

From the point A to B draw the straight line AB; (post. 1.)
upon AB describe the equilateral triangle ABD, (I. 1.)
and produce the straight lines DA, DB to E and F; (post. 2.)
from the center B, at the distance BC, describe the circle CGH, (post. 3.) cutting DF in the point G;
and from the center D, at the distance DG, describe the circle GKL, cutting AE in the point L.

Then the straight line AL shall be equal to BC.
Because the point B is the center of the circle CGH,
therefore BC is equal to BG; (def. 15.)
and because D is the center of the circle GKL,
therefore DL is equal to DG,
and DA, DB parts of them are equal; (I. 1.)
therefore the remainder AL is equal to the remainder BG; (ax. 3.)
but it has been shewn that BC is equal to BG,
wherefore AL and BC are each of them equal to BG;
and things that are equal to the same thing are equal to one another;
therefore the straight line AL is equal to BC. (ax. 1.)

Wherefore from the given point A, a straight line AL has been drawn equal to the given straight line BC. Which was to be done.

PROPOSITION III. PROBLEM.

From the greater of two given straight lines to cut off a part equal to the less.

Let AB and C be the two given straight lines, of which AB is the greater.

It is required to cut off from AB the greater, a part equal to C, the less.

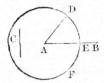

From the point A draw the straight line AD equal to C; (I. 2.) and from the center A, at the distance AD, describe the circle DEF (post. 3.) cutting AB in the point E.

Then AE shall be equal to C.
Because A is the center of the circle DEF,
therefore AE is equal to AD; (def. 15.)
but the straight line C is equal to AD; (constr.)
whence AE and C are each of them equal to AD;
wherefore the straight line AE is equal to C. (ax. 1.)

And therefore from AB the greater of two straight lines, a part AE has been cut off equal to C, the less. Which was to be done.

PROPOSITION IV. THEOREM.

If two triangles have two sides of the one equal to two sides of the other, each to each, and have likewise the angles contained by those sides equal to each other; they shall likewise have their bases or third *sides equal, and the two triangles shall be equal, and their other angles shall be equal, each to each, viz. those to which the equal sides are opposite.*

Let ABC, DEF be two triangles, which have the two sides AB, AC equal to the two sides DE, DF, each to each, viz. AB to DE, and AC to DF; and the included angle BAC equal to the included angle EDF.

Then shall the base *BC* be equal to the base *EF*; and the triangle *ABC* to the triangle *DEF*; and the other angles to which the equal sides are opposite shall be equal, each to each, viz. the angle *ABC* to the angle *DEF*, and the angle *ACB* to the angle *DFE*.

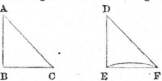

For, if the triangle *ABC* be applied to the triangle *DEF*,
so that the point *A* may be on *D*, and the straight line *AB* on *DE*;
then the point *B* shall coincide with the point *E*,
because *AB* is equal to *DE*;
and *AB* coinciding with *DE*,
the straight line *AC* shall fall on *DF*,
because the angle *BAC* is equal to the angle *EDF*;
therefore also the point *C* shall coincide with the point *F*,
because *AC* is equal to *DF*;
but the point *B* was shewn to coincide with the point *E*;
wherefore the base *BC* shall coincide with the base *EF*;
because the point *B* coinciding with *E*, and *C* with *F*,
if the base *BC* do not coincide with the base *EF*, the two straight lines *BC* and *EF* would enclose a space, which is impossible. (ax. 10.)
Therefore the base *BC* does coincide with *EF*, and is equal to it;
and the whole triangle *ABC* coincides with the whole triangle *DEF*, and is equal to it;
also the remaining angles of one triangle coincide with the remaining angles of the other, and are equal to them,
viz. the angle *ABC* to the angle *DEF*,
and the angle *ACB* to *DFE*.
Therefore, if two triangles have two sides of the one equal to two sides, &c.   Which was to be demonstrated.

∠ PROPOSITION V. THEOREM.

The angles at the base of an isosceles triangle are equal to each other; and if the equal sides be produced, the angles on the other side of the base shall be equal.

Let *ABC* be an isosceles triangle of which the side *AB* is equal to *AC*, and let the equal sides *AB*, *AC* be produced to *D* and *E*.
Then the angle *ABC* shall be equal to the angle *ACB*,
and the angle *DBC* to the angle *ECB*.
In *BD* take any point *F*;
from *AE* the greater, cut off *AG* equal to *AF* the less, (I. 3.)
and join *FC*, *GB*.
Because *AF* is equal to *AG*, (constr.) and *AB* to *AC*; (hyp.)
the two sides *FA*, *AC* are equal to the two *GA*, *AB*, each to each;
and they contain the angle *FAG* common to the two triangles *AFC*, *AGB*;

1*

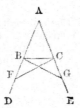

therefore the base FC is equal to the base GB, (I. 4.)
and the triangle AFC is equal to the triangle AGB,
also the remaining angles of the one are equal to the remaining angles of the other, each to each, to which the equal sides are opposite;
viz. the angle ACF to the angle ABG,
and the angle AFC to the angle AGB.
And because the whole AF is equal to the whole AG,
of which the parts AB, AC, are equal;
therefore the remainder BF is equal to the remainder CG; (ax. 3.)
and FC has been proved to be equal to GB;
hence, because the two sides BF, FC are equal to the two CG, GB, each to each;
and the angle BFC has been proved to be equal to the angle CGB,
also the base BC is common to the two triangles BFC, CGB;
wherefore these triangles are equal, (I. 4.)
and their remaining angles, each to each, to which the equal sides are opposite;
therefore the angle FBC is equal to the angle GCB,
and the angle BCF to the angle CBG.
And, since it has been demonstrated,
that the whole angle ABG is equal to the whole ACF,
the parts of which, the angles CBG, BCF are also equal;
therefore the remaining angle ABC is equal to the remaining angle ACB,
which are the angles at the base of the triangle ABC;
and it has also been proved.
that the angle FBC is equal to the angle GCB,
which are the angles upon the other side of the base.
Therefore the angles at the base, &c. Q.E.D.
Cor.   Hence an equilateral triangle is also equiangular.

PROPOSITION VI. THEOREM.

If two angles of a triangle be equal to each other; the sides also which subtend, or are opposite to, *the equal angles, shall be equal to one another.*

Let ABC be a triangle having the angle ABC equal to the angle ACB.
Then the side AB shall be equal to the side AC.

For, if AB be not equal to AC,
one of them is greater than the other.
If possible, let AB be greater than AC;
and from BA cut off BD equal to CA the less, (I. 3.) and join DC.
Then, in the triangles DBC, ABC,
because DB is equal to AC, and BC is common to both triangles,
the two sides DB, BC are equal to the two sides AC, CB, each to each;
and the angle DBC is equal to the angle ACB; (hyp.)
therefore the base DC is equal to the base AB, (I. 4.)
and the triangle DBC is equal to the triangle ABC,
the less equal to the greater, which is absurd. (ax. 9.)
Therefore AB is not unequal to AC, that is, AB is equal to AC.
Wherefore, if two angles, &c. Q.E.D.

Cor. Hence an equiangular triangle is also equilateral.

PROPOSITION VII. THEOREM.

Upon the same base, and on the same side of it, there cannot be two triangles that have their sides which are terminated in one extremity of the base, equal to one another, and likewise those which are terminated in the other extremity.

If it be possible, on the same base AB, and upon the same side of it, let there be two triangles ACB, ADB, which have their sides CA, DA, terminated in the extremity A of the base, equal to one another, and likewise their sides CB, DB, that are terminated in B.

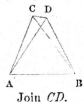

Join CD.

First. When the vertex of each of the triangles is without the other triangle.

Because AC is equal to AD in the triangle ACD,
therefore the angle ADC is equal to the angle ACD; (I. 5.)
but the angle ACD is greater than the angle BCD; (ax. 9.)
therefore also the angle ADC is greater than BCD;
much more therefore is the angle BDC greater than BCD.
Again, because the side BC is equal to BD in the triangle BCD, (hyp.)
therefore the angle BDC is equal to the angle BCD; (I. 5.)
but the angle BDC was proved greater than the angle BCD,
hence the angle BDC is both equal to, and greater than the angle BCD;
which is impossible.

Secondly. Let the vertex D of the triangle ADB fall within the triangle ACB.

Produce AC to E, and AD to F, and join CD.

Then because AC is equal to AD in the triangle ACD, therefore the angles ECD, FDC upon the other side of the base CD, are equal to one another; (I. 5.)

but the angle ECD is greater than the angle BCD; (ax. 9.)

therefore also the angle FDC is greater than the angle BCD;

much more then is the angle BDC greater than the angle BCD.

Again, because BC is equal to BD in the triangle BCD;

therefore the angle BDC is equal to the angle BCD. (I. 5.)

but the angle BDC has been proved greater than BCD,

wherefore the angle BDC is both equal to, and greater than the angle BCD; which is impossible.

Thirdly. The case in which the vertex of one triangle is upon a side of the other, needs no demonstration.

Therefore, upon the same base and on the same side of it, &c. Q.E.D.

PROPOSITION VIII. THEOREM.

If two triangles have two sides of the one equal to two sides of the other, each to each, and have likewise their bases equal; the angle which is contained by the two sides of the one shall be equal to the angle contained by the two sides equal to them, of the other.

Let ABC, DEF be two triangles, having the two sides AB, AC, equal to the two sides DE, DF, each to each, viz. AB to DE, and AC to DF, and also the base BC equal to the base EF.

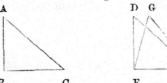

Then the angle BAC shall be equal to the angle EDF.

For, if the triangle ABC be applied to DEF, so that the point B be on E, and the straight line BC on EF;

then because BC is equal to EF, (hyp.)

therefore the point C shall coincide with the point F;

wherefore BC coinciding with EF,

BA and AC shall coincide with ED, DF;

for, if the base BC coincide with the base EF, but the sides BA, AC, do not coincide with the sides ED, DF, but have a different situation as EG, GF:

then, upon the same base, and upon the same side of it, there can be two triangles which have their sides which are terminated in one extremity of the base, equal to one another, and likewise those sides which are terminated in the other extremity; but this is impossible. (I. 7.)

Therefore, if the base BC coincide with the base EF, the sides BA, AC cannot but coincide with the sides ED, DF;

wherefore likewise the angle BAC coincides with the angle EDF, and is equal to it. (ax. 8.)

Therefore if two triangles have two sides, &c. Q.E.D.

BOOK I. PROP. IX., X.   13

PROPOSITION IX. PROBLEM.

To bisect a given rectilineal angle, that is, to divide it into two equal angles.

Let BAC be the given rectilineal angle.
It is required to bisect it.

In AB take any point D;
from AC cut off AE equal to AD, (I. 3.) and join DE;
on the side of DE remote from A,
describe the equilateral triangle DEF (I. 1), and join AF.
Then the straight line AF shall bisect the angle BAC.
Because AD is equal to AE, (constr.)
and AF is common to the two triangles DAF, EAF;
the two sides DA, AF, are equal to the two sides EA, AF, each to each;
and the base DF is equal to the base EF, (constr.)
therefore the angle DAF is equal to the angle EAF. (I. 8.)
Wherefore the angle BAC is bisected by the straight line AF.   Q.E.F.

PROPOSITION X. PROBLEM.

To bisect a given finite straight line, that is, to divide it into two equal parts.

Let AB be the given straight line.
It is required to divide AB into two equal parts.
Upon AB describe the equilateral triangle ABC; (I. 1.)

and bisect the angle ACB by the straight line CD meeting AB in the point D. (I. 9.)
Then AB shall be cut into two equal parts in the point D.
Because AC is equal to CB, (constr.)
and CD is common to the two triangles ACD, BCD;
the two sides AC, CD are equal to the two BC, CD, each to each;
and the angle ACD is equal to BCD; (constr.)
therefore the base AD is equal to the base BD. (I. 4.)
Wherefore the straight line AB is divided into two equal parts in the point D.   Q.E.F.

PROPOSITION XI. PROBLEM.

To draw a straight line at right angles to a given straight line, from a given point in the same.

Let AB be the given straight line, and C a given point in it.

It is required to draw a straight line from the point C at right angles to AB.

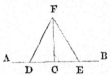

In AC take any point D, and make CE equal to CD; (I. 3.)
upon DE describe the equilateral triangle DEF (I. 1), and join CF.
Then CF drawn from the point C shall be at right angles to AB.
Because DC is equal to EC, and FC is common to the two triangles DCF, ECF;
the two sides DC, CF are equal to the two sides EC, CF, each to each;
and the base DF is equal to the base EF; (constr.)
therefore the angle DCF is equal to the angle ECF: (I. 8.)
and these two angles are adjacent angles.

But when the two adjacent angles which one straight line makes with another straight line, are equal to one another, each of them is called a right angle: (def. 10.)
therefore each of the angles DCF, ECF is a right angle.

Wherefore from the given point C, in the given straight line AB, FC has been drawn at right angles to AB. Q.E.F.

Cor. By help of this problem, it may be demonstrated that two straight lines cannot have a common segment.

If it be possible, let the segment AB be common to the two straight lines ABC, ABD.

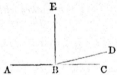

From the point B, draw BE at right angles to AB; (I. 11.)
then because ABC is a straight line,
therefore the angle ABE is equal to the angle EBC; (def. 10.)
Similarly, because ABD is a straight line,
therefore the angle ABE is equal to the angle EBD;
but the angle ABE is equal to the angle EBC,
wherefore the angle EBD is equal to the angle EBC, (ax. 1.)
the less equal to the greater angle, which is impossible.
Therefore two straight lines cannot have a common segment.

PROPOSITION XII. PROBLEM.

To draw a straight line perpendicular to a given straight line of unlimited length, from a given point without it.

BOOK I. PROP. XII., XIII.

Let *AB* be the given straight line, which may be produced any length both ways, and let *C* be a point without it.

It is required to draw a straight line perpendicular to *AB* from the point *C*.

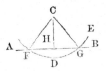

Upon the other side of *AB* take any point *D*, and from the center *C*, at the distance *CD*, describe the circle *EGF* meeting *AB*, produced if necessary, in *F* and *G* : (post. 3.) bisect *FG* in *H* (I. 10.) and join *CH*.

Then the straight line *CH* drawn from the given point *C*, shall be perpendicular to the given straight line *AB*.

Join *FC*, and *CG*.

Because *FH* is equal to *HG*, (constr.)
and *HC* is common to the triangles *FHC, GHC*;
the two sides *FH, HC*, are equal to the two *GH, HC*, each to each;
and the base *CF* is equal to the base *CG*; (def. 15.)
therefore the angle *FHC* is equal to the angle *GHC*; (I. 8.)
and these are adjacent angles.

But when a straight line standing on another straight line, makes the adjacent angles equal to one another, each of them is a right angle, and the straight line which stands upon the other is called a perpendicular to it. (def. 10.)

Therefore from the given point *C*, a perpendicular *CH* has been drawn to the given straight line *AB*. Q.E.F.

PROPOSITION XIII. THEOREM.

The angles which one straight line makes with another upon one side of it, are either two right angles, or are together equal to two right angles.

Let the straight line *AB* make with *CD*, upon one side of it, the angles *CBA, ABD*.

Then these shall be either two right angles,
or, shall be together, equal to two right angles.

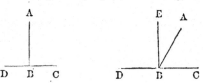

For if the angle *CBA* be equal to the angle *ABD*,
each of them is a right angle. (def. 10.)

But if the angle *CBA* be not equal to the angle *ABD*,
from the point *B* draw *BE* at right angles to *CD*. (I. 11.)

Then the angles *CBE, EBD* are two right angles. (def. 10.)

And because the angle *CBE* is equal to the angles *CBA*, *ABE*,
  add the angle *EBD* to each of these equals;
therefore the angles *CBE*, *EBD* are equal to the three angles *CBA*, *ABE*, *EBD*. (ax. 2.)
Again, because the angle *DBA* is equal to the two angles *DBE*, *EBA*,
  add to each of these equals the angle *ABC*;
therefore the angles *DBA*, *ABC* are equal to the three angles *DBE*, *EBA*, *ABC*.
But the angles *CBE*, *EBD* have been proved equal to the same three angles;
and things which are equal to the same thing are equal to one another;
therefore the angles *CBE*, *EBD* are equal to the angles *DBA*, *ABC*;
but the angles *CBE*, *EBD* are two right angles;
therefore the angles *DBA*, *ABC* are together equal to two right angles. (ax. 1.)
  Wherefore, when a straight line, &c. Q.E.D.

PROPOSITION XIV. THEOREM.

If at a point in a straight line, two other straight lines, upon the opposite sides of it, make the adjacent angles together equal to two right angles; then these two straight lines shall be in one and the same straight line.

At the point *B* in the straight line *AB*, let the two straight lines *BC*, *BD* upon the opposite sides of *AB*, make the adjacent angles *ABC*, *ABD* together equal to two right angles.
Then *BD* shall be in the same straight line with *BC*.

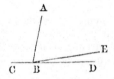

For, if *BD* be not in the same straight line with *BC*,
If possible, let *BE* be in the same straight line with it.
Then because *AB* meets the straight line *CBE*;
therefore the adjacent angles *CBA*, *ABE* are equal to two right angles; (I. 13.)
but the angles *CBA*, *ABD* are equal to two right angles; (hyp.)
therefore the angles *CBA*, *ABE* are equal to the angles *CBA*, *ABD*: (ax. 1.)
  take away from these equals the common angle *CBA*;
therefore the remaining angle *ABE* is equal to the remaining angle *ABD*; (ax. 3.)
  the less angle equal to the greater, which is impossible:
    therefore *BE* is not in the same straight line with *BC*.
And in the same manner it may be demonstrated, that no other can be in the same straight line with it but *BD*, which therefore is in the same straight line with *BC*.
  Wherefore, if at a point, &c. Q.E.D.

BOOK I. PROP. XV., XVI.

PROPOSITION XV. THEOREM.

If two straight lines cut one another, the vertical, or opposite angles shall be equal.

Let the two straight lines AB, CD cut one another in the point E.

Then the angle AEC shall be equal to the angle DEB, and the angle CEB to the angle AED.

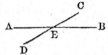

Because the straight line AE makes with CD at the point E, the adjacent angles CEA, AED;
  these angles are together equal to two right angles. (I. 13.)
Again, because the straight line DE makes with AB at the point E, the adjacent angles AED, DEB;
  these angles also are equal to two right angles;
but the angles CEA, AED have been shewn to be equal to two right angles;
wherefore the angles CEA, AED are equal to the angles AED, DEB;
  take away from each the common angle AED,
and the remaining angle CEA is equal to the remaining angle DEB. (ax. 3.)
In the same manner it may be demonstrated, that the angle CEB is equal to the angle AED.

Therefore, if two straight lines cut one another, &c. Q.E.D.

COR. 1. From this it is manifest, that, if two straight lines cut each other, the angles which they make at the point where they cut, are together equal to four right angles.

COR. 2. And consequently that all the angles made by any number of lines meeting in one point, are together equal to four right angles.

PROPOSITION XVI. THEOREM.

If one side of a triangle be produced, the exterior angle is greater than either of the interior opposite angles.

Let ABC be a triangle, and let the side BC be produced to D.

Then the exterior angle ACD shall be greater than either of the interior opposite angles CBA or BAC.

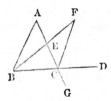

Bisect AC in E, (I. 10.) and join BE;
produce BE to F, making EF equal to BE, (I. 3.) and join FC.

Because AE is equal to EC, and BE to EF; (constr.)
the two sides AE, EB are equal to the two CE, EF, each to each, in the triangles ABE, CFE;
and the angle AEB is equal to the angle CEF,
because they are opposite vertical angles. (I. 15.)
therefore the base AB is equal to the base CF, (I. 4.)
and the triangle AEB to the triangle CEF,
and the remaining angles of one triangle to the remaining angles of the other, each to each, to which the equal sides are opposite ;
wherefore the angle BAE is equal to the angle ECF:
but the angle ECD or ACD is greater than the angle ECF;
therefore the angle ACD is greater than the angle BAE or BAC.
In the same manner, if the side BC be bisected, and AC be produced to G; it may be demonstrated that the angle BCG, that is, the angle ACD, (I. 15.) is greater than the angle ABC.

Therefore, if one side of a triangle, &c. Q.E.D.

PROPOSITION XVII. THEOREM.

Any two angles of a triangle are together less than two right angles.

Let ABC be any triangle.
Then any two of its angles together shall be less than two right angles.

Produce any side BC to D.
Then because ACD is the exterior angle of the triangle ABC, therefore the angle ACD is greater than the interior and opposite angle ABC. (I. 16.)
to each of these unequals add the angle ACB,
therefore the angles ACD, ACB are greater than the angles ABC, ACB;
but the angles ACD, ACB are equal to two right angles: (I. 13.)
therefore the angles ABC, ACB are less than two right angles.
In like manner it may be demonstrated,
that the angles BAC, ACB are less than two right angles,
as also the angles CAB, ABC.
Therefore any two angles of a triangle, &c. Q.E.D.

PROPOSITION XVIII. THEOREM.

The greater side of every triangle is opposite to the greater angle.

Let ABC be a triangle, of which the side AC is greater than the side AB.

Then the angle *ABC* shall be greater than the angle *ACB*.

Since the side *AC* is greater than the side *AB*, (hyp.)
make *AD* equal to *AB*, (I. 3.) and join *BD*.
Then, because *AD* is equal to *AB*, in the triangle *ABD*,
therefore the angle *ABD* is equal to the angle *ADB*, (I. 5.)
but because the side *CD* of the triangle *BDC* is produced to *A*,
therefore the exterior angle *ADB* is greater than the interior and opposite angle *DCB*; (I. 16.)
but the angle *ADB* has been proved equal to the angle *ABD*,
therefore the angle *ABD* is greater than the angle *DCB*;
wherefore much more is the angle *ABC* greater than the angle *ACB*.
Therefore the greater side, &c. Q.E.D.

PROPOSITION XIX. THEOREM.

The greater angle of every triangle is subtended by the greater side, or, has the greater side opposite to it.

Let *ABC* be a triangle of which the angle *ABC* is greater than the angle *BCA*.
Then the side *AC* shall be greater than the side *AB*.

For, if *AC* be not greater than *AB*,
AC must either be equal to, or less than *AB*;
if *AC* were equal to *AB*,
then the angle *ABC* would be equal to the angle *ACB*; (I. 5.)
but it is not equal; (hyp.)
therefore the side *AC* is not equal to *AB*.
Again, if *AC* were less than *AB*,
then the angle *ABC* would be less than the angle *ACB*; (I. 18.)
but it is not less, (hyp.)
therefore the side *AC* is not less than *AB*;
and *AC* has been shewn to be not equal to *AB*;
therefore *AC* is greater than *AB*.
Wherefore the greater angle, &c. Q.E.D.

PROPOSITION XX. THEOREM.

Any two sides of a triangle are together greater than the third side.

Let *ABC* be a triangle.
Then any two sides of it together shall be greater than the third side,
viz. the sides *BA*, *AC* greater than the side *BC*;

AB, *BC* greater than *AC*;
and *BC*, *CA* greater than *AB*.

Produce the side *BA* to the point *D*,
make *AD* equal to *AC*, (I. 3.) and join *DC*.
Then because *AD* is equal to *AC*, (constr.)
therefore the angle *ACD* is equal to the angle *ADC*; (I. 5.)
but the angle *BCD* is greater than the angle *ACD*; (ax. 9.)
therefore also the angle *BCD* is greater than the angle *ADC*.
And because in the triangle *DBC*,
the angle *BCD* is greater than the angle *BDC*,
and that the greater angle is subtended by the greater side; (I. 19.)
therefore the side *DB* is greater than the side *BC*;
but *DB* is equal to *BA* and *AC*,
therefore the sides *BA* and *AC* are greater than *BC*.
In the same manner it may be demonstrated,
that the sides *AB*, *BC* are greater than *CA*;
also that *BC*, *CA* are greater than *AB*.
Therefore any two sides, &c. Q.E.D.

PROPOSITION XXI. THEOREM.

If from the ends of a side of a triangle, there be drawn two straight lines to a point within the triangle; these shall be less than the other two sides of the triangle, but shall contain a greater angle.

Let *ABC* be a triangle, and from the points *B*, *C*, the ends of the side *BC*, let the two straight lines *BD*, *CD* be drawn to a point *D* within the triangle.
Then *BD* and *DC* shall be less than *BA* and *AC* the other two
sides of the triangle,
but shall contain an angle *BDC* greater than the angle *BAC*.

Produce *BD* to meet the side *AC* in *E*.
Because two sides of a triangle are greater than the third side, (I. 20.)
therefore the two sides *BA*, *AE* of the triangle *ABE* are greater
than *BE*;
to each of these unequals add *EC*;
therefore the sides *BA*, *AC* are greater than *BE*, *EC*. (ax. 4.)
Again, because the two sides *CE*, *ED* of the triangle *CED* are
greater than *DC*; (I. 20.)
add *DB* to each of these unequals;

therefore the sides *CE, EB* are greater than *CD, DB*. (ax. 4.)
But it has been shewn that *BA, AC* are greater than *BE, EC*;
much more then are *BA, AC* greater than *BD, DC*.

Again, because the exterior angle of a triangle is greater than the interior and opposite angle; (I. 16.)
therefore the exterior angle *BDC* of the triangle *CDE* is greater than the interior and opposite angle *CED*;
for the same reason, the exterior angle *CED* of the triangle *ABE* is greater than the interior and opposite angle *BAC*;
and it has been demonstrated,
that the angle *BDC* is greater than the angle *CEB*;
much more therefore is the angle *BDC* greater than the angle *BAC*.
Therefore, if from the ends of the side, &c. Q.E.D.

PROPOSITION XXII. PROBLEM.

To make a triangle of which the sides shall be equal to three given straight lines, but any two whatever of these must be greater than the third.

Let *A, B, C* be the three given straight lines,
of which any two whatever are greater than the third, (I. 20.)
namely, *A* and *B* greater than *C*;
A and *C* greater than *B*;
and *B* and *C* greater than *A*.

It is required to make a triangle of which the sides shall be equal to *A, B, C*, each to each.

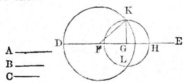

Take a straight line *DE* terminated at the point *D*, but unlimited towards *E*.

make *DF* equal to *A*, *FG* equal to *B*, and *GH* equal to *C*; (I. 3.)
from the center *F*, at the distance *FD*, describe the circle *DKL*; (post. 3.)
from the center *G*, at the distance *GH*, describe the circle *HLK*;
from *K* where the circles cut each other draw *KF, KG* to the points *F, G*;

Then the triangle *KFG* shall have its sides equal to the three straight lines *A, B, C*.

Because the point *F* is the center of the circle *DKL*,
therefore *FD* is equal to *FK*; (def. 15.)
but *FD* is equal to the straight line *A*;
therefore *FK* is equal to *A*.

Again, because *G* is the center of the circle *HKL*;
therefore *GH* is equal to *GK*, (def. 15.)
but *GH* is equal to *C*;
therefore also *GK* is equal to *C*; (ax. 1.)
and *FG* is equal to *B*;

therefore the three straight lines KF, FG, GK, are respectively equal to the three A, B, C:
and therefore the triangle KFG has its three sides KF, FG, GK, equal to the three given straight lines A, B, C. Q.E.F.

PROPOSITION XXIII. PROBLEM.

At a given point in a given straight line, to make a rectilineal angle equal to a given rectilineal angle.

Let AB be the given straight line, and A the given point in it, and DCE the given rectilineal angle.

It is required, at the given point A in the given straight line AB, to make an angle that shall be equal to the given rectilineal angle DCE.

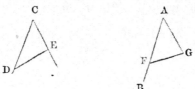

In CD, CE, take any points D, E, and join DE;
on AB, make the triangle AFG, the sides of which shall be equal to the three straight lines CD, DE, EC, so that AF be equal to CD, AG to CE, and FG to DE. (I. 22.)

Then the angle FAG shall be equal to the angle DCE.

Because FA, AG are equal to DC, CE, each to each, and the base FG is equal to the base DE;
therefore the angle FAG is equal to the angle DCE. (I. 8.)

Wherefore, at the given point A in the given straight line AB, the angle FAG is made equal to the given rectilineal angle DCE. Q.E.F.

PROPOSITION XXIV. THEOREM.

If two triangles have two sides of the one equal to two sides of the other, each to each, but the angle contained by the two sides of one of them greater than the angle contained by the two sides equal to them, of the other; the base of that which has the greater angle, shall be greater than the base of the other.

Let ABC, DEF be two triangles, which have the two sides AB, AC, equal to the two DE, DF, each to each, namely, AB equal to DE, and AC to DF; but the angle BAC greater than the angle EDF.

Then the base BC shall be greater than the base EF.

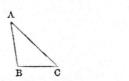

Of the two sides DE, DF, let DE be not greater than DF,
at the point D, in the line DE, and on the same side of it as DF,
make the angle EDG equal to the angle BAC; (I. 23.)
make DG equal to DF or AC, (I. 3.) and join EG, GF.
Then, because DE is equal to AB, and DG to AC,
the two sides DE, DG are equal to the two AB, AC, each to each,
and the angle EDG is equal to the angle BAC;
therefore the base EG is equal to the base BC. (I. 4.)
And because DG is equal to DF in the triangle DFG,
therefore the angle DFG is equal to the angle DGF; (I. 5.)
but the angle DGF is greater than the angle EGF; (ax. 9.)
therefore the angle DFG is also greater than the angle EGF;
much more therefore is the angle EFG greater than the angle EGF.
And because in the triangle EFG, the angle EFG is greater than the angle EGF,
and that the greater angle is subtended by the greater side; (I. 19.)
therefore the side EG is greater than the side EF;
but EG was proved equal to BC;
therefore BC is greater than EF.
Wherefore, if two triangles, &c. Q.E.D.

PROPOSITION XXV. THEOREM.

If two triangles have two sides of the one equal to two sides of the other, each to each, but the base of one greater than the base of the other; the angle contained by the sides of the one which has the greater base, shall be greater than the angle contained by the sides, equal to them, of the other.

Let ABC, DEF be two triangles which have the two sides AB, AC, equal to the two sides DE, DF, each to each, namely, AB equal to DE, and AC to DF; but the base BC greater than the base EF.
Then the angle BAC shall be greater than the angle EDF.

For, if the angle BAC be not greater than the angle EDF,
it must either be equal to it, or less than it.
If the angle BAC were equal to the angle EDF,
then the base BC would be equal to the base EF; (I. 4.)
but it is not equal, (hyp.)
therefore the angle BAC is not equal to the angle EDF.
Again, if the angle BAC were less than the angle EDF,
then the base BC would be less than the base EF; (I. 24.)
but it is not less, (hyp.)
therefore the angle BAC is not less than the angle EDF;
and it has been shown, that the angle BAC is not equal to the angle EDF;
therefore the angle BAC is greater than the angle EDF.
Wherefore, if two triangles, &c. Q.E.D.

PROPOSITION XXVI. THEOREM.

If two triangles have two angles of the one equal to two angles of the other, each to each, and one side equal to one side, viz. either the sides adjacent to the equal angles in each, or the sides opposite to them; then shall the other sides be equal, each to each, and also the third angle of the one equal to the third angle of the other.

Let ABC, DEF be two triangles which have the angles ABC, BCA, equal to the angles DEF, EFD, each to each, namely, ABC to DEF, and BCA to EFD; also one side equal to one side.

First, let those sides be equal which are adjacent to the angles that are equal in the two triangles, namely, BC to EF.

Then the other sides shall be equal, each to each, namely, AB to DE, and AC to DF, and the third angle BAC to the third angle EDF.

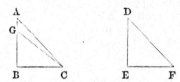

For, if AB be not equal to DE,
one of them must be greater than the other.
If possible, let AB be greater than DE,
make BG equal to ED, (I. 3.) and join GC.
Then in the two triangles GBC, DEF,
because GB is equal to DE, and BC to EF, (hyp.)
the two sides GB, BC are equal to the two DE, EF, each to each;
and the angle GBC is equal to the angle DEF;
therefore the base GC is equal to the base DF, (I. 4.)
and the triangle GBC to the triangle DEF,
and the other angles to the other angles, each to each, to which the equal sides are opposite;
therefore the angle GCB is equal to the angle DFE;
but the angle ACB is, by the hypothesis, equal to the angle DFE;
wherefore also the angle GCB is equal to the angle ACB; (ax. 1.)
the less angle equal to the greater, which is impossible;
therefore AB is not unequal to DE,
that is, AB is equal to DE.
Hence, in the triangles ABC, DEF;
because AB is equal to DE, and BC to EF, (hyp.)
and the angle ABC is equal to the angle DEF; (hyp.)
therefore the base AC is equal to the base DF, (I. 4.)
and the third angle BAC to the third angle EDF.

Secondly, let the sides which are opposite to one of the equal angles in each triangle be equal to one another, namely, AB equal to DE.

Then in this case likewise the other sides shall be equal, AC to DF, and BC to EF, and also the third angle BAC to the third angle EDF.

BOOK I. PROP. XXVI., XXVII. 25

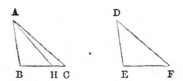

For if *BC* be not equal to *EF*,
one of them must be greater than the other.
If possible, let *BC* be greater than *EF*;
make *BH* equal to *EF*, (I. 3.) and join *AH*.
Then in the two triangles *ABH*, *DEF*,
because *AB* is equal to *DE*, and *BH* to *EF*,
and the angle *ABH* to the angle *DEF*; (hyp.)
therefore the base *AH* is equal to the base *DF*, (I. 4.)
and the triangle *ABH* to the triangle *DEF*,
and the other angles to the other angles, each to each, to which the equal sides are opposite;
therefore the angle *BHA* is equal to the angle *EFD*;
but the angle *EFD* is equal to the angle *BCA*; (hyp.)
therefore the angle *BHA* is equal to the angle *BCA*, (ax. 1.)
that is, the exterior angle *BHA* of the triangle *AHC*, is
equal to its interior and opposite angle *BCA*;
which is impossible; (I. 16.)
wherefore *BC* is not unequal to *EF*,
that is, *BC* is equal to *EF*.
Hence, in the triangles *ABC*, *DEF*;
because *AB* is equal to *DE*, and *BC* to *EF*, (hyp.)
and the included angle *ABC* is equal to the included angle *DEF*; (hyp.)
therefore the base *AC* is equal to the base *DF*, (I. 4.)
and the third angle *BAC* to the third angle *EDF*.
Wherefore, if two triangles, &c. Q.E.D.

PROPOSITION XXVII. THEOREM.

If a straight line falling on two other straight lines, make the alternate angles equal to each other; these two straight lines shall be parallel.

Let the straight line *EF*, which falls upon the two straight lines *AB*, *CD*, make the alternate angles *AEF*, *EFD*, equal to one another.
Then *AB* shall be parallel to *CD*.

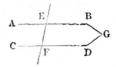

For, if *AB* be not parallel to *CD*,
then *AB* and *CD* being produced will meet, either towards *A* and *C*, or towards *B* and *D*.
Let *AB*, *CD* be produced and meet, if possible, towards *B* and *D*,
in the point *G*,
then *GEF* is a triangle.

And because a side GE of the triangle GEF is produced to A, therefore its exterior angle AEF is greater than the interior and opposite angle EFG; (I. 16.)
but the angle AEF is equal to the angle EFG; (hyp.)
therefore the angle AEF is greater than, and equal to, the angle EFG; which is impossible.

Therefore AB, CD being produced, do not meet towards B, D.

In like manner, it may be demonstrated, that they do not meet when produced towards A, C.

But those straight lines in the same plane, which meet neither way, though produced ever so far, are parallel to one another; (def. 35.)
therefore AB is parallel to CD.

Wherefore, if a straight line, &c. Q.E.D.

PROPOSITION XXVIII. THEOREM.

If a straight line falling upon two other straight lines, make the exterior angle equal to the interior and opposite upon the same side of the line; or make the interior angles upon the same side together equal to two right angles; the two straight lines shall be parallel to one another.

Let the straight line EF, which falls upon the two straight lines AB, CD, make the exterior angle EGB equal to the interior and opposite angle GHD, upon the same side of the line EF; or make the two interior angles BGH, GHD on the same side together equal to two right angles.

Then AB shall be parallel to CD.

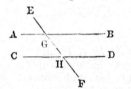

Because the angle EGB is equal to the angle GHD, (hyp.)
and the angle EGB is equal to the angle AGH, (I. 15.)
therefore the angle AGH is equal to the angle GHD; (ax. 1.)
and they are alternate angles,
therefore AB is parallel to CD. (I. 27.)

Again, because the angles BGH, GHD are together equal to two right angles, (hyp.)
and that the angles AGH, BGH are also together equal to two right angles; (I. 13.)
therefore the angles AGH, BGH are equal to the angles BGH, GHD; (ax. 1.)
take away from these equals, the common angle BGH;
therefore the remaining angle AGH is equal to the remaining angle GHD; (ax. 3.)
and they are alternate angles;
therefore AB is parallel to CD. (I. 27.)

Wherefore, if a straight line, &c. Q.E.D.

PROPOSITION XXIX. THEOREM.

If a straight line fall upon two parallel straight lines, it makes the alternate angles equal to one another; and the exterior angle equal to the interior and opposite upon the same side; and likewise the two interior angles upon the same side together equal to two right angles.

Let the straight line EF fall upon the parallel straight lines AB, CD.
Then the alternate angles AGH, GHD shall be equal to one another, the exterior angle EGB shall be equal to the interior and opposite angle GHD upon the same side of the line EF;
and the two interior angles BGH, GHD upon the same side of EF shall be together equal to two right angles.

First. For, if the angle AGH be not equal to the alternate angle GHD, one of them must be greater than the other;
if possible, let AGH be greater than GHD,
then because the angle AGH is greater than the angle GHD, add to each of these unequals the angle BGH;
therefore the angles AGH, BGH are greater than the angles BGH, GHD; (ax. 4.)
but the angles AGH, BGH are equal to two right angles; (I. 13.)
therefore the angles BGH, GHD are less than two right angles;
but those straight lines, which with another straight line falling upon them, make the two interior angles on the same side less than two right angles, will meet together if continually produced; (ax. 12.)
therefore the straight lines AB, CD, if produced far enough, will meet towards B, D;
but they never meet, since they are parallel by the hypothesis;
therefore the angle AGH is not unequal to the angle GHD,
that is, the angle AGH is equal to the alternate angle GHD.
Secondly, because the angle AGH is equal to the angle EGB, (I. 15.)
and the angle AGH is equal to the angle GHD,
therefore the exterior angle EGB is equal to the interior and opposite angle GHD, on the same side of the line.
Thirdly. Because the angle EGB is equal to the angle GHD,
add to each of them the angle BGH;
therefore the angles EGB, BGH are equal to the angles BGH, GHD; (ax. 2.)
but EGB, BGH are equal to two right angles; (I. 13.)
therefore also the two interior angles BGH, GHD on the same side of the line are equal to two right angles. (ax. 1.)
Wherefore, if a straight line, &c.   Q.E.D.

PROPOSITION XXX. THEOREM.

Straight lines which are parallel to the same straight line are parallel to each other.

Let the straight lines AB, CD, be each of them parallel to EF.
Then shall AB be also parallel to CD.

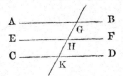

Let the straight line GHK cut AB, EF, CD.
Then because GHK cuts the parallel straight lines AB, EF, in G, H;
therefore the angle AGH is equal to the alternate angle GHF. (I. 29.)
Again, because GHK cuts the parallel straight lines EF, CD, in H, K;
therefore the exterior angle GHF is equal to the interior angle HKD;
and it was shewn that the angle AGH is equal to the angle GHF;
therefore the angle AGH is equal to the angle GKD;
and these are alternate angles;
therefore AB is parallel to CD. (I. 27.)
Wherefore, straight lines which are parallel, &c. Q.E.D.

PROPOSITION XXXI. PROBLEM.

To draw a straight line through a given point parallel to a given straight line.

Let A be the given point, and BC the given straight line.
It is required to draw, through the point A, a straight line parallel to the straight line BC.

In the line BC take any point D, and join AD,
at the point A in the straight line AD,
make the angle DAE equal to the angle ADC, (I. 23.) on the opposite side of AD;
and produce the straight line EA to F.
Then EF shall be parallel to BC.
Because the straight line AD meets the two straight lines EF, BC,
and makes the alternate angles EAD, ADC, equal to one another,
therefore EF is parallel to BC. (I. 27.)
Wherefore, through the given point A, has been drawn a straight line EAF parallel to the given straight line BC. Q.E.F.

PROPOSITION XXXII. THEOREM.

If a side of any triangle be produced, the exterior angle is equal to the two interior and opposite angles; and the three interior angles of every triangle are together equal to two right angles.

Let ABC be a triangle, and let one of its sides BC be produced to D.
Then the exterior angle ACD shall be equal to the two interior and opposite angles CAB, ABC:
and the three interior angles ABC, BCA, CAB shall be equal to two right angles.

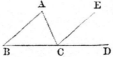

Through the point C draw CE parallel to the side BA. (I. 31.)
Then because CE is parallel to BA, and AC meets them,
therefore the angle ACE is equal to the alternate angle BAC. (I. 29.)
Again, because CE is parallel to AB, and BD falls upon them,
therefore the exterior angle ECD is equal to the interior and opposite angle ABC; (I. 29.)
but the angle ACE was shewn to be equal to the angle BAC;
therefore the whole exterior angle ACD is equal to the two interior and opposite angles CAB, ABC. (ax. 2.)
Again, because the angle ACD is equal to the two angles ABC, BAC,
to each of these equals add the angle ACB,
therefore the angles ACD and ACB are equal to the three angles ABC, BAC, and ACB; (ax. 2.)
but the angles ACD, ACB are equal to two right angles, (I. 13.)
therefore also the angles ABC, BAC, ACB are equal to two right angles. (ax. 1.)
Wherefore, if a side of any triangle be produced, &c. Q.E.D.

Cor. 1. All the interior angles of any rectilineal figure together with four right angles, are equal to twice as many right angles as the figure has sides.

For any rectilineal figure $ABCDE$ can be divided into as many triangles as the figure has sides, by drawing straight lines from a point F within the figure to each of its angles.

Then, because the three interior angles of a triangle are equal to two right angles, and there are as many triangles as the figure has sides,
therefore all the angles of these triangles are equal to twice as many right angles as the figure has sides;
but the same angles of these triangles are equal to the interior angles of the figure together with the angles at the point F:

and the angles at the point F, which is the common vertex of all the triangles, are equal to four right angles, (I. 15. Cor. 2.)

therefore the same angles of these triangles are equal to the angles of the figure together with four right angles;

but it has been proved that the angles of the triangles are equal to twice as many right angles as the figure has sides:

therefore all the angles of the figure together with four right angles, are equal to twice as many right angles as the figure has sides.

Cor. 2. All the exterior angles of any rectilineal figure, made by producing the sides successively in the same direction, are together equal to four right angles.

Since every interior angle ABC with its adjacent exterior angle ABD, is equal to two right angles, (I. 13.)

therefore all the interior angles, together with all the exterior angles, are equal to twice as many right angles as the figure has sides;

but it has been proved by the foregoing corollary, that all the interior angles together with four right angles are equal to twice as many right angles as the figure has sides;

therefore all the interior angles together with all the exterior angles, are equal to all the interior angles and four right angles, (ax. 1.)

take from these equals all the interior angles,

therefore all the exterior angles of the figure are equal to four right angles. (ax. 3.)

PROPOSITION XXXIII. THEOREM.

The straight lines which join the extremities of two equal and parallel straight lines towards the same parts, are also themselves equal and parallel.

Let AB, CD be equal and parallel straight lines, and joined towards the same parts by the straight lines AC, BD.

Then AC, BD shall be equal and parallel.

Join BC.

Then because AB is parallel to CD, and BC meets them, therefore the angle ABC is equal to the alternate angle BCD; (I. 29.)

and because AB is equal to CD, and BC common to the two triangles ABC, DCB; the two sides AB, BC, are equal to the two DC, CB, each to each, and the angle ABC was proved to be equal to the angle BCD:

therefore the base AC is equal to the base BD. (I. 4.)

and the triangle ABC to the triangle BCD,

and the other angles to the other angles, each to each, to which the equal sides are opposite;
therefore the angle ACB is equal to the angle CBD.
And because the straight line BC meets the two straight lines AC, BD, and makes the alternate angles ACB, CBD equal to one another;
therefore AC is parallel to BD; (I. 27.)
and AC was shewn to be equal to BD.
Therefore, straight lines which, &c. Q.E.D.

PROPOSITION XXXIV. THEOREM.

The opposite sides and angles of a parallelogram are equal to one another, and the diameter bisects it, that is, divides it into two equal parts.

Let $ACDB$ be a parallelogram, of which BC is a diameter.
Then the opposite sides and angles of the figure shall be equal to one another; and the diameter BC shall bisect it.

Because AB is parallel to CD, and BC meets them,
therefore the angle ABC is equal to the alternate angle BCD. (I. 29.)
And because AC is parallel to BD, and BC meets them,
therefore the angle ACB is equal to the alternate angle CBD. (I. 29.)
Hence in the two triangles ABC, CBD,
because the two angles ABC, BCA in the one, are equal to the two angles BCD, CBD in the other, each to each;
and one side BC, which is adjacent to their equal angles, common to the two triangles.
therefore their other sides are equal, each to each, and the third angle of the one to the third angle of the other, (I. 26.)
namely, the side AB to the side CD, and AC to BD, and the angle BAC to the angle BDC.
And because the angle ABC is equal to the angle BCD,
and the angle CBD to the angle ACB,
therefore the whole angle ABD is equal to the whole angle ACD; (ax. 2.)
and the angle BAC has been shewn to be equal to BDC;
therefore the opposite sides and angles of a parallelogram are equal to one another.
Also the diameter BC bisects it.
For since AB is equal to CD, and BC common, the two sides AB, BC, are equal to the two DC, CB, each to each,
and the angle ABC has been proved to be equal to the angle BCD;
therefore the triangle ABC is equal to the triangle BCD; (I. 4.) and the diameter BC divides the parallelogram $ACDB$ into two equal parts.
Q.E.D.

PROPOSITION XXXV. THEOREM

Parallelograms upon the same base, and between the same parallels, are equal to one another.

Let the parallelograms $ABCD$, $EBCF$ be upon the same base BC, and between the same parallels AF, BC.

Then the parallelogram $ABCD$ shall be equal to the parallelogram $EBCF$.

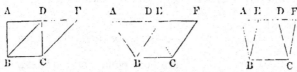

If the sides AD, DF of the parallelograms $ABCD$, $DBCF$, opposite to the base BC, be terminated in the same point D;

then it is plain that each of the parallelograms is double of the triangle BDC, (I. 34.)

and therefore the parallelogram $ABCD$ is equal to the parallelogram $DBCF$. (ax. 6.)

But if the sides AD, EF, opposite to the base BC, be not terminated in the same point;

Then, because $ABCD$ is a parallelogram,
therefore AD is equal to BC, (I. 34.)
and for a similar reason, EF is equal to BC;
wherefore AD is equal to EF, (ax. 1.)
and DE is common,
therefore the whole, or the remainder AE, is equal to the whole, or the remainder DF. (ax. 2 or 3.)
and AB is equal to DC, (I. 24.)
hence in the triangles EAB, FDC,
because FD is equal to EA, and DC to AB,
and the exterior angle FDC is equal to the interior and opposite angle EAB, (I. 29.)
therefore the base FC is equal to the base EB, (I. 4.)
and the triangle FDC is equal to the triangle EAB.
From the trapezium $ABCF$ take the triangle FDC,
and from the same trapezium take the triangle EAB,
and the remainders are equal. (ax. 3.)
therefore the parallelogram $ABCD$ is equal to the parallelogram $EBCF$.

Therefore, parallelograms upon the same, &c. Q.E.D.

PROPOSITION XXXVI. THEOREM.

Parallelograms upon equal bases and between the same parallels, are equal to one another.

Let $ABCD$, $EFGH$ be parallelograms upon equal bases BC, FG, and between the same parallels AH, BG.

Then the parallelogram $ABCD$ shall be equal to the parallelogram $EFGH$.

BOOK I. PROP. XXXVI., XXXVII.

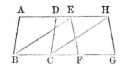

Join *BE*, *CH*.
Then because *BC* is equal to *FG*, (hyp.) and *FG* to *EH*, (I. 34.)
therefore *BC* is equal to *EH*; (ax. 1.)
and these lines are parallels, and joined towards the same parts by the straight lines *BE*, *CH*;
but straight lines which join the extremities of equal and parallel straight lines towards the same parts, are themselves equal and parallel; (I. 33.)
therefore *BE*, *CH* are both equal and parallel;
wherefore *EBCH* is a parallelogram. (def. A.)
And because the parallelograms *ABCD*, *EBCH*, are upon the same base *BC*, and between the same parallels *BC*, *AH*;
therefore the parallelogram *ABCD* is equal to the parallelogram *EBCH*. (I. 35.)
For the same reason, the parallelogram *EFGH* is equal to the parallelogram *EBCH*;
therefore, the parallelogram *ABCD* is equal to the parallelogram *EFGH*. (ax. 1.)
Therefore, parallelograms upon equal, &c. Q.E.D.

PROPOSITION XXXVII. THEOREM.

Triangles upon the same base and between the same parallels, are equal to one another.

Let the triangles *ABC*, *DBC* be upon the same base *BC*,
and between the same parallels *AD*, *BC*.
Then the triangle *ABC* shall be equal to the triangle *DBC*.

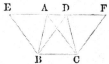

Produce *AD* both ways to the points *E*, *F*;
through *B* draw *BE* parallel to *CA*, (I. 31.)
and through *C* draw *CF* parallel to *BD*.
Then each of the figures *EBCA*, *DBCF* is a parallelogram;
and *EBCA* is equal to *DBCF*, (I. 35.) because they are upon the same base *BC*, and between the same parallels *BC*, *EF*.
And because the diameter *AB* bisects the parallelogram *EBCA*,
therefore the triangle *ABC* is half of the parallelogram *EBCA*; (I. 34.)
also because the diameter *DC* bisects the parallelogram *DBCF*,
therefore the triangle *DBC* is half of the parallelogram *DBCF*;
but the halves of equal things are equal; (ax. 7.)
therefore the triangle *ABC* is equal to the triangle *DBC*.
Wherefore, triangles, &c. Q.E.D.

PROPOSITION XXXVIII. THEOREM.

Triangles upon equal bases and between the same parallels, are equal to one another.

Let the triangles ABC, DEF be upon equal bases BC, EF, and between the same parallels BF, AD.

Then the triangle ABC shall be equal to the triangle DEF.

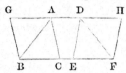

Produce AD both ways to the points G, H;
through B draw BG parallel to CA, (I. 31.)
and through F draw FH parallel to ED.

Then each of the figures $GBCA$, $DEFH$ is a parallelogram;
and they are equal to one another, (I. 36.)
because they are upon equal bases BC, EF,
and between the same parallels BF, GH.

And because the diameter AB bisects the parallelogram $GBCA$, therefore the triangle ABC is the half of the parallelogram $GBCA$; (I. 34.)
also, because the diameter DF bisects the parallelogram $DEFH$, therefore the triangle DEF is the half of the parallelogram $DEFH$;
but the halves of equal things are equal; (ax. 7.)
therefore the triangle ABC is equal to the triangle DEF.

Wherefore, triangles upon equal bases, &c.   Q.E.D.

PROPOSITION XXXIX. THEOREM.

Equal triangles upon the same base and upon the same side of it, are between the same parallels.

Let the equal triangles ABC, DBC be upon the same base BC and upon the same side of it.

Then the triangles ABC, DBC shall be between the same parallels.

Join AD; then AD shall be parallel to BC.

For if AD be not parallel to BC,
if possible, through the point A, draw AE parallel to BC, (I. 31.) meeting BD, or BD produced, in E, and join EC.

Then the triangle ABC is equal to the triangle EBC, (I. 37.)
because they are upon the same base BC,
and between the same parallels BC, AE:
but the triangle ABC is equal to the triangle DBC; (hyp.)
therefore the triangle DBC is equal to the triangle EBC,

the greater triangle equal to the less, which is impossible:
therefore AE is not parallel to BC.
In the same manner it can be demonstrated,
that no other line drawn from A but AD is parallel to BC;
AD is therefore parallel to BC.
Wherefore, equal triangles upon, &c. Q.E.D.

PROPOSITION XL. THEOREM.

Equal triangles upon equal bases in the same straight line, and towards the same parts, are between the same parallels.

Let the equal triangles ABC, DEF be upon equal bases BC, EF, in the same straight line BF, and towards the same parts.
Then they shall be between the same parallels.

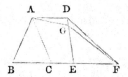

Join AD; then AD shall be parallel to BF.
For if AD be not parallel to BF,
if possible, through A draw AG parallel to BF, (I. 31.)
meeting ED, or ED produced in G, and join GF.
Then the triangle ABC is equal to the triangle GEF, (I. 38.)
because they are upon equal bases BC, EF,
and between the same parallels BF, AG;
but the triangle ABC is equal to the triangle DEF; (hyp.)
therefore the triangle DEF is equal to the triangle GEF, (ax. 1.)
the greater triangle equal to the less, which is impossible:
therefore AG is not parallel to BF.
And in the same manner it can be demonstrated,
that there is no other line drawn from A parallel to it but AD;
AD is therefore parallel to BF.
Wherefore, equal triangles upon, &c. Q.E.D.

PROPOSITION XLI. THEOREM.

If a parallelogram and a triangle be upon the same base, and between the same parallels; the parallelogram shall be double of the triangle.

Let the parallelogram $ABCD$, and the triangle EBC be upon the same base BC, and between the same parallels BC, AE.
Then the parallelogram $ABCD$ shall be double of the triangle EBC.

Join AC.
Then the triangle ABC is equal to the triangle EBC, (I. 37.)

because they are upon the same base BC, and between the same parallels BC, AE.

But the parallelogram $ABCD$ is double of the triangle ABC, because the diameter AC bisects it; (I. 34.)

wherefore $ABCD$ is also double of the triangle EBC.

Therefore, if a parallelogram and a triangle, &c.   Q.E.D.

PROPOSITION XLII. PROBLEM.

To describe a parallelogram that shall be equal to a given triangle, and have one of its angles equal to a given rectilineal angle.

Let ABC be the given triangle, and D the given rectilineal angle. It is required to describe a parallelogram that shall be equal to the given triangle ABC, and have one of its angles equal to D.

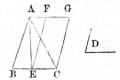

Bisect BC in E, (I. 10.) and join AE;
at the point E in the straight line EC,
make the angle CEF equal to the angle D; (I. 23.)
through C draw CG parallel to EF, and through A draw AFG parallel to BC, (I. 31.) meeting EF in F, and CG in G.

Then the figure $CEFG$ is a parallelogram.   (def. A.)

And because the triangles ABE, AEC are on the equal bases BE, EC, and between the same parallels BC, AG;
they are therefore equal to one another; (I. 38.)
and the triangle ABC is double of the triangle AEC;
but the parallelogram $FECG$ is double of the triangle AEC, (I. 41.)
because they are upon the same base EC, and between the same parallels EC, AG;
therefore the parallelogram $FECG$ is equal to the triangle ABC, (ax.6.)
and it has one of its angles CEF equal to the given angle D.

Wherefore, a parallelogram $FECG$ has been described equal to the given triangle ABC, and having one of its angles CEF equal to the given angle D.   Q.E.F.

PROPOSITION XLIII. THEOREM.

The complements of the parallelograms, which are about the diameter of any parallelogram, are equal to one another.

Let $ABCD$ be a parallelogram, of which the diameter is AC: and EH, GF the parallelograms about AC, that is, through which AC passes:
also BK, KD the other parallelograms which make up the whole figure $ABCD$, which are therefore called the complements.

Then the complement BK shall be equal to the complement KD.

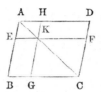

Because *ABCD* is a parallelogram, and *AC* its diameter,
therefore the triangle *ABC* is equal to the triangle *ADC*, (I. 34.)
Again, because *EKHA* is a parallelogram, and *AK* its diameter,
therefore the triangle *AEK* is equal to the triangle *AHK*; (I. 34.)
and for the same reason, the triangle *KGC* is equal to the triangle *KFC*.
Wherefore the two triangles *AEK*, *KGC* are equal to the two triangles *AHK*, *KFC*. (ax. 2.)
but the whole triangle *ABC* is equal to the whole triangle *ADC*;
therefore the remaining complement *BK* is equal to the remaining complement *KD*. (ax. 3.)
Wherefore the complements, &c. Q.E.D.

PROPOSITION XLIV. PROBLEM.

To a given straight line to apply a parallelogram, which shall be equal to a given triangle, and have one of its angles equal to a given rectilineal angle.

Let *AB* be the given straight line, and *C* the given triangle, and *D* the given rectilineal angle.

It is required to apply to the straight line *AB*, a parallelogram equal to the triangle *C*, and having an angle equal to the angle *D*.

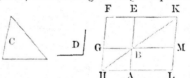

Make the parallelogram *BEFG* equal to the triangle *C*, and having the angle *EBG* equal to the angle *D*, (I. 42.)
so that *BE* be in the same straight line with *AB*;
produce *FG* to *H*,
through *A* draw *AH* parallel to *BG* or *EF*, (I. 31.) and join *HB*.
Then because the straight line *HF* falls upon the parallels *AH*, *EF*,
therefore the angles *AHF*, *HFE* are together equal to two right angles; (I. 29.)
wherefore the angles *BHF*, *HFE* are less than two right angles:
but straight lines which with another straight line, make the two interior angles upon the same side less than two right angles, do meet if produced far enough: (ax. 12.)
therefore *HB*, *FE* shall meet if produced;
let them be produced and meet in *K*,
through *K* draw *KL* parallel to *EA* or *FH*,
and produce *HA*, *GB* to meet *KL* in the points *L*, *M*.
Then *HLKF* is a parallelogram, of which the diameter is *HK*;

and AG, ME, are the parallelograms about HK;
also LB, BF are the complements;
therefore the complement LB is equal to the complement BF; (I. 43.)
but the complement BF is equal to the triangle C; (constr.)
wherefore LB is equal to the triangle C.

And because the angle GBE is equal to the angle ABM, (I. 15.) and likewise to the angle D; (constr.)
therefore the angle ABM is equal to the angle D. (ax. 1.)

Therefore to the given straight line AB, the parallelogram LB has been applied, equal to the triangle C, and having the angle ABM equal to the given angle D. Q.E.F.

PROPOSITION XLV. PROBLEM.

To describe a parallelogram equal to a given rectilineal figure, and having an angle equal to a given rectilineal angle.

Let $ABCD$ be the given rectilineal figure, and E the given rectilineal angle.

It is required to describe a parallelogram that shall be equal to the figure $ABCD$, and having an angle equal to the given angle E.

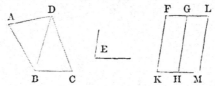

Join DB.

Describe the parallelogram FH equal to the triangle ADB, and having the angle FKH equal to the angle E; (I. 42.)
to the straight line GH, apply the parallelogram GM equal to the triangle DBC, having the angle GHM equal to the angle E. (I. 44.)

Then the figure $FKML$ shall be the parallelogram required.

Because each of the angles FKH, GHM, is equal to the angle E, therefore the angle FKH is equal to the angle GHM;
add to each of these equals the angle KHG;
therefore the angles FKH, KHG are equal to the angles KHG, GHM;
but FKH, KHG are equal to two right angles; (I. 29.)
therefore also KHG, GHM are equal to two right angles;
and because at the point H, in the straight line GH, the two straight lines KH, HM, upon the opposite sides of it, make the adjacent angles KHG, GHM equal to two right angles,
therefore HK is in the same straight line with HM. (I. 14.)

And because the line HG meets the parallels KM, FG,
therefore the angle MHG is equal to the alternate angle HGF; (I. 29.)
add to each of these equals the angle HGL;
therefore the angles MHG, HGL are equal to the angles HGF, HGL;
but the angles MHG, HGL are equal to two right angles; (I. 29.)
therefore also the angles HGF, HGL are equal to two right angles,
and therefore FG is in the same straight line with GL. (I. 14.)

And because KF is parallel to HG, and HG to ML,
therefore KF is parallel to ML; (I. 30.)
and FL has been proved parallel to KM,
wherefore the figure $FKML$ is a parallelogram;
and since the parallelogram HF is equal to the triangle ABD,
and the parallelogram GM to the triangle BDC;
therefore the whole parallelogram $KFLM$ is equal to the whole rectilineal figure $ABCD$.

Therefore the parallelogram $KFLM$ has been described equal to the given rectilineal figure $ABCD$, having the angle FKM equal to the given angle E. Q.E.F.

Cor. From this it is manifest how, to a given straight line, to apply a parallelogram which shall have an angle equal to a given rectilineal angle, and shall be equal to a given rectilineal figure; viz. by applying to the given straight line a parallelogram equal to the first triangle ABD, (I. 44.) and having an angle equal to the given angle.

PROPOSITION XLVI. PROBLEM.

To describe a square upon a given straight line.

Let AB be the given straight line.

It is required to describe a square upon AB.
From the point A draw AC at right angles to AB; (I. 11.)
make AD equal to AB; (I. 3.)
through the point D draw DE parallel to AB; (I. 31.)
and through B, draw BE parallel to AD, meeting DE in E;
therefore $ABED$ is a parallelogram;
whence AB is equal to DE, and AD to BE; (I. 34.)
but AD is equal to AB,
therefore the four lines AB, BE, ED, DA are equal to one another and the parallelogram $ABED$ is equilateral.
It has likewise all its angles right angles;
since AD meets the parallels AB, DE,
therefore the angles BAD, ADE are equal to two right angles; (I. 29.)
but BAD is a right angle; (constr.)
therefore also ADE is a right angle.
But the opposite angles of parallelograms are equal; (I. 34.)
therefore each of the opposite angles ABE, BED is a right angle;
wherefore the figure $ABED$ is rectangular,
and it has been proved to be equilateral;
therefore the figure $ABED$ is a square, (def. 30.)
and it is described upon the given straight line AB. Q.E.F.

Cor. Hence, every parallelogram that has one of its angles a right angle, has all its angles right angles.

PROPOSITION XLVII. THEOREM.

In any right-angled triangle, the square which is described upon the side subtending the right angle, is equal to the squares described upon the sides which contain the right angle.

Let ABC be a right-angled triangle, having the right angle BAC.
Then the square described upon the side BC, shall be equal to the squares described upon BA, AC.

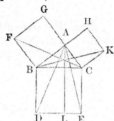

On BC describe the square $BDEC$, (I. 46.)
and on BA, AC the squares GB, HC;
through A draw AL parallel to BD or CE; (I. 31.)
and join AD, FC.
Then because the angle BAC is a right angle, (hyp.)
and that the angle BAG is a right angle, (def. 30.)
the two straight lines AC, AG upon the opposite sides of AB, make with it at the point A, the adjacent angles equal to two right angles;
therefore CA is in the same straight line with AG. (I. 14.)
For the same reason, BA and AH are in the same straight line.
And because the angle DBC is equal to the angle FBA,
each of them being a right angle,
add to each of these equals the angle ABC,
therefore the whole angle ABD is equal to the whole angle FBC. (ax. 2.)
And because the two sides AB, BD, are equal to the two sides FB, BC, each to each, and the included angle ABD is equal to the included angle FBC,
therefore the base AD is equal to the base FC. (I. 4.)
and the triangle ABD to the triangle FBC.
Now the parallelogram BL is double of the triangle ABD, (I. 41.)
because they are upon the same base BD, and between the same parallels BD, AL;
also the square GB is double of the triangle FBC,
because these also are upon the same base FB, and between the same parallels FB, GC.
But the doubles of equals are equal to one another: (ax. 6.)
therefore the parallelogram BL is equal to the square GB.
Similarly, by joining AE, BK, it can be proved,
that the parallelogram CL is equal to the square HC.

BOOK I. PROP. XLVIII. 41

Therefore the whole square $BDEC$ is equal to the two squares GB, HC; (ax. 2.)
and the square $BDEC$ is described upon the straight line BC,
and the squares GB, HC, upon AB, AC:
therefore the square upon the side BC, is equal to the squares upon the sides AB, AC.
Therefore, in any right-angled triangle, &c. Q.E.D.

PROPOSITION XLVIII. THEOREM.

If the square described upon one of the sides of a triangle, be equal to the squares described upon the other two sides of it; the angle contained by these two sides is a right angle.

Let the square described upon BC, one of the sides of the triangle ABC, be equal to the squares upon the other two sides, AB, AC.
Then the angle BAC shall be a right angle.

From the point A draw AD at right angles to AC, (I. 11.)
make AD equal to AB, and join DC.
Then, because AD is equal to AB,
the square on AD is equal to the square on AB;
to each of these equals add the square on AC;
therefore the squares on AD, AC are equal to the squares on AB, AC:
but the squares on AD, AC are equal to the square on DC, (I. 47.)
because the angle DAC is a right angle;
and the square on BC, by hypothesis, is equal to the squares on BA, AC;
therefore the square on DC is equal to the square on BC;
and therefore the side DC is equal to the side BC.
And because the side AD is equal to the side AB,
and AC is common to the two triangles DAC, BAC;
the two sides DA, AC, are equal to the two BA, AC, each to each;
and the base DC has been proved to be equal to the base BC;
therefore the angle DAC is equal to the angle BAC; (I. 8.)
but DAC is a right angle;
therefore also BAC is a right angle.
Therefore, if the square described upon, &c. Q.E.D.

NOTES TO BOOK I.

ON THE DEFINITIONS

Geometry is one of the most perfect of the deductive Sciences, and seems to rest on the simplest inductions from experience and observation.

The first principles of Geometry are therefore in this view consistent hypotheses founded on facts cognizable by the senses, and it is a subject of primary importance to draw a distinction between the conception of things and the things themselves. These hypotheses do not involve any property contrary to the real nature of the things, and consequently cannot be regarded as arbitrary, but in certain respects, agree with the conceptions which the things themselves suggest to the mind through the medium of the senses. The essential definitions of Geometry therefore being inductions from observation and experience, rest ultimately on the evidence of the senses.

It is by experience we become acquainted with the existence of individual forms of magnitudes; but by the mental process of abstraction, which begins with a particular instance, and proceeds to the general idea of all objects of the same kind, we attain to the general conception of those forms which come under the same general idea.

The essential definitions of Geometry express generalized conceptions of real existences in their most perfect ideal forms: the laws and appearances of nature, and the operations of the human intellect being supposed uniform and consistent.

But in cases where the subject falls under the class of simple ideas, the terms of the definitions so called, are no more than merely equivalent expressions. The simple idea described by a proper term or terms, does not in fact admit of definition properly so called. The definitions in Euclid's Elements may be divided into two classes, those which merely explain the meaning of the terms employed, and those which, besides explaining the meaning of the terms, suppose the existence of the things described in the definitions.

Definitions in Geometry cannot be of such a form as to explain the nature and properties of the figures defined: it is sufficient that they give marks whereby the thing defined may be distinguished from every other of the same kind. It will at once be obvious, that the definitions of Geometry, one of the pure sciences, being abstractions of space, are not like the definitions in any one of the physical sciences. The discovery of any new physical facts may render necessary some alteration or modification in the definitions of the latter.

Def. 1. Simson has adopted Theon's definition of a point. Euclid's definition is, σημεῖον ἐστιν οὗ μέρος οὐδέν, "A point is that, of which there is no part," or which cannot be parted or divided, as it is explained by Proclus. The Greek term σημεῖον, literally means, a visible *sign* or *mark* on a surface, in other words, *a physical point*. The English term *point*, means the sharp end of any thing, or a mark made by it. The word *point* comes from the Latin *punctum*, through the French word *point*. Neither of these terms, in its literal sense, appears to give a very exact notion of what is to be understood by a point in Geometry. Euclid's definition of a point merely expresses a negative property, which excludes the proper and literal meaning of the Greek term, as applied to denote a physical point, or a mark which is visible to the senses.

Pythagoras defined a point to be μονὰς θέσιν ἔχουσα, "a monad having position." By uniting the positive idea of position, with the negative idea of defect of magnitude, the conception of a point in Geometry may be rendered perhaps more intelligible. A point is defined to be that which has no magnitude, but position only.

Def. II. Every visible line has both length and breadth, and it is impossible to draw any line whatever which shall have no breadth. The definition requires the conception of the length only of the line to be considered, abstracted from, and independently of, all idea of its breadth.

Def. III. This definition renders more intelligible the exact meaning of the definition of a point; and we may add, that, in the Elements, Euclid supposes that the intersection of two lines is a point, and that two lines can intersect each other in one point only.

Def. IV. The straight line or right line is a term so clear and intelligible as to be incapable of becoming more so by formal definition. Euclid's definition is Εὐθεῖα γραμμή ἐστιν, ἥτις ἐξ ἴσου τοῖς ἐφ' ἑαυτῆς σημείοις κεῖται, wherein he states it to lie *evenly*, or *equally*, or *upon an equality* (ἐξ ἴσου) between its extremities, and which Proclus explains as being stretched between its extremities, ἡ ἐπ' ἄκρων τεταμένη.

If the line be conceived to be drawn on a plane surface, the words ἐξ ἴσου may mean, that no part of the line which is called a straight line deviates either from one side or the other of the direction which is fixed by the extremities of the line; and thus it may be distinguished from a curved line, which does not lie, in this sense, evenly between its extreme points. If the line be conceived to be drawn in space, the words ἐξ ἴσου must be understood to apply to every direction on every side of the line between its extremities.

Every straight line situated in a plane, is considered to have two sides; and when the direction of a line is known, the line is said to be given in position; also, when the length is known or can be found, it is said to be given in magnitude.

From the definition of a straight line, it follows, that two points fix a straight line in position, which is the foundation of the first and second postulates. Hence straight lines which are proved to coincide in two or more points, are called, "one and the same straight line," Prop. 14, Book I, or, which is the same thing, that "two straight lines cannot have a common segment," as Simson shews in his Corollary to Prop. 11, Book I.

The following definition of straight lines has also been proposed: "Straight lines are those which, if they coincide in any two points, coincide as far as they are produced." But this is rather a criterion of straight lines, and analogous to the eleventh axiom, which states that, "all right angles are equal to one another," and suggests that all straight lines may be made to coincide wholly, if the lines be equal, or partially, if the lines be of unequal lengths. A definition should properly be restricted to the description of the thing defined, as it exists, independently of any comparison of its properties or of tacitly assuming the existence of axioms.

Def. VII. Euclid's definition of a plane surface is Ἐπίπεδος ἐπιφάνειά ἐστιν ἥτις ἐξ ἴσου ταῖς ἐφ' ἑαυτῆς εὐθείαις κεῖται, "A plane surface is that which lies evenly or equally with the straight lines in it," instead of which Simson has given the definition which was originally proposed by Hero the Elder. A plane superficies may be supposed to be situated in any position, and to be continued in every direction to any extent.

Def. VIII. Simson remarks that this definition seems to include the angles formed by two curved lines, or a curve and a straight line, as well as that formed by two straight lines.

Angles made by straight lines only, are treated of in Elementary Geometry.

Def. IX. It is of the highest importance to attain a clear conception of an angle, and of the sum and difference of two angles. The literal meaning of the term *angulus* suggests the Geometrical conception of an angle, which may be regarded as formed by the divergence of two straight lines from a point. In the definition of an angle, the magnitude of the angle is independent of the lengths of the two lines by which it is included; their mutual divergence from the point at which they meet, is the criterion of the magnitude of an angle, as it is pointed out in the succeeding definitions. The point at which the two lines meet is called the angular point or the vertex of the angle, and must not be confounded with the magnitude of the angle itself. The right angle is fixed in magnitude, and, on this account, it is made the standard with which all other angles are compared.

Two straight lines which actually intersect one another, or which when produced would intersect, are said to be inclined to one another, and the inclination of the two lines is determined by the angle which they make with one another.

Def. X. It may be here observed that in the Elements, Euclid always assumes that when one line is perpendicular to another line, the latter is also perpendicular to the former; and always calls *a right angle*, ὀρθὴ γωνία; but *a straight line*, εὐθεῖα γραμμή.

Def. XIX. This has been restored from Proclus, as it seems to have a meaning in the construction of Prop. 14, Book II, the first case of Prop. 33, Book III, and Prop. 13, Book VI. The definition of the segment of a circle is not once alluded to in Book I, and is not required before the discussion of the properties of the circle in Book III. Proclus remarks on this definition "Hence you may collect that the center has three places, for it is either within the figure, as in the circle, or in its perimeter, as in the semicircle, or without the figure, as in certain conic lines."

Def. XXIV–XXIX. Triangles are divided into three classes, by reference to the relations of their sides, and into three other classes, by reference to their angles. A further classification may be made by considering both the relation of the sides and angles in each triangle.

In Simson's definition of the isosceles triangle, the word *only* must be omitted, as in the Cor. Prop. 5, Book I, an isosceles triangle may be equilateral, and an equilateral triangle is considered isosceles in Prop. 15, Book IV. Objection has been made to the definition of an acute-angled triangle. It is said that it cannot be admitted as a definition, that all the three angles of a triangle are acute, which is supposed in Def. 29. It may be replied, that the definitions of the three kinds of angles point out and seem to supply a foundation for a similar distinction of triangles.

Def. XXX–XXXIV. The definitions of quadrilateral figures are liable to objection. All of them, except the trapezium, fall under the general idea of a parallelogram; but as Euclid defined parallel straight lines after he had defined four-sided figures, no other arrangement could be adopted than the one he has followed; and for which there appeared to him, without doubt, some probable reasons. Sir Henry Savile, in his Seventh Lecture, remarks on some of the definitions of Euclid, "Nec dissimulandum aliquot harum in manibus exiguum esse usum in Geometriâ." A few verbal emendations have been made in some of them.

A square is a four-sided plane figure having all its sides equal, and one angle a right angle; because it is proved in Prop. 46, Book I, that if a parallelogram have one angle a right angle, all its angles are right angles.

An oblong, in the same manner, may be defined as a plane figure of four sides, having only its opposite sides equal, and one of its angles a right angle.

A rhomboid is a four-sided plane figure having only its opposite sides equal to one another and its angles not right angles

Sometimes an irregular four-sided figure which has two sides parallel, is called a trapezoid

Def xxxv. It is possible for two right lines never to meet when produced, and not be parallel.

Def. A The term parallelogram literally implies a figure formed by parallel straight lines, and may consist of four, six, eight, or any even number of sides, where every two of the opposite sides are parallel to one another. In the Elements, however, the term is restricted to four-sided figures, and includes the four species of figures named in the Definitions XXX–XXXIII.

The synthetic method is followed by Euclid not only in the demonstrations of the propositions, but also in laying down the definitions He commences with the simplest abstractions, defining a point, a line, an angle, a superficies, and their different varieties. This mode of proceeding involves the difficulty, almost insurmountable, of defining satisfactorily the elementary abstractions of Geometry. It has been observed, that it is necessary to consider a solid, that is, a magnitude which has length, breadth, and thickness, in order to understand aright the definitions of a point, a line, and a superficies A solid or volume considered apart from its physical properties, suggests the idea of the surfaces by which it is bounded a surface, the idea of the line or lines which form its boundaries and a finite line, the points which form its extremities. A solid is therefore bounded by surfaces; a surface is bounded by lines, and a line is terminated by two points A point marks position only, a line has one dimension, length only, and defines distance; a superficies has two dimensions, length and breadth, and defines extension and a solid has three dimensions, length, breadth, and thickness, and defines some portion of space

It may also be remarked that two points are sufficient to determine the position of a straight line, and three points not in the same straight line, are necessary to fix the position of a plane

ON THE POSTULATES

The definitions assume the possible existence of straight lines and circles, and the postulates predicate the possibility of drawing and of producing straight lines, and of describing circles. The postulates form the principles of construction assumed in the Elements, and are, in fact, problems, the possibility of which is admitted to be self-evident, and to require no proof.

It must, however, be carefully remarked, that the third postulate only admits that when any line is given in position and magnitude, a circle may be described from either extremity of the line as a center, and with a radius equal to the length of the line, as in Euc i, 1. It does not admit the description of a circle with any other point as a center than one of the extremities of the given line.

Euc I 2, shews how, from any given point, to draw a straight line equal to another straight line which is given in magnitude and position.

ON THE AXIOMS.

Axioms are usually defined to be self-evident truths, which cannot be rendered more evident by demonstration; in other words, the axioms of Geometry are theorems, the truth of which is admitted without proof. It is by experience we first become acquainted with the different forms of geometrical magnitudes, and the axioms, or the fundamental ideas of their equality or inequality, appear to rest on the same basis. The conception of the truth of the axioms does not appear to be more removed from experience than the conception of the definitions.

These axioms, or first principles of demonstration, are such theorems as cannot be resolved into simpler theorems, and no theorem ought to be admitted as a first principle of reasoning which is capable of being demonstrated. An axiom, and (when it is convertible) its converse, should both be of such a nature as that neither of them should require a formal demonstration.

The first and most simple idea, derived from experience is, that every magnitude fills a certain space, and that several magnitudes may successively fill the same space.

All the knowledge we have of magnitude is purely relative, and the most simple relations are those of equality and inequality. In the comparison of magnitudes, some are considered as given or known, and the unknown are compared with the known, and conclusions are synthetically deduced with respect to the equality or inequality of the magnitudes under consideration. In this manner we form our idea of equality, which is thus formally stated in the eighth axiom. "Magnitudes which coincide with one another, that is, which exactly fill the same space, are equal to one another."

Every specific definition is referred to this universal principle. With regard to a few more general definitions which do not furnish an equality, it will be found that some hypothesis is always made reducing them to that principle, before any theory is built upon them. As for example, the definition of a straight line is to be referred to the tenth axiom; the definition of a right angle to the eleventh axiom; and the definition of parallel straight lines to the twelfth axiom.

The eighth axiom is called the principle of superposition, or, the mental process by which one Geometrical magnitude may be conceived to be placed on another, so as exactly to coincide with it, in the parts which are made the subject of comparison. Thus, if one straight line be conceived to be placed upon another, so that their extremities are coincident, the two straight lines are equal. If the directions of two lines which include one angle, coincide with the directions of the two lines which contain another angle, where the points, from which the angles diverge, coincide, then the two angles are equal: the lengths of the lines not affecting in any way the magnitudes of the angles. When one plane figure is conceived to be placed upon another, so that the boundaries of one exactly coincide with the boundaries of the other, then the two plane figures are equal. It may also be remarked, that the converse of this proposition is not universally true, namely, that when two magnitudes are equal, they coincide with one another: since two magnitudes may be equal in area, as two parallelograms or two triangles, Euc. I. 35, 37; but their boundaries may not be equal, and consequently, by superposition, the figures could not exactly coincide: all such figures, however, having equal areas, by a different arrangement of their parts, may be made to coincide exactly.

NOTES TO BOOK I.

This axiom is the criterion of Geometrical equality, and is essentially different from the criterion of Arithmetical equality. Two geometrical magnitudes are equal, when they coincide or may be made to coincide; two abstract numbers are equal, when they contain the same aggregate of units; and two concrete numbers are equal, when they contain the same number of units of the same kind of magnitude. It is at once obvious, that Arithmetical representations of Geometrical magnitudes are not admissible in Euclid's criterion of Geometrical Equality, as he has not fixed the unit of magnitude of either the straight line, the angle, or the superficies. Perhaps Euclid intended that the first seven axioms should be applicable to numbers as well as to Geometrical magnitudes; and this is in accordance with the words of Proclus, who calls the axioms, *common notions*, not peculiar to the subject of Geometry.

Several of the axioms may be generally exemplified thus:

Axiom I. If the straight line AB be equal to the straight line CD, and if the straight line EF be also equal to the straight line CD, then the straight line AB is equal to the straight line EF.

Axiom II. If the line AB be equal to the line CD; and if the line EF be also equal to the line GH, then the sum of the lines AB and EF is equal to the sum of the lines CD and GH.

Axiom III. If the line AB be equal to the line CD, and if the line EF be also equal to the line GH; then the difference of AB and EF, is equal to the difference of CD and GH.

Axiom IV. admits of being exemplified under the two following forms:

1. If the line AB be equal to the line CD, and if the line EF be greater than the line GH, then the sum of the lines AB and EF is greater than the sum of the lines CD and GH.

2. If the line AB be equal to the line CD, and if the line EF be less than the line GH, then the sum of the lines AB and EF is less than the sum of the lines CD and GH.

Axiom V. also admits of two forms of exemplification.

1. If the line AB be equal to the line CD, and if the line EF be greater than the line GH, then the difference of the lines AB and EF is greater than the difference of CD and GH.

2. If the line AB be equal to the line CD, and if the line EF be less than the line GH, then the difference of the lines AB and EF is less than the difference of the lines CD and GH.

The axiom, "If unequals be taken from equals, the remainders are unequal," may be exemplified in the same manner.

Axiom VI. If the line AB be double of the line CD; and if the line EF be also double of the line CD; then the line AB is equal to the line EF.

Axiom VII. If the line AB be the half of the line CD; and if the line EF be also the half of the line CD, then the line AB is equal to the line EF.

It may be observed that when equal magnitudes are taken from unequal magnitudes, the greater remainder exceeds the less remainder by as much as the greater of the unequal magnitudes exceeds the less.

If unequals be taken from unequals, the remainders are not always unequal; they may be equal: also if unequals be added to unequals the wholes are not always unequal, they may also be equal.

Axiom IX. The whole is greater than its part, and conversely, the part is less than the whole. This axiom appears to assert the contrary of the eighth axiom, namely, that two magnitudes, of which one is greater than the other, cannot be made to coincide with one another.

Axiom X. The property of straight lines expressed by the tenth axiom, namely, "that two straight lines cannot enclose a space," is obviously implied in the definition of straight lines; for if they enclosed a space, they could not coincide between their extreme points, when the two lines are equal.

Axiom XI. This axiom has been asserted to be a demonstrable theorem. As an angle is a species of magnitude, this axiom is only a particular application of the eighth axiom to right angles.

Axiom XII. See the notes on Prop. XXIX. Book I.

ON THE PROPOSITIONS.

WHENEVER a judgment is formally expressed, there must be something respecting which the judgment is expressed, and something else which constitutes the judgment. The former is called the *subject* of the proposition, and the latter, the *predicate*, which may be anything which can be affirmed or denied respecting the *subject*.

The propositions in Euclid's Elements of Geometry may be divided into two classes, *problems* and *theorems*. A proposition, as the term imports, is something proposed; it is a *problem*, when some Geometrical *construction* is required to be *effected*: and it is a *theorem* when some Geometrical *property* is to be *demonstrated*. Every proposition is naturally divided into two parts; a problem consists of the *data*, or *things given;* and the *quæsita*, or *things required:* a theorem consists of the *subject* or *hypothesis*, and the *conclusion*, or *predicate*. Hence the distinction between a problem and a theorem is this, that a problem consists of the data and the quæsita, and requires solution: and a theorem consists of the hypothesis and the predicate, and requires demonstration.

All propositions are *affirmative* or *negative;* that is, they either assert some property, as Euc. I. 4, or deny the existence of some property, as Euc. I. 7; and every proposition which is affirmatively stated has a contradictory corresponding proposition. If the affirmative be proved to be true, the contradictory is false.

All propositions may be viewed as (1) *universally affirmative*, or *universally negative;* (2) as *particularly affirmative*, or *particularly negative*.

The connected course of reasoning by which any Geometrical truth is established is called a demonstration. It is called a *direct* demonstration when the predicate of the proposition is inferred directly from the premises, as the conclusion of a series of successive deductions. The demonstration is called *indirect*, when the conclusion shows that the introduction of any other supposition contrary to the hypothesis stated in the proposition, necessarily leads to an absurdity.

It has been remarked by Pascal, that "Geometry is almost the only subject as to which we find truths wherein all men agree; and one cause of this is, that Geometers alone regard the true laws of demonstration."

NOTES TO BOOK I. 49

These are enumerated by him as eight in number "1. To define nothing which cannot be expressed in clearer terms than those in which it is already expressed 2. To leave no obscure or equivocal terms undefined 3 To employ in the definition no terms not already known 4 To omit nothing in the principles from which we argue, unless we are sure it is granted 5 To lay down no axiom which is not perfectly evident. 6 To demonstrate nothing which is as clear already as we can make it 7 To prove every thing in the least doubtful by means of self-evident axioms, or of propositions already demonstrated 8 To substitute mentally the definition instead of the thing defined" Of these rules, he says, "the first, fourth and sixth are not absolutely necessary to avoid error, but the other five are indispensable; and though they may be found in books of logic, none but the Geometers have paid any regard to them"

The course pursued in the demonstrations of the propositions in Euclid's Elements of Geometry, is always to refer directly to some expressed principle, to leave nothing to be inferred from vague expressions, and to make every step of the demonstrations the object of the understanding

It has been maintained by some philosophers, that a genuine definition contains some property or properties which can form a basis for demonstration, and that the science of Geometry is deduced from the definitions, and that on them alone the demonstrations depend Others have maintained that a definition explains only the meaning of a term, and does not embrace the nature and properties of the thing defined

If the propositions usually called postulates and axioms are either tacitly assumed or expressly stated in the definitions, in this view, demonstrations may be said to be legitimately founded on definitions. If, on the other hand, a definition is simply an explanation of the meaning of a term, whether abstract or concrete, by such marks as may prevent a misconception of the thing defined; it will be at once obvious that some constructive and theoretic principles must be assumed, besides the definitions to form the ground of legitimate demonstration These principles we conceive to be the postulates and axioms The postulates describe constructions which may be admitted as possible by direct appeal to our experience; and the axioms assert general theoretic truths so simple and self-evident as to require no proof, but to be admitted as the assumed first principles of demonstration Under this view all Geometrical reasonings proceed upon the admission of the hypotheses assumed in the definitions, and the unquestioned possibility of the postulates, and the truth of the axioms

Deductive reasoning is generally delivered in the form of an enthymeme, or an argument wherein one enunciation is not expressed, but is readily supplied by the reader and it may be observed, that although this is the ordinary mode of speaking and writing, it is not in the strictly syllogistic form, as either the *major* or the *minor* premiss only is formally stated before the conclusion Thus in Euc 1, 1

Because the point A is the center of the circle BCD,

therefore the straight line AB is equal to the straight line AC

The premiss here omitted, is all straight lines drawn from the center of a circle to the circumference are equal

In a similar way may be supplied the reserved premiss in every enthymeme The conclusion of two enthymemes may form the major and minor premiss of a third syllogism, and so on, and thus any process of reasoning is reduced to the strictly syllogistic form And in this way it is shewn

3

that the general theorems of Geometry are demonstrated by means of syllogisms founded on the axioms and definitions.

Every syllogism consists of three propositions, of which, two are called the premisses, and the third, the conclusion. These propositions contain three terms, the subject and predicate of the conclusion, and the middle term which connects the predicate and the conclusion together. The subject of the conclusion is called *the minor*, and the predicate of the conclusion is called *the major* term, of the syllogism. The major term appears in one premiss, and the minor term in the other, with the middle term, which is in both premisses. That premiss which contains the middle term and the major term, is called the *major premiss*, and that which contains the middle term and the minor term, is called the *minor premiss* of the syllogism. As an example, we may take the syllogism in the demonstration of Prop 1, Book 1, wherein it will be seen that the middle term is the subject of the major premiss and the predicate of the minor.

Major premiss. Because the straight line AB is equal to the straight line AC,
Minor premiss. and, because the straight line BC is equal to the straight line AB,
Conclusion. therefore the straight line BC is equal to the straight line AC.

Here, BC is the subject, and AC the predicate of the conclusion.
BC is the subject, and AB the predicate of the minor premiss.
AB is the subject, and AC the predicate of the major premiss.

Also, AC is the major term, BC the minor term, and AB the middle term of the syllogism.

In this syllogism, it may be remarked that the definition of a straight line is assumed, and the definition of the Geometrical equality of two straight lines, also that a general theoretic truth, or axiom, forms the ground of the conclusion. And further, though it be impossible to make any point, mark or sign ($\sigma\eta\mu\epsilon\tilde{\iota}o\nu$) which has not both length and breadth, and any line which has not both length and breadth, the demonstrations in Geometry do not on this account become invalid. For they are pursued on the hypothesis that the point has no parts, but position only: and the line has length only, but no breadth or thickness also that the surface has length and breadth only, but no thickness: and all the conclusions at which we arrive are independent of every other consideration.

The truth of the conclusion in the syllogism depends upon the truth of the premisses. If the premisses, or only one of them be not true, the conclusion is false. The conclusion is said *to follow from* the premisses; whereas, in truth, it is *contained in* the premisses. The expression must be understood of the mind apprehending in succession, the truth of the premisses, and subsequent to that, the truth of the conclusion, so that the conclusion *follows from* the premisses in order of time as far as reference is made to the mind's apprehension of the whole argument.

Every proposition, when complete, may be divided into six parts, as Proclus has pointed out in his commentary.

1 *The proposition* or *general enunciation*, which states in general terms the conditions of the problem or theorem.

2. *The exposition* or *particular enunciation*, which exhibits the *subject* of the proposition in particular terms as a fact, and refers it to some diagram described.

3 *The determination* contains the *predicate* in particular terms, as it is pointed out in the diagram, and directs attention to the demonstration, by pronouncing the thing sought.

4. *The construction* applies the postulates to prepare the diagram for the demonstration

5. *The demonstration* is the connexion of syllogisms, which prove the truth or falsehood of the theorem, the possibility or impossibility of the problem, in that particular case exhibited in the diagram

6. *The conclusion* is merely the repetition of the general enunciation, wherein the predicate is asserted as a demonstrated truth

Prop. I In the first two Books, the circle is employed as a mechanical instrument, in the same manner as the straight line, and the use made of it rests entirely on the third postulate No properties of the circle are discussed in these books beyond the definition and the third postulate When two circles are described, one of which has its center in the circumference of the other, the two circles being each of them partly within and partly without the other, their circumferences must intersect each other in two points, and it is obvious from the two circles cutting each other, in two points, one on each side of the given line, that two equilateral triangles may be formed on the given line.

Prop. II. When the given point is neither in the line, nor in the line produced, this problem admits of eight different lines being drawn from the given point in different directions, every one of which is a solution of the problem For, 1 The given line has two extremities, to each of which a line may be drawn from the given point. 2 The equilateral triangle may be described on either side of this line. 3 And the side BD of the equilateral triangle ABD may be produced either way

But when the given point lies either in the line or in the line produced, the distinction which arises from joining the two ends of the line with the given point, no longer exists, and there are only four cases of the problem.

The construction of this problem assumes a neater form, by first describing the circle CGH with center B and radius BC, and producing DB the side of the equilateral triangle DBA to meet the circumference in G. next, with center D and radius DG, describing the circle GKL, and then producing DA to meet the circumference in L.

By a similar construction the less of two given straight lines may be produced, so that the less together with the part produced may be equal to the greater.

Prop III. This problem admits of two solutions, and it is left undetermined from which end of the greater line the part is to be cut off

By means of this problem, a straight line may be found equal to the sum or the difference of two given lines.

Prop iv This forms the first case of equal triangles, two other cases are proved in Prop. VIII and Prop XXVI.

The term *base* is obviously taken from the idea of a building, and the same may be said of the term *altitude* In Geometry, however, these terms are not restricted to one particular position of a figure, as in the case of a building, but may be in any position whatever.

Prop. v. Proclus has given, in his commentary, a proof for the equality of the angles at the base, without producing the equal sides The construction follows the same order, taking in AB one side of the isosceles triangle ABC, a point D and cutting off from AC a part AE equal to AD, and then joining CD and BE

A corollary is a theorem which results from the demonstration of a proposition.

Prop. vi. is the converse of one part of Prop v. One proposition is defined to be the *converse* of another when the hypothesis of the former becomes the predicate of the latter, and vice versa.

There is besides this, another kind of conversion, when a theorem has several hypotheses and one predicate, by assuming the predicate and one, or more than one of the hypotheses, some one of the hypotheses may be inferred as the predicate of the converse. In this manner, Prop VIII is the converse of Prop IV. It may here be observed, that converse theorems are not universally true as for instance, the following direct proposition is universally true, "If two triangles have their three sides respectively equal, the three angles of each shall be respectively equal." But the converse is not universally true, namely, "If two triangles have the three angles in each respectively equal, the three sides are respectively equal." Converse theorems require, in some instances, the consideration of other conditions than those which enter into the proof of the direct theorem. Converse and *contrary* propositions are by no means to be confounded, the *contrary* proposition denies what is asserted, or asserts what is denied, in the *direct* proposition, but the subject and predicate in each are the same. A *contrary proposition is a completely contradictory proposition*, and the distinction consists in this—that *two contrary propositions* may both be false, but of *two contradictory propositions*, one of them must be true, and the other false. It may here be remarked, that one of the most common intellectual mistakes of learners, is to imagine that the denial of a proposition is a legitimate ground for affirming the contrary as true, whereas the rules of sound reasoning allow that the affirmation of a proposition as true, only affords a ground for the denial of the contrary as false.

Prop VI is the first instance of indirect demonstrations, and they are more suited for the proof of converse propositions. All those propositions which are demonstrated ex absurdo, are properly analytical demonstrations, according to the Greek notion of analysis, which first supposed the thing required, to be done, or to be true, and then shewed the consistency or inconsistency of this construction or hypothesis with truths admitted or already demonstrated

In indirect demonstrations, where hypotheses are made which are not true and contrary to the truth stated in the proposition, it seems desirable that a form of expression should be employed different from that in which the hypotheses are true. In all cases therefore, whether noted by Euclid or not, the words *if possible* have been introduced, or some such qualifying expression, as in Euc I 6, so as not to leave upon the mind of the learner, the impression that the hypothesis which contradicts the proposition, is really true

Prop VIII When the three sides of one triangle are shewn to coincide with the three sides of any other, the equality of the triangles is at once obvious This, however, is not stated at the conclusion of Prop VIII or of Prop XXVI. For the equality of the areas of two coincident triangles, reference is always made by Euclid to Prop IV

A direct demonstration may be given of this proposition, and Prop VII. may be dispensed with altogether.

Let the triangles ABC, DEF be so placed that the base BC may coincide with the base EF, and the vertices A, D may be on opposite sides of EF. Join AD Then because EAD is an isosceles triangle, the angle EAD is equal to the angle EDA, and because CDA is an isosceles triangle, the angle CAD is equal to the angle CDA. Hence

NOTES TO BOOK I. 53

the angle EAF is equal to the angle EDF, (ax. 2 or 3) or the angle BDC is equal to the angle EDF.

Prop IX If BA, AC be in the same straight line. This problem then becomes the same as Prob XI, which may be regarded as drawing a line which bisects an angle equal to two right angles.

If EA be produced in the fig Prop 9, it bisects the angle which is the defect of the angle BAC *from four right angles*.

By means of this problem, any angle may be divided into four, eight, sixteen, &c. equal angles.

Prop X. A finite straight line may, by this problem, be divided into four, eight, sixteen, &c equal parts

Prop XI. When the point is at the extremity of the line; by the second postulate the line may be produced, and then the construction applies. See note on Euc. III 31

The distance between two points is the straight line which joins the points; but the distance between a point and a straight line, is *the shortest line* which can be drawn from the point to the line

From this Prop it follows that only one perpendicular can be drawn from a given point to a given line; and this perpendicular may be shewn to be less than any other line which can be drawn from the given point to the given line· and of the rest, the line which is nearer to the perpendicular is less than one more remote from it also only two equal straight lines can be drawn from the same point to the line, one on each side of the perpendicular or the least. This property is analogous to Euc. III. 7, 8.

The corollary to this proposition is not in the Greek text, but was added by Simson, who states that it "is necessary to Prop 1, Book XI, and otherwise"

Prop. XII. The third postulate requires that the line CD should be drawn before the circle can be described with the center C, and radius CD

Prop XIV. is the converse of Prop. XIII. "Upon the opposite sides of it." If these words were omitted, it is possible for two lines to make with a third, two angles, which together are equal to two right angles, in such a manner that the two lines shall not be in the same straight line

The line BE may be supposed to fall above, as in Euclid's figure, or below the line BD, and the demonstration is the same in form

Prop XV is the development of the definition of an angle If the lines at the angular point be produced, the produced lines have the same inclination to one another as the original lines, but in a different position

The converse of this Proposition is not proved by Euclid, namely — If the vertical angles made by four straight lines at the same point be respectively equal to each other, each pair of opposite lines shall be in the same straight line

Prop XVII appears to be only a corollary to the preceding proposition, and it seems to be introduced to explain Axiom XII, of which it is the converse. The exact truth respecting the angles of a triangle is proved in Prop XXXII.

Prop XVIII. It may here be remarked, for the purpose of guarding the student against a very common mistake, that in this proposition, and in the converse of it, the *hypothesis* is stated before the *predicate*

Prop. XIX. is the converse of Prop XVIII It may be remarked, that Prop XIX bears the same relation to Prop. XVIII, as Prop. VI does to Prop V

Prop. xx. The following corollary arises from this proposition :—

A straight line is the shortest distance between two points. For the straight line BC is always less than BA and AC, however near the point A may be to the line BC.

It may be easily shewn from this proposition, that the difference of any two sides of a triangle is less than the third side.

Prop. xxii. When the sum of two of the lines is equal to, and when it is less than the third line, let the diagrams be described and they will exhibit the impossibility implied by the restriction laid down in the Proposition.

The same remark may be made here, as was made under the first Proposition, namely,—if one circle lies partly within and partly without another circle, the circumferences of the circles intersect each other in two points.

Prop. xxiii. CD might be taken equal to CE, and the construction effected by means of an isosceles triangle. It would, however, be less general than Euclid's, but is more convenient in practice.

Prop. xxiv. Simson makes the angle EDG at D in the line ED, the side which is not the greater of the two ED, DF, otherwise, three different cases would arise, as may be seen by forming the different figures. The point G might fall below or upon the base EF produced as well as above it. Prop. xxiv and Prop. xxv. bear to each other the same relation as Prop. iv and Prop. viii.

Prop. xxvi. This forms the third case of the equality of two triangles. Every triangle has three sides and three angles, and when any three of one triangle are given equal to any three of another, the triangles may be proved to be equal to one another, whenever the three magnitudes given in the hypothesis are independent of one another. Prop. iv contains the first case, when the hypothesis consists of two sides and the included angle of each triangle. Prop. viii contains the second, when the hypothesis consists of the three sides of each triangle. Prop. xxvi contains the third, when the hypothesis consists of two angles, and one side either adjacent to the equal angles, or opposite to one of the equal angles in each triangle. There is another case, not proved by Euclid, when the hypothesis consists of two sides and one angle in each triangle, but these not the angles included by the two given sides in each triangle. This case however is only true under a certain restriction, thus :—

If two triangles have two sides of one of them equal to two sides of the other, each to each, and have also the angles opposite to one of the equal sides in each triangle, equal to one another, and if the angles opposite to the other equal sides be both acute, or both obtuse angles, then shall the third sides be equal in each triangle, as also the remaining angles of the one to the remaining angles of the other.

Let ABC, DEF be two triangles which have the sides AB, AC equal to the two sides DE, DF, each to each, and the angle ABC equal to the angle DEF; then, if the angles ACB, DEF, be both acute, or both obtuse angles, the third side BC shall be equal to the third side EF, and also the angle BCA to the angle EFD, and the angle BAC to the angle EDF.

First. Let the angles ACB, DFE, opposite to the equal sides AB, DE, be both acute angles.

If BC be not equal to EF, let BC be the greater, and from BC, cut off BG equal to EF, and join AG.

Then in the triangles ABG, DEF, Euc. 1. 4. AG is equal to DF

and the angle AGB to DFE. But since AC is equal to DF, AG is equal to AC, and therefore the angle ACG is equal to the angle AGC, which is also an acute angle. But because AGC, AGB are together equal to two right angles, and that AGC is an acute angle, AGB must be an obtuse angle, which is absurd. Wherefore, BC is not unequal to EF, that is, BC is equal to EF, and also the remaining angles of one triangle to the remaining angles of the other.

Secondly. Let the angles ACB, DFE, be both *obtuse angles*. By proceeding in a similar way, it may be shewn that BC cannot be otherwise equal to EF.

If ACB, DFE be *both right angles* the case falls under Euc. I. 26.

Prop. XXVII. Alternate angles are defined to be the two angles which two straight lines make with another at its extremities, but upon opposite sides of it.

When a straight line intersects two other straight lines, two pairs of alternate angles are formed by the lines at their intersections, as in the figure, BEF, EFC are alternate angles as well as the angles AEF, EFD.

Prop. XXVIII. One angle is called "the exterior angle," and another "the interior and opposite angle," when they are formed on the same side of a straight line which falls upon or intersects two other straight lines. It is also obvious that on each side of the line, there will be two exterior and two interior and opposite angles. The exterior angle EGB has the angle GHD for its corresponding interior and opposite angle; also the exterior angle FHD has the angle HGB for its interior and opposite angle.

Prop. XXIX. is the converse of Prop. XXVII and Prop. XXVIII.

As the definition of parallel straight lines simply describes them by a statement of the negative property, that they never meet, it is necessary that some positive property of parallel lines should be assumed as an axiom, on which reasonings on such lines may be founded.

Euclid has assumed the statement in the twelfth axiom, which has been objected to, as not being self-evident. A stronger objection appears to be, that the converse of it forms Euc. I. 17, for both the assumed axiom and its converse, should be so obvious as not to require formal demonstration.

Simson has attempted to overcome the objection, not by any improved definition and axiom respecting parallel lines, but by considering Euclid's twelfth axiom to be a theorem, and for its proof, assuming two definitions and one axiom, and then demonstrating five subsidiary Propositions.

Instead of Euclid's twelfth axiom, the following has been proposed as a more simple property for the foundation of reasonings on parallel lines namely, "If a straight line fall on two parallel straight lines, the alternate angles are equal to one another." In whatever this may exceed Euclid's definition in simplicity, it is liable to a similar objection, being the converse of Euc. I. 27.

Professor Playfair has adopted in his Elements of Geometry, that "Two straight lines which intersect one another cannot be both parallel to the same straight line." This apparently more simple axiom follows as a direct inference from Euc. I. 30.

But one of the least objectionable of all the definitions which have been proposed on this subject, appears to be that which simply expresses the conception of equidistance. It may be formally stated thus:—"Parallel lines are such as lie in the same plane, and which neither recede from, nor approach to, each other." This includes the conception stated by Euclid, that parallel lines never meet. Dr. Wallis observes on this subject, " Parallelismus et æquidistantia vel idem sunt, vel certe se mutuo comitantur."

As an additional reason for this definition being preferred, it may be remarked that the meaning of the terms γραμμαὶ παράλληλοι, suggests the exact idea of such lines.

An account of thirty methods which have been proposed at different times for avoiding the difficulty in the twelfth axiom, will be found in the appendix to Colonel Thompson's "Geometry without Axioms."

Prop. xxx. In the diagram, the two lines AB and CD are placed one on each side of the line EF; the proposition may also be proved when both AB and CD are on the same side of EF.

Prop. xxxii. From this proposition, it is obvious that if one angle of a triangle be equal to the sum of the other two angles, that angle is a right angle, as is shewn in Euc. III. 31, and that each of the angles of an equilateral triangle, is equal to two thirds of a right angle, as it is shewn in Euc. iv. 15. Also, if one angle of an isosceles triangle be a right angle, then each of the equal angles is half a right angle, as in Euc. II. 9.

The three angles of a triangle may be shewn to be equal to two right angles without producing a side of the triangle, by drawing through any angle of the triangle a line parallel to the opposite side, as Proclus has remarked in his Commentary on this proposition. It is manifest from this proposition, that the third angle of a triangle is not independent of the sum of the other two, but is known if the sum of any two is known. Cor. 1 may be also proved by drawing lines from any one of the angles of the figure to the other angles. If any of the sides of the figure bent inwards and form what are called re-entering angles, the enunciation of these two corollaries will require some modification. As Euclid gives no definition of re-entering angles, it may fairly be concluded, he did not intend to enter into the proofs of the properties of figures which contain such angles.

Prop. xxxiii. The words "towards the same parts" are a necessary restriction, for if they were omitted, it would be doubtful whether the extremities A, C, and B, D, were to be joined by the lines AC and BD, or the extremities A, D, and B, C, by the lines AD and BC.

Prop. xxxiv. If the other diameter be drawn, it may be shewn that the diameters of a parallelogram bisect each other, as well as bisect the area of the parallelogram. If the parallelogram be right-angled, the diagonals are equal, if the parallelogram be a square or a rhombus, the diagonals bisect each other at right angles. The converse of this Prop, namely, " If the opposite sides or opposite angles of a quadrilateral figure be equal, the opposite sides shall also be parallel; that is, the figure shall be a parallelogram," is not proved by Euclid.

Prop. xxxv. The latter part of the demonstration is not expressed very intelligibly. Simson, who altered the demonstration, seems in fact to consider two trapeziums of the same form and magnitude, and from one of them, to take the triangle ABE, and from the other, the triangle DCF, and then the remainders are equal by the third axiom; that is, the parallelogram $ABCD$ is equal to the parallelogram $EBCF$. Otherwise, the triangle, whose base is DE, (fig. 2,) is taken twice from the trapezium, which would appear to be impossible, if the sense in which Euclid applies the third axiom, is to be retained here.

It may be observed, that the two parallelograms exhibited in fig 2 partially lie on one another, and that the triangle whose base is *BC* is a common part of them, but that the triangle whose base is *DE* is entirely without both the parallelograms. After having proved the triangle *ABE* equal to the triangle *DCF*, if we take from these equals (fig 2) the triangle whose base is *DE*, and to each of the remainders add the triangle whose base is *BC*, then the parallelogram *ABCD* is equal to the parallelogram *EBCF*. In fig 3, the equality of the parallelograms *ABCD*, *EBCF*, is shewn by adding the figure *EBCD* to each of the triangles *ABE*, *DCF*.

In this proposition, the word *equal* assumes a new meaning, and is no longer restricted to mean coincidence in all the parts of two figures

Prop xxxvIII In this proposition, it is to be understood that the bases of the two triangles are in the same straight line. If in the diagram the point *E* coincide with *C*, and *D* with *A*, then the angle of one triangle is supplemental to the other. Hence the following property —If two triangles have two sides of the one respectively equal to two sides of the other, and the contained angles supplemental, the two triangles are equal

A distinction ought to be made between *equal* triangles and *equivalent* triangles, the former including those whose sides and angles mutually coincide the latter those whose areas only are equivalent.

Prop xxxix If the vertices of all the equal triangles which can be described upon the same base, or upon the equal bases as in Prop 40, be joined, the line thus formed will be a straight line, and is called the locus of the vertices of equal triangles upon the same base, or upon equal bases

A locus in plane Geometry is a straight line or a plane curve, every point of which and none else satisfies a certain condition. With the exception of the straight line and the circle, the two most simple loci, all other loci, perhaps including also the Conic Sections, may be more readily and effectually investigated algebraically by means of their rectangular or polar equations

Prop xLI The converse of this proposition is not proved by Euclid; viz. If a parallelogram is double of a triangle, and they have the same base, or equal bases upon the same straight line, and towards the same parts, they shall be between the same parallels. Also, it may easily be shewn that if two equal triangles are between the same parallels, they are either upon the same base, or upon equal bases.

Prop xLIV. A parallelogram described on a straight line is said to be *applied* to that line

Prop xLV The problem is solved only for a rectilineal figure of four sides. If the given rectilineal figure have more than four sides, it may be divided into triangles by drawing straight lines from any angle of the figure to the opposite angles, and then a parallelogram equal to the third triangle can be applied to *LM*, and having an angle equal to *E* and so on for all the triangles of which the rectilineal figure is composed.

Prop xLVI The square being considered as an equilateral rectangle, its area or surface may be expressed numerically if the number of lineal units in a side of the square be given, as is shewn in the note on Prop 1, Book II.

The student will not fail to remark the analogy which exists between the *area of a square* and *the product of two equal numbers*, and between the *side of a square* and *the square root of a number*. There is, however, this distinction to be observed it is always possible to find the product of two equal numbers, (or *to find the square of a number*, as it is usually called,) and to describe a square on a given line, but conversely, though the side of a given square is known from the figure itself, the exact number of units in the side of a square of given area, can only be found exactly, in such cases where the given number is a square number. For example, if the area of a square contain 9 square units, then the square root of 9 or 3, indicates the number of lineal units in the side of that square. Again, if the area of a square contain 12 square units, the side of the square is greater than 3, but less than 4 lineal units, and there is no number which will exactly express the side of that square; an approximation to the true length, however, may be obtained to any assigned degree of accuracy.

Prop XLVII. In a right-angled triangle, the side opposite to the right angle is called the hypotenuse, and the other two sides, the base and perpendicular, according to their position.

In the diagram the three squares are described on the *outer* sides of the triangle ABC. The Proposition may also be demonstrated (1) when the three squares are described upon the *inner* sides of the triangle. (2) when one square is described on the outer side and the other two squares on the inner sides of the triangle. (3) when one square is described on the inner side and the other two squares on the outer sides of the triangle.

As one instance of the third case. If the square BE on the hypotenuse be described on the inner side of BC and the squares BG, HC on the outer sides of AB, AC, the point D falls on the side IG (Euclid's fig.) of the square BG, and KH produced meets CE in E. Let LA meet BC in M. Join DA, then the square GB and the oblong LB are each double of the triangle DAB, (Euc. I. 41,) and similarly by joining EA, the square HC and oblong LC are each double of the triangle EAC. Whence it follows that the squares on the sides AB, AC are together equal to the square on the hypotenuse BC.

By this proposition may be found a square equal to the sum of any given squares, or equal to any multiple of a given square: or equal to the difference of two given squares.

The truth of this proposition may be exhibited to the eye in some particular instances. As in the case of that right-angled triangle whose three sides are 3, 4, and 5 units respectively. If through the points of division of two contiguous sides of each of the squares upon the sides, lines be drawn parallel to the sides, (see the notes on Book II.,) it will be obvious, that the squares will be divided into 9, 16, and 25 small squares, each of the same magnitude; and that the number of the small squares into which the squares on the perpendicular and base are divided is equal to the number into which the square on the hypotenuse is divided.

Prop XLVIII is the converse of Prop XLVII. In this Prop is assumed the Corollary that "the squares described upon two equal lines are equal," and the converse, which properly ought to have been appended to Prop. XLVI.

The First Book of Euclid's Elements, it has been seen, is conversant with the construction and properties of rectilineal figures. It first lays down the definitions which limit the subjects of discussion in the First Book, next the three postulates, which restrict the instruments by which the constructions in Plane Geometry are effected; and thirdly, the twelve axioms, which express the principles by which a comparison is made between the ideas of the things defined.

This Book may be divided into three parts. The first part treats of the origin and properties of triangles, both with respect to their sides and angles, and the comparison of these mutually, both with regard to equality and inequality. The second part treats of the properties of parallel lines and of parallelograms. The third part exhibits the connection of the properties of triangles and parallelograms, and the equality of the squares on the base and perpendicular of a right-angled triangle to the square on the hypotenuse.

When the propositions of the First Book have been read with the notes, the student is recommended to use different letters in the diagrams, and where it is possible, diagrams of a form somewhat different from those exhibited in the text, for the purpose of testing the accuracy of his knowledge of the demonstrations. And further, when he has become sufficiently familiar with the method of geometrical reasoning, he may dispense with the aid of letters altogether, and acquire the power of expressing in general terms the process of reasoning in the demonstration of any proposition. Also, he is advised to answer the following questions before he attempts to apply the principles of the First Book to the solution of Problems and the demonstration of Theorems.

QUESTIONS ON BOOK I.

1. What is the name of the Science of which Euclid gives the Elements? What is meant by *Solid Geometry?* Is there any distinction between *Plane Geometry*, and the *Geometry of Planes?*

2. Define the term *magnitude*, and specify the different kinds of magnitude considered in Geometry. What dimensions of space belong to figures treated of in the first six Books of Euclid?

3. Give Euclid's definition of a "straight line." What does he really use as his test of rectilineaity, and where does he first employ it? What objections have been made to it, and what substitute has been proposed as an available definition? How many points are necessary to fix the position of a straight line in a plane? When is one straight line said to *cut*, and when to *meet* another?

4. What positive property has a Geometrical point? From the definition of a straight line, shew that the intersection of two lines is a point.

5. Give Euclid's definition of a plane rectilineal angle. What are the limits of the angles considered in Geometry? Does Euclid consider angles greater than two right angles?

6. When is a straight line said to be drawn at *right angles*, and when *perpendicular*, to a given straight line?

7. Define a *triangle*, shew how many kinds of triangles there are according to the variation both of the *angles*, and of the *sides*.

8. What is Euclid's definition of a circle? Point out the assumption involved in your definition. Is any axiom applied in it? Shew that in this, as in all other definitions, some geometrical fact is assumed as somehow previously known.

9. Define the quadrilateral figures mentioned by Euclid.

10. Describe briefly the use and foundation of definitions, axioms, and postulates: give illustrations by an instance of each.

11. What objection may be made to the method and order in which Euclid has laid down the elementary abstractions of the Science of Geometry? What other method has been suggested?

12. What distinctions may be made between definitions in the Science of Geometry and in the Physical Sciences?

13. What is necessary to constitute an exact definition? Are definitions propositions? Are they arbitrary? Are they convertible? Does a Mathematical definition admit of proof on the principles of the Science to which it relates?

14. Enumerate the principles of construction assumed by Euclid.

15. Of what instruments may the use be considered to meet approximately the demands of Euclid's postulates? Why only *approximately*?

16. "A circle may be described from any center, with any straight line as radius." How does this postulate differ from Euclid's, and which of his problems is assumed in it?

17. What principles in the Physical Sciences correspond to axioms in Geometry?

18. Enumerate Euclid's twelve axioms, and point out those which have special reference to Geometry. State the converse of those which admit of being so expressed.

19. What two tests of equality are assumed by Euclid? Is the assumption of the principle of superposition (ax. 8), essential to all Geometrical reasoning? Is it correct to say, that it is "an appeal, though of the most familiar sort, to external observation"?

20. Could any, and if any, which of the axioms of Euclid be turned into definitions; and with what advantages or disadvantages?

21. Define the terms, Problem, Postulate, Axiom, and Theorem. Are any of Euclid's axioms improperly so called?

22. Of what two parts does the enunciation of a Problem, and of a Theorem consist? Distinguish them in Euc. 1. 4, 5, 18, 19.

23. When is a problem said to be indeterminate? Give an example.

24. When is one proposition said to be the converse or reciprocal of another? Give examples. Are converse propositions universally true? If not, under what circumstances are they necessarily true? Why is it necessary to demonstrate converse propositions? How are they proved?

25. Explain the meaning of the word *proposition*. Distinguish between *converse* and *contrary* propositions, and give examples.

26. State the grounds as to whether Geometrical reasonings depend for their conclusiveness upon axioms or definitions.

27. Explain the meaning of *enthymeme* and *syllogism*. How is the enthymeme made to assume the form of the syllogism? Give examples.

28. What constitutes a demonstration? State the laws of demonstration.

29. What are the principal parts, in the entire process of establishing a proposition?

30. Distinguish between a *direct* and *indirect* demonstration.

31. What is meant by the term *synthesis*, and what by the term *analysis*? Which of these modes of reasoning does Euclid adopt in his Elements of Geometry?

32. In what sense is it true that the conclusions of Geometry are necessary truths?

33. Enunciate those Geometrical definitions which are used in the proof of the propositions of the First Book.

34. If in Euclid 1. 1, an equal triangle be described on the other side of the given line, what figure will the two triangles form?

35. In the diagram, Euclid 1. 2, if DB a side of the equilateral triangle DAB be produced both ways and cut the circle whose center is B and radius BC in two points G and H, shew that either of the distances, DG, DH

may be taken as the radius of the second circle; and give the proof in each case

36. Explain how the propositions Euc. 1. 2, 3, are rendered necessary by the restriction imposed by the third postulate. Is it necessary for the proof, that the triangle described in Euc. 1. 2, should be equilateral? Could we, at this stage of the subject, describe an isosceles triangle on a given base?

37. State how Euc. 1. 2, may be extended to the following problem: "From a given point to draw a straight line *in a given direction* equal to a given straight line."

38. How would you cut off from a straight line unlimited in both directions, a length equal to a given straight line?

39. In the proof of Euclid 1. 4, how much depends upon Definition, how much upon Axiom?

40. Draw the figure for the third case of Euc. 1. 7, and state why it needs no *demonstration*.

41. In the construction Euclid 1. 9, is it indifferent in all cases on which side of the joining line the equilateral triangle is described?

42. Shew how a given straight line may be bisected by Euc. 1. 1.

43. In what cases do the lines which bisect the interior angles of plane triangles, also bisect one, or more than one of the corresponding opposite sides of the triangles?

44. "Two straight lines cannot have a common segment." Has this corollary been tacitly assumed in any preceding proposition?

45. In Euc. 1. 12, must the given line necessarily be "of unlimited length"?

46. Shew that (fig. Euc. 1. 11) every point without the perpendicular drawn from the middle point of every straight line *DE*, is at unequal distances from the extremities *D, E*, of that line.

47. From what proposition may it be inferred that a straight line is the shortest distance between two points?

48. Enunciate the propositions you employ in the proof of Euc. 1. 16.

49. Is it essential to the truth of Euc. 1. 21, that the two straight lines be drawn from the extremities of the base?

50. In the diagram, Euc. 1. 21, by how much does the greater angle *BDC* exceed the less *BAC*?

51. To form a triangle with three straight lines, any two of them must be greater than the third. Is a similar limitation necessary with respect to the three angles?

52. Is it possible to form a triangle with three lines whose lengths are 1, 2, 3 units; or one with three lines whose lengths are 1, ½, ⅓?

53. Is it possible to construct a triangle whose angles shall be as the numbers 1, 2, 3? Prove or disprove your answer.

54. What is the reason of the limitation in the construction of Euc. 1. 24, viz. "that *DE* is that side which is not greater than the other"?

55. Quote the first proposition in which the equality of two areas which cannot be superposed on each other is considered.

56. Is the following proposition universally true? "If two plane triangles have three elements of the one respectively equal to three elements of the other, the triangles are equal in every respect." Enumerate all the cases in which this equality is proved in the First Book. What case is omitted?

57. What parts of a triangle must be given in order that the triangle may be described?

58. State the converse of the second case of Euc. I. 26. Under what limitations is it true? Prove the proposition so limited.

59. Shew that the angle contained between the perpendiculars drawn to two given straight lines which meet each other, is equal to the angle contained by the lines themselves.

60. Are two triangles necessarily equal in all respects, where a side and two angles of the one are equal to a side and two angles of the other each to each?

61. Illustrate fully the difference between analytical and synthetical proofs. What propositions in Euclid are demonstrated analytically?

62. Can it be properly predicated of any two straight lines that they never meet if indefinitely produced either way, antecedently to our knowledge of some other property of such lines, which makes the property first predicated of them a necessary conclusion from it?

63. Enunciate Euclid's definition and axiom relating to parallel straight lines, and state in what Props. of Book I. they are used.

64. What proposition is the converse to the twelfth axiom of the First Book? What other two propositions are complementary to these?

65. If lines being produced ever so far do not meet, can they be otherwise than parallel? If so, under what circumstances?

66. Define *adjacent angles, opposite angles, vertical angles,* and *alternate angles*, and give examples from the First Book of Euclid.

67. Can you suggest any thing to justify the assumption in the twelfth axiom upon which the proof of Euc. I. 29, depends?

68. What objections have been urged against the definition and the doctrine of parallel straight lines as laid down by Euclid? Where does the difficulty originate? What other assumptions have been suggested, and for what reasons?

69. Assuming as an axiom that two straight lines which cut one another cannot both be parallel to the same straight line, deduce Euclid's twelfth axiom as a corollary of Euc. I. 29.

70. From Euc. I. 27, shew that the distance between two parallel straight lines is constant.

71. If two straight lines be not parallel, shew that all straight lines falling on them, make alternate angles, which differ by the same angle.

72. Taking as the definition of parallel straight lines that they are equally inclined to the same straight line towards the same parts, prove that "being produced ever so far both ways they do not meet." Prove also Euclid's axiom 12, by means of the same definition.

73. What is meant by *exterior* and *interior* angles? Point out examples.

74. Can the three angles of a triangle be proved equal to two right angles without producing a side of the triangle?

75. Shew how the corners of a triangular piece of paper may be turned down, so as to exhibit to the eye that the three angles of a triangle are equal to two right angles.

76. Explain the meaning of the term *corollary*. Enunciate the two corollaries appended to Euc. I. 32, and give another proof of the first. What other corollaries may be deduced from this proposition?

77. Shew that the two lines which bisect the exterior and interior angles of a triangle, as well as those which bisect any two interior angles of a parallelogram, contain a right angle.

78. The opposite sides and angles of a parallelogram are equal to one another, and the diameters bisect it. State and prove the converse of this proposition. Also shew that a quadrilateral figure, is a paral-

lelogram, when its diagonals bisect each other: and when its diagonals divide it into four triangles, which are equal, two and two, viz. those which have the same vertical angles.

79. If two straight lines join the extremities of two parallel straight lines, but *not* towards the same parts, when are the joining lines equal, and when are they unequal?

80. If either diameter of a four-sided figure divide it into two equal triangles, is the figure necessarily a parallelogram? Prove your answer.

81. Shew how to divide one of the parallelograms in Euc. 1. 35, by straight lines so that the parts when properly arranged shall make up the other parallelogram.

82. Distinguish between *equal* triangles and *equivalent* triangles, and give examples from the First Book of Euclid.

83. What is meant by the locus of a point? Adduce instances of loci from the First Book of Euclid.

84. How is it shewn that equal triangles upon the same base or equal bases have equal altitudes, whether they are situated on the same or opposite sides of the same straight line?

85. In Euc. 1. 37, 38, if the triangles are not towards the same parts, shew that the straight line joining the vertices of the triangles is bisected by the line containing the bases.

86. If the complements (fig. Euc. 1. 43) be squares, determine their relation to the whole parallelogram.

87. What is meant by a parallelogram being applied to a straight line?

88. Is the proof of Euc. 1. 45, perfectly general?

89. Define a square without including superfluous conditions, and explain the mode of constructing a square upon a given straight line in conformity with such a definition.

90. The sum of the angles of a square is equal to four right angles. Is the converse true? If not, why?

91. Conceiving a square to be a figure bounded by four equal straight lines not necessarily in the same plane, what condition respecting the angles is necessary to complete the definition?

92. In Euclid 1. 47, why is it necessary to prove that one side of each square described upon each of the sides containing the right angle, should be in the same straight line with the other side of the triangle?

93. On what assumption is an analogy shewn to exist between the product of two equal numbers and the surface of a square?

94. Is the triangle whose sides are 3, 4, 5 right-angled or not?

95. Can the side and diagonal of a square be represented simultaneously by any finite numbers?

96. By means of Euc. 1. 47, the square roots of the natural numbers, 1, 2, 3, 4, &c may be represented by straight lines.

97. If the square on the hypotenuse in the fig. Euc. 1. 47, be described on the other side of it: shew from the diagram how the squares on the two sides of the triangle may be made to cover exactly the square on the hypotenuse.

98. If Euclid II. 2, be assumed, enunciate the form in which Euc. 1. 47 may be expressed.

99. Classify all the properties of *triangles* and *parallelograms*, proved in the First Book of Euclid.

100. Mention any propositions in Book I which are included in more general ones which follow.

ON THE ANCIENT GEOMETRICAL ANALYSIS.

SYNTHESIS, or the method of composition, is a mode of reasoning which begins with something given, and ends with something required, either to be done or to be proved. This may be termed a *direct process*, as it leads from principles to consequences.

Analysis, or the method of resolution, is the reverse of synthesis, and thus it may be considered an *indirect process*, a method of reasoning from consequences to principles.

The synthetic method is pursued by Euclid in his Elements of Geometry. He commences with certain assumed principles, and proceeds to the solution of problems and the demonstration of theorems by undeniable and successive inferences from them.

The Geometrical Analysis was a process employed by the ancient Geometers both for the discovery of the solution of problems and for the investigation of the truth of theorems. In the analysis of a *problem*, the quæsita, or what is required to be done, is supposed to have been effected, and the consequences are traced by a series of geometrical constructions and reasonings, till at length they terminate in the data of the problem, or in some previously demonstrated or admitted truth, whence the direct solution of the problem is deduced.

In the Synthesis of a *problem*, however, the last consequence of the analysis is assumed as the first step of the process, and by proceeding in a contrary order through the several steps of the analysis until the process terminate in the quæsita, the solution of the problem is effected.

But if, in the analysis, we arrive at a consequence which contradicts any truth demonstrated in the Elements, or which is inconsistent with the data of the problem, the problem must be impossible; and further, if in certain relations of the given magnitudes the construction be possible, while in other relations it is impossible, the discovery of these relations will become a necessary part of the solution of the problem.

In the analysis of a *theorem*, the question to be determined is, whether by the application of the geometrical truths proved in the Elements, the predicate is consistent with the hypothesis. This point is ascertained by assuming the predicate to be true, and by deducing the successive consequences of this assumption combined with proved geometrical truths, till they terminate in the hypothesis of the theorem or some demonstrated truth. The theorem will be proved synthetically by retracing, in order, the steps of the investigation pursued in the analysis, til they terminate in the predicate, which was assumed in the analysis. This process will constitute the demonstration of the theorem.

If the assumption of the truth of the predicate in the analysis lead to some consequence which is inconsistent with any demonstrated truth, the false conclusion thus arrived at, indicates the falsehood of the predicate; and by reversing the process of the analysis, it may be demonstrated, that the theorem cannot be true.

It may here be remarked, that the geometrical analysis is more extensively useful in discovering the solution of problems than for investigating the demonstration of theorems.

From the nature of the subject, it must be at once obvious, that no general rules can be prescribed, which will be found applicable in all cases, and infallibly lead to the solution of every problem. The conditions of problems must suggest what constructions may be possible; and the consequences which follow from these constructions and the assumed solution, will shew the possibility or impossibility of arriving at some known property consistent with the data of the problem.

Though the data of a problem may be given in magnitude and position, certain ambiguities will arise, if they are not properly restricted. Two points may be considered as situated on the same side, or one on each side of a given line; and there may be two lines drawn from a given point making equal angles with a line given in position; and to avoid ambiguity, it must be stated on which side of the line the angle is to be formed.

A problem is said to be *determinate* when, with the prescribed conditions, it admits of one definite solution, the same construction which may be made on the other side of any given line, not being considered a different solution—and a problem is said to be *indeterminate* when it admits of more than one definite solution. This latter circumstance arises from the data not *absolutely fixing*, but *merely restricting* the quæsita, leaving certain points or lines not fixed in one position only. The number of given conditions may be insufficient for a single determinate solution, or relations may subsist among some of the given conditions from which one or more of the remaining given conditions may be deduced.

If the base of a right-angled triangle be given, and also the difference of the squares of the hypotenuse and perpendicular, the triangle is indeterminate. For though apparently here are three things given, the right angle, the base, and the difference of the squares of the hypotenuse and perpendicular, it is obvious that these three apparent conditions are in fact reducible to two; for since in a right-angled triangle, the sum of the squares on the base and on the perpendicular, is equal to the square on the hypotenuse, it follows that the difference of the squares of the hypotenuse and perpendicular, is equal to the square of the base of the triangle, and therefore the base is known from the difference of the squares of the hypotenuse and perpendicular being known. The conditions therefore are insufficient to determine a right-angled triangle; an indefinite number of triangles may be found with the prescribed conditions, whose vertices will lie in the line which is perpendicular to the base.

If a problem relate to the determination of *a single point*, and the data be sufficient to determine the position of that point, the problem is *determinate:* but if one or more of the conditions be omitted, the data which remain may be sufficient for the determination of more than one point, each of which satisfies the conditions of the problem; in that case, the problem is *indeterminate* and in general, such points are found to be situated in some line, and hence such line is called the locus of the point which satisfies the conditions of the problem.

If any two given points A and B (fig. Euc. iv. 5) be joined by a straight line AB, and this line be bisected in D, then if a perpendicular be drawn from the point of bisection, it is manifest that a circle described with *any* point in the perpendicular as a center, and a radius equal to its distance from one of the given points, will pass through the other point, and the perpendicular will be the locus of all the circles which can be described passing through the two given points.

Again, if a third point C be taken, but not in the same straight line with the other two, and this point be joined with the first point, A; then the perpendicular drawn from the bisection E of this line will be the locus of the centers of all circles which pass through the first and third points A and C. But the perpendicular at the bisection of the first and second points A and B is the locus of the centers of circles which pass through these two points. Hence the intersection F of these two perpendiculars, will be the center of a circle which passes through the three points and is called the intersection of the two loci. Sometimes this method of solving geometrical problems may be pursued with advantage, by constructing the locus of every two points separately, which are given in the conditions of the problem. In the Geometrical Exercises which follow, only those local problems are given where the locus is either a straight line or a circle.

Whenever the quæsitum is a point, the problem on being rendered indeterminate, becomes a locus, whether the deficient datum be of the essential or of the accidental kind. When the quæsitum is a straight line or a circle, (which were the only two loci admitted into the ancient Elementary Geometry,) the problem *may* admit of an *accidentally indeterminate* case, but will not *invariably* or even very frequently do so. This will be the case, when the line or circle shall be so far arbitrary in its position, as depends upon the deficiency of a *single* condition to fix it perfectly; —that is, (for instance,) one point in the line, or two points in the circle, may be determined from the given conditions, but the remaining one is indeterminate from the accidental relations among the data of the problem.

Determinate Problems become indeterminate by the merging of some one datum in the results of the remaining ones. This may arise in three different ways: first, from the coincidence of two points, secondly, from that of two straight lines, and thirdly, from that of two circles. These, further, are the only three ways in which this accidental coincidence of data can produce this indeterminateness; that is, in other words, convert the problem into a Porism.

In the original Greek of Euclid's Elements, the corollaries to the propositions are called porisms, (πορισματα,) but this scarcely explains the nature of *porisms*, as it is manifest that they are different from simple deductions from the demonstrations of propositions. Some analogy, however, we may suppose them to have to the porisms or corollaries in the Elements. Pappus (Coll. Math. Lib vii. pref.) informs us that Euclid wrote three books on Porisms. He defines "a porism to be something between a problem and a theorem, or that in which something is proposed to be investigated." Dr Simson, to whom is due the merit of having restored the porisms of Euclid, gives the following definition of that class of propositions "Porisma est propositio in qua proponitur demonstrare rem aliquam, vel plures datas esse, cui, vel quibus, ut et cuilibet ex rebus innumeris, non quidem, datis, sed quæ ad ea quæ data sunt eandem habent relationem, convenire ostendendum est affectionem quandam communem in propositione descriptam." That is, "A Porism is a proposition in which it is proposed to demonstrate that some one thing, or more things than one, are given, to which, as also to each of innumerable other things, not given indeed, but which have the same relation to those which are given, it is to be shewn that there belongs some common affection described in the proposition." Professor Dugald Stewart defines a porism to be "A proposition affirming the possibility of finding one or more of the conditions of an indeterminate theorem." Professor Playfair in a paper (from which the following account is taken) on Porisms, printed in the Transactions of the Royal Society of Edinburgh, for the year 1792, defines a porism to be "A proposition affirming the possibility of finding such conditions as will render a certain problem indeterminate or capable of innumerable solutions."

It may without much difficulty be perceived that this definition represents a porism as almost the same as an indeterminate problem. There is a large class of indeterminate problems which are, in general, loci, and satisfy certain defined conditions. Every indeterminate problem containing a locus may be made to assume the form of a porism, but not the converse. Porisms are of a more general nature than indeterminate problems which involve a locus.

The ancient geometers appear to have undertaken the solution of problems with a scrupulous and minute attention, which would scarcely allow any of the collateral truths to escape their observation. They never considered a problem as solved till they had distinguished all its varieties, and evolved separately every different case that could occur, carefully distinguishing whatever change might arise in the construction from any change that was supposed to take place among the magnitudes which were given. This cautious method of proceeding soon led them to see that there were circumstances in which the solution of a problem would cease to be possible; and this always happened when one of the conditions of the data was inconsistent with the rest. Such instances would occur in the simplest problems, but in the analysis of more complex problems, they must have remarked that their constructions failed, for a reason directly contrary to that assigned. Instances would be found where the lines, which, by their intersection, were to determine the thing sought, instead of intersecting one another, as they did in general, or of not meeting at all, would coincide with one another entirely, and consequently leave the question unresolved. The confusion thus arising would soon be cleared up, by observing, that a problem before determined by the intersection of two lines, would now become capable of an indefinite number of solutions. This was soon perceived to arise from one of the conditions of the problem involving another, or from two parts of the data becoming one, so that there was not left a sufficient number of independent conditions to confine the problem to a single solution, or any determinate number of solutions. It was not difficult afterwards to perceive that these cases of problems formed very curious propositions, of an indeterminate nature between problems and theorems, and that they admitted of being enunciated separately. It was to such propositions so enunciated that the ancient geometers gave the name of *Porisms*.

Besides, it will be found, that some problems are possible within certain limits, and that certain magnitudes increase while others decrease within those limits, and after having reached a certain value, the former begin to decrease, while the latter increase. This circumstance gives rise to questions of *maxima* and *minima*, or the greatest and least values which certain magnitudes may admit of in determinate problems

In the following collection of problems and theorems, most will be found to be of so simple a character, (being almost obvious deductions from propositions in the Elements,) as scarcely to admit of the principle of the Geometrical Analysis being applied in their solution.

It must however be recollected that a clear and exact knowledge of the first principles of Geometry must necessarily precede any intelligent application of them. Indistinctness or defectiveness of understanding with respect to these, will be a perpetual source of error and confusion. The learner is therefore recommended to understand the principles of the Science, and their connection fully, before he attempt any applications of them. The following directions may assist him in his proceedings

ANALYSIS OF THEOREMS.

1. Assume that the Theorem is true.

2. Proceed to examine any consequences that result from this admission, by the aid of other truths respecting the diagram which have been already proved.

3. Examine whether any of these consequences are already known to be *true*, or to be *false*.

4 It any one of them be false, we have arrived at a *reductio ad absurdum*, which proves that the theorem itself is false, as in Euc. 1 25.

5 If none of the consequences so deduced be *known* to be either true or false, proceed to deduce other consequences from all or any of these, as in (2)

6. Examine these results, and proceed as in (3) and (4); and if still without any conclusive indications of the truth or falsehood of the alleged theorem, proceed still further, until such are obtained.

ANALYSIS OF PROBLEMS.

1. In general, any given problem will be found to depend on several problems and theorems, and these ultimately on some problem or theorem in Euclid.

2. Describe the diagram as directed in the enunciation, and suppose the solution of the problem effected.

3. Examine the relations of the lines, angles, triangles, &c in the diagram, and find the dependence of the assumed solution on some theorem or problem in the Elements.

4. If such cannot be found, draw other lines parallel or perpendicular as the case may require, join given points, or points assumed in the solution, and describe circles it need be, and then proceed to trace the dependence of the assumed solution on some theorem or problem in Euclid

5 Let not the first unsuccessful attempts at the solution of a Problem be considered as of no value, such attempts have been found to lead to the discovery of other theorems and problems.

GEOMETRICAL EXERCISES ON BOOK I.

PROPOSITION I. PROBLEM.

To trisect a given straight line.

ANALYSIS. Let AB be the given straight line, and suppose it divided into three equal parts in the points D, E.

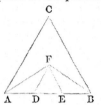

On DE describe an equilateral triangle DEF,
then DF is equal to AD, and FE to EB.
On AB describe an equilateral triangle ABC,
and join AF, FB.
Then because AD is equal to DF,
therefore the angle AFD is equal to the angle DAF,
and the two angles DAF, DFA are double of one of them DAF.
But the angle FDE is equal to the angles DAF, DFA,
and the angle FDE is equal to DAC, each being an angle of an equilateral triangle;
therefore the angle DAC is double the angle DAF;
wherefore the angle DAC is bisected by AF.
Also because the angle FAC is equal to the angle FAD,
and the angle FAD to DFA;
therefore the angle CAF is equal to the alternate angle AFD:
and consequently FD is parallel to AC.

Synthesis. Upon AB describe an equilateral triangle ABC, bisect the angles at A and B by the straight lines AF, BF, meeting in F; through F draw FD parallel to AC, and FE parallel to BC.
Then AB is trisected in the points D, E.
For since AC is parallel to FD and FA meets them,
therefore the alternate angles FAC, AFD are equal;
but the angle FAD is equal to the angle FAC,
hence the angle DAF is equal to the angle AFD,
and therefore DF is equal to DA.
But the angle FDE is equal to the angle CAB,
and FED to CBA; (I. 29.)
therefore the remaining angle DFE is equal to the remaining angle ACB.
Hence the three sides of the triangle DFE are equal to one another,
and DF has been shewn to be equal to DA,
therefore AD, DE, EB are equal to one another.
Hence the following theorem.

If the angles at the base of an equilateral triangle be bisected by two lines which meet at a point within the triangle; the two lines drawn from this point parallel to the sides of the triangle, divide the base into three equal parts.

Note. There is another method whereby a line may be divided into three equal parts :—by drawing from one extremity of the given line, another making an acute angle with it, and taking three equal distances from the extremity, then joining the extremities, and through the other two points of division, drawing lines parallel to this line through the other two points of division, and to the given line ; the three triangles thus formed are equal in all respects. This may be extended for any number of parts, and is a particular case of Euc. vi.10.

PROPOSITION II. THEOREM.

If two opposite sides of a parallelogram be bisected, and two lines be drawn from the points of bisection to the opposite angles, these two lines trisect the diagonal.

Let $ABCD$ be a parallelogram of which the diagonal is AC.
Let AB be bisected in E, and DC in F,
also let DE, FB be joined cutting the diagonal in G, H.
Then AC is trisected in the points G, H.

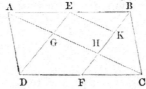

Through E draw EK parallel to AC and meeting FB in K,
Then because EB is the half of AB, and DF the half of DC,
therefore EB is equal to DF;
and these equal and parallel straight lines are joined towards the same parts by DE and FB;
therefore DE and FB are equal and parallel. (i. 33.)
And because AEB meets the parallels EK, AC,
therefore the exterior angle BEK is equal to the interior angle EAG.
For a similar reason, the angle EBK is equal to the angle AEG.
Hence in the triangles AEG, EBK, there are the two angles GAE, AEG in the one, equal to the two angles KEB, EBK, in the other, and one side adjacent to the equal angles in each triangle, namely AE equal to EB;
therefore AG is equal to EK, (i. 26.)
but EK is equal to GH, (i. 34.) therefore AG is equal to GH.
By a similar process, it may be shewn that GH is equal to HC.
Hence AG, GH, HC are equal to one another,
and therefore AC is trisected in the points G, H.
It may also be proved that BF is trisected in H and K.

PROPOSITION III. PROBLEM.

Draw through a given point, between two straight lines not parallel, a straight line which shall be bisected in that point.

Analysis. Let BC, BD be the two lines meeting in B, and let A be the given point between them.

Suppose the line EAF drawn through A, so that EA is equal to AF,

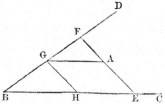

through A draw AG parallel to BC, and GH parallel to EF.
Then $AGHE$ is a parallelogram, wherefore AE is equal to GH,
but EA is equal to AF by hypothesis; therefore GH is equal to AF.
Hence in the triangles BHG, GAF,
the angles HBG, AGF are equal, as also BGH, GFA, (I. 29.)
also the side GH is equal to AF;
whence the other parts of the triangles are equal, (I. 26.)
therefore BG is equal to GF.
Synthesis. Through the given point A, draw AG parallel to BC,
on GD, take GF equal to GB;
then F is a second point in the required line:
join the points F, A, and produce FA to meet BC in E;
then the line FE is bisected in the point A;
draw GH parallel to AE.
Then in the triangles BGH, GFA, the side BG is equal to GF,
and the angles GBH, BGH are respectively equal to FGA, GFA;
wherefore GH is equal to AF, (I. 26.)
but GH is equal to AE, (I. 34.)
therefore AE is equal to AF, or EF is bisected in A.

PROPOSITION IV. PROBLEM.

From two given points on the same side of a straight line given in position, draw two straight lines which shall meet in that line, and make equal angles with it; also prove, that the sum of these two lines is less than the sum of any other two lines drawn to any other point in the line.

Analysis. Let A, B be the two given points, and CD the given line.
Suppose G the required point in the line, such that AG and BG being joined, the angle AGC is equal to the angle BGD.

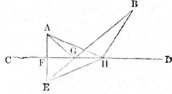

Draw AF perpendicular to CD and meeting BG produced in E.
Then, because the angle BGD is equal to AGF, (hyp.)
and also to the vertical angle FGE, (I. 15.)
therefore the angle AGF is equal to the angle EGF;

also the right angle *AFG* is equal to the right angle *EFG*,
and the side *FG* is common to the two triangles *AFG, EFG*,
therefore *AG* is equal to *EG*, and *AF* to *FE*.

Hence the point *E* being known, the point *G* is determined by the intersection of *CD* and *BE*.

Synthesis. From *A* draw *AF* perpendicular to *CD*, and produce it to *E*, making *FE* equal to *AF*, and join *BE* cutting *CD* in *G*.
Join also *AG*.

Then *AG* and *BG* make equal angles with *CD*.

For since *AF* is equal to *FE*, and *FG* is common to the two triangles *AGF, EGF*, and the included angles *AFG, EFG* are equal;
therefore the base *AG* is equal to the base *EG*,
and the angle *AGF* to the angle *EGF*,
but the angle *EGF* is equal to the vertical angle *BGD*,
therefore the angle *AGF* is equal to the angle *BGD*;
that is, the straight lines *AG* and *BG* make equal angles with the straight line *CD*.

Also the sum of the lines *AG, GB* is a minimum.

For take any other point *H* in *CD*, and join *EH, HB, AH*.
Then since any two sides of a triangle are greater than the third side, therefore *EH, HB* are greater than *EB* in the triangle *EHB*.

But *EG* is equal to *AG*, and *EH* to *AH*;
therefore *AH, HB* are greater than *AG, GB*.

That is, *AG, GB* are less than any other two lines which can be drawn from *A, B*, to any other point *H* in the line *CD*.

By means of this Proposition may be found the shortest path from one given point to another, subject to the condition, that it shall meet two given lines.

PROPOSITION V. PROBLEM.

Given one angle, a side opposite to it, and the sum of the other two sides, construct the triangle.

Analysis. Suppose *BAC* the triangle required, having *BC* equal to the given side, *BAC* equal to the given angle opposite to *BC*, also *BD* equal to the sum of the other two sides.

Join *DC*.

Then since the two sides *BA, AC* are equal to *BD*, by taking *BA* from these equals, the remainder *AC* is equal to the remainder *AD*.

Hence the triangle *ACD* is isosceles, and therefore the angle *ADC* is equal to the angle *ACD*.

But the exterior angle *BAC* of the triangle *ADC* is equal to the two interior and opposite angles *ACD* and *ADC*:

Wherefore the angle *BAC* is double the angle *BDC*, and *BDC* is the half of the angle *BAC*.

Hence the synthesis.

At the point D in BD, make the angle BDC equal to half the
given angle,
and from B the other extremity of BD, draw BC equal to the
given side, and meeting DC in C,
at C in CD make the angle DCA equal to the angle CDA, so
that CA may meet BD in the point A.
Then the triangle ABC shall have the required conditions.

PROPOSITION VI. PROBLEM.

To bisect a triangle by a line drawn from a given point in one of the sides.

Analysis. Let ABC be the given triangle, and D the given
point in the side AB.

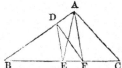

Suppose DF the line drawn from D which bisects the triangle;
therefore the triangle DBF is half of the triangle ABC.
Bisect BC in E, and join AE, DE, AF,
then the triangle ABE is half of the triangle ABC:
hence the triangle ABE is equal to the triangle DBF;
take away from these equals the triangle DBE,
therefore the remainder ADE is equal to the remainder DEF.
But ADE, DEF are equal triangles upon the same base DE, and
on the same side of it,
they are therefore between the same parallels, (I. 39.)
that is, AF is parallel to DE,
therefore the point F is determined.
Synthesis. Bisect the base BC in E, join DE,
from A, draw AF parallel to DE, and join DF.
Then because DE is parallel to AF,
therefore the triangle ADE is equal to the triangle DEF;
to each of these equals, add the triangle BDE,
therefore the whole triangle ABE is equal to the whole DBF,
but ABE is half of the whole triangle ABC;
therefore DBF is also half of the triangle ABC.

PROPOSITION VII. THEOREM.

*If from a point without a parallelogram lines be drawn to the extremities
of two adjacent sides, and of the diagonal which they include: of the triangles thus formed, that, whose base is the diagonal, is equal to the sum of
the other two.*

Let ABCD be a parallelogram of which AC is one of the diagonals, and let P be any point without it: and let AP, PC, BP, PD
be joined.
Then the triangles APD, APB are together equivalent to the
triangle APC.

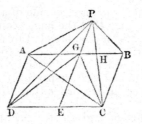

Draw PGE parallel to AD or BC, and meeting AB in G, and DC in E; and join DG, GC.

Then the triangles CBP, CBG are equal: (I. 37.)
and taking the common part CBH from each,
the remainders PHB, CHG are equal.

Again, the triangles DAP, DAG are equal; (I. 37.)
also the triangles DAG, AGC are equal, being on the same base AG, and between the same parallels AG, DC:
therefore the triangle DAP is equal to the triangle AGC:
but the triangle PHB is equal to the triangle CHG,
wherefore the triangles PHB, DAP are equal to AGC, CHG, or ACH, add to these equals the triangle APH,
therefore the triangles APH, PHB, DAP are equal to APH, ACH, that is, the triangles APB, DAP are together equal to the triangle PAC.

If the point P be within the parallelogram, then the *difference* of the triangles APB, DAP may be proved to be equal to the triangle PAC.

I.

8. Describe an isosceles triangle upon a given base and having each of the sides double of the base, without using any proposition of the Elements subsequent to the first three. If the base and sides be given, what condition must be fulfilled with regard to the magnitude of each of the equal sides in order that an isosceles triangle may be constructed?

9. In the fig. Euc. I. 5. If FC and BG meet in H, then prove that AH bisects the angle BAC.

10. In the fig. Euc. I. 5. If the angle FBG be equal to the angle ABC, and BG, CF, intersect in O; the angle BOF is equal to twice the angle BAC.

11. From the extremities of the base of an isosceles triangle straight lines are drawn perpendicular to the sides, the angles made by them with the base are each equal to half the vertical angle.

12. A line drawn bisecting the angle contained by the two equal sides of an isosceles triangle, bisects the third side at right angles.

13. If a straight line drawn bisecting the vertical angle of a triangle also bisect the base, the triangle is isosceles.

14. Given two points, one on each side of a given straight line; find a point in the line such that the angle contained by two lines drawn to the given points may be bisected by the given line.

15. In the fig. Euc. i. 5, let F and G be the points in the sides AB and AC produced, and let lines FH and GK be drawn perpendicular and equal to FC and GB respectively; also if BH, CK, or these lines produced meet in O, prove that BH is equal to CK, and BO to CO.

16. From every point of a given straight line, the straight lines drawn to each of two given points on opposite sides of the line are equal: prove that the line joining the given points will cut the given line at right angles.

17. If A be the vertex of an isosceles triangle ABC, and BA be produced so that AD is equal to BA, and DC be drawn; shew that BCD is a right angle.

18. The straight line EDF, drawn at right angles to BC the base of an isosceles triangle ABC, cuts the side AB in D, and CA produced in E; shew that AED is an isosceles triangle.

19. In the fig. Euc. i. 1, if AB be produced both ways to meet the circles in D and E, and from C, CD and CE be drawn; the figure CDE is an isosceles triangle having each of the angles at the base, equal to one-fourth of the angle at the vertex of the triangle.

20. From a given point, draw two straight lines making equal angles with two given straight lines intersecting one another.

21. From a given point to draw a straight line to a given straight line, that shall be bisected by another given straight line.

22. Place a straight line of given length between two given straight lines which meet, so that it shall be equally inclined to each of them.

23. To determine that point in a straight line from which the straight lines drawn to two other given points shall be equal, provided the line joining the two given points is not perpendicular to the given line.

24. In a given straight line to find a point equally distant from two given straight lines. In what case is this impossible?

25. If a line intercepted between the extremity of the base of an isosceles triangle, and the opposite side (produced if necessary) be equal to a side of the triangle, the angle formed by this line and the base produced, is equal to three times either of the equal angles of the triangle.

26. In the base BC of an isosceles triangle ABC, take a point D, and in CA take CE equal to CD, let ED produced meet AB produced in F; then $3\,AEF = 2$ right angles $+ AFE$, or $= 4$ right angles $+ AFE$.

27. If from the base to the opposite sides of an isosceles triangle, three straight lines be drawn, making equal angles with the base, viz., one from its extremity, the other two from any other point in it, these two shall be together equal to the first.

28. A straight line is drawn, terminated by one of the sides of an isosceles triangle, and by the other side produced, and bisected by the base, prove that the straight lines, thus intercepted between the

vertex of the isosceles triangle, and this straight line, are together equal to the two equal sides of the triangle.

29. In a triangle, if the lines bisecting the angles at the base be equal, the triangle is isosceles, and the angle contained by the bisecting lines is equal to an exterior angle at the base of the triangle.

30 In a triangle, if the two straight lines drawn from the extremities of the base, (1) perpendicular to the sides, (2) bisecting the sides, (3) making equal angles with the sides, the triangle is isosceles: and then these lines which respectively join the intersections of the sides, are parallel to the base.

II.

31. ABC is a triangle right-angled at B, and having the angle A double the angle C; shew that the side BC is less than double the side AB

32. If one angle of a triangle be equal to the sum of the other two, the greatest side is double of the distance of its middle point from the opposite angle

33. If from the right angle of a right-angled triangle, two straight lines be drawn, one perpendicular to the base, and the other bisecting it, they will contain an angle equal to the difference of the two acute angles of the triangle.

34. If the vertical angle CAB of a triangle ABC be bisected by AD, to which the perpendiculars CE, BF are drawn from the remaining angles bisect the base BC in G, join GE, GF, and prove these lines equal to each other

35. The difference of the angles at the base of any triangle, is double the angle contained by a line drawn from the vertex perpendicular to the base, and another bisecting the angle at the vertex.

36 If one angle at the base of a triangle be double of the other, the less side is equal to the sum or difference of the segments of the base made by the perpendicular from the vertex, according as the angle is greater or less than a right angle.

37. If two exterior angles of a triangle be bisected, and from the point of intersection of the bisecting lines, a line be drawn to the opposite angle of the triangle, it will bisect that angle

38 From the vertex of a scalene triangle draw a right line to the base, which shall exceed the less side as much as it is exceeded by the greater

39 Divide a right angle into three equal angles

40. One of the acute angles of a right-angled triangle is three times as great as the other; trisect the smaller of these.

41. Prove that the sum of the distances of any point within a triangle from the three angles is greater than half the perimeter of the triangle.

42. The perimeter of an isosceles triangle is less than that of any other equal triangle upon the same base.

43. If from the angles of a triangle ABC, straight lines ADE, BDF, CDG be drawn through a point D to the opposite sides, prove that the sides of the triangle are together greater than the three

lines drawn to the point D, and less than twice the same, but greater than two-thirds of the lines drawn through the point to the opposite sides.

44. In a plane triangle an angle is right, acute or obtuse, according as the line joining the vertex of the angle with the middle point of the opposite side is equal to, greater or less than half of that side.

45 If the straight line AD bisect the angle A of the triangle ABC, and BDE be drawn perpendicular to AD and meeting AC or AC produced in E, shew that $BD = DE$

46. The side BC of a triangle ABC is produced to a point D. The angle ACB is bisected by a line CE which meets AB in E. A line is drawn through E parallel to BC and meeting AC in F, and the line bisecting the exterior angle ACD, in G. Shew that EF is equal to FG.

47 The sides AB, AC, of a triangle are bisected in D and E respectively, and BE, CD, are produced until $EF = EB$, and $GD = DC$; shew that the line GF passes through A.

48 In a triangle ABC. AD being drawn perpendicular to the straight line BD which bisects the angle B, shew that a line drawn from D parallel to BC will bisect AC.

49. If the sides of a triangle be trisected and lines be drawn through the points of section adjacent to each angle so as to form another triangle, this shall be in all respects equal to the first triangle.

50. Between two given straight lines it is required to draw a straight line which shall be equal to one given straight line, and parallel to another.

51. If from the vertical angle of a triangle three straight lines be drawn, one bisecting the angle, another bisecting the base, and the third perpendicular to the base, the first is always intermediate in magnitude and position to the other two.

52. In the base of a triangle, find the point from which, lines drawn parallel to the sides of the triangle and limited by them, are equal.

53. In the base of a triangle, to find a point from which if two lines be drawn, (1) perpendicular, (2) parallel, to the two sides of the triangle, their sum shall be equal to a given line.

III.

54. In the figure of Euc 1 1, the given line is produced to meet either of the circles in P, shew that P and the points of intersection of the circles, are the angular points of an equilateral triangle.

55. If each of the equal angles of an isosceles triangle be one-fourth of the third angle, and from one of them a line be drawn at right angles to the base meeting the opposite side produced, then will the part produced, the perpendicular, and the remaining side, form an equilateral triangle.

56 In the figure Euc 1 1, if the sides CA, CB of the equilateral triangle ABC be produced to meet the circles in F, G, respectively, and if C' be the point in which the circles cut one another on the

other side of AB; prove the points F, C, G to be in the same straight line; and the figure CFG to be an equilateral triangle.

57. ABC is a triangle and the exterior angles at B and C are bisected by lines BD, CD respectively, meeting in D; shew that the angle BDC and half the angle BAC make up a right angle

58. If the exterior angle of a triangle be bisected, and the angles of the triangle made by the bisectors be bisected, and so on, the triangles so formed will tend to become eventually equilateral

59. If in the three sides AB, BC, CA of an equilateral triangle ABC, distances AE. BF, CG be taken, each equal to a third of one of the sides, and the points E, F, G be respectively joined (1) with each other, (2) with the opposite angles: shew that the two triangles so formed, are equilateral triangles.

IV.

60. Describe a right-angled triangle upon a given base. having given also the perpendicular from the right angle upon the hypotenuse.

61. Given one side of a right-angled triangle, and the difference between the hypotenuse and the sum of the other two sides, to construct the triangle

62 Construct an isosceles right-angled triangle, having given (1) the sum of the hypotenuse and one side; (2) their difference.

63 Describe a right-angled triangle of which the hypotenuse and the difference between the other two sides are given

64. Given the base of an isosceles triangle, and the sum or difference of a side and the perpendicular from the vertex on the base. Construct the triangle.

65. Make an isosceles triangle of given altitude whose sides shall pass through two given points and have its base on a given straight line.

66. Construct an equilateral triangle, having given the length of the perpendicular drawn from one of the angles on the opposite side.

67 Having given the straight lines which bisect the angles at the base of an equilateral triangle, determine a side of the triangle.

68 Having given two sides and an angle of a triangle, construct the triangle, distinguishing the different cases

69 Having given the base of a triangle, the difference of the sides, and the difference of the angles at the base; to describe the triangle

70 Given the perimeter and the angles of a triangle, to construct it.

71. Having given the base of a triangle, and half the sum and half the difference of the angles at the base; to construct the triangle.

72. Having given two lines, which are not parallel, and a point between them, describe a triangle having two of its angles in the respective lines, and the third at the given point; and such that the sides shall be equally inclined to the lines which they meet.

73. Construct a triangle, having given the three lines drawn from the angles to bisect the sides opposite.

74. Given one of the angles at the base of a triangle, the base itself, and the sum of the two remaining sides, to construct the triangle.

75. Given the base, an angle adjacent to the base, and the difference of the sides of a triangle, to construct it.

76. Given one angle, a side opposite to it, and the difference of the other two sides; to construct the triangle.

77. Given the base and the sum of the two other sides of a triangle, construct it so that the line which bisects the vertical angle shall be parallel to a given line.

V.

78. From a given point without a given straight line, to draw a line making an angle with the given line equal to a given rectilineal angle.

79. Through a given point A, draw a straight line ABC meeting two given parallel straight lines in B and C, such that BC may be equal to a given straight line.

80. If the line joining two parallel lines be bisected, all the lines drawn through the point of bisection and terminated by the parallel lines are also bisected in that point.

81. Three given straight lines issue from a point; draw another straight line cutting them so that the two segments of it intercepted between them may be equal to one another.

82. AB, AC are two straight lines, B and C given points in the same; BD is drawn perpendicular to AC, and DE perpendicular to AB; in like manner CF is drawn perpendicular to AB, and FG to AC. Shew that EG is parallel to BC.

83. ABC is a right-angled triangle, and the sides AC, AB are produced to D and F; bisect FBC and BCD by the lines BE, CE, and from E let fall the perpendiculars EF, ED. Prove (without assuming any properties of parallels) that $ADEF$ is a square.

84. Two pairs of equal straight lines being given, shew how to construct with them the greatest parallelogram.

85. With two given lines as diagonals describe a parallelogram which shall have an angle equal to a given angle. Within what limits must the given angle lie?

86. Having given one of the diagonals of a parallelogram, the sum of the two adjacent sides and the angle between them, construct the parallelogram.

87. One of the diagonals of a parallelogram being given, and the angle which it makes with one of the sides, complete the parallelogram, so that the other diagonal may be parallel to a given line.

88. $ABCD$, $A'B'C'D'$ are two parallelograms whose corresponding sides are equal, but the angle A is greater than the angle A', prove that the diameter AC is less than $A'C'$ but BD greater than $B'D'$.

89. If in the diagonal of a parallelogram any two points equidistant from its extremities be joined with the opposite angles, a figure will be formed which is also a parallelogram.

90. From each angle of a parallelogram a line is drawn making

the same angle towards the same parts with an adjacent side, taken always in the same order; shew that these lines form another parallelogram *similar* to the original one

91. Along the sides of a parallelogram taken in order, measure $AA' = BB' = CC'' = DD'$. the figure $A'B'C'D'$ will be a parallelogram.

92. On the sides AB, BC, CD, DA, of a parallelogram, set off AE, BF, CG, DH, equal to each other, and join AF, BG, CH, DE: these lines form a parallelogram, and the difference of the angles AFB, BGC, equals the difference of any two proximate angles of the two parallelograms.

93. OB, OC are two straight lines at right angles to each other, through any point P any two straight lines are drawn intersecting OB, OC, in B, B', C, C', respectively. If D and D' be the middle points of BB' and CC', shew that the angle $B'PD'$ is equal to the angle DOD'.

94. $ABCD$ is a parallelogram of which the angle C is opposite to the angle A. If through A any straight line be drawn, then the distance of C is equal to the sum or difference of the distances of B and of D from that straight line, according as it lies without or within the parallelogram.

95. Upon stretching two chains AC, BD, across a field $ABCD$, I find that BD and AC make equal angles with DC, and that AC makes the same angle with AD that BD does with BC; hence prove that AB is parallel to CD.

96. To find a point in the side or side produced of any parallelogram, such that the angle it makes with the line joining the point and one extremity of the opposite side, may be bisected by the line joining it with the other extremity.

97. When the corner of the leaf of a book is turned down a second time, so that the lines of folding are parallel and equidistant, the space in the second fold is equal to three times that in the first.

VI.

98. If the points of bisection of the sides of a triangle be joined, the triangle so formed shall be one-fourth of the given triangle.

99. If in the triangle ABC, BC be bisected in D, AD joined and bisected in E, BE joined and bisected in F, and CF joined and bisected in G; then the triangle EFG will be equal to one-eighth of the triangle ABC.

100. Shew that the areas of the two equilateral triangles in Prob. 59, p. 78, are, respectively, one-third and one-seventh of the area of the original triangle.

101. To describe a triangle equal to a given triangle, (1) when the base, (2) when the altitude of the required triangle is given.

102. To describe a triangle equal to the sum or difference of two given triangles.

103. Upon a given base describe an isosceles triangle equal to a given triangle.

104. Describe an equilateral triangle equal to a given triangle.

105. To a given straight line apply a triangle which shall be equal

to a given parallelogram and have one of its angles equal to a given rectilineal angle.

106. Transform a given rectilineal figure into a triangle whose vertex shall be in a given angle of the figure, and whose base shall be in one of the sides.

107. Divide a triangle by two straight lines into three parts which when properly arranged shall form a parallelogram whose angles are of a given magnitude.

108. Shew that a scalene triangle cannot be divided into two parts which will coincide.

109. If two sides of a triangle be given, the triangle will be greatest when they contain a right angle

110. Of all triangles having the same vertical angle, and whose bases pass through a given point, the least is that whose base is bisected in the given point.

111. Of all triangles having the same base and the same perimeter, that is the greatest which has the two undetermined sides equal.

112. Divide a triangle into three equal parts, (1) by lines drawn from a point in one of the sides: (2) by lines drawn from the angles to a point within the triangle: (3) by lines drawn from a given point within the triangle. In how many ways can the third case be done?

113. Divide an equilateral triangle into nine equal parts.

114. Bisect a parallelogram, (1) by a line drawn from a point in one of its sides. (2) by a line drawn from a given point within or without it: (3) by a line perpendicular to one of the sides: (4) by a line drawn parallel to a given line.

115. From a given point in one side produced of a parallelogram, draw a straight line which shall divide the parallelogram into two equal parts.

116. To trisect a parallelogram by lines drawn (1) from a given point in one of its sides, (2) from one of its angular points.

VII.

117. To describe a rhombus which shall be equal to any given quadrilateral figure.

118. Describe a parallelogram which shall be equal in area and perimeter to a given triangle.

119. Find a point in the diagonal of a square produced, from which if a straight line be drawn parallel to any side of the square, and meeting another side produced, it will form together with the produced diagonal and produced side, a triangle equal to the square.

120. If from any point within a parallelogram, straight lines be drawn to the angles, the parallelogram shall be divided into four triangles of which each two opposite are together equal to one-half of the parallelogram.

121. If $ABCD$ be a parallelogram, and E any point in the diagonal AC, or AC produced; shew that the triangles EBC, EDC, are equal, as also the triangles EBA and EBD.

122. $ABCD$ is a parallelogram, draw DFG meeting BC in F,

and AB produced in G; join AF, CG; then will the triangles ABF, CFG be equal to one another.

123. $ABCD$ is a parallelogram, E the point of intersection of its diagonals, and K any point in AD. If KB, KC be joined, shew that the figure $BKEC$ is one-fourth of the parallelogram.

124. Let $ABCD$ be a parallelogram, and O any point within it, through O draw lines parallel to the sides of $ABCD$, and join OA, OC, prove that the difference of the parallelograms DO, BO is twice the triangle OAC.

125. The diagonals AC, BD of a parallelogram intersect in O, an P is a point within the triangle AOB; prove that the difference of the triangles APB, CPD is equal to the sum of the triangles APC, BPD.

126. If K be the common angular point of the parallelograms about the diameter AC (fig Euc I 43) and BD be the other diameter, the difference of these parallelograms is equal to twice the triangle BKD.

127. The perimeter of a square is less than that of any other parallelogram of equal area.

128. Shew that of all equiangular parallelograms of equal perimeters, that which is equilateral is the greatest.

129. Prove that the perimeter of an isosceles triangle is greater than that of an equal right-angled parallelogram of the same altitude.

VIII.

130. If a quadrilateral figure is bisected by one diagonal, the second diagonal is bisected by the first.

131. If two opposite angles of a quadrilateral figure are equal, shew that the angles between opposite sides produced are equal.

132. Prove that the sides of any four-sided rectilinear figure are together greater than the two diagonals.

133. The sum of the diagonals of a trapezium is less than the sum of any four lines which can be drawn to the four angles, from any point within the figure, except their intersection.

134. The longest side of a given quadrilateral is opposite to the shortest; shew that the angles adjacent to the shortest side are together greater than the sum of the angles adjacent to the longest side.

135. Give any two points in the opposite sides of a trapezium, inscribe in it a parallelogram having two of its angles at these points.

136. Shew that, in every quadrilateral plane figure, two parallelograms can be described upon two opposite sides as diagonals, such that the other two diagonals shall be in the same straight line and equal.

137. Describe a quadrilateral figure whose sides shall be equal to four given straight lines. What limitation is necessary?

138. If the sides of a quadrilateral figure be bisected and the points of bisection joined, the included figure is a parallelogram, and equal in area to half the original figure.

139. A trapezium is such, that the perpendiculars let fall on a diagonal from the opposite angles are equal. Divide the trapezium into four equal triangles, by straight lines drawn to the angles from a point within it.

140. If two opposite sides of a trapezium be parallel to one another, the straight line joining their bisections, bisects the trapezium.

141. If of the four triangles into which the diagonals divide a trapezium, any two opposite ones are equal, the trapezium has two of its opposite sides parallel.

142. If two sides of a quadrilateral are parallel but not equal, and the other two sides are equal but not parallel, the opposite angles of the quadrilateral are together equal to two right angles: and conversely.

143. If two sides of a quadrilateral be parallel, and the line joining the middle points of the diagonals be produced to meet the other sides; the line so produced will be equal to half the sum of the parallel sides, and the line between the points of bisection equal to half their difference.

144. To bisect a trapezium, (1) by a line drawn from one of its angular points, (2) by a line drawn from a given point in one side.

145. To divide a square into four equal portions by lines drawn from any point in one of its sides.

146. It is impossible to divide a quadrilateral figure (except it be a parallelogram) into equal triangles by lines drawn from a point within it to its four corners.

IX.

147. If the greater of the acute angles of a right-angled triangle, be double the other, the square on the greater side is three times the square on the other.

148. Upon a given straight line construct a right-angled triangle such that the square of the other side may be equal to seven times the square on the given line.

149. If from the vertex of a plane triangle, a perpendicular fall upon the base or the base produced, the difference of the squares on the sides is equal to the difference of the squares on the segments of the base.

150. If from the middle point of one of the sides of a right-angled triangle, a perpendicular be drawn to the hypotenuse, the difference of the squares on the segments into which it is divided, is equal to the square on the other side.

151. If a straight line be drawn from one of the acute angles of a right-angled triangle, bisecting the opposite side, the square upon that line is less than the square upon the hypotenuse by three times the square upon half the line bisected.

152. If the sum of the squares of the three sides of a triangle be equal to eight times the square on the line drawn from the vertex to the point of bisection of the base, then the vertical angle is a right angle.

153. If a line be drawn parallel to the hypotenuse of a right-angled triangle, and each of the acute angles be joined with the points where this line intersects the sides respectively opposite to them, the squares on the joining lines are together equal to the squares on the hypotenuse and on the line drawn parallel to it.

154. Let ACB, ADB be two right-angled triangles having a common hypotenuse AB, join CD, and on CD produced both ways draw perpendiculars AE, BF. Shew that $CE^2 + CF^2 = DE^2 + DF^2$.

155. If perpendiculars AD, BE, CF drawn from the angles on the opposite sides of a triangle intersect in G, the squares on AB, BC, and CA, are together three times the squares on AG, BG, and CG.

156. If ABC be a triangle of which the angle A is a right angle; and BE, CF be drawn bisecting the opposite sides respectively: shew that four times the sum of the squares on BE and CF is equal to five times the square on BC.

157. If ABC be an isosceles triangle, and CD be drawn perpendicular to AB; the sum of the squares on the three sides is equal to

$$AD^2 + 2\,BD^2 + 3.CD^2.$$

158. The sum of the squares described upon the sides of a rhombus is equal to the squares described on its diameters.

159. A point is taken within a square, and straight lines drawn from it to the angular points of the square, and perpendicular to the sides, the squares on the first are double the sum of the squares on the last. Shew that these sums are least when the point is in the centre of the square.

160. In the figure Euc. I. 47,

(*a*) Shew that the diagonals FA, AK of the squares on AB, AC, lie in the same straight line.

(*b*) If DF, EK be joined, the sum of the angles at the bases of the triangles BFD, CEK is equal to one right angle.

(*c*) If BG and CH be joined, those lines will be parallel.

(*d*) If perpendiculars be let fall from F and K on BC produced, the parts produced will be equal; and the perpendiculars together will be equal to BC.

(*e*) Join GH, KE, FD, and prove that each of the triangles so formed, equals the given triangle ABC.

(*f*) The sum of the squares on GH, KE, and FD will be equal to six times the square on the hypotenuse.

(*g*) The difference of the squares on AB, AC, is equal to the difference of the squares on AD, AE.

161. The area of any two parallelograms described on the two sides of a triangle, is equal to that of a parallelogram on the base, whose side is equal and parallel to the line drawn from the vertex of the triangle, to the intersection of the two sides of the former parallelograms produced to meet.

162. If one angle of a triangle be a right angle, and another equal to two-thirds of a right-angle, prove from the First Book of Euclid, that the equilateral triangle described on the hypotenuse, is equal to the sum of the equilateral triangles described upon the sides which contain the right angle.

BOOK II.

DEFINITIONS.

I.

EVERY right-angled parallelogram is called a *rectangle*, and is said to be contained by any two of the straight lines which contain one of the right angles.

II.

In every parallelogram, any of the parallelograms about a diameter together with the two complements, is called a gnomon.

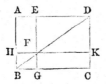

"Thus the parallelogram *HG* together with the complements *AF, FC*, is the gnomon, which is more briefly expressed by the letters *AGK*, or *EHC*, which are at the opposite angles of the parallelograms which make the gnomon."

PROPOSITION I. THEOREM.

If there be two straight lines, one of which is divided into any number of parts; the rectangle contained by the two straight lines, is equal to the rectangles contained by the undivided line, and the several parts of the divided line.

Let *A* and *BC* be two straight lines;
and let *BC* be divided into any parts *BD, DE, EC,* in the points *D, E*.
Then the rectangle contained by the straight lines *A* and *BC*, shall be equal to the rectangle contained by *A* and *BD*, together with that contained by *A* and *DE*, and that contained by *A* and *EC*.

From the point B, draw BF at right angles to BC, (I. 11.) and make BG equal to A; (I. 3.) through G draw GH parallel to BC, (I. 31.) and through D, E, C, draw DK, EL, CH parallel to BG, meeting GH in K, L, H.

Then the rectangle BH is equal to the rectangles BK, DL, EH.

And BH is contained by A and BC, for it is contained by GB, BC, and GB is equal to A:

and the rectangle BK is contained by A, BD, for it is contained by GB, BD, of which GB is equal to A:

also DL is contained by A, DE, because DK, that is, BG, (I. 34.) is equal to A;

and in like manner the rectangle EH is contained by A, EC:

therefore the rectangle contained by A, BC, is equal to the several rectangles contained by A, BD, and by A, DE, and by A, EC.

Wherefore, if there be two straight lines, &c. Q.E.D.

PROPOSITION II. THEOREM.

If a straight line be divided into any two parts, the rectangles contained by the whole and each of the parts, are together equal to the square on the whole line.

Let the straight line AB be divided into any two parts in the point C.

Then the rectangle contained by AB, BC, together with that contained by AB, AC, shall be equal to the square on AB.

Upon AB describe the square $ADEB$, (I. 46.) and through C draw CF parallel to AD or BE, (I. 31.) meeting DE in F.

Then AE is equal to the rectangles AF, CE.

And AE is the square on AB;

and AF is the rectangle contained by BA, AC;

for it is contained by DA, AC, of which DA is equal to AB:

and CE is contained by AB, BC, for BE is equal to AB:

therefore the rectangle contained by AB, AC, together with the rectangle AB, BC is equal to the square on AB.

If therefore a straight line, &c. Q.E.D.

PROPOSITION III. THEOREM.

If a straight line be divided into any two parts, the rectangle contained by the whole and one of the parts, is equal to the rectangle contained by the two parts, together with the square on the aforesaid part.

Let the straight line AB be divided into any two parts in the point C.
Then the rectangle AB, BC, shall be equal to the rectangle AC, CB, together with the square on BC.

Upon BC describe the square $CDEB$, (I. 46.) and produce ED to F, through A draw AF parallel to CD or BE, (I. 31.) meeting EF in F.
Then the rectangle AE is equal to the rectangles AD, CE.
And AE is the rectangle contained by AB, BC,
for it is contained by AB, BE, of which BE is equal to BC:
and AD is contained by AC, CB, for CD is equal to CB:
and CE is the square on BC:
therefore the rectangle AB, BC, is equal to the rectangle AC, CB, together with the square on BC.
If therefore a straight line be divided, &c. Q.E.D.

PROPOSITION IV. THEOREM.

If a straight line be divided into any two parts, the square on the whole line is equal to the squares on the two parts, together with twice the rectangle contained by the parts.

Let the straight line AB be divided into any two parts in C.
Then the square on AB shall be equal to the squares on AC, and CB, together with twice the rectangle contained by AC, CB.

Upon AB describe the square $ADEB$, (I. 46.) join BD,
through C draw CGF parallel to AD or BE, (I. 31.) meeting BD in G and DE in F;
and through G draw HGK parallel to AB or DE, meeting AD in H, and BE in K;
Then, because CF is parallel to AD and BD falls upon them, therefore the exterior angle BGC is equal to the interior and opposite angle BDA; (I. 29.)
but the angle BDA is equal to the angle DBA, (I. 5.)
because BA is equal to AD, being sides of a square;

wherefore the angle BGC is equal to the angle DBA or GBC;
and therefore the side BC is equal to the side CG; (I. 6.)
but BC is equal also to GK, and CG to BK; (I. 34.)
wherefore the figure $CGKB$ is equilateral.

It is likewise rectangular;
for, since CG is parallel to BK, and BC meets them,
therefore the angles KBC, BCG are equal to two right angles; (I. 29.)
but the angle KBC is a right angle; (def. 30. constr.)
wherefore BCG is a right angle:
and therefore also the angles CGK, GKB, opposite to these, are right angles; (I. 34.)
wherefore $CGKB$ is rectangular:
but it is also equilateral, as was demonstrated;
wherefore it is a square, and it is upon the side CB.
For the same reason HF is a square,
and it is upon the side HG, which is equal to AC. (I. 34.)
Therefore the figures HF, CK, are the squares on AC, CB.
And because the complement AG is equal to the complement GE, (I. 43.)
and that AG is the rectangle contained by AC, CB,
for GC is equal to CB;
therefore GE is also equal to the rectangle AC, CB;
wherefore AG, GE are equal to twice the rectangle AC, CB;
and HF, CK are the squares on AC, CB;
wherefore the four figures HF, CK, AG, GE, are equal to the squares on AC, CB, and twice the rectangle AC, CB:
but HF, CK, AG, GE make up the whole figure $ADEB$, which is the square on AB;
therefore the square on AB is equal to the squares on AC, CB, and twice the rectangle AC, CB.
Wherefore, if a straight line be divided, &c. Q.E.D.

Cor. From the demonstration, it is manifest, that the parallelograms about the diameter of a square, are likewise squares.

PROPOSITION V. THEOREM.

If a straight line be divided into two equal parts, and also into two unequal parts; the rectangle contained by the unequal parts, together with the square on the line between the points of section, is equal to the square on half the line.

Let the straight line AB be divided into two equal parts in the point C, and into two unequal parts in the point D.
Then the rectangle AD, DB, together with the square on CD, shall be equal to the square on CB.

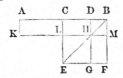

Upon *CB* describe the square *CEFB*, (I. 46.) join *BE*,
through *D* draw *DHG* parallel to *CE* or *BF*, (I. 31.) meeting *DE* in *H*, and *EF* in *G*.
and through *H* draw *KLM* parallel to *CB* or *EF*, meeting *CE* in *L*, and *BF* in *M*;
also through *A* draw *AK* parallel to *CL* or *BM*, meeting *MLK* in *K*.
Then because the complement *CH* is equal to the complement *HF*, (I. 43.) to each of these equals add *DM*;
  therefore the whole *CM* is equal to the whole *DF*;
  but because the line *AC* is equal to *CB*,
  therefore *AL* is equal to *CM*, (I. 36.)
  therefore also *AL* is equal to *DF*;
  to each of these equals add *CH*,
and therefore the whole *AH* is equal to *DF* and *CH*:
but *AH* is the rectangle contained by *AD*, *DB*, for *DH* is equal to *DB*;
 and *DF* together with *CH* is the gnomon *CMG*;
therefore the gnomon *CMG* is equal to the rectangle *AD*, *DB*:
to each of these equals add *LG*, which is equal to the square on *CD*; (II. 4. Cor.)
therefore the gnomon *CMG*, together with *LG*, is equal to the rectangle *AD*, *DB*, together with the square on *CD*:
but the gnomon *CMG* and *LG* make up the whole figure *CEFB*, which is the square on *CB*;
therefore the rectangle *AD*, *DB*, together with the square on *CD* is equal to the square on *CB*.
  Wherefore, if a straight line, &c. Q.E.D.
Cor. From this proposition it is manifest, that the difference of the squares on two unequal lines *AC*, *CD*, is equal to the rectangle contained by their sum *AD* and their difference *DB*.

PROPOSITION VI. THEOREM.

If a straight line be bisected, and produced to any point; the rectangle contained by the whole line thus produced, and the part of it produced, together with the square on half the line bisected, is equal to the square on the straight line which is made up of the half and the part produced.

Let the straight line *AB* be bisected in *C*, and produced to the point *D*.
Then the rectangle *AD*, *DB*, together with the square on *CB*, shall be equal to the square on *CD*.

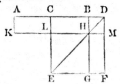

Upon *CD* describe the square *CEFD*, (I. 46.) and join *DE*,
through *B* draw *BHG* parallel to *CE* or *DF*, (I. 31.) meeting *DE* in *H*, and *EF* in *G*;
through *H* draw *KLM* parallel to *AD* or *EF*, meeting *DF* in *M*, and *CE* in *L*;
and through *A* draw *AK* parallel to *CL* or *DM*, meeting *MLK* in *K*.

Then because the line AC is equal to CB,
therefore the rectangle AL is equal to the rectangle CH, (I. 36.)
but CH is equal to HF; (I. 43.)
therefore AL is equal to HF;
to each of these equals add CM;
therefore the whole AM is equal to the gnomon CMG:
but AM is the rectangle contained by AD, DB,
for DM is equal to DB: (II. 4. Cor.)
therefore the gnomon CMG is equal to the rectangle AD, DB:
to each of these equals add LG which is equal to the square on CB;
therefore the rectangle AD, DB, together with the square on
CB, is equal to the gnomon CMG, and the figure LG;
but the gnomon CMG and LG make up the whole figure $CEFD$,
which is the square on CD;
therefore the rectangle AD, DB, together with the square on
CB, is equal to the square on CD.
Wherefore, if a straight line, &c. Q.E.D.

PROPOSITION VII. THEOREM.

If a straight line be divided into any two parts, the squares on the whole line, and on one of the parts, are equal to twice the rectangle contained by the whole and that part, together with the square on the other part.

Let the straight line AB be divided into any two parts in the point C.
Then the squares on AB, BC shall be equal to twice the rectangle AB, BC, together with the square on AC.

Upon AB describe the square $ADEB$, (I. 46.) and join BD;
through C draw CF parallel to AD or BE (I. 31.) meeting BD
    in G, and DE in F;
through G draw HGK parallel to AB or DE, meeting AD in H,
    and BE in K.
Then because AG is equal to GE, (I. 43.)
    add to each of them CK;
therefore the whole AK is equal to the whole CE;
and therefore AK, CE, are double of AK:
but AK, CE, are the gnomon AKF and the square CK;
therefore the gnomon AKF and the square CK are double of AK:
but twice the rectangle AB, BC, is double of AK,
    for BK is equal to BC; (II. 4. Cor.)
therefore the gnomon AKF and the square CK, are equal to
    twice the rectangle AB, BC:
to each of these equals add HF, which is equal to the square on AC,
therefore the gnomon AKF, and the squares CK, HF, are equal
    to twice the rectangle AB, BC, and the square on AC;
but the gnomon AKF, together with the squares CK, HF, make

up the whole figure $ADEB$ and CK, which are the squares on AB and BC;

therefore the squares on AB and BC are equal to twice the rectangle AB, BC, together with the square on AC.

Wherefore, if a straight line, &c. Q.E.D.

PROPOSITION VIII. THEOREM.

If a straight line be divided into any two parts, four times the rectangle contained by the whole line, and one of the parts, together with the square on the other part, is equal to the square on the straight line, which is made up of the whole and that part.

Let the straight line AB be divided into any two parts in the point C.

Then four times the rectangle AB, BC, together with the square on AC, shall be equal to the square on the straight line made up of AB and BC together.

Produce AB to D, so that BD be equal to CB, (I. 3.) upon AD describe the square $AEFD$, (I. 46.) and join DE, through B, C, draw BL, CH parallel to AE or DF, and cutting DE in the points K, P respectively, and meeting EF in L, H; through K, P, draw $MGKN$, $XPRO$ parallel to AD or EF.

Then because CB is equal to BD, CB to GK, and BD to KN;

therefore GK is equal to KN;

for the same reason, PR is equal to RO;

and because CB is equal to BD, and GK to KN,

therefore the rectangle CK is equal to BN, and GR to RN; (I. 36.)

but CK is equal to RN, (I. 43.)

because they are the complements of the parallelogram CO;

therefore also BN is equal to GR;

and the four rectangles BN, CK, GR, RN, are equal to one another, and so are quadruple of one of them CK.

Again, because CB is equal to BD, and BD to BK, that is, to CG;

and because CB is equal to GK, that is, to GP;

therefore CG is equal to GP.

And because CG is equal to GP, and PR to RO,

therefore the rectangle AG is equal to MP, and PL to RF;

but the rectangle MP is equal to PL, (I. 43.)

because they are the complements of the parallelogram ML:

wherefore also AG is equal to RF:

therefore the four rectangles AG, MP, PL, RF, are equal to one another, and so are quadruple of one of them AG.

And it was demonstrated, that the four CK, BN, GR, and RN, are quadruple of CK:

therefore the eight rectangles which contain the gnomon AOH, are quadruple of AK.
And because AK is the rectangle contained by AB, BC, for BK is equal to BC,
therefore four times the rectangle AB, BC is quadruple of AK:
but the gnomon AOH was demonstrated to be quadruple of AK;
therefore four times the rectangle AB, BC is equal to the gnomon AOH;
to each of these equals add XH, which is equal to the square on AC;
therefore four times the rectangle AB, BC, together with the square on AC, is equal to the gnomon AOH and the square XH;
but the gnomon AOH and XH make up the figure $AEFD$, which is the square on AD;
therefore four times the rectangle AB, BC together with the square on AC, is equal to the square on AD, that is, on AB and BC added together in one straight line.
Wherefore, if a straight line, &c. Q.E.D.

PROPOSITION IX. THEOREM.

If a straight line be divided into two equal, and also into two unequal parts; the squares on the two unequal parts are together double of the square on half the line, and of the square on the line between the points of section.

Let the straight line AB be divided into two equal parts in the point C, and into two unequal parts in the point D.
Then the squares on AD, DB together, shall be double of the squares on AC, CD.

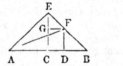

From the point C draw CE at right angles to AB, (I. 11.)
make CE equal to AC or CB, (I. 3.) and join EA, EB;
through D draw DF parallel to CE, meeting EB in F, (I. 31.)
through F draw FG parallel to BA, and join AF.
Then, because AC is equal to CE,
therefore the angle AEC is equal to the angle EAC; (I. 5.)
and because ACE is a right angle,
therefore the two other angles AEC, EAC of the triangle are together equal to a right angle, (I. 32.)
and since they are equal to one another;
therefore each of them is half a right angle.
For the same reason, each of the angles CEB, EBC is half a right angle;
and therefore the whole AEB is a right angle.
And because the angle GEF is half a right angle,
and EGF a right angle,
for it is equal to the interior and opposite angle ECB, (I. 29.)
therefore the remaining angle EFG is half a right angle;
wherefore the angle GEF is equal to the angle EFG,
and the side GF equal to the side EG. (I. 6.)

Again, because the angle at B is half a right angle,
and FDB a right angle,
for it is equal to the interior and opposite angle ECB, (I. 29.)
therefore the remaining angle BFD is half a right angle;
wherefore the angle at B is equal to the angle BFD,
and the side DF equal to the side DB. (I. 6.)
And because AC is equal to CE,
the square on AC is equal to the square on CE;
therefore the squares on AC, CE are double of the square on AC;
but the square on AE is equal to the squares on AC, CE, (I. 47.)
because ACE is a right angle;
therefore the square on AE is double of the square on AC.
Again, because EG is equal to GF,
the square on EG is equal to the square on GF;
therefore the squares on EG, GF are double of the square on GF;
but the square on EF is equal to the squares on EG, GF; (I. 47.)
therefore the square on EF is double of the square on GF;
and GF is equal to CD; (I. 34.)
therefore the square on EF is double of the square on CD;
but the square on AE is double of the square on AC;
therefore the squares on AE, EF are double of the squares on AC, CD;
but the square on AF is equal to the squares on AE, EF,
because AEF is a right angle; (I. 47.)
therefore the square on AF is double of the squares on AC, CD;
but the squares on AD, DF are equal to the square on AF;
because the angle ADF is a right angle; (I. 47.)
therefore the squares on AD, DF are double of the squares on AC, CD;
and DF is equal to DB;
therefore the squares on AD, DB are double of the squares on AC, CD.
If therefore a straight line be divided, &c. Q.E.D.

PROPOSITION X. THEOREM.

If a straight line be bisected, and produced to any point, the square on the whole line thus produced, and the square on the part of it produced, are together double of the square on half the line bisected, and of the square on the line made up of the half and the part produced.

Let the straight line AB be bisected in C, and produced to the point D.

Then the squares on AD, DB, shall be double of the squares on AC, CD.

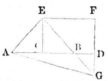

From the point C draw CE at right angles to AB, (I. 11.)
make CE equal to AC or CB, (I. 3.) and join AE, EB;
through E draw EF parallel to AB, (I. 31.)
and through D draw DF parallel to CE, meeting EF in F.

Then because the straight line *EF* meets the parallels *CE, FD*, therefore the angles *CEF, EFD* are equal to two right angles; (I. 29.) and therefore the angles *BEF, EFD* are less than two right angles.

But straight lines, which with another straight line make the interior angles upon the same side of a line, less than two right angles, will meet if produced far enough; (I. ax 12)

therefore *EB, FD* will meet, if produced towards *B, D*; let them be produced and meet in *G*, and join *AG*.

Then, because *AC* is equal to *CE*, therefore the angle *CEA* is equal to the angle *EAC*; (I 5.) and the angle *ACE* is a right angle, therefore each of the angles *CEA, EAC* is half a right angle (I. 32.) For the same reason, each of the angles *CEB, EBC* is half a right angle; therefore the whole *AEB* is a right angle. And because *EBC* is half a right angle, therefore *DBG* is also half a right angle. (I. 15.) for they are vertically opposite; but *BDG* is a right angle, because it is equal to the alternate angle *DCE*; (I 29.) therefore the remaining angle *DGB* is half a right angle; and is therefore equal to the angle *DBG*; wherefore also the side *BD* is equal to the side *DG*. (I. 6)

Again, because *EGF* is half a right angle, and the angle at *F* is a right angle, being equal to the opposite angle *ECD*, (I. 34.) therefore the remaining angle *FEG* is half a right angle, and therefore equal to the angle *EGF*; wherefore also the side *GF* is equal to the side *FE*. (I. 6.)

And because *EC* is equal to *CA*; the square on *EC* is equal to the square on *CA*, therefore the squares on *EC, CA* are double of the square on *CA*; but the square on *EA* is equal to the squares on *EC, CA*; (I. 47.) therefore the square on *EA* is double of the square on *AC*.

Again, because *GF* is equal to *FE*, the square on *GF* is equal to the square on *FE*; therefore the squares on *GF, FE* are double of the square on *FE*; but the square on *EG* is equal to the squares on *GF, FE*; (I 47.) therefore the square on *EG* is double of the square on *FE*; and *FE* is equal to *CD*; (I. 34.) wherefore the square on *EG* is double of the square on *CD* but it was demonstrated, that the square on *EA* is double of the square on *AC*; therefore the squares on *EA, EG* are double of the squares on *AC, CD*; but the square on *AG* is equal to the squares on *EA, EG*; (I. 47.) therefore the square on *AG* is double of the squares on *AC, CD*: but the squares on *AD, DG* are equal to the square on *AG*; therefore the squares on *AD, DG* are double of the squares on *AC, CD*; but *DG* is equal to *DB*, therefore the squares on *AD, DB* are double of the squares on *AC, CD*. Wherefore, if a straight line, &c. Q.E.D.

PROPOSITION XI. PROBLEM.

To divide a given straight line into two parts, so that the rectangle contained by the whole and one of the parts, shall be equal to the square on the other part.

Let AB be the given straight line.

It is required to divide AB into two parts, so that the rectangle contained by the whole line and one of the parts, shall be equal to the square on the other part.

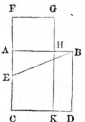

Upon AB describe the square $ACDB$; (I. 46.)
  bisect AC in E, (I. 10.) and join BE,
 produce CA to F, and make EF equal to EB, (I. 3.)
  upon AF describe the square $FGHA$. (I. 46.)

Then AB shall be divided in H, so that the rectangle AB, BH is equal to the square on AH.

Produce GH to meet CD in K.

Then because the straight line AC is bisected in E, and produced to F,
therefore the rectangle CF, FA together with the square on AE,
 is equal to the square on EF; (II. 6.)
   but EF is equal to EB;
therefore the rectangle CF, FA together with the square on AE,
 is equal to the square on EB;
but the squares on BA, AE are equal to the square on EB, (I. 47.)
  because the angle EAB is a right angle;
therefore the rectangle CF, FA, together with the square on AE,
 is equal to the squares on BA, AE;
  take away the square on AE, which is common to both;
therefore the rectangle contained by CF, FA is equal to the square on BA.

But the figure FK is the rectangle contained by CF, FA,
  for FA is equal to FG;
  and AD is the square on AB;
  therefore the figure FK is equal to AD;
   take away the common part AK,
therefore the remainder FH is equal to the remainder HD;
 but HD is the rectangle contained by AB, BH,
  for AB is equal to BD;
  and FH is the square on AH;
therefore the rectangle AB, BH, is equal to the square on AH.

Wherefore the straight line AB is divided in H, so that the rectangle AB, BH is equal to the square on AH. Q.E.F.

PROPOSITION XII. THEOREM.

In obtuse-angled triangles, if a perpendicular be drawn from either of the acute angles to the opposite side produced, the square on the side subtending the obtuse angle, is greater than the squares on the sides containing the obtuse angle, by twice the rectangle contained by the side upon which, when produced, the perpendicular falls, and the straight line intercepted without the triangle between the perpendicular and the obtuse angle.

Let ABC be an obtuse-angled triangle, having the obtuse angle ACB, and from the point A, let AD be drawn perpendicular to BC produced.

Then the square on AB shall be greater than the squares on AC, CB, by twice the rectangle BC, CD.

Because the straight line BD is divided into two parts in the point C,
therefore the square on BD is equal to the squares on BC, CD, and twice the rectangle BC, CD; (II. 4.)
to each of these equals add the square on DA;
therefore the squares on BD, DA are equal to the squares on BC, CD, DA, and twice the rectangle BC, CD;
but the square on BA is equal to the squares on BD, DA, (I. 47.)
because the angle at D is a right angle;
and the square on CA is equal to the squares on CD, DA;
therefore the square on BA is equal to the squares on BC, CA, and twice the rectangle BC, CD;
that is, the square on BA is greater than the squares on BC, CA, by twice the rectangle BC, CD.

Therefore in obtuse-angled triangles, &c. Q.E.D.

PROPOSITION XIII. THEOREM.

In every triangle, the square on the side subtending either of the acute angles, is less than the squares on the sides containing that angle, by twice the rectangle contained by either of these sides, and the straight line intercepted between the acute angle and the perpendicular let fall upon it from the opposite angle.

Let ABC be any triangle, and the angle at B one of its acute angles, and upon BC, one of the sides containing it, let fall the perpendicular AD from the opposite angle. (I. 12.)

Then the square on AC opposite to the angle B, shall be less than the squares on CB, BA, by twice the rectangle CB, BD.

BOOK II. PROP. XIII. 97

First, let AD fall within the triangle ABC.
Then because the straight line CB is divided into two parts in D,
the squares on CB, BD are equal to twice the rectangle contained by
CB, BD, and the square on DC; (II. 7.)
to each of these equals add the square on AD;
therefore the squares on CB, BD, DA, are equal to twice the
rectangle $CB.BD$, and the squares on AD, DC;
but the square on AB is equal to the squares on BD, DA, (I. 47.)
because the angle BDA is a right angle;
and the square on AC is equal to the squares on AD, DC;
therefore the squares on CB, BA are equal to the square on AC,
and twice the rectangle CB, BD:
that is, the square on AC alone is less than the squares on CB, BA,
by twice the rectangle CB, BD.
Secondly, let AD fall without the triangle ABC.

Then, because the angle at D is a right angle,
the angle ACB is greater than a right angle; (I. 16.)
and therefore the square on AB is equal to the squares on AC, CB,
and twice the rectangle BC, CD; (II. 12.)
to each of these equals add the square on BC;
therefore the squares on AB, BC are equal to the square on AC,
twice the square on BC, and twice the rectangle BC, CD;
but because BD is divided into two parts in C,
therefore the rectangle DB, BC is equal to the rectangle BC, CD,
and the square on BC; (II. 3.)
and the doubles of these are equal;
that is, twice the rectangle DB, BC is equal to twice the rectangle
BC, CD and twice the square on BC:
therefore the squares on AB, BC are equal to the square on AC,
and twice the rectangle DB, BC:
wherefore the square on AC alone is less than the squares on AB, BC;
by twice the rectangle DB, BC.
Lastly, let the side AC be perpendicular to BC.

Then BC is the straight line between the perpendicular and the
acute angle at B;
and it is manifest, that the squares on AB, BC, are equal to the
square on AC, and twice the square on BC. (I. 47.)
Therefore in any triangle, &c. Q.E.D.

PROPOSITION XIV. PROBLEM.

To describe a square that shall be equal to a given rectilineal figure.

Let A be the given rectilineal figure.
It is required to describe a square that shall be equal to A.

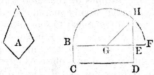

Describe the rectangular parallelogram $BCDE$ equal to the rectilineal figure A. (I. 45.)
  Then, if the sides of it, BE, ED, are equal to one another,
    it is a square, and what was required is now done.
  But if BE, ED, are not equal,
    produce one of them BE to F, and make EF equal to ED,
      bisect BF in G; (I. 10.)
from the center G, at the distance GB, or GF, describe the semicircle BHF,
    and produce DE to meet the circumference in H.
  The square described upon EH shall be equal to the given rectilineal figure A.
      Join GH.
  Then because the straight line BF is divided into two equal parts in the point G, and into two unequal parts in the point E;
    therefore the rectangle BE, EF, together with the square on EG,
      is equal to the square on GF; (II. 5.)
        but GF is equal to GH; (def. 15.)
  therefore the rectangle BE, EF, together with the square on EG, is equal to the square on GH;
but the squares on HE, EG are equal to the square on GH; (I. 47.)
  therefore the rectangle BE, EF, together with the square on EG,
    is equal to the squares on HE, EG;
      take away the square on EG, which is common to both;
  therefore the rectangle BE, EF is equal to the square on HE.
  But the rectangle contained by BE, EF is the parallelogram BD, because EF is equal to ED;
      therefore BD is equal to the square on EH;
        but BD is equal to the rectilineal figure A; (constr.)
      therefore the square on EH is equal to the rectilineal figure A.
  Wherefore a square has been made equal to the given rectilineal figure A, namely, the square described upon EH. Q.E.F.

NOTES TO BOOK II.

In Book I., Geometrical magnitudes of the same kind, lines, angles and surfaces, more particularly triangles and parallelograms, are compared, either as being absolutely equal, or unequal to one another.

In Book II., the properties of right-angled parallelograms, but without reference to their magnitudes, are demonstrated, and an important extension is made of Euc. I., 47, to acute-angled and obtuse-angled triangles. Euclid has given no definition of *a rectangular parallelogram* or *rectangle* probably, because the Greek expression παραλληλόγραμμον ὀρθογώνιον, οἱ ὀρθογώνιον simply, is a definition of the figure. In English, the term *rectangle*, formed from *rectus angulus*, ought to be defined before its properties are demonstrated. A rectangle may be defined to be a parallelogram having one angle a right-angle, or a right-angled parallelogram; and a square is a rectangle having all its sides equal.

As the squares in Euclid's demonstrations are squares described or supposed to be described on straight lines, the expression "*the square on AB*," is a more appropriate abbreviation for "*the square described on the line AB*," than "*the square of AB*." The latter expression more fitly expresses the arithmetical or algebraical equivalent for the square on the line AB.

In Euc. I., 35, it may be seen that there may be an indefinite number of parallelograms on the same base and between the same parallels whose areas are always equal to one another; but that one of them has all its angles right angles, and the length of its boundary less than the boundary of any other parallelogram upon the same base and between the same parallels. The area of this rectangular parallelogram is therefore determined by the two lines which contain one of its right angles. Hence it is stated in Def. I, that every right-angled parallelogram *is said to be contained* by any two of the straight lines which contain one of the right angles. No distinction is made in Book II., between *equality* and *identity*, as the rectangle may be said to be contained by two lines which are equal respectively to the two which contain one right angle of the figure. It may be remarked that the rectangle itself *is bounded* by four straight lines.

It is of primary importance to discriminate the Geometrical conception of a rectangle from the Arithmetical or Algebraical representation of it. The subject of Geometry is *magnitude* not *number*, and therefore it would be a departure from strict reasoning on space, to substitute in Geometrical demonstrations, the Arithmetical or Algebraical representation of a rectangle for the rectangle itself. It is, however, absolutely necessary that the connexion of *number* and *magnitude* be clearly understood, as far as regards the representation of lines and areas.

All lines are measured by lines, and all surfaces by surfaces. Some one line of definite length is arbitrarily assumed as the linear unit, and the length of every other line is represented by the number of linear units contained in it. The square is the figure assumed for the measure of surfaces. The square unit or the unit of area is assumed to be that square, the side of which is one unit in length, and the magnitude of every surface is represented by the number of square units contained in it. But here it may be remarked, that the properties of rectangles and squares in the Second Book of Euclid are proved independently of the consideration, whether the sides of the rectangles can be represented by any multiples of the same linear unit. If, however, the sides of rectangles are supposed to be divisible into an exact number of linear units, a numerical representation for the area of a rectangle may be deduced.

On two lines at right angles to each other, take AB equal to 4, and AD equal to 3 linear units.

Complete the rectangle $ABCD$, and through the points of division of AB, AD, draw EL, FM, GN parallel to AD; and HP, KQ parallel to AB respectively.

Then the whole rectangle AC is divided into squares, all equal to each other.

And AC is equal to the sum of the rectangles AL, EM, FN, GC; (II. 1.)
also these rectangles are equal to one another, (I. 36.)
therefore the whole AC is equal to four times one of them AL.

Again, the rectangle AL is equal to the rectangles EH, HR, RD, and these rectangles, by construction, are squares described upon the equal lines AH, HK, KD, and are equal to one another.

Therefore the rectangle AL is equal to 3 times the square on AH,
but the whole rectangle AC is equal to 4 times the rectangle AL,
therefore the rectangle AC is 4 × 3 times the square on AH, or 12 square units:

that is, the product of the two numbers which express the number of linear units in the two sides, will give the number of square units in the rectangle, and therefore will be an arithmetical representation of its area.

And generally, if AB, AD, instead of 4 and 3, consisted of a and b linear units respectively, it may be shewn in a similar manner, that the area of the rectangle AC would contain ab square units; and therefore the product ab is a proper representation for the area of the rectangle AC.

Hence, it follows, that the term *rectangle* in Geometry corresponds to the term *product* in Arithmetic and Algebra, and that a similar comparison may be made between the products of the two numbers which represent the sides of rectangles, as between the areas of the rectangles themselves. This forms the basis of what are called Arithmetical or Algebraical proofs of Geometrical properties.

If the two sides of the rectangle be equal, or if b be equal to a, the figure is a square, and the area is represented by aa or a^2.

Also, since a triangle is equal to the half of a parallelogram of the same base and altitude;

Therefore the area of a triangle will be represented by half the rectangle which has the same base and altitude as the triangle: in other words, if the length of the base be a units, and the altitude be b units;

Then the area of the triangle is algebraically represented by $\frac{1}{2}ab$.

The demonstrations of the first eight propositions, exemplify the obvious axiom, that, "the whole area of every figure in each case, is equal to all the parts of it taken together."

Def. 2. The parallelogram EK together with the complements AF,

NOTES TO BOOK II. 101

FC, is also a *gnomon*, as well as the parallelogram HG together with the same complements.

Prop. I. For the sake of brevity of expression, "the rectangle contained by the straight lines AB, BC," is called "the rectangle AB, BC," and sometimes "the rectangle ABC."

To this proposition may be added the corollary. If two straight lines be divided into any number of parts, the rectangle contained by the two straight lines, is equal to the rectangles contained by the several parts of one line and the several parts of the other respectively.

The method of reasoning on the properties of rectangles by means of the products which indicate the number of square units contained in their areas is foreign to Euclid's ideas of rectangles, as discussed in his Second Book, which have no reference to any particular unit of length or measure of surface.

Prop. I. The figures BH, BK, DL, EH are rectangles, as may readily be shewn. For, by the parallels, the angle CEL is equal to EDK, and the angle EDK is equal to BDG (Euc. I. 29.) But BDG is a right angle. Hence one of the angles in each of the figures BH, BK, DL, EH is a right angle, and therefore (Euc. I. 46, Cor.) these figures are rectangular.

Prop. I. Algebraically. (fig. Prop. I.)

Let the line BC contain a linear units, and the line A, b linear units of the same length.

Also suppose the parts BD, DE, EC to contain m, n, p linear units respectively.

Then $a = m + n + p$,

multiply these equals by b,

therefore $ab = bm + bn + bp$

That is, the product of two numbers, one of which is divided into any number of parts, is equal to the sum of the products of the undivided number, and the several parts of the other;

or, if the Geometrical interpretation of the products be restored,

The number of square units expressed by the product ab, is equal to the number of square units expressed by the sum of the products bm, bn, bp.

Prop. II. Algebraically. (fig. Prop. II.)

Let AB contain a linear units, and AC, CB, m and n linear units respectively.

Then $m + n = a$,

multiply these equals by a,

therefore $am + an = a^2$

That is, if a number be divided into any two parts, the sum of the products of the whole and each of the parts is equal to the square of the whole number.

Prop. III. Algebraically. (fig. Prop. III.)

Let AB contain a linear units, and let BC contain m, and AC, n linear units.

Then $a = m + n$,

multiply these equals by m,

therefore $ma = m^2 + mn$

That is, if a number be divided into any two parts, the product of the whole number and one of the parts, is equal to the square of that part, and the product of the two parts.

Prop IV might have been deduced from the two preceding propositions; but Euclid has preferred the method of exhibiting, in the demonstrations of the second book, the equality of the spaces compared.

In the corollary to Prop XLVI Book I it is stated that a parallelogram which has one right angle, has all its angles right angles. By applying this corollary, the demonstration of Prop IV. may be considerably shortened.

If the two parts of the line be equal, then the square on the whole line is equal to four times the square on half the line.

Also, if a line be divided into any three parts, the square on the whole line is equal to the squares on the three parts, and twice the rectangles contained by every two parts.

Prop IV. Algebraically. (fig Prop IV.)

Let the line AB contain a linear units, and the parts of it AC and BC, m and n linear units respectively.

$$\text{Then } a = m + n,$$
$$\text{squaring these equals, } \therefore a^2 = (m+n)^2,$$
$$\text{or } a^2 = m^2 + 2mn + n^2.$$

That is, if a number be divided into any two parts, the square of the number is equal to the squares of the two parts together with twice the product of the two parts.

From Euc II, 4, may be deduced a proof of Euc I, 47. In the fig take DL on DE, and EM on EB, each equal to BC, and join CH, HL, LM, MC. Then the figure $HLMC$ is a square, and the four triangles CAH, HDL, LEM, MBC are equal to one another, and together are equal to the two rectangles AG, GE.

Now AG, GE, FH, CK are together equal to the whole figure $ADEB$, and $HLMC$, with the four triangles CAH, HDL, LEB, MBC also make up the whole figure $ADEB$,

Hence AG, GE, FH, CK are equal to $HLMC$ together with the four triangles.

but AG, GE are equal to the four triangles,

wherefore FH, CK are equal to $HLMC$,

that is, the squares on AC, AH are together equal to the square on CH.

Prop V. It must be kept in mind, that the sum of two straight lines in Geometry, means the straight line formed by joining the two lines together, so that both may be in the same straight line.

The following simple properties respecting the equal and unequal division of a line are worthy of being remembered.

I Since $AB = 2BC = 2 (BD + DC) = 2BD + 2DC$, (fig Prop v.)
and $AB = AD + DB$;
$\therefore 2CD + 2DB = AD + DB$,

and by subtracting $2DB$ from these equals,
$\therefore 2CD = AD - DB$,
and $CD = \frac{1}{2} (AD - DB)$

That is, if a line AB be divided into two equal parts in C, and into two unequal parts in D, the part CD of the line between the points of section is equal to half the difference of the unequal parts AD and DB

II. Here $AD = AC + CD$, the sum of the unequal parts, (fig. Prop. v.)
and $DB = AC - CD$ their difference

Hence by adding these equals together,
$$AD + DB = 2AC,$$
or the sum and difference of two lines AC, CD, are together equal to twice the greater line.

And the halves of these equals are equal,
$$\tfrac{1}{2} AD + \tfrac{1}{2} DB = AC,$$
or, half the sum of two unequal lines AC, CD added to half their difference is equal to the greater line AC

III. Again, since $AD = AC + CD$, and $DB = AC - CD$, by subtracting these equals,
$$AD - DB = 2CD,$$
or, the difference between the sum and difference of two unequal lines is equal to twice the less line

And the halves of these equals are equal,
$$\tfrac{1}{2} AD - \tfrac{1}{2} DB = CD,$$
or, half the difference of two lines subtracted from half their sum is equal to the less of the two lines

IV. Since $AC - CD = DB$ the difference,
$$\therefore AC = CD + DB,$$
and adding CD the less to each of these equals,
$$\therefore AC + CD = 2CD + DB,$$
or, the sum of two unequal lines is equal to twice the less line together with the difference between the lines

Prop. v. Algebraically

Let AB contain $2a$ linear units,

its half BC will contain a linear units

And let CD the line between the points of section contain m linear units Then AD the greater of the two unequal parts, contains $a + m$ linear units;

and DB the less contains $a - m$ units.

Also m is half the difference of $a + m$ and $a - m$;
$$(a + m)(a - m) = a^2 - m^2,$$
to each of these equals add m^2,
$$(a + m)(a - m) + m^2 = a^2$$

That is, if a number be divided into two equal parts, and also into two unequal parts, the product of the unequal parts together with the square of half their difference, is equal to the square of half the number.

Bearing in mind that AC, CD are respectively half the sum and half the difference of the two lines AD, DB; the corollary to this proposition may be expressed in the following form "The rectangle contained by two straight lines is equal to the difference on the squares of half their sum and half their difference"

The rectangle contained by AD and DB, and the square on BC are each bounded by the same extent of line, but the spaces enclosed differ by the square on CD

A given straight line is said *to be produced* when it has its length increased in either direction, and the increase it receives, is called the *part produced*

If a point be taken in a line or in a line produced, the line is said to be divided *internally* or *externally*, and the distances of the point from the ends of the line are called the internal or external segments of the line, according as the point of section is in the line or the line produced

Prop. vi. Algebraically.

Let AB contain $2a$ linear units, then its half BC contains a units; and let BD contain m units.

Then AD contains $2a + m$ units,
and $(2a + m) m = 2am + m^2$;
to each of these equals add a^2,
$\therefore (2a + m) m + a^2 = a^2 + 2am + m^2$.
But $a^2 + 2am + m^2 = (a + m)^2$,
$\therefore (2a + m) m + a^2 = (a + m)^2$.

That is, If a number be divided into two equal numbers, and another number be added to the whole and to one of the parts, the product of the whole number thus increased and the other number, together with the square of half the given number, is equal to the square of the number which is made up of half the given number increased.

The algebraical results of Prop. v and Prop. vi are identical, as it is obvious that the difference of $a + m$ and $a - m$ in Prop. v is equal to the difference of $2a + m$ and m in Prop. vi, and one algebraical result expresses the truth of both propositions.

This arises from the two ways in which the difference between two unequal lines may be represented geometrically, when they are in the same direction.

In the diagram (fig. to Prop. v), the difference DB of the two unequal lines AC and CD is exhibited by producing the less line CD, and making CB equal to AC the greater.

Then the part produced DB is the difference between AC and CD, for AC is equal to CB, and taking CD from each, the difference of AC and CD is equal to the difference of CB and CD.

In the diagram (fig. to Prop. vi), the difference DB of the two unequal lines CD and CA is exhibited by cutting off from CD the greater, a part CB equal to CA the less.

Prop. vii. Either of the two parts AC, CB of the line AB may be taken: and it is equally true, that the squares on AB and AC are equal to twice the rectangle AB, AC, together with the square on BC.

Prop. vii. Algebraically.

Let AB contain a linear units, and let the parts AC and CB contain m and n linear units respectively.

Then $a = m + n$;
squaring these equals,
$\therefore a^2 = m^2 + 2mn + n^2$,
add n^2 to each of these equals,
$\therefore a^2 + n^2 = m^2 + 2mn + 2n^2$.
But $2mn + 2n^2 = 2(m + n) n = 2an$,
$\therefore a^2 + n^2 = m^2 + 2an$.

That is, If a number be divided into any two parts, the square of the whole number and of one of the parts, is equal to twice the product of the whole number and that part, together with the square of the other part.

Prop. viii. As in Prop. vii either part of the line may be taken, and it is also true in this Proposition, that four times the rectangle contained by AB, AC together with the square on BC, is equal to the square on the straight line made up of AB and AC together.

The truth of this proposition may be deduced from Euc. II. 4 and 7.

For the square on AD (by Prop 8) is equal to the squares on AB, BD, and twice the rectangle AB, BD, (Euc. II. 4) or the squares on AB, BC, and twice the rectangle AB, BC, because BC is equal to BD and the squares on AB, BC are equal to twice the rectangle AB, BC with the square on AC (Euc. II 7) therefore the square on AD is equal to four times the rectangle AB, BC together with the square on AC.

Prop VIII Algebraically

Let the whole line AB contain a linear units of which the parts AC, CB contain m, n units respectively.

Then $m + n = a$,

and subtracting or taking n from each,

$$m = a - n,$$

squaring these equals,

$$m^2 = a^2 - 2an + n^2,$$

and adding $4an$ to each of these equals,

$$4an + m^2 = a^2 + 2an + n^2$$

But $a^2 + 2an + n^2 = (a + n)^2$,

$$\therefore 4an + m^2 = (a + n)^2$$

That is, If a number be divided into any two parts, four times the product of the whole number and one of the parts, together with the square of the other part, is equal to the square of the number made of the whole and the part first taken.

Prop VIII. may be put under the following form The square on the sum of two lines exceeds the square on their difference, by four times the rectangle contained by the lines.

Prop IX The demonstration of this proposition may be deduced from Euc II 4 and 7.

For (Euc II 4) the square on AD is equal to the squares on AC, CD and twice the rectangle AC, CD, (by Prop 4) and adding the square on DB to each, therefore the squares on AD, DB are equal to the squares on AC, CD and twice the rectangle AC, CD together with the square on DB, or to the squares on BC, CD and twice the rectangle BC, CD with the square on DB, because BC is equal to AC.

But the squares on BC, CD are equal to twice the rectangle BC, CD, with the square on DB (Euc II 7).

Wherefore the squares on AD, DB are equal to twice the squares on BC and CD.

Prop IX. Algebraically

Let AB contain $2a$ linear units, its half AC or BC will contain a units, and let CD the line between the points of section contain m units.

Also AD the greater of the two unequal parts contains $a + m$ units,

and DB the less contains $a - m$ units.

Then $(a + m)^2 = a^2 + 2am + m^2$,

and $(a - m)^2 = a^2 - 2am + m^2$

Hence by adding these equals,

$$\therefore (a + m)^2 + (a - m)^2 = 2a^2 + 2m^2$$

That is, If a number be divided into two equal parts, and also into two unequal parts, the sum of the squares of the two unequal parts is equal to twice the square of half the number itself, and twice the square of half the difference of the unequal parts.

The proof of Prop. x. may be deduced from Euc. ii. 4, 7, as Prop. ix.

Prop. x. Algebraically.

Let the line AB contain $2a$ linear units, of which its half AC or CB will contain a units,

and let BD contain m units.

Then the whole line and the part produced will contain $2a + m$ units,

and half the line and the part produced will contain $a + m$ units,

$$. (2a + m)^2 = 4a^2 + 4am + m^2,$$

add m^2 to each of these equals,

$$.. (2a + m)^2 + m^2 = 4a^2 + 4am + 2m^2.$$

Again, $(a + m)^2 = a^2 + 2am + m^2$,

add a^2 to each of these equals,

$$.. (a + m)^2 + a^2 = 2a^2 + 2am + m^2,$$

and doubling these equals,

$$\therefore 2(a + m)^2 + 2a^2 = 4a^2 + 4am + 2m^2.$$

But $(2a + m)^2 + m^2 = 4a^2 + 4am + 2m^2$.

Hence $(2a + m)^2 + m^2 = 2a^2 + 2(a + m)^2$.

That is, If a number be divided into two equal parts, and the whole number and one of the parts be increased by the addition of another number, the squares of the whole number thus increased, and of the number by which it is increased, are equal to double the squares of half the number, and of half the number increased.

The algebraical results of Prop. ix. and Prop. x. are identical, (the enunciations of the two Props. arising, as in Prop. v. and Prop. vi., from the two ways of exhibiting the difference between two lines,) and both may be included under the following proposition. The square on the sum of two lines and the square on their difference, are together equal to double the sum of the squares on the two lines.

Prop. xi. Two series of lines, one series decreasing and the other series increasing in magnitude, and each line divided in the same manner, may be found by means of this proposition.

(1) To find the decreasing series.

In the fig. Euc. ii. 11, $AB = AH + BH$,

and since $AB \cdot BH = AH^2$, $\cdot (AH + BH) \cdot BH = AH^2$,

$\therefore BH^2 = AH^2 - AH \cdot BH = AH (AH - BH)$

If now in HA, HL be taken equal to BH,

then $HL^2 = AH (AH - HL)$, or $AH \cdot AL = HL^2$ ·

that is, AH is divided in L, so that the rectangle contained by the whole line AH and one part, is equal to the square on the other part HL. By a similar process, HL may be so divided, and so on, by always taking from the greater part of the divided line, a part equal to the less.

(2) To find the increasing series.

From the fig. it is obvious that $CF \cdot FA = CA^2$.

Hence CF is divided in A, in the same manner as AB is divided in H, by adding AF a line equal to the greater segment, to the given line CA or

AB. And by successively adding to the last line thus divided, its greater segment, a series of lines increasing in magnitude may be found similarly divided to AB.

It may also be shewn that the squares on the whole line and on the less segment are equal to three times the square on the greater segment. (Euc XIII. 4.)

To solve Prop. XI. algebraically, or to find the point H in AB such that the rectangle contained by the whole line AB and the part HB shall be equal to the square on the other part AH.

Let AB contain a linear units, and AH one of the unknown parts contain x units,

then the other part HB contains $a - x$ units.

And $\therefore a(a - x) = x^2$, by the problem,

or $x^2 + ax = a^2$, a quadratic equation.

Whence $x = \dfrac{\pm a \sqrt{5} - a}{2}$.

The former of these values of x determines the point H

So that $x = \dfrac{\sqrt{5} - 1}{2} \cdot AB = AH$, one part,

and $a - x = a - AH = \dfrac{3 - \sqrt{5}}{2} \cdot AB = HB$, the other part.

It may be observed that the parts AH and HB cannot be numerically expressed by any rational number. Approximation to their true values in terms of AB, may be made to any required degree of accuracy, by extending the extraction of the square root of 5 to any number of decimals

To ascertain the meaning of the other result $x = -\dfrac{\sqrt{5} + 1}{2} \cdot a$.

In the equation $a(a - x) = x^2$,

for x write $-x$, then $a(a + x) = x^2$,

which when translated into words gives the following problem.

To find the length to which a given line must be produced so that the rectangle contained by the given line and the line made up of the given line and the part produced, may be equal to the square on the part produced

Or, the problem may also be expressed as follows:

To find two lines having a given difference, such that the rectangle contained by the difference and one of them may be equal to the square on the other

It may here be remarked that Prop XI Book II affords a simple Geometrical construction for a quadratic equation.

Prop XII Algebraically.

Assuming the truth of Euc I 47

Let BC, CA, AB contain a, b, c linear units respectively,

and let CD, DA, contain m, n units,

then BD contains $a + m$ units.

And therefore, $c^2 = (a + m)^2 + n^2$, from the right-angled triangle ABD,

also $b^2 = m^2 + n^2$ from ACD;

$\therefore c^2 - b^2 = (a + m)^2 - m^2$

$= a^2 + 2am + m^2 - m^2$

$$= a^2 + 2am,$$
$$\therefore c^2 = b^2 + a^2 + 2am,$$
that is, c^2 is greater than $b^2 + a^2$ by $2am$.

Prop. XIII. Case II may be proved more simply as follows.

Since BD is divided into two parts in the point D,
therefore the squares on CB, BD are equal to twice the rectangle contained by CB, BD and the square on CD, (II 7)
add the square on AD to each of these equals,
therefore the squares on CB, BD, DA are equal to twice the rectangle CB, BD, and the squares on CD and DA,
but the squares on BD, DA are equal to the square on AB, (I 47)
and the squares on CD, DA are equal to the square on AC,
therefore the squares on CB, BA are equal to the square on AC, and twice the rectangle CB, BD. That is, &c

Prop XIII Algebraically

Let BC, CA, AB contain respectively a, b, c linear units, and let BD and AD also contain m and n units

Case I. Then DC contains $a - m$ units

Therefore $c^2 = n^2 + m^2$ from the right-angled triangle ABD,

and $b^2 = n^2 + (a - m)^2$ from ADC.

$\therefore c^2 - b^2 = m^2 - (a - m)^2$
$$= m^2 - a^2 + 2am - m^2$$
$$= -a^2 + 2am,$$
$\therefore a^2 + c^2 = b^2 + 2am,$

or $b^2 + 2am = a^2 + c^2$,

that is, b^2 is less than $a^2 + c^2$ by $2am$.

Case II. $DC = m - a$ units.

$\therefore c^2 = m^2 + n^2$ from the right-angled triangle ABD,

and $b^2 = (m - a)^2 + n^2$ from ACD,

$\therefore c^2 - b^2 = m^2 - (m - a)^2$,
$$= m^2 - m^2 + 2am - a^2$$
$$= 2am - a^2,$$
$\therefore a^2 + c^2 = b^2 + 2am,$

or $b^2 + 2am = a^2 + c^2$,

that is, b^2 is less than $a^2 + c^2$ by $2am$.

Case III Here m is equal to a.

And $b^2 + a^2 = c^2$, from the right-angled triangle ABC.

Add to each of these equals a^2,

$$b^2 + 2a^2 = c^2 + a^2,$$

that is, b^2 is less than $c^2 + a^2$ by $2a^2$, or $2aa$.

These two propositions, Euc II 12, 13, with Euc I 47, exhibit the relations which subsist between the sides of an obtuse-angled, an acute-angled, and right-angled triangle respectively.

NOTE ON THE ABBREVIATIONS AND ALGEBRAICAL SYMBOLS EMPLOYED IN GEOMETRY.

The ancient Geometry of the Greeks admitted no symbols besides the diagrams and ordinary language. In later times, after symbols of operation had been devised by writers on Algebra, they were very soon adopted and employed on account of their brevity and convenience, in writings purely geometrical. Dr Barrow was one of the first who introduced algebraical symbols into the language of Elementary Geometry, and distinctly states in the preface to his Euclid, that his object is "to content the desires of those who are delighted more with symbolical than verbal demonstrations." As algebraical symbols are employed in almost all works on the mathematics, whether geometrical or not, it seems proper in this place to give some brief account of the marks which may be regarded as the alphabet of symbolical language.

The mark $=$ was first used by Robert Recorde, in his treatise on Algebra entitled, "The Whetstone of Witte," 1557. He remarks: "And to avoide the tediouse repetition of these woordes *is equalle to*, I will sette as I doe often in woorke use, a paire of parallels, or Gemowe lines of one lengtke, thus: $=$, bicause noe 2 thynges can be more equalle." It was employed by him as simply affirming the equality of two numerical or algebraical expressions. Geometrical equality is not exactly the same as numerical equality, and when this symbol is used in geometrical reasonings, it must be understood as having reference to pure geometrical equality.

The signs of relative magnitude, $>$ meaning, *is greater than*, and $<$, *is less than*, were first introduced into algebra by Thomas Harriot, in his "Artis Analyticæ Praxis," which was published after his death in 1631.

The signs $+$ and $-$ were first employed by Michael Stifel, in his "Arithmetica Integra," which was published in 1544. The sign $+$ was employed by him for the word *plus*, and the sign $-$, for the word *minus*. These signs were used by Stifel strictly as the arithmetical or algebraical signs of addition and subtraction.

The sign of multiplication $\times$ was first introduced by Oughtred in his "Clavis Mathematica," which was published in 1631. In algebraical multiplication he either connects the letters which form the factors of a product by the sign $\times$, or writes them as words without any sign or mark between them, as had been done before by Harriot, who first introduced the small letters to designate known and unknown quantities. However concise and convenient the notation $AB \times BC$ or $AB \cdot BC$ may be in practice for "*the rectangle contained by the lines AB and BC*", the student is cautioned against the use of it, in the early part of his geometrical studies, as its use is likely to occasion a misapprehension of Euclid's meaning, by confounding the idea of Geometrical equality with that of Arithmetical equality. Later writers on Geometry who employed the Latin language, explained the notation $AB \times BC$, by "$AB\ ductum\ in\ BC$", that is, if the line AB be carried along the line BC in a normal position to it, until it come to the end C, it will then form with BC, the rectangle contained by AB and BC. Dr Barrow sometimes expresses "*the rectangle contained by AB and BC*" by "*the rectangle ABC*."

Michael Stifel was the first who introduced integral exponents to denote the powers of algebraical symbols of quantity, for which he employed capital letters. Vieta afterwards used the vowels to denote known, and the consonants, unknown quantities, but used words to designate the powers. Simon

Stevin, in his treatise on Algebra, which was published in 1605, improved the notation of Stifel, by placing the figures that indicated the powers within small circles. Peter Ramus adopted the initial letters l, q, c, bq of *latus, quadratus, cubus, biquadratus*, as the notation of the first four powers. Harriot exhibited the different powers of algebraical symbols by repeating the symbol, two, three, four, &c. times, according to the order of the power. Descartes restored the numerical exponents of powers, placing them at the right of the numbers, or symbols of quantity, as at the present time. Dr. Barrow employed the notation ABq, for "*the square on the line AB*," in his edition of Euclid. The notations AB^2, AB^3, for "*the square and cube on the line whose extremities are A and B*," as well as $AB \times BC$, for "*the rectangle contained by AB and BC*," are used as abbreviations in almost all works on the Mathematics, though not wholly consistent with the algebraical notations a^2 and a^3.

The symbol $\sqrt{}$, being originally the initial letter of the word *radix*, was first used by Stifel to denote the square root of the number, or of the symbol, before which it is placed.

The Hindus, in their treatises on Algebra, indicated the ratio of two numbers, or of two algebraical symbols, by placing one above the other, without any line of separation. The line was first introduced by the Arabians, from whom it passed to the Italians, and from them to the rest of Europe. This notation has been employed for the expression of geometrical ratios by almost all writers on the Mathematics, on account of its great convenience. Oughtred first used points to indicate proportion, thus, $a \;.\; b \;:\; c \;.\; d$, means that a bears the same proportion to b, as c does to d.

QUESTIONS ON BOOK II.

1. Is *rectangle* the same as *rectus angulus*? Explain the distinction, and give the corresponding Greek terms.

2. What is meant by *the sum* of two, or more than two straight lines in Geometry?

3. Is there any difference between the straight lines by which a rectangle is said *to be contained*, and those by which *it is bounded*?

4. Define a *gnomon*. How many *gnomons* appear from the same construction in the same rectangle? Find the difference between them.

5. What axiom is assumed in proving the first eight propositions of the Second Book of Euclid?

6. Of equal squares and equal rectangles, which must *necessarily* coincide?

7. How may a rectangle be dissected so as to form an equivalent rectangle of any proposed length?

8. When the adjacent sides of a rectangle are commensurable, the area of the rectangle is properly represented by the product of the number of units in two adjacent sides of the rectangle. Illustrate this by considering the case when the two adjacent sides contain 3 and 4 units respectively, and distinguish between the units of the factors and the units of the product. Shew generally that a rectangle whose adjacent sides are represented by the integers a and b, is represented by ab. Also shew, that in the same sense, the rectangle is represented by $\dfrac{ab}{mn}$, if the sides be represented by $\dfrac{a}{m}, \dfrac{b}{n}$.

9. Why may not Algebraical or Arithmetical proofs be substituted (as being shorter) for the demonstrations of the Propositions in the Second Book of Euclid?

10. In what sense is the *area* of a triangle said to be equal to half the product of its base and its altitude? What two propositions of Euclid may be adduced to prove it?

11. How do you shew that the area of a rhombus is equal to half the rectangle contained by the diagonals?

12. How may a rule be deduced for finding a numerical expression for the area of any parallelogram, when two adjacent sides are given?

13. The area of a trapezium which has two of its sides parallel is equal to that of a rectangle contained by its altitude and half the sum of its parallel sides. What propositions of the First and Second Books of Euclid are employed to prove this? Of what service is the above in the mensuration of fields with irregular borders?

14. From what propositions of Euclid may be deduced the following rule for finding the area of any quadrilateral figure :—"Multiply the sum of the perpendiculars drawn from opposite angles of the figure upon the diagonal joining the other two angles, and take half the product."

15. In Euclid II 3, where must be the point of division of the line, so that the rectangle contained by the two parts may be a maximum? Exemplify in the case where the line is 12 inches long.

16. How may the demonstration of Euclid II 4, be legitimately shortened? Give the Algebraical proof, and state on what suppositions it can be regarded as a proof.

17. Shew that the proof of Euc II 4, can be deduced from the two previous propositions without any geometrical construction.

18. Shew that if the two complements be together equal to the two squares, the given line is bisected.

19. If the line AB, as in Euc II 4, be divided into any three parts, enunciate and prove the analogous proposition.

20. Prove geometrically that if a straight line be trisected, the square on the whole line equals nine times the square on a third part of it.

21. Deduce from Euc II 4, a proof of Euc I 47.

22. If a straight line be divided into two parts, when is the rectangle contained by the parts, *the greatest possible?* and when is the sum of the squares of the parts, *the least possible?*

23. Shew that if a line be divided into two equal parts and into two unequal parts; the part of the line between the points of section is equal to half the difference of the unequal parts.

24. If half the sum of two unequal lines be increased by half their difference, the sum will be equal to the greater line, and if the sum of two lines be diminished by half their difference, the remainder will be equal to the less line.

25. Explain what is meant by the *internal* and *external segments* of a line, and shew that the sum of the external segments of a line or the difference of the internal segments is double the distance between the points of section and bisection of the line.

26. Shew how Euc. II 6, may be deduced immediately from the preceding Proposition.

27. Prove Geometrically that the squares on the sum and difference of two lines are equal to twice the squares on the lines themselves.

28. A given rectangle is divided by two straight lines into four rectangles. Given the areas of the two which have not common sides, find the areas of the other two.

29. In how many ways may the difference of two lines be exhibited? Enunciate the propositions in Book II which depend on that circumstance.

30. How may a series of lines be found similarly divided to the line AB in Euc. II. 11?

31. Divide Algebraically a given line (a) into two parts, such that the rectangle contained by the whole and one part may be equal to the square of the other part. Deduce Euclid's construction from one solution, and explain the other.

32. Given the lesser segment of a line, divided as in Euc. II. 11, find the greater.

33. Enunciate the Arithmetical theorems expressed by the following Algebraical formulæ,
$$(a+b)^2 = a^2 + 2ab + b^2 \quad a^2 - b^2 = (a+b)(a-b) \quad (a-b)^2 = a^2 - 2ab + b^2,$$
and state the corresponding Geometrical propositions.

34. Shew that the first of the Algebraical propositions,
$$(a+x)(a-x) + x^2 = a^2 \quad (a+x)^2 + (a-x)^2 = 2a^2 + 2x^2,$$
is equivalent to the two propositions V and VI, and the second of them, to the two propositions IX and X of the Second Book of Euclid.

35. Prove Euc. II. 12, when the perpendicular BE is drawn from B on AC produced to E, and shew that the rectangle BC, CD is equal to the rectangle AC, CE.

36. Include the first two cases of Euc. II. 13, in one proof.

37. In the second case of Euc. II. 13, draw a perpendicular CE from the obtuse angle C upon the side AB, and prove that the square on AB is equal to the rectangle AB, AE together with the rectangle BC, BD.

38. Enunciate Euc. II. 13, and give an Algebraical or Arithmetical proof of it.

39. The sides of a triangle are as 3, 4, 5. Determine whether the angles between 3, 4, 4, 5, and 3, 5, respectively are greater than, equal to, or less than, a right angle.

40. Two sides of a triangle are 4 and 5 inches in length, if the third side be $6\tfrac{7}{16}$ inches, the triangle is acute-angled, but if it be $6\tfrac{9}{16}$ inches, the triangle is obtuse-angled.

41. A triangle has its sides 7, 8, 9 units respectively, a strip of breadth 2 units being taken off all round from the triangle, find the area of the remainder.

42. If the original figure, Euc. II. 14, were a right-angled triangle, whose sides were represented by 8 and 9, what number would represent the side of a square of the same area? Shew that the perimeter of the square is less than the perimeter of the triangle.

43. If the sides of a rectangle are 8 feet and 2 feet, what is the side of the equivalent square?

44. "All plane rectilineal figures admit of quadrature." Point out the succession of steps by which Euclid establishes the truth of this proposition.

45. Explain the construction (without proof) for making a square equal to a plane polygon.

46. Shew from Euc. II. 14 that any algebraical surd as $\sqrt{a}$ can be represented by a line, if the unit be a line.

47. Could any of the *propositions* of the Second Book be made *corollaries* to other propositions, with advantage? Point out any such propositions, and give your reasons for the alterations you would make.

GEOMETRICAL EXERCISES ON BOOK II.

PROPOSITION I. PROBLEM.

Divide a given straight line into two parts such, that their rectangle may be equal to a given square; and determine the greatest square which the rectangle can equal.

Let AB be the given straight line, and let M be the side of the given square.

It is required to divide the line AB into two parts, so that the rectangle contained by them may be equal to the square on M.

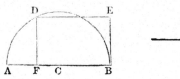

Bisect AB in C, with center C, and radius CA or CB, describe the semicircle ADB.

At the point B draw BE at right angles to AB and equal to M.

Through E, draw ED parallel to AB and cutting the semicircle in D;

and draw DF parallel to EB meeting AB in F.

Then AB is divided in F, so that the rectangle AF, FB is equal to the square on M. (II. 14.)

The square will be the greatest, when ED touches the semicircle, or when M is equal to half of the given line AB.

PROPOSITION II. THEOREM.

The square on the excess of one straight line above another is less than the squares on the two lines by twice their rectangle.

Let AB, BC be the two straight lines, whose difference is AC.

Then the square on AC is less than the squares on AB and BC by twice the rectangle contained by AB and BC.

Constructing as in Prop. 4. Book II.
Because the complement AG is equal to GE,
add to each CK,
therefore the whole AK is equal to the whole CE;

and AK, CE together are double of AK;
but AK, CE are the gnomon AKF and CK,
and AK is the rectangle contained by AB, BC;
therefore the gnomon AKF and CK
are equal to twice the rectangle AB, BC,
but AE, CK are equal to the squares on AB, BC;
taking the former equals from these equals,
therefore the difference of AE and the gnomon AKF is equal to the difference between the squares on AB, BC, and twice the rectangle AB, BC;
but the difference AE and the gnomon AKF is the figure HF which is equal to the square on AC.

Wherefore the square on AC is equal to the difference between the squares on AB, BC, and twice the rectangle AB, BC.

PROPOSITION III. THEOREM.

In any triangle the squares on the two sides are together double of the squares on half the base and on the straight line joining its bisection with the opposite angle.

Let ABC be a triangle, and AD the line drawn from the vertex A to the bisection D of the base BC.

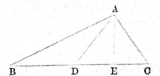

From A draw AE perpendicular to BC.
Then, in the obtuse angled triangle ABD, (II. 12.);
the square on AB exceeds the squares on AD, DB, by twice the rectangle BD, DE:
and in the acute-angled triangle ADC. (II. 13.);
the square on AC is less than the squares on AD, DC, by twice the rectangle CD, DE:
wherefore, since the rectangle BD, DE is equal to the rectangle CD, DE; it follows that the squares on AB, AC are double of the squares on AD, DB.

PROPOSITION IV. THEOREM.

If straight lines be drawn from each angle of a triangle bisecting the opposite sides, four times the sum of the squares on these lines is equal to three times the sum of the squares on the sides of the triangle.

Let ABC be any triangle, and let AD, BE, CF be drawn from A, B, C, to D, E, F, the bisections of the opposite sides of the triangle: draw AG perpendicular to BC.

ON BOOK II.

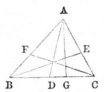

Then the square on AB is equal to the squares on BD, DA together with twice the rectangle BD, DG, (II. 12.)
  and the square on AC is equal to the squares on CD, DA diminished by twice the rectangle CD, DG; (II. 13.)
  therefore the squares on AB, AC are equal to twice the square on BD, and twice the square on AD; for DC is equal to BD:
  and twice the squares on AB, AC are equal to the square on BC, and four times the square on AD: for BC is twice BD.
  Similarly, twice the squares on AB, BC are equal to the square on AC, and four times the square on BE:
  also twice the squares on BC, CA are equal to the square on AB, and four times the square on FC:
    hence, by adding these equals,
  four times the squares on AB, AC, BC are equal to four times the squares on AD, BE, CF together with the squares on AB, AC, BC:
  and taking the squares on AB, AC, BC from these equals,
  therefore three times the squares on AB, AC, BC are equal to four times the squares on AD, BE, CF.

PROPOSITION V. THEOREM.

The sum of the perpendiculars let fall from any point within an equilateral triangle, will be equal to the perpendicular let fall from one of its angles upon the opposite side. Is this proposition true when the point is in one of the sides of the triangle? In what manner must the proposition be enunciated when the point is without the triangle?

Let ABC be an equilateral triangle, and P any point within it: and from P let fall PD, PE, PF perpendiculars on the sides AB, BC, CA respectively, also from A let fall AG perpendicular on the base BC.
  Then AG is equal to the sum of PD, PE, PF.

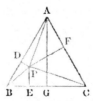

From P draw PA, PB, PC to the angles A, B, C.
Then the triangle ABC is equal to the three triangles PAB, PBC, PCA.

But since every rectangle is double of a triangle of the same base and altitude, (I. 41.)

therefore the rectangle AG, BC, is equal to the three rectangles AB, PD, AC, PF and BC, PE.

Whence the line AG is equal to the sum of the lines PD, PE, PF. If the point P fall on one side of the triangle, or coincide with E

then the triangle ABC is equal to the two triangles APC, BPA

whence AG is equal to the sum of the two perpendiculars PD, PF.

If the point P fall without the base BC of the triangle

then the triangle ABC is equal to the difference between the sum of the two triangles APC, BPA, and the triangle PCB.

Whence AG is equal to the difference between the sum of PD, PF, and PE.

I.

6. If the straight line AB be divided into two unequal parts in D, and into two unequal parts in E, the rectangle contained by AE, EB, will be greater or less than the rectangle contained by AD, DB, according as E is nearer to, or further from, the middle point of AB, than D.

7. Produce a given straight line in such a manner that the square on the whole line thus produced, shall be equal to twice the square on the given line

8. If AB be the line so divided in the points C and E, (fig. Euc. II. 5.) Shew that $AB^2 = 4.CD^2 + 4.AD.DB$.

9. Divide a straight line into two parts, such that the sum of their squares may be the least possible

10. Divide a line into two parts, such that the sum of their squares shall be double the square on another line.

11. Shew that the difference between the squares on the two unequal parts (fig. Euc. II. 9.) is equal to twice the rectangle contained by the whole line, and the part between the points of section

12. Shew how in all the possible cases, a straight line may be *geometrically* divided into two such parts, that the sum of their squares shall be equal to a given square

13. Divide a given straight line into two parts, such that the squares on the whole line and on one of the parts shall be equal to twice the square on the other part

14. Any rectangle is the half of the rectangle contained by the diameters of the squares on its two sides.

15. If a straight line be divided into two equal and into two unequal parts, the squares on the two unequal parts are equal to twice the rectangle contained by the two unequal parts, together with four times the square on the line between the points of section

16. If the points C, D be equidistant from the extremities of the straight line AB, shew that the squares constructed on AD and AC, exceed twice the rectangle AC, AD by the square constructed on CD.

17. If any point be taken in the plane of a parallelogram from which perpendiculars are let fall on the diagonal, and on the sides which include it, the rectangle of the diagonal and the perpendicular

on it, is equal to the sum or difference of the rectangles of the sides and the perpendiculars on them.

18. $ABCD$ is a rectangular parallelogram, of which A, C are opposite angles, E any point in BC, F any point in CD. Prove that twice the area of the triangle AEF together with the rectangle BE, DF is equal to the parallelogram AC.

II.

19. Shew how to produce a given line, so that the rectangle contained by the whole line thus produced, and the produced part, shall be equal to the square (1) on the given line (2) on the part produced.

20. If in the figure Euc. II. 11, we join BF and CH, and produce CH to meet BF in L, CL is perpendicular to BF.

21. If a line be divided, as in Euc. II. 11, the squares on the whole line and one of the parts are together three times the square on the other part.

22. If in the fig Euc. II. 11, the points F, D be joined cutting AHB, GHK in f, d respectively; then shall $Ff = Dd$.

III.

23. If from the three angles of a triangle, lines be drawn to the points of bisection of the opposite sides, the squares on the distances between the angles and the common intersection, are together one-third of the squares on the sides of the triangle.

24. ABC is a triangle of which the angle at C is obtuse, and the angle at B is half a right angle; D is the middle point of AB, and CE is drawn perpendicular to AB. Shew that the square on AC is double of the squares on AD and DE.

25. If an angle of a triangle be two-thirds of two right angles, shew that the square on the side subtending that angle is equal to the squares on the sides containing it, together with the rectangle contained by those sides.

26. The square described on a straight line drawn from one of the angles at the base of a triangle to the middle point of the opposite side, is equal to the sum or difference of the square on half the side bisected, and the rectangle contained between the base and that part of it, or of it produced, which is intercepted between the same angle and a perpendicular drawn from the vertex.

27. ABC is a triangle of which the angle at C is obtuse, and the angle at B is half a right angle; D is the middle point of AB, and CE is drawn perpendicular to AB. Shew that the square on AC is double of the squares on AD and DE.

28. Produce one side of a scalene triangle, so that the rectangle under it and the produced part may be equal to the difference of the squares on the other two sides.

29. Given the base of any triangle, the area, and the line bisecting the base, construct the triangle.

IV.

30. Shew that the square on the hypotenuse of a right-angled triangle, is equal to four times the area of the triangle together with the square on the difference of the sides.

31. In the triangle ABC, if AD be the perpendicular let fall upon the side BC, then the square on AC together with the rectangle contained by BC, BD is equal to the square on AB together with the rectangle CB, CD.

32. ABC is a triangle, right-angled at C, and CD is the perpendicular let fall from C upon AB; if HK is equal to the sum of the sides AC, CB, and LM to the sum of AB, CD shew that the square on HK together with the square on CD is equal to the square on LM.

33. ABC is a triangle having the angle at B a right angle; it is required to find in AB a point P such that the square on AC may exceed the squares on AP and PC by half the square on AB.

34. In a right-angled triangle, the square on that side which is the greater of the two sides containing the right angle, is equal to the rectangle by the sum and difference of the other sides.

35. The hypotenuse AB of a right-angled triangle ABC is trisected in the points D, E; prove that if CD, CE be joined the sum of the squares on the sides of the triangle CDE is equal to two-thirds of the square on AB.

36. From the hypotenuse of a right-angled triangle portions are cut off equal to the adjacent sides; shew that the square on the middle segment is equivalent to twice the rectangle under the extreme segments.

V.

37. Prove that the square on any straight line drawn from the vertex of an isosceles triangle to the base, is less than the square on a side of the triangle by the rectangle contained by the segments of the base—and conversely.

38. If from one of the equal angles of an isosceles triangle a perpendicular be drawn to the opposite side, the rectangle contained by that side and the segment of it intercepted between the perpendicular and base, is equal to the half of the square described upon the base.

39. If in an isosceles triangle a perpendicular be let fall from one of the equal angles to the opposite side, the square on the perpendicular is equal to the square on the line intercepted between the other equal angle and the perpendicular, together with twice the rectangle contained by the segments of that side.

40. The square on the base of an isosceles triangle whose vertical angle is a right angle, is equal to four times the area of the triangle.

41. Describe an isosceles obtuse-angled triangle, such that the square on the side subtending the obtuse angle may be three times the square on either of the sides containing the obtuse angle.

42. If AB, one of the sides of an isosceles triangle ABC, be produced beyond the base to D, so that $BD = AB$, shew that
$$CD^2 = AB^2 + 2.BC^2.$$

43. If ABC be an isosceles triangle, and DE be drawn parallel to the base BC, and EB be joined; prove that $BE^2 = BC \times DE + CE^2$.

44. If ABC be an isosceles triangle of which the angles at B and C are each double of A; then the square on AC is equal to the square on BC together with the rectangle contained by AC and BC.

VI.

45. Shew that in a parallelogram the squares on the diagonals are equal to the sum of the squares on all the sides.

46. If $ABCD$ be any rectangle, A and C being opposite angles, and O any point either within or without the rectangle:
$$OA^2 + OC^2 = OB^2 + OD^2.$$

47. In any quadrilateral figure, the sum of the squares on the diagonals together with four times the square on the line joining their middle points, is equal to the sum of the squares on all the sides.

48. In any trapezium, if the opposite sides be bisected, the sum of the squares on the other two sides, together with the squares on the diagonals, is equal to the sum of the squares on the bisected sides, together with four times the square on the line joining the points of bisection.

49. The squares on the diagonals of a trapezium are together double the squares on the two lines joining the bisections of the opposite sides.

50. In any trapezium two of whose sides are parallel, the squares on the diagonals are together equal to the squares on its two sides which are not parallel, and twice the rectangle contained by the sides which are parallel.

51. It the two sides of a trapezium be parallel, shew that its area is equal to that of a triangle contained by its altitude and half the sum of the parallel sides.

52. If a trapezium have two sides parallel, and the other two equal, shew that the rectangle contained by the two parallel sides, together with the square on one of the other sides, will be equal to the square on the straight line joining two opposite angles of the trapezium.

53. If squares be described on the sides of any triangle and the angular points of the squares be joined; the sum of the squares on the sides of the hexagonal figure thus formed is equal to four times the sum of the squares on the sides of the triangle.

VII.

54. Find the side of a square equal to a given equilateral triangle.

55. Find a square which shall be equal to the sum of two given rectilineal figures.

56. To divide a given straight line so that the rectangle under its segments may be equal to a given rectangle.

57. Construct a rectangle equal to a given square and having the difference of its sides equal to a given straight line.

58. Shew how to describe a rectangle equal to a given square, and having one of its sides equal to a given straight line.

BOOK III.

DEFINITIONS.

I.

EQUAL circles are those of which the diameters are equal, or from the centers of which the straight lines to the circumferences are equal.

This is not a definition, but a theorem, the truth of which is evident; for, if the circles be applied to one another, so that their centers coincide, the circles must likewise coincide since the straight lines from the centers are equal.

II.

A straight line is said to touch a circle when it meets the circle, and being produced does not cut it.

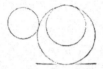

III.

Circles are said to touch one another, which meet, but do not cut one another.

IV.

Straight lines are said to be equally distant from the center of a circle, when the perpendiculars drawn to them from the center are equal.

V.

And the straight line on which the greater perpendicular falls, is said to be further from the center.

VI.

A segment of a circle is the figure contained by a straight line, and *the arc* or the part of the circumference which it cuts off.

VII.

The angle of a segment is that which is contained by a straight line and a part of the circumference.

VIII.

An angle in a segment is any angle contained by two straight lines drawn from any point in the arc of the segment, to the extremities of the straight line which is the base of the segment.

IX.

An angle is said to insist or stand upon the part of the circumference intercepted between the straight lines that contain the angle.

X.

A sector of a circle is the figure contained by two straight lines drawn from the center and the arc between them.

XI.

Similar segments of circles are those in which the angles are equal, or which contain equal angles.

PROPOSITION I. PROBLEM.

To find the center of a given circle.

Let ABC be the given circle: it is required to find its center

Draw within it any straight line AB to meet the circumference A, B; and bisect AB in D; (I. 10.) from the point D draw DC at right angles to AB, (I. 11.) meeting the circumference in C, produce CD to E to meet the circumference again in E, and bisect CE in F.
Then the point F shall be the center of the circle ABC.
For, if it be not, if possible, let G be the center, and join GA, GD, GB.
Then, because DA is equal to DB, (constr.)
and DG common to the two triangles ADG, BDG,
the two sides AD, DG, are equal to the two BD, DG, each to each;
and the base GA is equal to the base GB, (I. def. 15.)
because they are drawn from the center G:
therefore the angle ADG is equal to the angle GDB: (I. 8.)
but when a straight line standing upon another straight line makes the adjacent angles equal to one another, each of the angles is a right angle; (I. def. 10.)
therefore the angle GDB is a right angle:
but FDB is likewise a right angle; (constr.)
wherefore the angle FDB is equal to the angle GDB, (ax. 1.)
the greater angle equal to the less, which is impossible;
therefore G is not the center of the circle ABC.
In the same manner it can be shewn that no other point out of the line CE is the center;
and since CE is bisected in F,
any other point in CE divides CE into unequal parts, and cannot be the center.
Therefore no point but F is the center of the circle ABC.
Which was to be found.

Cor. From this it is manifest, that if in a circle a straight line bisects another at right angles, the center of the circle is in the line which bisects the other.

PROPOSITION II. THEOREM.

If any two points be taken in the circumference of a circle, the straight line which joins them shall fall within the circle.

Let ABC be a circle, and A, B any two points in the circumference. Then the straight line drawn from A to B shall fall within the circle.

For if AB do not fall within the circle,
let it fall, if possible, without the circle as AEB;
find D the center of the circle ABC, (III. 1.) and join DA, DB;
in the circumference AB take any point F,
join DF, and produce it to meet AB in E.
Then, because DA is equal to DB, (I. def. 15.)
therefore the angle DBA is equal to the angle DAB; (I. 5.)
and because AE, a side of the triangle DAE, is produced to B,
the exterior angle DEB is greater than the interior and opposite angle DAE; (I. 16.)
but DAE was proved to be equal to the angle DBE;
therefore the angle DEB is greater than the angle DBE;
but to the greater angle the greater side is opposite, (I. 19.)
therefore DB is greater than DE:
but DB is equal to DF; (I. def. 15.)
wherefore DF is greater than DE,
the less than the greater, which is impossible;
therefore the straight line drawn from A to B does not fall without the circle.
In the same manner, it may be demonstrated that it does not fall upon the circumference;
therefore it falls within it.
Wherefore, if any two points, &c. Q.E.D.

PROPOSITION III. THEOREM.

If a straight line drawn through the center of a circle bisect a straight line in it which does not pass through the center, it shall cut it at right angles: and conversely, if it cut it at right angles, it shall bisect it.

Let ABC be a circle; and let CD, a straight line drawn through the center, bisect any straight line AB, which does not pass through the center, in the point F.

Then CD shall cut AB at right angles.

Take E the center of the circle, (III. 1.) and join EA, EB.
Then, because AF is equal to FB, (hyp.)
and FE common to the two triangles AFE, BFE,

there are two sides in the one equal to two sides in the other, each to each;
and the base EA is equal to the base EB; (I. def. 15.)
therefore the angle AFE is equal to the angle BFE; (I. 8.)
but when a straight line standing upon another straight line makes the adjacent angles equal to one another,
each of them is a right angle; (I. def. 10.)
therefore each of the angles AFE, BFE, is a right angle:
wherefore the straight line CD, drawn through the center, bisecting another AB that does not pass through the center, cuts the same at right angles.

Conversely, let CD cut AB at right angles.
Then CD shall also bisect AB, that is, AF shall be equal to FB.
The same construction being made,
because, EB, EA, from the center are equal to one another, (I. def. 15.)
therefore the angle EAF is equal to the angle EBF; (I. 5.)
and the right angle AFE is equal to the right angle BFE; (I. def. 10.)
therefore, in the two triangles, EAF, EBF,
there are two angles in the one equal to two angles in the other, each to each;
and the side EF, which is opposite to one of the equal angles in each, is common to both;
therefore the other sides are equal; (I. 26.)
therefore AF is equal to FB.
Wherefore, if a straight line, &c. Q.E.D.

PROPOSITION IV. THEOREM.

If in a circle two straight lines cut one another, which do not both pass through the center, they do not bisect each other.

Let $ABCD$ be a circle, and AC, BD two straight lines in it which cut one another in the point E, and do not both pass through the center.
Then AC, BD, shall not bisect one another.

For, if it be possible, let AE be equal to EC, and BE to ED.
If one of the lines pass through the center,
it is plain that it cannot be bisected by the other which does not pass through the center:
but if neither of them pass through the center,
find F the center of the circle, (III. 1.) and join EF.
Then because FE, a straight line drawn through the center, bisects another AC which does not pass through the center, (hyp.)
therefore FE cuts AC at right angles: (III. 3.)
wherefore FEA is a right angle.

Again, because the straight line *FE* bisects the straight line *BD*, which does not pass through the center, (hyp.)
therefore *FE* cuts *BD* at right angles : (III. 3.)
wherefore *FEB* is a right angle :
but *FEA* was shewn to be a right angle ;
therefore the angle *FEA* is equal to the angle *FEB*, (ax. 1.)
the less equal to the greater, which is impossible :
therefore *AC*, *BD* do not bisect one another.
Wherefore, if in a circle, &c. Q.E.D.

PROPOSITION V. THEOREM.

If two circles cut one another, they shall not have the same center.

Let the two circles *ABC*, *CDG*, cut one another in the points *B*, *C*. They shall not have the same center.

If possible, let *E* be the center of the two circles ; join *EC*, and draw any straight line *EFG* meeting the circumferences in *F* and *G*.
And because *E* is the center of the circle *ABC*,
therefore *EF* is equal to *EC* : (I. def. 15.)
again, because *E* is the center of the circle *CDG*,
therefore *EG* is equal to *EC* : (I. def. 15.)
but *EF* was shewn to be equal to *EC* ;
therefore *EF* is equal to *EG*, (ax. 1.)
the less line equal to the greater, which is impossible.
Therefore *E* is not the center of the circles *ABC*, *CDG*.
Wherefore, if two circles, &c. Q.E.D.

PROPOSITION VI. THEOREM.

If one circle touch another internally, they shall not have the same center.

Let the circle *CDE* touch the circle *ABC* internally in the point *C*. They shall not have the same center.

If possible, let *F* be the center of the two circles : join *FC*, and draw any straight line *FEB*, meeting the circumferences in *E* and *B*.
And because *F* is the center of the circle *ABC*,
FB is equal to *FC* ; (I. def. 15.)

also, because F is the center of the circle CDE,
FE is equal to FC: (I. def. 15.)
but FB was shewn to be equal to FC;
therefore FE is equal to FB, (ax. 1.)
the less line equal to the greater, which is impossible:
therefore F is not the center of the circles ABC, CDE.
Therefore, if two circles, &c. Q.E.D.

PROPOSITION VII. THEOREM.

If any point be taken in the diameter of a circle which is not the center, of all the straight lines which can be drawn from it to the circumference, the greatest is that in which the center is, and the other part of that diameter is the least; and, of the rest, that which is nearer to the line which passes through the center is always greater than one more remote: and from the same point there can be drawn only two equal straight lines to the circumference one upon each side of the diameter.

Let $ABCD$ be a circle, and AD its diameter, in which let any point F be taken which is not the center:
let the center be E.
Then, of all the straight lines FB, FC, FG, &c. that can be drawn from F to the circumference,
FA, that in which the center is, shall be the greatest,
and FD, the other part of the diameter AD, shall be the least:
and of the rest, FB, the nearer to FA, shall be greater than FC the more remote, and FC greater than FG.

Join BE, CE, GE.
Because two sides of a triangle are greater than the third side, (I. 20.)
therefore BE, EF are greater than BF:
but AE is equal to BE; (I. def. 15.)
therefore AE, EF, that is, AF is greater than BF.
Again, because BE is equal to CE,
and FE common to the triangles BEF, CEF,
the two sides BE, EF are equal to the two CE, EF, each to each;
but the angle BEF is greater than the angle CEF; (ax. 9.)
therefore the base BF is greater than the base CF. (I. 24.)
For the same reason CF is greater than GF.
Again, because GF, FE are greater than EG, (I. 20.)
and EG is equal to ED:
therefore GF, FE are greater than ED:
take away the common part FE,
and the remainder GF is greater than the remainder FD. (ax. 5.)

Therefore, *FA* is the greatest,
and *FD* the least of all the straight lines from *F* to the circumference;
and *BF* is greater than *CF*, and *CF* than *GF*.

Also, there can be drawn only two equal straight lines from the point *F* to the circumference, one upon each side of the diameter.

At the point *E*, in the straight line *EF*, make the angle *FEH* equal to the angle *FEG*, (I. 23.) and join *FH*.

Then, because *GE* is equal to *EH*, (I. def. 15.)
and *EF* common to the two triangles *GEF*, *HEF*;
the two sides *GE*, *EF* are equal to the two *HE*, *EF*, each to each;
and the angle *GEF* is equal to the angle *HEF*; (constr.)
therefore the base *FG* is equal to the base *FH*: (I. 4.)
but, besides *FH*, no other straight line can be drawn from *F* to the circumference equal to *FG*:
for, if possible, let it be *FK*:
and because *FK* is equal to *FG*, and *FG* to *FH*,
therefore *FK* is equal to *FH*; (ax. 1.)
that is, a line nearer to that which passes through the center, is equal to one which is more remote;
which has been proved to be impossible.
Therefore, if any point be taken, &c.   Q.E.D

PROPOSITION VIII.   THEOREM.

If any point be taken without a circle, and straight lines be drawn from it to the circumference, whereof one passes through the center; of those which fall upon the concave part of the circumference, the greatest is that which passes through the center; and of the rest, that which is nearer to the one passing through the center is always greater than one more remote: but of those which fall upon the convex part of the circumference, the least is that between the point without the circle and the diameter; and of the rest, that which is nearer to the least is always less than one more remote; and only two equal straight lines can be drawn from the same point to the circumference, one upon each side of the line which passes through the center.

Let *ABC* be a circle, and *D* any point without it, from which let the straight lines *DA*, *DE*, *DF*, *DC* be drawn to the circumference, whereof *DA* passes through the center.

Of those which fall upon the concave part of the circumference *AEFC*, the greatest shall be *DA*; which passes through the center;

and any line nearer to it shall be greater than one more remote,
viz. DE shall be greater than DF, and DF greater than DC;
but of those which fall upon the convex part of the circumference $HLKG$, the least shall be DG between the point D and the diameter AG;
and any line nearer to it shall be less than one more remote,
viz DK less than DL, and DL less than DH.

Take M the center of the circle ABC, (iii 1.)
and join ME, MF, MC, MK, ML, MH.
And because AM is equal to ME,
add MD to each of these equals,
therefore AD is equal to EM, MD (ax 2.)
but EM, MD are greater than ED, (i 20.)
therefore also AD is greater than ED.

Again, because ME is equal to MF, and MD common to the triangles EMD, FMD, EM, MD, are equal to FM, MD, each to each;
but the angle EMD is greater than the angle FMD; (ax 9.)
therefore the base ED is greater than the base FD. (i 24.)
In like manner it may be shewn that FD is greater than CD.
Therefore DA is the greatest;
and DE greater than DF, and DF greater than DC.

And, because MK, KD are greater than MD, (i. 20.)
and MK is equal to MG, (i. def. 15.)
the remainder KD is greater than the remainder GD, (ax. 5.)
that is, GD is less than KD:
and because MLD is a triangle, and from the points M, D, the extremities of its side MD, the straight lines MK, DK are drawn to the point K within the triangle,
therefore MK, KD are less than ML, LD: (i. 21.)
but MK is equal to ML, (i. def. 15.)
therefore, the remainder DK is less than the remainder DL. (ax. 5.)
In like manner it may be shewn, that DL is less than DH.
Therefore, DG is the least, and DK less than DL, and DL less than DH.

Also, there can be drawn only two equal straight lines from the point D to the circumference, one upon each side of the line which passes through the center.

At the point M, in the straight line MD,
make the angle DMB equal to the angle DMK, (i. 23.) and join DB.
And because MK is equal to MB, and MD common to the triangles KMD, BMD,
the two sides KM, MD are equal to the two BM, MD, each to each;
and the angle KMD is equal to the angle BMD, (constr.)
therefore the base DK is equal to the base DB. (i. 4.)
but, besides DB, no straight line equal to DK can be drawn from D to the circumference,
for, if possible, let it be DN;
and because DK is equal to DN, and also to DB,
therefore DB is equal to DN,
that is, a line nearer to the least is equal to one more remote, which has been proved to be impossible.
If therefore, any point, &c.   Q.E.D.

PROPOSITION IX. THEOREM.

If a point be taken within a circle, from which there fall more than two equal straight lines to the circumference, that point is the center of the circle.

Let the point D be taken within the circle ABC, from which to the circumference there fall more than two equal straight lines, viz. DA, DB, DC.

Then the point D shall be the center of the circle.

For, if not, let E, if possible, be the center:
join DE, and produce it to meet the circumference in F, G;
then FG is a diameter of the circle ABC: (I. def. 17.)
and because in FG, the diameter of the circle ABC, there is taken the point D, which is not the center,
therefore DG is the greatest line drawn from it to the circumference, and DC is greater than DB, and DB greater than DA: (III. 7.)
but these lines are likewise equal, (hyp.) which is impossible:
therefore E is not the center of the circle ABC.
In like manner it may be demonstrated,
that no other point but D is the center;
D therefore is the center.
Wherefore, if a point be taken, &c. Q.E.D.

PROPOSITION X. THEOREM.

One circumference of a circle cannot cut another in more than two points.

If it be possible let the circumference ABC cut the circumference DEF in more than two points, viz. in B, G, F.

Take the center K of the circle ABC, (III. 3.) and join KB, KG, KF.
Then because K is the center of the circle ABC,
therefore KB, KG, KF are all equal to each other: (I. def. 15.)
and because within the circle DEF there is taken the point K, from which to the circumference DEF fall more than two equal straight lines KB, KG, KF;
therefore the point K is the center of the circle DEF: (III. 9.)
but K is also the center of the circle ABC; (constr.)

therefore the same point is the center of two circles that cut one another, which is impossible. (III. 5.)

Therefore, one circumference of a circle cannot cut another in more than two points. Q.E.D.

PROPOSITION XI. THEOREM.

If one circle touch another internally in any point, the straight line which joins their centers being produced, shall pass through that point of contact.

Let the circle ADE touch the circle ABC internally in the point A; and let F be the center of the circle ABC, and G the center of the circle ADE;
then the straight line which joins the centers F, G, being produced, shall pass through the point A.

For, if FG produced do not pass through the point A, let it fall otherwise, if possible, as $FGDH$, and join AF, AG.

Then, because two sides of a triangle are together greater than the third side, (I. 20.)
therefore FG, GA are greater than FA:
but FA is equal to FH; (I. def. 15.)
therefore FG, GA are greater than FH:
take away from these unequals the common part FG;
therefore the remainder AG is greater than the remainder GH; (ax. 5.)
but AG is equal to GD; (I. def. 15.)
therefore GD is greater than GH,
the less than the greater, which is impossible.
Therefore the straight line which joins the points F, G, being produced, cannot fall otherwise than upon the point A,
that is, it must pass through it.
Therefore, if one circle, &c. Q.E.D.

PROPOSITION XII. THEOREM.

If two circles touch each other externally in any point, the straight line which joins their centers, shall pass through that point of contact.

Let the two circles ABC, ADE, touch each other externally in the point A;
and let F be the center of the circle ABC, and G the center of ADE.
Then the straight line which joins the points F, G, shall pass through the point of contact A.

BOOK III. PROP. XIII. 131

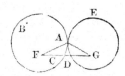

If not, let it pass otherwise, if possible, as *FCDG*, and join *FA*, *AG*.
And because *F* is the center of the circle *ABC*,
FA is equal to *FC*:
also, because *G* is the center of the circle *ADE*,
GA is equal to *GD*:
therefore *FA*, *AG* are equal to *FC*, *DG*; (ax. 2.)
wherefore the whole *FG* is greater than *FA*, *AG*:
but *FG* is less than *FA*, *AG*; (I. 20.) which is impossible.
therefore the straight line which joins the points *F*, *G*, cannot pass otherwise than through *A* the point of contact,
that is, *FG* must pass through the point *A*.
Therefore, if two circles, &c. Q.E.D.

PROPOSITION XIII. THEOREM.

One circle cannot touch another in more points than one, whether it touches it on the inside or outside.

For, if it be possible, let the circle *EBF* touch the circle *ABC* in more points than one.
and first on the inside, in the points *B, D*.

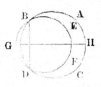 

Join *BD*, and draw *GH* bisecting *BD* at right angles. (I. 11.)
Because the points *B, D* are in the circumferences of each of the circles,
therefore the straight line *BD* falls within each of them; (III. 2.)
therefore their centers are in the straight line *GH* which bisects *BD* at right angles: (III. 1. Cor.)
therefore *GH* passes through the point of contact: (III. 11.)
but it does not pass through it,
because the points *B, D* are without the straight line *GH*;
which is absurd:
therefore one circle cannot touch another on the inside in more points than one.
Nor can two circles touch one another on the outside in more than one point.
For, if it be possible,
let the circle *ACK* touch the circle *ABC* in the points *A, C*;
join *AC*.

132   EUCLID'S ELEMENTS.

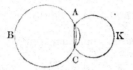

Because the two points A, C are in the circumference of the circle ACK,
therefore the straight line AC which joins them, falls within the circle ACK: (III. 2.)
but the circle ACK is without the circle ABC; (hyp.)
therefore the straight line AC is without this last circle:
but, because the points A, C are in the circumference of the circle ABC,
the straight line AC must be within the same circle, (III. 2.)
which is absurd:
therefore one circle cannot touch another on the outside in more than one point:
and it has been shown, that they cannot touch on the inside in more points than one.
Therefore, one circle, &c.   Q.E.D.

PROPOSITION XIV. THEOREM.

Equal straight lines in a circle are equally distant from the center; and conversely, those which are equally distant from the center, are equal to one another.

Let the straight lines AB, CD, in the circle $ABDC$, be equal to one another.
Then AB and CD shall be equally distant from the center.

Take E the center of the circle $ABDC$, (III. 1.)
from E draw EF, EG perpendiculars to AB, CD, (I 12.) and join EA, EC.
Then, because the straight line EF passing through the center, cuts AB, which does not pass through the center, at right angles;
EF bisects AB in the point F: (III. 3.)
therefore AF is equal to FB, and AB double of AF.
For the same reason CD is double of CG:
but AB is equal to CD: (hyp.)
therefore AF is equal to CG.   (ax. 7.)
And because AE is equal to EC, (I. def. 15.)
the square on AE is equal to the square on EC:
but the squares on AF, FE are equal to the square on AE, (I. 47.)
because the angle AFE is a right angle;

and for the same reason, the squares on EG, GC are equal to the square on EC;

therefore the squares on AF, FE are equal to the squares on CG, GE: (ax. 1.)

but the square on AF is equal to the square on CG,
because AF is equal to CG;

therefore the remaining square on EF is equal to the remaining square on EG, (ax. 3.)

and the straight line EF is therefore equal to EG:

but straight lines in a circle are said to be equally distant from the center, when the perpendiculars drawn to them from the center are equal: (III. def. 4.)

therefore AB, CD are equally distant from the center.

Conversely, let the straight lines AB, CD be equally distant from the center, (III. def. 4.)

that is, let FE be equal to EG;
then AB shall be equal to CD.

For the same construction being made,
it may, as before, be demonstrated,
that AB is double of AF, and CD double of CG,
and that the squares on FE, AF are equal to the squares on EG, GC:

but the square on FE is equal to the square on EG,
because FE is equal to EG; (hyp.)

therefore the remaining square on AF is equal to the remaining square on CG: (ax. 3.)

and the straight line AF is therefore equal to CG:

but AB was shown to be double of AF, and CD double of CG:
wherefore AB is equal to CD. (ax. 6.)

Therefore equal straight lines, &c. Q.E.D.

PROPOSITION XV. THEOREM.

The diameter is the greatest straight line in a circle; and of the rest, that which is nearer to the center is always greater than one more remote: and conversely the greater is nearer to the center than the less.

Let $ABCD$ be a circle of which the diameter is AD, and the center E;
and let BC be nearer to the center than FG.

Then AD shall be greater than any straight line BC, which is not diameter, and BC shall be greater than FG.

From E draw EH, perpendicular to BC, and EK to FG, (I. 12.)
and join EB, EC, EF.

And because AE is equal to EB, and ED to EC, (I. def. 15.)
therefore AD is equal to EB, EC: (ax. 2.)
but EB, EC are greater than BC; (I. 20.)
wherefore also AD is greater than BC.

And, because *BC* is nearer to the center than *FG*, (hyp.)
therefore *EH* is less than *EK* : (III. def. 5.)
but, as was demonstrated in the preceding proposition,
BC is double of *BH*, and *FG* double of *FK*,
and the squares on *EH*, *HB* are equal to the squares on *EK*, *KF*:
but the square on *EH* is less than the square on *EK*,
because *EH* is less than *EK*;
therefore the square on *BH* is greater than the square on *FK*,
and the straight line *BH* greater than *FK*,
and therefore *BC* is greater than *FG*.

Next, let *BC* be greater than *FG*;
then *BC* shall be nearer to the center than *FG*, that is, the same construction being made, *EH* shall be less than *EK*. (III. def. 5.)
Because *BC* is greater than *FG*,
BH likewise is greater than *KF*:
and the squares on *BH*, *HE* are equal to the squares on *FK*, *KE*
of which the square on *BH* is greater than the square on *FK*,
because *BH* is greater than *FK*:
therefore the square on *EH* is less than the square on *EK*,
and the straight line *EH* less than *EK*:
and therefore *BC* is nearer to the center than *FG*. (III. def. 5.)
Wherefore the diameter, &c. Q.E.D.

PROPOSITION XVI. THEOREM.

The straight line drawn at right angles to the diameter of a circle, from the extremity of it, falls without the circle; and no straight line can be drawn from the extremity between that straight line and the circumference, so as not to cut the circle: or, which is the same thing, no straight line can make so great an acute angle with the diameter at its extremity, or so small an angle with the straight line which is at right angles to it, as not to cut the circle.

Let *ABC* be a circle, the center of which is *D*, and the diameter *AB*.
Then the straight line drawn at right angles to *AB* from its extremity *A*, shall fall without the circle.

For, if it does not, let it fall, if possible, within the circle, as *AC*;
and draw *DC* to the point *C*, where it meets the circumference.
And because *DA* is equal to *DC*, (I. def. 15.)
the angle *DAC* is equal to the angle *ACD*: (I. 5.)
but *DAC* is a right angle; (hyp.)
therefore *ACD* is a right angle;
and therefore the angles *DAC*, *ACD* are equal to two right angles;
which is impossible: (I. 17.)
therefore the straight line drawn from *A* at right angles to *BA*, does not fall within the circle.

In the same manner it may be demonstrated,
that it does not fall upon the circumference;
therefore it must fall without the circle, as AE.
Also, between the straight line AE and the circumference, no straight line can be drawn from the point A which does not cut the circle.
For, if possible, let AF fall between them,

and from the point D, let DG be drawn perpendicular to AF, (I. 12.)
and let it meet the circumference in H.
And because AGD is a right angle,
and DAG less than a right angle, (I. 17.)
therefore DA is greater than DG: (I. 19.)
but DA is equal to DH; (I. def. 15.)
therefore DH is greater than DG,
the less than the greater, which is impossible:
therefore no straight line can be drawn from the point A, between AE and the circumference, which does not cut the circle:
or, which amounts to the same thing, however great an acute angle a straight line makes with the diameter at the point A, or however small an angle it makes with AE, the circumference must pass between that straight line and the perpendicular AE. Q.E.D.

Cor. From this it is manifest, that the straight line which is drawn at right angles to the diameter of a circle from the extremity of it touches the circle: (III. def. 2.) and that it touches it only in one point, because, if it did meet the circle in two, it would fall within it. (III. 2.) "Also, it is evident, that there can be but one straight line which touches the circle in the same point."

PROPOSITION XVII. PROBLEM.

To draw a straight line from a given point, either without or in the circumference, which shall touch a given circle.

First, let A be a given point without the given circle BCD;
it is required to draw a straight line from A which shall touch the circle.

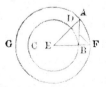

Find the center E of the circle, (III. 1.) and join AE;
and from the center E, at the distance EA, describe the circle AFG;
from the point D draw DF at right angles to EA, (I. 11.) meeting the circumference of the circle AFG in F;
and join EBF, AB.

Then AB shall touch the circle BCD in the point B.
Because E is the center of the circles BCD, AFG. (I. def. 15.)
therefore EA is equal to EF, and ED to EB;
therefore the two sides AE, EB, are equal to the two FE, ED, each to each;
and they contain the angle at E common to the two triangles AEB, FED;
therefore the base DF is equal to the base AB, (I. 4.)
and the triangle FED to the triangle AEB,
and the other angles to the other angles:
therefore the angle EBA is equal to the angle EDF:
but EDF is a right angle, (constr.)
wherefore EBA is a right angle: (ax. 1.)
and EB is drawn from the center:
but a straight line drawn from the extremity of a diameter, at right angles to it, touches the circle: (III. 16. Cor.)
therefore AB touches the circle;
and it is drawn from the given point A.
Secondly, if the given point be in the circumference of the circle, as the point D,
draw DE to the center E, and DF at right angles to DE:
then DF touches the circle. (III. 16. Cor.) Q.E.F.

PROPOSITION XVIII. THEOREM.

If a straight line touch a circle, the straight line drawn from the center to the point of contact, shall be perpendicular to the line touching the circle.

Let the straight line DE touch the circle ABC in the point C;
take the center F, and draw the straight line FC. (III. 1.)
Then FC shall be perpendicular to DE.

If FC be not perpendicular to DE; from the point F, if possible, let FBG be drawn perpendicular to DE.
And because FGC is a right angle,
therefore GCF is an acute angle; (I. 17.)
and to the greater angle the greater side is opposite: (I. 19.)
therefore FC is greater than FG:
but FC is equal to FB; (I. def. 15.)
therefore FB is greater than FG,
the less than the greater, which is impossible:
therefore FG is not perpendicular to DE.
In the same manner it may be shewn,
that no other line is perpendicular to DE besides FC,
that is, FC is perpendicular to DE.
Therefore, if a straight line, &c. Q.E.D.

PROPOSITION XIX. THEOREM.

If a straight line touch a circle, and from the point of contact a straight line be drawn at right angles to the touching line, the center of the circle shall be in that line.

Let the straight line *DE* touch the circle *ABC* in *C*, and from *C* let *CA* be drawn at right angles to *DE*.
Then the center of the circle shall be in *CA*.

For, if not, let *F* be the center, if possible, and join *CF*.
Because *DE* touches the circle *ABC*,
and *FC* is drawn from the center to the point of contact,
therefore *FC* is perpendicular to *DE*; (III. 18.)
therefore *FCE* is a right angle:
but *ACE* is also a right angle; (hyp.)
therefore the angle *FCE* is equal to the angle *ACE*, (ax. 1.)
the less to the greater, which is impossible:
therefore *F* is not the center of the circle *ABC*.
In the same manner it may be shewn,
that no other point which is not in *CA*, is the center;
that is, the center of the circle is in *CA*.
Therefore, if a straight line, &c. Q.E.D.

PROPOSITION XX. THEOREM.

The angle at the center of a circle is double of the angle at the circumference upon the same base, that is, upon the same part of the circumference.

Let *ABC* be a circle, and *BEC* an angle at the center, and *BAC* an angle at the circumference, which have *BC* the same part of the circumference for their base.
Then the angle *BEC* shall be double of the angle *BAC*.

Join *AE*, and produce it to *F*.
First, let the center of the circle be within the angle *BAC*.
Because *EA* is equal to *EB*,
therefore the angle *EBA* is equal to the angle *EAB*; (I. 5.)
therefore the angles *EAB*, *EBA* are double of the angle *EAB*:
but the angle *BEF* is equal to the angles *EAB*, *EBA*; (I. 32.)

therefore also the angle *BEF* is double of the angle *EAB*:
for the same reason, the angle *FEC* is double of the angle *EAC*:
therefore the whole angle *BEC* is double of the whole angle *BAC*.
Secondly, let the center of the circle be without the angle *BAC*.

It may be demonstrated, as in the first case,
that the angle *FEC* is double of the angle *FAC*,
and that *FEB*, a part of the first, is double of *FAB*, a part of the other;
therefore the remaining angle *BEC* is double of the remaining
angle *BAC*.
Therefore the angle at the center, &c. Q.E.D.

PROPOSITION XXI. THEOREM.

The angles in the same segment of a circle are equal to one another.

Let *ABCD* be a circle,
and *BAD*, *BED* angles in the same segment *BAED*.
Then the angles *BAD*, *BED* shall be equal to one another.
First, let the segment *BAED* be greater than a semicircle.

Take *F*, the center of the circle *ABCD*, (III. 1.) and join *BF*, *FD*.
Because the angle *BFD* is at the center, and the angle *BAD* at the circumference, and that they have the same part of the circumference. viz. the arc *BCD* for their base;
therefore the angle *BFD* is double of the angle *BAD*: (III. 20.)
for the same reason the angle *BFD* is double of the angle *BED*:
therefore the angle *BAD* is equal to the angle *BED*. (ax. 7.)
Next, let the segment *BAED* be not greater than a semicircle.

Draw *AF* to the center, and produce it to *C*, and join *CE*.
Because *AC* is a diameter of the circle,
therefore the segment *BADC* is greater than a semicircle;
and the angles in it *BAC*, *BEC* are equal, by the first case:

for the same reason, because *CBED* is greater than a semicircle,
the angles *CAD*, *CED*, are equal:
therefore the whole angle *BAD* is equal to the whole angle *BED*. (ax. 2.)
Wherefore the angles in the same segment, &c. Q.E.D.

PROPOSITION XXII. THEOREM.

The opposite angles of any quadrilateral figure inscribed in a circle, are together equal to two right angles.

Let *ABCD* be a quadrilateral figure in the circle *ABCD*.
Then any two of its opposite angles shall together be equal to two right angles.

Join *AC*, *BD*.
And because the three angles of every triangle are equal to two right angles, (I. 32.)
the three angles of the triangle *CAB*, viz. the angles *CAB*, *ABC*, *BCA*, are equal to two right angles:
but the angle *CAB* is equal to the angle *CDB*, (III. 21.)
because they are in the same segment *CDAB*;
and the angle *ACB* is equal to the angle *ADB*,
because they are in the same segment *ADCB*:
therefore the two angles *CAB*, *ACB* are together equal to the whole angle *ADC*: (ax. 2.)
to each of these equals add the angle *ABC*;
therefore the three angles *ABC*, *CAB*, *BCA* are equal to the two angles *ABC*, *ADC*: (ax. 2.)
but *ABC*, *CAB*, *BCA*, are equal to two right angles;
therefore also the angles *ABC*, *ADC* are equal to two right angles.
In the same manner, the angles *BAD*, *DCB*, may be shewn to be equal to two right angles.
Therefore, the opposite angles, &c. Q.E.D.

PROPOSITION XXIII. THEOREM.

Upon the same straight line, and upon the same side of it, there cannot be two similar segments of circles, not coinciding with one another.

If it be possible, upon the same straight line *AB*, and upon the same side of it, let there be two similar segments of circles, *ACB*, *ADB*, not coinciding with one another.

Then, because the circumference ACB cuts the circumference ADB in the two points A, B, they cannot cut one another in any other point; (III. 10.)
therefore one of the segments must fall within the other;
let ACB fall within ADB,
draw the straight line BCD, and join CA, DA.
Because the segment ACB is similar to the segment ADB, (hyp.)
and that similar segments of circles contain equal angles, (III. def. 11.)
therefore the angle ACB is equal to the angle ADB,
the exterior angle to the interior, which is impossible. (I. 16.)
Therefore, there cannot be two similar segments of circles upon the same side of the same line, which do not coincide. Q.E.D.

PROPOSITION XXIV. THEOREM.

Similar segments of circles upon equal straight lines, are equal to one another.

Let AEB, CFD be similar segments of circles upon the equal straight lines AB, CD.
Then the segment AEB shall be equal to the segment CFD.

For if the segment AEB be applied to the segment CFD, so that the point A may be on C, and the straight line AB upon CD, then the point B shall coincide with the point D,
because AB is equal to CD;
therefore, the straight line AB coinciding with CD,
the segment AEB must coincide with the segment CFD, (III. 23.)
and therefore is equal to it. (I. ax. 8.)
Wherefore similar segments, &c. Q.E.D.

PROPOSITION XXV. PROBLEM.

A segment of a circle being given, to describe the circle of which it is the segment.

Let ABC be the given segment of a circle.
It is required to describe the circle of which it is the segment.
Bisect AC in D, (I. 10.) and from the point D draw DB at right angles to AC, (I. 11.) and join AB.
First, let the angles ABD, BAD be equal to one another:

then the straight line DA is equal to DB, (I. 6.) and therefore, to DC;
and because the three straight lines DA, DB, DC are all equal,
therefore D is the center of the circle. (III. 9.)
From the center D, at the distance of any of the three DA, DB, DC, describe a circle;
this shall pass through the other points;
and the circle of which ABC is a segment has been described:

BOOK III. PROP. XXVI. 141

and because the center D is in AC, the segment ABC is a semicircle.
But if the angles ABD, BAD are not equal to one another:

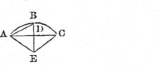

at the point A, in the straight line AB,
make the angle BAE equal to the angle ABD, (I. 23.)
and produce BD, if necessary, to meet AE in E, and join EC.
  Because the angle ABE is equal to the angle BAE,
  therefore the straight line EA is equal to EB: (I. 6.)
and because AD is equal to DC, and DE common to the triangles ADE, CDE,
the two sides AD, DE, are equal to the two CD, DE, each to each;
  and the angle ADE is equal to the angle CDE,
    for each of them is a right angle; (constr.)
  therefore the base EA is equal to the base EC: (I. 4.)
    but EA was shewn to be equal to EB:
    wherefore also EB is equal to EC: (ax. 1.)
and therefore the three straight lines EA, EB, EC are equal to one another:
  wherefore E is the center of the circle. (III. 9.)
From the center E, at the distance of any of the three EA, EB, EC, describe a circle;
  this shall pass through the other points;
  and the circle of which ABC is a segment, is described.
  And it is evident, that if the angle ABD be greater than the angle BAD, the center E falls without the segment ABC, which therefore is less than a semicircle:
  but if the angle ABD be less than BAD, the center E falls within the segment ABC, which is therefore greater than a semicircle.
Wherefore a segment of a circle being given, the circle is described of which it is a segment. Q.E.F.

PROPOSITION XXVI. THEOREM.

In equal circles, equal angles stand upon equal arcs, whether the angles be at the centers or circumferences.

Let ABC, DEF be equal circles,
  and let the angles BGC, EHF at their centers,
and BAC, EDF at their circumferences be equal to each other.
Then the arc BKC shall be equal to the arc ELF.

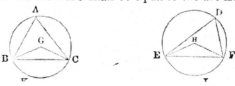

Join BC, EF.
And because the circles ABC, DEF are equal,
the straight lines drawn from their centers are equal;. (III. def. 1.)
therefore the two sides BG, GC, are equal to the two EH, HF, each to each:
and the angle at G is equal to the angle at H; (hyp.)
therefore the base BC is equal to the base EF. (I. 4.)
And because the angle at A is equal to the angle at D, (hyp.)
the segment BAC is similar to the segment EDF: (III. def. 11.)
and they are upon equal straight lines BC, EF:
but similar segments of circles upon equal straight lines, are equal to one another, (III. 24.)
therefore the segment BAC is equal to the segment EDF:
but the whole circle ABC is equal to the whole DEF; (hyp.)
therefore the remaining segment BKC is equal to the remaining segment ELF, (I. ax. 3.)
and the arc BKC to the arc ELF.
Wherefore, in equal circles, &c. Q.E.D.

PROPOSITION XXVII. THEOREM.

In equal circles, the angles which stand upon equal arcs, are equal to one another, whether they be at the centers or circumferences.

Let ABC, DEF be equal circles,
and let the angles BGC, EHF at their centers,
and the angles BAC, EDF at their circumferences,
stand upon the equal arcs BC, EF.
Then the angle BGC shall be equal to the angle EHF,
and the angle BAC to the angle EDF.

If the angle BGC be equal to the angle EHF,
it is manifest that the angle BAC is also equal to EDF. (III. 20. and I. ax. 7.)
But, if not, one of them must be greater than the other:
if possible, let the angle BGC be greater than EHF,
and at the point G, in the straight line BG,
make the angle BGK equal to the angle EHF. (I. 23.)
Then because the angle BGK is equal to the angle EHF,
and that equal angles stand upon equal arcs, when they are at the centers; (III. 26.)
therefore the arc BK is equal to the arc EF:
but the arc EF is equal to the arc BC; (hyp.)
therefore also the arc BK is equal to the arc BC,
the less equal to the greater, which is impossible: (I. ax. 1.)

therefore the angle BGC is not unequal to the angle EHF;
that is, it is equal to it:
but the angle at A is half of the angle BGC, (III. 20.)
and the angle at D, half of the angle EHF;
therefore the angle at A is equal to the angle at D. (I. ax. 7.)
Wherefore, in equal circles, &c. Q.E.D.

PROPOSITION XXVIII. THEOREM.

In equal circles, equal straight lines cut off equal arcs, the greater equal to the greater, and the less to the less.

Let ABC, DEF be equal circles,
and BC, EF equal straight lines in them, which cut off the two greater arcs BAC, EDF, and the two less BGC, EHF.
Then the greater arc BAC shall be equal to the greater EDF,
and the less arc BGC to the less EHF.

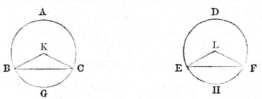

Take K, L, the centers of the circles, (III. 1.) and join BK, KC, EL, LF.
Because the circles ABC, DEF are equal,
the straight lines from their centers are equal: (III. def. 1.)
therefore BK, KC are equal to EL, LF, each to each:
and the base BC is equal to the base EF, in the triangles BCK, EFL;
therefore the angle BKC is equal to the angle ELF: (I. 8.)
but equal angles stand upon equal arcs, when they are at the centers: (III. 26.)
therefore the arc BGC is equal to the arc EHF:
but the whole circumference ABC is equal to the whole EDF; (hyp.)
therefore the remaining part of the circumference,
viz. the arc BAC, is equal to the remaining part EDF. (I. ax. 3.)
Therefore, in equal circles, &c. Q.E.D.

PROPOSITION XXIX. THEOREM.

In equal circles, equal arcs are subtended by equal straight lines.

Let ABC, DEF be equal circles,
and let the arcs BGC, EHF also be equal,
and joined by the straight lines BC, EF.
Then the straight line BC shall be equal to the straight line EF.

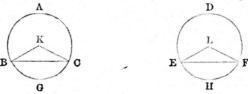

Take K, L, (III. 1) the centers of the circles, and join BK, KC, EL, LF.
Because the arc BGC is equal to the arc EHF,
therefore the angle BKC is equal to the angle ELF (III. 27)
and because the circles ABC, DEF, are equal,
the straight lines from their centers are equal: (III. def. 1)
therefore BK, KC, are equal to EL, LF, each to each:
and they contain equal angles in the triangles BCK, EFL;
therefore the base BC is equal to the base EF. (I. 4.)
Therefore, in equal circles, &c.   Q E D.

PROPOSITION XXX. PROBLEM.

To bisect a given arc, that is, to divide it into two equal parts.

Let ADB be the given arc:
it is required to bisect it.

Join AB, and bisect it in C; (I. 10.)
from the point C draw CD at right angles to AB. (I. 11.)
Then the arc ADB shall be bisected in the point D.
Join AD, DB.
And because AC is equal to CB,
and CD common to the triangles ACD, BCD,
the two sides AC, CD are equal to the two BC, CD, each to each;
and the angle ACD is equal to the angle BCD,
because each of them is a right angle:
therefore the base AD is equal to the base BD. (I 4.)
But equal straight lines cut off equal arcs, (III 28)
the greater arc equal to the greater, and the less arc to the less;
and the arcs AD, DB are each of them less than a semicircle,
because DC, if produced, passes through the center: (III. 1. Cor)
therefore the arc AD is equal to the arc DB.
Therefore the given arc ADB is bisected in D.   Q.E.F.

PROPOSITION XXXI THEOREM.

In a circle, the angle in a semicircle is a right angle; but the angle in a segment greater than a semicircle is less than a right angle, and the angle in a segment less than a semicircle is greater than a right angle

Let $ABCD$ be a circle, of which the diameter is BC, and center E, and let CA be drawn, dividing the circle into the segments ABC, ADC.
Join BA, AD, DC.
Then the angle in the semicircle BAC shall be a right angle:
and the angle in the segment ABC, which is greater than a semicircle, shall be less than a right angle,
and the angle in the segment ADC, which is less than a semicircle, shall be greater than a right angle

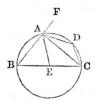

Join *AE*, and produce *BA* to *F*.
First, because *EB* is equal to *EA*, (I. def. 15.)
the angle *EAB* is equal to *EBA*; (I. 5.)
also, because *EA* is equal to *EC*,
the angle *ECA* is equal to *EAC*;
wherefore the whole angle *BAC* is equal to the two angles *EBA*, *ECA*; (I. ax. 2.)
but *FAC*, the exterior angle of the triangle *ABC*, is equal to the two angles *EBA*, *ECA*; (I. 32.)
therefore the angle *BAC* is equal to the angle *FAC*; (ax. 1.)
and therefore each of them is a right angle; (I. def. 10.)
wherefore the angle *BAC* in a semicircle is a right angle.
Secondly, because the two angles *ABC*, *BAC* of the triangle *ABC* are together less than two right angles, (I. 17.)
and that *BAC* has been proved to be a right angle;
therefore *ABC* must be less than a right angle:
and therefore the angle in a segment *ABC* greater than a semicircle, is less than a right angle.
And lastly, because *ABCD* is a quadrilateral figure in a circle, any two of its opposite angles are equal to two right angles: (III. 22.)
therefore the angles *ABC*, *ADC*, are equal to two right angles:
and *ABC* has been proved to be less than a right angle;
wherefore the other *ADC* is greater than a right angle.
Therefore, in a circle the angle in a semicircle is a right angle; &c. Q.E.D.

Cor. From this it is manifest, that if one angle of a triangle be equal to the other two, it is a right angle: because the angle adjacent to it is equal to the same two; (I. 32.) and when the adjacent angles are equal, they are right angles. (I. def. 10.)

PROPOSITION XXXII. THEOREM.

If a straight line touch a circle, and from the point of contact a straight line be drawn meeting the circle; the angles which this line makes with the line touching the circle shall be equal to the angles which are in the alternate segments of the circle.

Let the straight line *EF* touch the circle *ABCD* in *B*,
and from the point *B* let the straight line *BD* be drawn, meeting the circumference in *D*, and dividing it into the segments *DCB*, *DAB*, of which *DCB* is less than, and *DAB* greater than a semicircle.
Then the angles which *BD* makes with the touching line *EF*, shall be equal to the angles in the alternate segments of the circle;
that is, the angle *DBF* shall be equal to the angle which is in the segment *DAB*,

146   EUCLID'S ELEMENTS.

and the angle *DBE* shall be equal to the angle in the alternate segment *DCB*.

From the point *B* draw *BA* at right angles to *EF*, (I. 11.) meeting the circumference in *A*;
take any point *C* in the arc *DB*, and join *AD*, *DC*, *CB*.
Because the straight line *EF* touches the circle *ABCD* in the point *B*,
and *BA* is drawn at right angles to the touching line from the point of contact *B*,
the center of the circle is in *BA* : (III. 19.)
therefore the angle *ADB* in a semicircle is a right angle: (III. 31.)
and consequently the other two angles *BAD*, *ABD*, are equal to a right angle; (I. 32.)
but *ABF* is likewise a right angle; (constr.)
therefore the angle *ABF* is equal to the angles *BAD*, *ABD*: (I. ax. 1.)
take from these equals the common angle *ABD*:
therefore the remaining angle *DBF* is equal to the angle *BAD*, (I. ax. 3.)
which is in *BDA*, the alternate segment of the circle.
And because *ABCD* is a quadrilateral figure in a circle,
the opposite angles *BAD*, *BCD* are equal to two right angles: (III. 22.)
but the angles *DBF*, *DBE* are likewise equal to two right angles; (I. 13.)
therefore the angles *DBF*, *DBE* are equal to the angles *BAD*, *BCD*, (I. ax. 1.)
and *DBF* has been proved equal to *BAD*;
therefore the remaining angle *DBE* is equal to the angle *BCD* in *BDC*, the alternate segment of the circle. (I. ax. 2.)
Wherefore, if a straight line, &c.   Q.E.D.

PROPOSITION XXXIII. PROBLEM.

Upon a given straight line to describe a segment of a circle, which shall contain an angle equal to a given rectilineal angle.

Let *AB* be the given straight line,
and the angle *C* the given rectilineal angle.
It is required to describe upon the given straight line *AB*, a segment of a circle, which shall contain an angle equal to the angle *C*.
First, let the angle *C* be a right angle.

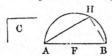

BOOK III. PROP. XXXIII., XXXIV. 147

Bisect AB in F. (I. 10.)
and from the center F, at the distance FB, describe the semicircle AHB, and draw AH, BH to any point H in the circumference.

Therefore the angle AHB in a semicircle is equal to the right angle C. (III. 31.)

But if the angle C be not a right angle:

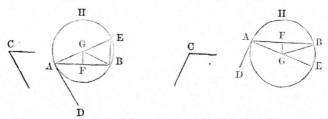

at the point A, in the straight line AB,
make the angle BAD equal to the angle C, (I. 23.)
and from the point A draw AE at right angles to AD; (I. 11.)
bisect AB in F, (I. 10.)
and from F draw FG at right angles to AB, (I. 11.) and join GB.

Because AF is equal to FB, and FG common to the triangles AFG, BFG,
the two sides AF, FG are equal to the two BF, FG, each to each,
and the angle AFG is equal to the angle BFG; (I. def. 10.)
therefore the base AG is equal to the base GB; (I. 4.)
and the circle described from the center G, at the distance GA,
shall pass through the point B:
let this be the circle AHB.

The segment AHB shall contain an angle equal to the given rectilineal angle C.

Because from the point A the extremity of the diameter AE, AD is drawn at right angles to AE,
therefore AD touches the circle: (III. 16. Cor.)
and because AB, drawn from the point of contact A, cuts the circle,
the angle DAB is equal to the angle in the alternate segment AHB: (III. 32.)
but the angle DAB is equal to the angle C: (constr.)
therefore the angle C is equal to the angle in the segment AHB.

Wherefore, upon the given straight line AB, the segment AHB of a circle is described, which contains an angle equal to the given angle C. Q.E.F.

PROPOSITION XXXIV. PROBLEM.

From a given circle to cut off a segment, which shall contain an angle equal to a given rectilineal angle.

Let ABC be the given circle, and D the given rectilineal angle.

It is required to cut off from the circle ABC a segment that shall contain an angle equal to the given angle D.

148 EUCLID'S ELEMENTS.

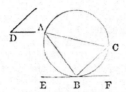

Draw the straight line *EF* touching the circle *ABC* in any point *B*, (III. 17.)
and at the point *B*, in the straight line *BF*, make the angle *FBC* equal to the angle *D*. (I. 23.)
Then the segment *BAC* shall contain an angle equal to the given angle *D*.

Because the straight line *EF* touches the circle *ABC*,
and *BC* is drawn from the point of contact *B*,
therefore the angle *FBC* is equal to the angle in the alternate segment *BAC* of the circle: (III. 32.)
but the angle *FBC* is equal to the angle *D*; (constr.)
therefore the angle in the segment *BAC* is equal to the angle *D*. (I. ax. 1.)

Wherefore from the given circle *ABC*, the segment *BAC* is cut off, containing an angle equal to the given angle *D*. Q.E.F.

PROPOSITION XXXV. THEOREM.

If two straight lines cut one another within a circle, the rectangle contained by the segments of one of them, is equal to the rectangle contained by the segments of the other.

Let the two straight lines *AC*, *BD*, cut one another in the point *E*, within the circle *ABCD*.

Then the rectangle contained by *AE*, *EC* shall be equal to the rectangle contained by *BE*, *ED*.

First, if *AC*, *BD* pass each of them through the center, so that *E* is the center;
it is evident that since *AE*, *EC*, *BE*, *ED*, being all equal, (I. def. 15.)
therefore the rectangle *AE*, *EC* is equal to the rectangle *BE*, *ED*.

Secondly, let one of them *BD* pass through the center, and cut the other *AC*, which does not pass through the center, at right angles, in the point *E*.

Then, if BD be bisected in F,
F is the center of the circle $ABCD$.
Join AF.
Because BD which passes through the center, cuts the straight line AC, which does not pass through the center, at right angles in E, therefore AE is equal to EC: (III. 3.)
and because the straight line BD is cut into two equal parts in the point F, and into two unequal parts in the point E,
therefore the rectangle BE, ED, together with the square on EF, is equal to the square on FB; (II. 5.)
that is, to the square on FA:
but the squares on AE, EF, are equal to the square on FA: (I. 47.)
therefore the rectangle BE, ED, together with the square on EF, is equal to the squares on AE, EF: (I. ax. 1.)
take away the common square on EF,
and the remaining rectangle BE, ED is equal to the remaining square on AE; (I. ax. 3.)
that is, to the rectangle AE, EC.

Thirdly, let BD, which passes through the center, cut the other AC, which does not pass through the center, in E, but not at right angles.

Then, as before, if BD be bisected in F,
F is the center of the circle.
Join AF, and from F draw FG perpendicular to AC; (I. 12.)
therefore AG is equal to GC; (III. 3.)
wherefore the rectangle AE, EC, together with the square on EG, is equal to the square on AG: (II. 5.)
to each of these equals add the square on GF;
therefore the rectangle AE, EC, together with the squares on EG, GF, is equal to the squares on AG, GF; (I. ax. 2.)
but the squares on EG, GF, are equal to the square on EF; (I. 47.)
and the squares on AG, GF are equal to the square on AF;
therefore the rectangle AE, EC, together with the square on EF, is equal to the square on AF;
that is, to the square on FB:
but the square on FB is equal to the rectangle BE, ED, together with the square on EF; (II. 5.)
therefore the rectangle AE, EC, together with the square on EF, is equal to the rectangle BE, ED, together with the square on EF; (I. ax. 1.)
take away the common square on EF,
and the remaining rectangle AE, EC, is therefore equal to the remaining rectangle BE, ED. (ax. 3.)

Lastly, let neither of the straight lines AC, BD pass through the center.

Take the center F, (III. 1.)
and through E the intersection of the straight lines AC, DB,
draw the diameter $GEFH$.

And because the rectangle AE, EC is equal, as has been shewn, to the rectangle GE, EH;
and for the same reason, the rectangle BE, ED is equal to the same rectangle GE, EH;
therefore the rectangle AE, EC is equal to the rectangle BE, ED. (I. ax. 1.)

Wherefore, if two straight lines, &c.   Q.E.D.

PROPOSITION XXXVI. THEOREM.

If from any point without a circle two straight lines be drawn, one of which cuts the circle, and the other touches it; the rectangle contained by the whole line which cuts the circle, and the part of it without the circle, shall be equal to the square on the line which touches it.

Let D be any point without the circle ABC,
and let DCA, DB be two straight lines drawn from it,
of which DCA cuts the circle, and DB touches the same.
Then the rectangle AD, DC shall be equal to the square on DB.
Either DCA passes through the center, or it does not:
first, let it pass through the center E.

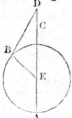

Join EB,
therefore the angle EBD is a right angle. (III. 18.)
And because the straight line AC is bisected in E, and produced to the point D,
therefore rectangle AD, DC. together with the square on EC, is equal to the square on ED: (II. 6.)
but CE is equal to EB;
therefore the rectangle AD, DC. together with the square on EB, is equal to the square on ED:
but the square on ED is equal to the squares on EB, BD, (I. 47.)
because EBD is a right angle:
therefore the rectangle AD, DC. together with the square on EB, is equal to the squares on EB, BD: (ax. 1.)

BOOK III. PROP. XXXVI. 151

take away the common square on EB;
therefore the remaining rectangle AD, DC is equal to the square on the tangent DB. (ax. 3.)
Next, if DCA does not pass through the center of the circle ABC.

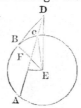

Take E the center of the circle, (III. 1.)
draw EF perpendicular to AC, (I. 12.) and join EB, EC, ED.
Because the straight line EF, which passes through the center, cuts the straight line AC, which does not pass through the center, at right angles; it also bisects AC, (III. 3.)
therefore AF is equal to FC;
and because the straight line AC is bisected in F, and produced to D, the rectangle AD, DC, together with the square on FC,
is equal to the square on FD: (II. 6.)
to each of these equals add the square on FE;
therefore the rectangle AD, DC, together with the squares on CF, FE, is equal to the squares on DF, FE: (I. ax. 2.)
but the square on ED is equal to the squares on DF, FE, (I. 47.)
because EFD is a right angle;
and for the same reason,
the square on EC is equal to the squares on CF, FE;
therefore the rectangle AD, DC, together with the square on EC,
is equal to the square on ED: (ax. 1.)
but CE is equal to EB;
therefore the rectangle AD, DC, together with the square on EB,
is equal to the square on ED:
but the squares on EB, BD, are equal to the square on ED, (I. 47.)
because EBD is a right angle:
therefore the rectangle AD, DC, together with the square on EB,
is equal to the squares on EB, BD;
take away the common square on EB;
and the remaining rectangle AD, DC is equal to the square on DB. (I. ax. 3.)
Wherefore, if from any point, &c. Q.E.D.
Cor. If from any point without a circle, there be drawn two straight

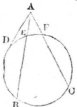

lines cutting it, as AB, AC, the rectangles contained by the whole lines and the parts of them without the circle, are equal to one another, viz. the rectangle BA, AE, to the rectangle CA, AF: for each of them is equal to the square on the straight line AD, which touches the circle.

PROPOSITION XXXVII. THEOREM.

If from a point without a circle there be drawn two straight lines, one of which cuts the circle, and the other meets it; if the rectangle contained by the whole line which cuts the circle, and the part of it without the circle, be equal to the square on the line which meets it, the line which meets, shall touch the circle.

Let any point D be taken without the circle ABC, and from it let two straight lines DCA and DB be drawn, of which DCA cuts the circle in the points C, A, and DB meets it in the point B.

If the rectangle AD, DC be equal to the square on DB; then DB shall touch the circle.

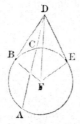

Draw the straight line DE, touching the circle ABC, in the point E; (III. 17.)

find F, the center of the circle, (III. 1.)
and join FE, FB, FD.

Then FED is a right angle: (III. 18.)
and because DE touches the circle ABC, and DCA cuts it,
therefore the rectangle AD, DC is equal to the square on DE; (III. 36.)
but the rectangle AD, DC, is, by hypothesis,
equal to the square on DB:
therefore the square on DE is equal to the square on DB; (I. ax. 1.)
and the straight line DE equal to the straight line DB:
and FE is equal to FB; (I. def. 15.)
wherefore DE, EF are equal to DB, BF, each to each:
and the base FD is common to the two triangles DEF, DBF;
therefore the angle DEF is equal to the angle DBF: (I. 8.)
but DEF was shewn to be a right angle;
therefore also DBF is a right angle: (I. ax. 1.)
and BF, if produced, is a diameter;
and the straight line which is drawn at right angles to a diameter, from the extremity of it, touches the circle; (III. 16. Cor.)
therefore DB touches the circle ABC.

Wherefore, if from a point, &c. Q.E.D.

NOTES TO BOOK III.

In the Third Book of the Elements are demonstrated the most elementary properties of the circle, assuming all the properties of figures demonstrated in the First and Second Books.

It may be worthy of remark, that the word *circle* will be found sometimes taken to mean *the surface* included within the circumference, and sometimes *the circumference itself*. Euclid has employed the word (περιφέρεια) *periphery*, both for the whole, and for a part of the circumference of a circle. If the word *circumference* were restricted to mean *the whole* circumference, and the word *arc* to mean a *part of it*, ambiguity might be avoided when speaking of the circumference of a circle, where only a part of it is the subject under consideration. A circle is said to be given in position, when the position of its center is known, and in magnitude, when its radius is known.

Def. I. And it may be added, or of which the circumferences are equal. And conversely, if two circles be equal, their diameters and radii are equal, as also their circumferences.

Def. I. states the criterion of equal circles. Simson calls it a theorem, and Euclid seems to have considered it as one of those theorems, or axioms, which might be admitted as a basis for reasoning on the equality of circles.

Def. II. There seems to be tacitly assumed in this definition, that a straight line, when it meets a circle and does not touch it, must necessarily, when produced, cut the circle.

A straight line which touches a circle, is called a *tangent* to the circle, and a straight line which cuts a circle is called a *secant*.

Def. IV. The distance of a straight line from the center of a circle is the distance of a point from a straight line, which has been already explained in note to Prop. II. page 53.

Def. VI. X. An *arc* of a circle is any portion of the circumference; and a *chord* is the straight line joining the extremities of an arc. Every chord except a diameter divides a circle into two unequal segments, one greater than, and the other less than a semicircle. And in the same manner, two radii drawn from the center to the circumference, divide the circle into two unequal sectors, which become equal when the two radii are in the same straight line. As Euclid, however, does not notice re-entering angles, a sector of the circle seems necessarily restricted to the figure which is less than a semicircle. A quadrant is a sector whose radii are perpendicular to one another, and which contains a fourth part of the circle.

Def. VII. No use is made of this definition in the Elements.

Def. XI. The definition of similar segments of circles as employed in the Third Book is restricted to such segments as are also equal. Props. XXIII and XXIV are the only two instances, in which reference is made to similar segments of circles.

Prop. I. "Lines drawn in a circle," always mean in Euclid, such lines only as are terminated at their extremities by the circumference.

If the point G be in the diameter CE, but not coinciding with the point F, the demonstration given in the text does not hold good. At the same time, it is obvious that G cannot be the center of the circle, because GC is not equal to GE.

Indirect demonstrations are more frequently employed in the Third Book than in the First Book of the Elements. Of the demonstrations of the forty-eight propositions of the First Book, nine are indirect; but of the thirty-seven of the Third Book, no less than fifteen are indirect demonstrations. The *indirect* is, in general, less readily appreciated by the learner, than the *direct* form of demonstration. The indirect form, however, is equally satisfactory, as it excludes every assumed hypothesis as false, except that which is made in the enunciation of the proposition. It may be here remarked that Euclid employs three methods of demonstrating converse propositions. First, by indirect demonstrations as in Euc. i. 6, iii. 1, &c. Secondly, by shewing that neither side of a possible alternative can be true, and thence inferring the truth of the proposition, as in Euc. i. 19, 25. Thirdly, by means of a construction, thereby avoiding the indirect mode of demonstration, as in Euc. i. 47, iii. 37.

Prop. ii. In this proposition, the circumference of a circle is proved to be essentially different from a straight line, by shewing that every straight line joining any two points in the arc falls entirely within the circle, and can neither coincide with any part of the circumference, nor meet it except in the two assumed points. It excludes the idea of the circumference of a circle being flexible, or capable, under any circumstances, of admitting the possibility of the line falling outside the circle.

If the line could fall partly within and partly without the circle, the circumference of the circle would intersect the line at some point between its extremities, and any part *without* the circle has been shewn to be impossible, and the part *within* the circle is in accordance with the enunciation of the Proposition. If the line could fall upon the circumference and coincide with it, it would follow that a straight line coincides with a curved line.

From this proposition follows the corollary, that "a straight line cannot cut the circumference of a circle in more points than two."

Commandine's direct demonstration of Prop. ii. depends on the following axiom, "If a point be taken nearer to the center of a circle than the circumference, that point falls within the circle."

Take any point E in AB, and join DA, DE, DB (fig. Euc. iii. 2.)
Then because DA is equal to DB in the triangle DAB;
therefore the angle DAB is equal to the angle DBA; (i. 5.)
but since the side AE of the triangle DAE is produced to B,
therefore the exterior angle DEB is greater than the interior and opposite angle DAE, (i. 16.)
but the angle DAE is equal to the angle DBE,
therefore the angle DEB is greater than the angle DBE.
And in every triangle, the greater side is subtended by the greater angle;
therefore the side DB is greater than the side DE,
but DB from the center meets the circumference of the circle,
therefore DE does not meet it.
Wherefore the point E falls within the circle;
and E is any point in the straight line AB,
therefore the straight line AB falls within the circle.

Prop. vii. and Prop. viii. exhibit the same property; in the former, the point is taken in the diameter, and in the latter in the diameter produced.

Prop. viii. An arc of a circle is said to be *convex* or *concave* with respect to a point, according as the straight lines drawn from the point meet the *outside* or *inside* of the circular arc; and the two points found in the circumference of a circle by two straight lines drawn from a given point to touch the circle, divide the circumference into two portions, one of which is *convex* and the other *concave*, with respect to the given point

Prop. ix. This appears to follow as a Corollary from Euc. iii. 7.

Prop. xi. and Prop. xii. In the enunciation it is not asserted that the contact of two circles is confined to a single point. The meaning appears to be, that supposing two circles to touch each other in any point, the straight line which joins their centers being produced, shall pass through that point in which the circles touch each other. In Prop. xiii. it is proved that a circle cannot touch another in more points than one, by assuming two points of contact, and proving that this is impossible.

Prop. xiii. The following is Euclid's demonstration of the case, in which one circle touches another on the inside.

If possible, let the circle EBF touch the circle ABC on the inside, in more points than in one point, namely in the points B, D (fig. Euc. iii. 13.) Let P be the center of the circle ABC, and Q the center of EBF. Join P, Q, then PQ produced shall pass through the points of contact B, D. For since P is the center of the circle ABC, PB is equal to PD, but PB is greater than QD, much more then is QB greater than QD. Again, since the point Q is the center of the circle EBF, QB is equal to QD, but QB has been shewn to be greater than QD, which is impossible. One circle therefore cannot touch another on the inside in more points than in one point.

Prop. xvi. may be demonstrated *directly* by assuming the following axiom. "If a point be taken further from the center of a circle than the circumference, that point falls without the circle."

If one circle touch another, either *internally* or *externally*, the two circles can have, at the point of contact, only one common tangent.

Prop. xvii. When the given point is without the circumference of the given circle, it is obvious that two equal tangents may be drawn from the given point to touch the circle, as may be seen from the diagram to Prop. viii.

The best practical method of drawing a tangent to a circle from a given point without the circumference, is the following. join the given point and the center of the circle, upon this line describe a semicircle cutting the given circle, then the line drawn from the given point to the intersection will be the tangent required.

Circles are called *concentric circles* when they have the same center.

Prop. xviii. appears to be nothing more than the converse to Prop. xvi., because a tangent to any point of a circumference of a circle is a straight line at right angles at the extremity of the diameter which meets the circumference in that point.

Prop. xx. This proposition is proved by Euclid only in the case in which the angle at the circumference is less than a right angle, and the demonstration is free from objection. If, however, the angle at the circumference be a right angle, the angle at the center disappears, by the two straight lines from the center to the extremities of the arc becoming one straight line. And, if the angle at the circumference be an obtuse angle, the angle formed by the two lines from the center, does not stand on the same arc, but upon the arc which the assumed arc wants of the whole circumference.

If Euclid's definition of an angle be strictly observed, Prop. xx. is geometrically true, only when the angle at the center is less than two right angles. If, however, the defect of an angle from four right angles may be regarded as an angle, the proposition is universally true, as may be proved by drawing a line from the angle in the circumference through the center, and thus forming two angles at the center, in Euclid's strict sense of the term

In the first case, it is assumed that, if there be four magnitudes, such that the first is double of the second, and the third double of the fourth, then the first and third together shall be double of the second and fourth together: also in the second case, that if one magnitude be double of another, and a part taken from the first be double of a part taken from the second, the remainder of the first shall be double the remainder of the second, which is, in fact, a particular case of Prop v Book v

Prop xxi   Hence, the locus of the vertices of all triangles upon the same base, and which have the same vertical angle, is a circular arc

Prop xxii   The converse of this Proposition, namely If the opposite angles of a quadrilateral figure be equal to two right angles, a circle can be described about it, is not proved by Euclid

It is obvious from the demonstration of this proposition, that if any side of the inscribed figure be produced, the exterior angle is equal to the opposite angle of the figure

Prop xxiii   It is obvious from this proposition that of two circular segments upon the same base, the larger is that which contains the smaller angle.

Prop xxv   The three cases of this proposition may be reduced to one, by drawing any two contiguous chords to the given arc, bisecting them, and from the points of bisection drawing perpendiculars   The point in which they meet will be the center of the circle   This problem is equivalent to that of finding a point equally distant from three given points

Props xxvi—xxix   The properties predicated in these four propositions with respect to *equal circles*, are also true when predicated of the *same circle*

Prop xxxi suggests a method of drawing a line at right angles to another when the given point is at the extremity of the given line   And that if the diameter of a circle be one of the equal sides of an isosceles triangle, the base is bisected by the circumference

Prop xxxv   The most general case of this Proposition might have been first demonstrated, and the other more simple cases deduced from it   But this is not Euclid's method   He always commences with the more simple case and proceeds to the more difficult afterwards   The following process is the reverse of Euclid's method

Assuming the construction in the last fig to Euc iii 35   Join FA, FD, and draw FK perpendicular to AC, and FL perpendicular to BD Then (Euc ii 5) the rectangle AE, EC with square on EK is equal to the square on AK add to these equals the square on FK therefore the rectangle AE, EC, with the squares on EK, FK is equal to the squares on AK, FK. But the squares on EK, FK are equal to the square on EF, and the squares on AK, FK are equal to the square on AF Hence the rectangle AE, EC, with the square on EF is equal to the square on AF.

In a similar way may be shewn, that the rectangle BE, ED with the square on EF is equal to the square on FD And the square on FD is equal to the square on AD Wherefore the rectangle AE, EC, with the square on EF is equal to the rectangle BE, ED with the square on EF. Take from these equals the square on EF, and the rectangle AE, EC is equal to the rectangle BE, ED.

The other more simple cases may easily be deduced from this general case.

The converse is not proved by Euclid, namely,—If two straight lines intersect one another, so that the rectangle contained by the parts of one is equal to the rectangle contained by the parts of the other, then a circle may be described passing through the extremities of the two lines. Or, in other words:—If the diagonals of a quadrilateral figure intersect one another, so that the rectangle contained by the segments of one of them is equal to the rectangle contained by the segments of the other; then a circle may be described about the quadrilateral.

Prop. XXXVI. The converse of the corollary to this proposition may be thus stated:—If there be two straight lines, such that, when produced to meet, the rectangle contained by one of the lines produced, and the part produced, be equal to the rectangle contained by the other line produced and the part produced; then a circle can be described passing through the extremities of the two straight lines. Or, If two opposite sides of a quadrilateral figure be produced to meet, and the rectangle contained by one of the sides produced and the part produced, be equal to the rectangle contained by the other side produced and the part produced; then a circle may be described about the quadrilateral figure.

Prop. XXXVII. The demonstration of this theorem may be made shorter by a reference to the note on Euclid III. Def. 2: for if DB meet the circle in B and do not touch it at that point, the line must, when produced, cut the circle in two points.

It is a circumstance worthy of notice, that in this proposition, as well as in Prop. XLVIII. Book I. Euclid departs from the ordinary *ex absurdo* mode of proof of converse propositions.

QUESTIONS ON BOOK III.

1. Define accurately the terms *radius, arc, circumference, chord, secant*.
2. How does a *sector* differ in form from a *segment* of a circle? Are they in any case coincident?
3. What is Euclid's criterion of the equality of two circles? What is meant by a given circle? How many points are necessary to determine the *magnitude* and *position* of a circle?
4. When are segments of circles said to be similar? Enunciate the propositions of the Third Book of Euclid, in which this definition is employed. Is it employed in a restricted or general form?
5. In how many points can a circle be cut by a straight line and by another circle?
6. When are straight lines equally distant from the center of a circle?
7. Shew the necessity of an indirect demonstration in Euc. III. 1.
8. Find the center of a given circle without bisecting any straight line.
9. Shew that if the circumference of one of two equal circles pass through the center of the other, the portions of the two circles, each of which lies without the circumference of the other circle, are equal.
10. If a straight line passing through the center of a circle bisect a straight line in it, it shall cut it at right angles. Point out the exception, and shew that if a straight line bisect the arc and base of a segment of a circle, it will, when produced, pass through the center.
11. If any point be taken within a circle, and a right line be drawn from

it to the circumference, how many lines can generally be drawn equal to it? Draw them

12. Find the shortest distance between a circle and a given straight line without it

13. Shew that a circle can only have one center, stating the axioms upon which your proof depends

14. Why would not the demonstration of Euc. III. 9, hold good, if there were only two such equal straight lines?

15. Two parallel chords in a circle are respectively six and eight inches in length, and one inch apart; how many inches is the diameter in length?

16. Which is the greater chord in a circle whose diameter is 10 inches, that whose length is 5 inches, or that whose distance from the center is 4 inches?

17. What is the locus of the middle points of all equal straight lines in a circle?

18. The radius of a circle $BCDGF$, (fig Euc. III. 15.) whose center is E, is equal to five inches. The distance of the line FG from the center is four inches, and the distance of the line BC from the center is three inches, required the lengths of the lines FG, BC.

19. If the chord of an arc be twelve inches long, and be divided into two segments of eight and four inches by another chord, what is the length of the latter chord, if one of its segments be two inches?

20. What is the radius of that circle of which the chords of an arc and of double the arc are five and eight inches respectively?

21. If the chord of an arc of a circle whose diameter is 8½ inches, be five inches, what is the length of the chord of double the arc of the same circle?

22. State when a straight line is said to touch a circle, and shew from your definition that a straight line cannot be drawn to touch a circle from a point within it

23. Can more circles than one touch a straight line in the same point?

24. Shew from the construction, Euc. III. 17, that *two* equal straight lines, and only two, can be drawn touching a given circle from a given point without it, and one, and only one, from a point in the circumference

25. What is the locus of the centers of all the circles which touch a straight line in a given point?

26. How may a tangent be drawn at a given point in the circumference of a circle, without knowing the center?

27. In a circle place two chords of given length at right angles to each other

28. From Euc. III. 19, shew how many circles equal to a given circle may be drawn to touch a straight line in the same point

29. Enunciate Euc. III. 20. Is this true, when the base is greater than a semicircle? If so, why has Euclid omitted this case?

30. The angle at the center of a circle is double of that at the circumference. How will it appear hence that the angle in a semicircle is a right angle?

31. What conditions are essential to the possibility of the inscription and circumscription of a circle in and about a quadrilateral figure?

32. What conditions are requisite in order that a parallelogram may be inscribed in a circle? Are there any analogous conditions requisite that a parallelogram may be described about a circle?

33. Define the angle *in* a segment of a circle, and the angle *on* a seg-

ment; and shew, that in the same circle, they are together equal to two right angles

34. State and prove the converse of Euc. III. 22.

35. All circles which pass through two given points have their centers in a certain straight line.

36. Describe the circle of which a given segment is a part. Give Euclid's more simple method of solving the same problem independently of the magnitude of the given segment.

37. In the same circle equal straight lines cut off equal circumferences. If these straight lines have any point common to one another, it must not be in the circumference. Is the enunciation given complete?

38. Enunciate Euc. III. 31, and deduce the proof of it from Euc. III. 20.

39. What is the locus of the vertices of all right-angled triangles which can be described upon the same hypotenuse?

40. How may a perpendicular be drawn to a given straight line from one of its extremities *without producing the line?*

41. If the angle in a semicircle be a right angle, what is the angle in a quadrant?

42. The sum of the squares of any two lines drawn from any point in a semicircle to the extremity of the diameter is constant. Express that *constant* in terms of the radius.

43. In the demonstration of Euc. III. 30, it is stated that "equal straight lines cut off equal circumferences, the greater equal to the greater, and the less to the less." explain by reference to the diagram the meaning of this statement.

44. How many circles may be described so as to pass through one, two, and three given points? In what case is it possible for a circle to pass through three given points?

45. Compare the circumference of the segment (Euc. III. 33.) with the whole circumference when the angle contained in it is a right angle and a half.

46. Include the four cases of Euc. III. 35, in one general proof.

47. Enunciate the propositions which are converse to Props. 32, 35, of Book III.

48. If the position of the center of a circle be known with respect to a given point outside a circle, and the distance of the circumference to the point be ten inches, what is the length of the diameter of the circle, if a tangent drawn from the given point be fifteen inches?

49. If two straight lines be drawn from a point without a circle, and be both terminated by the concave part of the circumference, and if one of the lines pass through the center, and a portion of the other line intercepted by the circle, be equal to the radius: find the diameter of the circle, if the two lines meet the convex part of the circumference, a, b, units respectively from the given point.

50. Upon what propositions depends the demonstration of Euc. III. 35? Is any extension made of this proposition in the Third Book?

51. What conditions must be fulfilled that a circle may pass through four given points?

52. Why is it considered necessary to demonstrate all the separate cases of Euc. III. 35, 36, geometrically, which are comprehended in one formula, when expressed by Algebraic symbols?

53. Enunciate the converse propositions of the Third Book of Euclid which are not demonstrated *ex absurdo*: and state the three methods which Euclid employs in the demonstration of converse propositions in the First and Third Books of the Elements.

GEOMETRICAL EXERCISES ON BOOK III.

PROPOSITION I. THEOREM.

If AB, CD be chords of a circle at right angles to each other, prove that the sum of the arcs AC, BD is equal to the sum of the arcs AD, BC.

Draw the diameter FGH parallel to AB, and cutting CD in H.

Then the arcs FDG and FCG are each half the circumference.
Also since CD is bisected in the point H,
the arc FD is equal to the arc FC,
and the arc FD is equal to the arcs FA, AD, of which, AF is equal to BG,
therefore the arcs AD, BG are equal to the arc FC;
add to each CG,
therefore the arcs AD, BC are equal to the arcs FC, CG, which make up the half circumference.
Hence also the arcs AC, DB are equal to half the circumference.
Wherefore the arcs AD, BC are equal to the arcs AC, DB.

PROPOSITION II. PROBLEM.

The diameter of a circle having been produced to a given point, it is required to find in the part produced a point, from which if a tangent be drawn to the circle, it shall be equal to the segment of the part produced, that is, between the given point and the point found.

Analysis. Let AEB be a circle whose center is C, and whose diameter AB is produced to the given point D.
Suppose that G is the point required, such that the segment GD is equal to the tangent GE drawn from G to touch the circle in E.

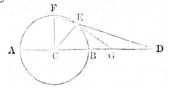

Join DE and produce it to meet the circumference again in F;
join also CE and CF.
Then in the triangle GDE, because GD is equal to GE,
therefore the angle GED is equal to the angle GDE;

and because CE is equal to CF,
the angle CEF is equal to the angle CFE;
therefore the angles CEF, GED are equal to the angles CFE, GDE:
but since GE is a tangent at E,
therefore the angle CEG is a right angle, (III. 18.)
hence the angles CEF, GEF are equal to a right angle,
and consequently, the angles CFE, EDG are also equal to a right angle,
wherefore the remaining angle FCD of the triangle CFD is a right angle,
and therefore CF is perpendicular to AD.

Synthesis. From the center C, draw CF perpendicular to AD meeting the circumference of the circle in F:
join DF cutting the circumference in E,
join also CE, and at E draw EG perpendicular to CE and intersecting BD in G.
Then G will be the point required.
For in the triangle CFD, since FCD is a right angle, the angles CFD, CDF are together equal to a right angle;
also since CEG is a right angle,
therefore the angles CEF, GED are together equal to a right angle;
therefore the angles CEF, GED are equal to the angles CFD, CDF;
but because CE is equal to CF,
the angle CEF is equal to the angle CFD,
wherefore the remaining angle GED is equal to the remaining angle CDF,
and the side GD is equal to the side GE of the triangle EGD,
therefore the point G is determined according to the required conditions.

PROPOSITION III. THEOREM.

If a chord of a circle be produced till the part produced be equal to the radius, and if from its extremity a line be drawn through the centre and meeting the convex and concave circumferences, the convex is one-third of the concave circumference.

Let AB any chord be produced to C, so that BC is equal to the radius of the circle:

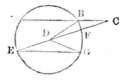

and let CE be drawn from C through the center D, and meeting the convex circumference in F, and the concave in E.
Then the arc BF is one-third of the arc AE.

Draw *EG* parallel to *AB*, and join *DB, DG*.
Since the angle *DEG* is equal to the angle *DGE*; (I. 5.)
and the angle *GDF* is equal to the angles *DEG, DGE*; (I. 32.)
therefore the angle *GDC* is double of the angle *DEG*.
But the angle *BDC* is equal to the angle *BCD*, (I. 5.)
and the angle *CEG* is equal to the alternate angle *ACE*; (I. 29.)
therefore the angle *GDC* is double of the angle *CDB*,
add to these equals the angle *CDB*,
therefore the whole angle *GDB* is treble of the angle *CDB*,
but the angles *GDB, CDB* at the center *D*, are subtended by the arcs *BF, BG*, of which *BG* is equal to *AE*.
Wherefore the circumference *AE* is treble of the circumference *BF*, and *BF* is one-third of *AE*.

Hence may be solved the following problem:

AE, BF are two arcs of a circle intercepted between a chord and a given diameter. Determine the position of the chord, so that one arc shall be triple of the other.

PROPOSITION IV. THEOREM.

AB, AC and *ED* are tangents to the circle CFB; at whatever point between C and B the tangent EFD is drawn, the three sides of the triangle AED are equal to twice AB or twice AC: also the angle subtended by the tangent EFD at the center of the circle, is a constant quantity.

Take *G* the center of the circle, and join *GB, GE, GF, GD, GC*.
Then *EB* is equal to *EF*, and *DC* to *DF*; (III. 37.)

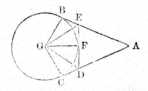

therefore *ED* is equal to *EB* and *DC*;
to each of these add *AE, AD*,
wherefore *AD, AE, ED* are equal to *AB, AC*;
and *AB* is equal to *AC*,
therefore *AD, AE, ED* are equal to twice *AB*, or twice *AC*;
or the perimeter of the triangle *AED* is a constant quantity.
Again, the angle *EGF* is half of the angle *BGF*,
and the angle *DGF* is half of the angle *CGF*,
therefore the angle *DGE* is half of the angle *CGB*,
or the angle subtended by the tangent *ED* at *G*, is half of the angle contained between the two radii which meet the circle at the points where the two tangents *AB, AC* meet the circle.

PROPOSITION V. PROBLEM.

Given the base, the vertical angle, and the perpendicular in a plane triangle, to construct it.

Upon the given base AB describe a segment of a circle containing an angle equal to the given angle. (III. 33.)

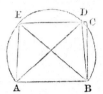

At the point B draw BC perpendicular to AB, and equal to the altitude of the triangle. (I. 11, 3.)

Through C, draw CDE parallel to AB, and meeting the circumference in D and E. (I. 31.)

Join DA, DB; also EA, EB;
then EAB or DAB is the triangle required.

It is also manifest, that if CDE touch the circle, there will be only one triangle which can be constructed on the base AB with the given altitude.

PROPOSITION VI. THEOREM.

If two chords of a circle intersect each other at right angles either within or without the circle, the sum of the squares described upon the four segments, is equal to the square described upon the diameter.

Let the chords AB, CD intersect at right angles in E.

Draw the diameter AF, and join AC, AD, CF, DB.
Then the angle ACF in a semicircle is a right angle, (III. 31.)
and equal to the angle AED:
also the angle ADC is equal to the angle AFC. (III. 21.)
Hence in the triangles ADE, AFC, there are two angles in the one respectively equal to two angles in the other,
consequently, the third angle CAF is equal to the third angle DAB;
therefore the arc DB is equal to the arc CF, (III. 26.)
and therefore also the chord DB is equal to the chord CF. (III. 29.)
Because AEC is a right-angled triangle,
the squares on AE, EC are equal to the square on AC; (I. 47.)
similarly, the squares on DE, EB are equal to the square on DB;
therefore the squares on AE, EC, DE, EB, are equal to the squares on AC, DB;
but DB was proved equal to FC,
and the squares on AC, FC are equal to the square on AF,

wherefore the squares on AE, EC, DE, EB, are equal to the square on AF, the diameter of the circle.

When the chords meet without the circle, the property is proved in a similar manner.

I.

7. Through a given point within a circle, to draw a chord which shall be bisected in that point, and prove it to be the least.

8. To draw that diameter of a given circle which shall pass at a given distance from a given point.

9. Find the locus of the middle points of any system of parallel chords in a circle.

10. The two straight lines which join the opposite extremities of two parallel chords, intersect in a point in that diameter which is perpendicular to the chords.

11. The straight lines joining towards the same parts, the extremities of any two lines in a circle equally distant from the center, are parallel to each other.

12. A, B, C, A', B', C' are points on the circumference of a circle; if the lines AB, AC be respectively parallel to $A'B'$, $A'C'$, shew that BC' is parallel to $B'C$.

13. Two chords of a circle being given in position and magnitude, describe the circle.

14. Two circles are drawn, one lying within the other; prove that no chord to the outer circle can be bisected in the point in which it touches the inner, unless the circles are concentric, or the chord be perpendicular to the common diameter. If the circles have the same center, shew that every chord which touches the inner circle is bisected in the point of contact.

15. Draw a chord in a circle, so that it may be double of its perpendicular distance from the center.

16. The arcs intercepted between any two parallel chords in a circle are equal.

17. If any point P be taken in the plane of a circle, and PA, PB, PC, ..be drawn to any number of points A, B, C...situated symmetrically in the circumference, the sum of PA, PB,..is least when P is at the center of the circle.

II.

18. The sum of the arcs subtending the vertical angles made by any two chords that intersect, is the same, as long as the angle of intersection is the same.

19. From a point without a circle two straight lines are drawn cutting the convex and concave circumferences, and also respectively parallel to two radii of the circle. Prove that the difference of the concave and convex arcs intercepted by the cutting lines, is equal to twice the arc intercepted by the radii.

20. In a circle with center O, any two chords, AB, CD are drawn

cutting in E, and OA, OB, OC, OD are joined; prove that the angles $AOC + BOD = 2 AEC$, and $AOD + BOC = 2.AED$

21. If from any point without a circle, lines be drawn cutting the circle and making equal angles with the longest line, they will cut off equal segments.

22. If the corresponding extremities of two intersecting chords of a circle be joined, the triangles thus formed will be equiangular.

23. Through a given point within or without a circle, it is required to draw a straight line cutting off a segment containing a given angle.

24. If on two lines containing an angle, segments of circles be described containing angles equal to it, the lines produced will touch the segments.

25. Any segment of a circle being described on the base of a triangle, to describe on the other sides segments similar to that on the base.

26. If an arc of a circle be divided into three equal parts by three straight lines drawn from one extremity of the arc, the angle contained by two of the straight lines is bisected by the third.

27. If the chord of a given circular segment be produced to a fixed point, describe upon it when so produced a segment of a circle which shall be similar to the given segment, and shew that the two segments have a common tangent.

28. If AD, CE be drawn perpendicular to the sides BC, AB of the triangle ABC, and DE be joined, prove that the angles ADE, and ACE are equal to each other.

29. If from any point in a circular arc, perpendiculars be let fall on its bounding radii, the distance of their feet is invariable.

III.

30. If both tangents be drawn, (fig Euc. III. 17.) and the points of contact joined by a straight line which cuts EA in H, and on HA as diameter a circle be described, the lines drawn through E to touch this circle will meet it on the circumference of the given circle.

31. Draw, (1) perpendicular, (2) parallel to a given line, a line touching a given circle.

32. If two straight lines intersect, the centers of all circles that can be inscribed between them, he in two lines at right angles to each other

33. Draw two tangents to a given circle, which shall contain an angle equal to a given rectilineal angle

34. Describe a circle with a given radius touching a given line, and so that the tangents drawn to it from two given points in this line may be parallel, and shew that, if the radius vary, the locus of the centers of the circles so described is a circle.

35. Determine the distance of a point from the center of a given circle, so that if tangents be drawn from it to the circle, the concave part of the circumference may be double of the convex

36. In a chord of a circle produced, it is required to find a point, from which if a straight line be drawn touching the circle, the line so drawn shall be equal to a given straight line.

37. Find a point without a given circle, such that the sum of the two lines drawn from it touching the circle, shall be equal to the line drawn from it through the center to meet the circle.

38. If from a point without a circle two tangents be drawn, the straight line which joins the points of contact will be bisected at right angles by a line drawn from the center to the point without the circle.

39. If tangents be drawn at the extremities of any two diameters of a circle, and produced to intersect one another, the straight lines joining the opposite points of intersection will both pass through the center.

40. If from any point without a circle two lines be drawn touching the circle, and from the extremities of any diameter, lines be drawn to the point of contact cutting each other within the circle, the line drawn from the points without the circle to the point of intersection, shall be perpendicular to the diameter.

41. If any chord of a circle be produced equally both ways, and tangents to the circle be drawn on opposite sides of it from its extremities, the line joining the points of contact bisects the given chord.

42. AB is a chord, and AD is a tangent to a circle at A: DPQ, any secant parallel to AB meeting the circle in P and Q. Shew that the triangle PAD is equiangular with the triangle QAB.

43. If from any point in the circumference of a circle a chord and tangent be drawn, the perpendiculars dropped upon them from the middle point of the subtended arc, are equal to one another.

IV.

44. In a given straight line to find a point at which two other straight lines being drawn to two given points, shall contain a right angle. Shew that if the distance between the two given points be *greater* than the sum of their distances from the given line, there will be two such points; if *equal*, there may be only one; if *less*, the problem may be impossible.

45. Find the point in a given straight line at which the tangents to a given circle will contain the greatest angle.

46. Of all straight lines which can be drawn from two given points to meet in the convex circumference of a given circle, the sum of those two will be the least, which make equal angles with the tangent at the point of concourse.

47. DF is a straight line touching a circle, and terminated by AD, BF, the tangents at the extremities of the diameter AB; shew that the angle which DF subtends at the center is a right angle.

48. If tangents Am, Bn be drawn at the extremities of the diameter of a semicircle, and any line mPn crossing them and touching the circle in P, and if AN, BM be joined intersecting in O and cutting the semicircle in E and F, shew that O, P, and the point of intersection of the tangents at E and F, are in the same straight line.

49. If from a point P without a circle, any straight line be drawn cutting the circumference in A and B, shew that the straight lines joining the points A and B with the bisection of the chord of contact of the tangents from P, make equal angles with that chord.

V.

50. Describe a circle which shall pass through a given point and which shall touch a given straight line in a given point.

51. Draw a straight line which shall touch a given circle, and make a given angle with a given straight line.

52. Describe a circle the circumference of which shall pass through a given point, and touch a given circle in a given point.

53. Describe a circle with a given center, such that the circle so described and a given circle may touch one another internally.

54. Describe the circles which shall pass through a given point and touch two given straight lines.

55. Describe a circle with a given center, cutting a given circle in the extremities of a diameter.

56. Describe a circle which shall have its center in a given straight line, touch another given line, and pass through a fixed point in the first given line.

57. The center of a given circle is equidistant from two given straight lines: to describe another circle which shall touch the two straight lines and shall cut off from the given circle a segment containing an angle equal to a given rectilineal angle.

VI.

58. If any two circles, the centers of which are given, intersect each other, the greatest line which can be drawn through either point of intersection and terminated by the circles, is independent of the diameters of the circles.

59. Two equal circles intersect, the lines joining the points in which any straight line through one of the points of section, which meets the circles with the other point of section, are equal.

60. Draw through one of the points in which any two circles cut one another, a straight line which shall be terminated by their circumferences and bisected in their point of section.

61. Describe two circles with given radii which shall cut each other, and have the line between the points of section equal to a given line.

62. Two circles cut each other, and from the points of intersection straight lines are drawn parallel to one another, the portions intercepted by the circumferences are equal.

63. ACB, ADB are two segments of circles on the same base AB, take any point C in the segment ACB, join AC, BC, and produce them to meet the segment ADB in D and E respectively: shew that the arc DE is constant.

64. ADB, ACB are the arcs of two equal circles cutting one another in the straight line AB, draw the chord ACD cutting the inner circumference in C and the outer in D, such that AD and DB together may be double of AC and CB together.

65. If from two fixed points in the circumference of a circle, straight lines be drawn intercepting a given arc and meeting without the circle, the locus of their intersections is a circle.

66. If two circles intersect, the common chord produced bisects the common tangent.

67. Shew that, if two circles cut each other, and from any point in the straight line produced, which joins their intersections, two tangents be drawn, one to each circle, they shall be equal to one another.

68. Two circles intersect in the points A and B, through A and B any two straight lines CAD, EBF, are drawn cutting the circles in the points C, D, E, F, prove that CE is parallel to DF.

69. Two equal circles are drawn intersecting in the points A and B, a third circle is drawn with center A and any radius not greater than AB intersecting the former circles in D and C. Shew that the three points B, C, D lie in one and the same straight line.

70. If two circles cut each other, the straight line joining their centers will bisect their common chord at right angles.

71. Two circles cut one another, if through a point of intersection a straight line be drawn bisecting the angle between the diameters at that point, this line cuts off similar segments in the two circles.

72. ACB, APB are two equal circles, the center of APB being on the circumference of ACB. AB being the common chord, if any chord AC of ACB be produced to cut APB in P, the triangle PBC is equilateral.

VII

73. If two circles touch each other externally, and two parallel lines be drawn, so touching the circles in points A and B respectively that neither circle is cut, then a straight line AB will pass through the point of contact of the circles.

74. A common tangent is drawn to two circles which touch each other externally, if a circle be described on that part of it which lies between the points of contact, as diameter, this circle will pass through the point of contact of the two circles, and will touch the line which joins their centers.

75. If two circles touch each other externally or internally, and parallel diameters be drawn, the straight line joining the extremities of these diameters will pass through the point of contact.

76. If two circles touch each other internally, and any circle be described touching both, prove that the sum of the distances of its center from the centers of the two given circles will be invariable.

77. If two circles touch each other, any straight line passing through the point of contact, cuts off similar parts of their circumferences.

78. Two circles touch each other externally, the diameter of one being double of the diameter of the other; through the point of contact any line is drawn to meet the circumferences of both, shew that the part of the line which lies in the larger circle is double of that in the smaller.

79. If a circle roll within another of twice its size, any point in its circumference will trace out a diameter of the first.

80. With a given radius to describe a circle touching two given circles.

81. Two equal circles touch one another externally, and through the point of contact chords are drawn, one to each circle, at right angles to each; prove that the straight line joining the other extremities of these chords is equal and parallel to the straight line joining the centres of the circles.

82. Two circles can be described, each of which shall touch a given circle, and pass through two given points outside the circle; shew that the angles which the two given points subtend at the two points of contact, are one greater and the other less than that which they subtend at any other point in the given circle.

VIII.

83. Draw a straight line which shall touch two given circles; (1) on the same side, (2) on the alternate sides.

84. If two circles do not touch each other, and a segment of the line joining their centers be intercepted between the convex circumferences, any circle whose diameter is not less than that segment may be so placed as to touch both the circles.

85. Given two circles it is required to find a point from which tangents may be drawn to each, equal to two given straight lines.

86. Two circles are traced on a plane; draw a straight line cutting them in such a manner that the chords intercepted within the circles shall have given lengths.

87. Draw a straight line which shall touch one of two given circles and cut off a given segment from the other. Of how many solutions does this problem admit?

88. If from the point where a common tangent to two circles meets the line joining their centers, any line be drawn cutting the circles, it will cut off similar segments.

89. To find a point P, so that tangents drawn from it to the outsides of two equal circles which touch each other, may contain an angle equal to a given angle.

90. Describe a circle which shall touch a given straight line at a given point, and bisect the circumference of a given circle.

91. A circle is described to pass through a given point and cut a given circle orthogonally; shew that the locus of the center is a certain straight line.

92. Through two given points to describe a circle bisecting the circumference of a given circle.

93. Describe a circle through a given point, and touching a given straight line, so that the chord joining the given point and point of contact, may cut off a segment containing a given angle.

94. To describe a circle through two given points to cut a straight line given in position, so that a diameter of the circle drawn through the point of intersection, shall make a given angle with the line.

95. Describe a circle which should pass through two given points and cut a given circle, so that the chord of intersection may be of a given length.

IX.

96. The circumference of one circle is wholly within that of another. Find the greatest and the least straight lines that can be drawn touching the former and terminated by the latter.

97. Draw a straight line through two concentric circles, so that the chord terminated by the exterior circumference may be double that terminated by the interior. What is the least value of the radius of the interior circle for which the problem is possible?

98. If a straight line be drawn cutting any number of concentric circles, shew that the segments so cut off are not similar.

99. If from any point in the circumference of the exterior of two concentric circles, two straight lines be drawn touching the interior and meeting the exterior, the distance between the points of contact will be half that between the points of intersection.

100. Shew that all equal straight lines in a circle will be touched by another circle.

101. Through a given point draw a straight line so that the part intercepted by the circumference of a circle, shall be equal to a given straight line not greater than the diameter.

102. Two circles are described about the same center, draw a chord to the outer circle, which shall be divided into three equal parts by the inner one. How is the possibility of the problem limited?

103. Find a point without a given circle from which if two tangents be drawn to it, they shall contain an angle equal to a given angle, and shew that the locus of this point is a circle concentric with the given circle.

104. Draw two concentric circles such that those chords of the outer circle which touch the inner, may be equal to its diameter.

105. Find a point in a given straight line from which the tangent drawn to a given circle, is of given length.

106. If any number of chords be drawn in the inner of two concentric circles, from the same point A in its circumference, and each of the chords be then produced beyond A to the circumference of the outer circle, the rectangle contained by the whole line so produced and the part of it produced, shall be constant for all the cases.

X.

107. The circles described on the sides of any triangle as diameters will intersect in the sides, or sides produced, of the triangle.

108. The circles which are described upon the sides of a right-angled triangle as diameters, meet the hypotenuse in the same point; and the line drawn from the point of intersection to the center of either of the circles will be a tangent to the other circle.

109. If on the sides of a triangle circular arcs be described containing angles whose sum is equal to two right angles, the triangle formed by the lines joining their centers, has its angles equal to those in the segments.

110. The perpendiculars let fall from the three angles of any triangle upon the opposite sides, intersect each other in the same point.

111. If AD, CE be drawn perpendicular to the sides BC, AB of

the triangle ABC, prove that the rectangle contained by BC and BD, is equal to the rectangle contained by BA and BE

112. The lines which bisect the vertical angles of all triangles on the same base and with the same vertical angle, all intersect in one point.

113. Of all triangles on the same base and between the same parallels, the isosceles has the greatest vertical angle.

114. It is required within an isosceles triangle to find a point such that its distance from one of the equal angles may be double its distance from the vertical angle.

115. To find within an acute-angled triangle, a point from which, if straight lines be drawn to the three angles of the triangle, they shall make equal angles with each other.

116. A flag-staff of a given height is erected on a tower whose height is also given at what point on the horizon will the flag-staff appear under the greatest possible angle?

117. A ladder is gradually raised against a wall; find the locus of its middle point.

118. The triangle formed by the chord of a circle (produced or not) the tangent at its extremity, and any line perpendicular to the diameter through its other extremity will be isosceles.

119. AD, BE are perpendiculars from the angles A and B on the opposite sides of a triangle, BF perpendicular to ED or ED produced; shew that the angle $FBD = EBA$.

XI.

120. If three equal circles have a common point of intersection, prove that a straight line joining any two of the points of intersection, will be perpendicular to the straight line joining the other two points of intersection.

121. Two equal circles cut one another, and a third circle touches each of these two equal circles externally; the straight line which joins the points of section will, if produced, pass through the centre of the third circle.

122. A number of circles touch each other at the same point, and a straight line is drawn from it cutting them; the straight lines joining each point of intersection with the centre of the circle will be all parallel.

123. If three circles intersect one another, two and two, the three chords joining the points of intersection shall all pass through one point.

124. If three circles touch each other externally, and the three common tangents be drawn, these tangents shall intersect in a point equidistant from the points of contact of the circles.

125. If two equal circles intersect one another in A and B, and from one of the points of intersection as a center, a circle be described which shall cut both of the equal circles, then will the other point of intersection, and the two points in which the third circle cuts the other two on the same side of AB, be in the same straight line.

XII.

126. Given the base, the vertical angle, and the difference of the sides, to construct the triangle.

127. Describe a triangle, having given the vertical angle, and the segments of the base made by a line bisecting the vertical angle.

128. Given the perpendicular height, the vertical angle and the sum of the sides, to construct the triangle.

129. Construct a triangle in which the vertical angle and the difference of the two angles at the base shall be respectively equal to two given angles, and whose base shall be equal to a given straight line.

130. Given the vertical angle, the difference of the two sides containing it, and the difference of the segments of the base made by a perpendicular from the vertex; construct the triangle.

131. Given the vertical angle, and the lengths of two lines drawn from the extremities of the base to the points of bisection of the sides, to construct the triangle.

132. Given the base, and vertical angle, to find the triangle whose area is a maximum.

133. Given the base, the altitude, and the sum of the two remaining sides, construct the triangle.

134. Describe a triangle of given base, area, and vertical angle.

135. Given the base and vertical angle of a triangle, find the locus of the intersection of perpendiculars to the sides from the extremities of the base.

XIII.

136. Shew that the perpendiculars to the sides of a quadrilateral inscribed in a circle from their middle points intersect in a fixed point.

137. The lines bisecting any angle of a quadrilateral figure inscribed in a circle, and the opposite exterior angle, meet in the circumference of the circle.

138. If two opposite sides of a quadrilateral figure inscribed in a circle be equal, prove that the other two are parallel.

139. The angles subtended at the center of a circle by any two opposite sides of a quadrilateral figure circumscribed about it, are together equal to two right angles.

140. Four circles are described so that each may touch internally three of the sides of a quadrilateral figure, or one side and the adjacent sides produced; shew that the centers of these four circles will all lie in the circumference of a circle.

141. One side of a trapezium capable of being inscribed in a given circle is given, the sum of the remaining three sides is given; and also one of the angles opposite to the given side construct it.

142. If the sides of a quadrilateral figure inscribed in a circle be produced to meet, and from each of the points of intersection a straight line be drawn, touching the circle, the squares of these tangents are together equal to the square of the straight line joining the points of intersection.

143. If a quadrilateral figure be described about a circle, the sums of the opposite sides are equal, and each sum equal to half the perimeter of the figure.

144. A quadrilateral $ABCD$ is inscribed in a circle, BC and DO

are produced to meet AD and AB produced in E and F. The angles ABC and ADC are together equal to AFC, AEB, and twice the angle BAC.

145. If the hypotenuse AB of a right-angled triangle ABC be bisected in D, and EDF drawn perpendicular to AB, and DE DF cut off each equal to DA, and CE, CF joined, prove that the last two lines will bisect the angle at C and its supplement respectively.

146. $ABCD$ is a quadrilateral figure inscribed in a circle. Through its angular points tangents are drawn so as to form another quadrilateral figure $FBLCHDEA$ circumscribed about the circle. Find the relation which exists between the angles of the exterior and the angles of the interior figure.

147. The angle contained by the tangents drawn at the extremities of any chord in a circle is equal to the difference of the angles in segments made by the chord: and also equal to twice the angle contained by the same chord and a diameter drawn from either of its extremities.

148. If $ABCD$ be a quadrilateral figure, and the lines AB, AC, AD be equal, shew that the angle BAD is double of CBD and CDB together.

149. If the sides of a quadrilateral figure circumscribing a circle, touch the circle at the angular points of an inscribed quadrilateral figure; all the diagonals will intersect in the same point.

150. In a quadrilateral figure $ABCD$ is inscribed a second quadrilateral by joining the middle points of its adjacent sides; a third is similarly inscribed in the second, and so on. Shew that each of the series of quadrilaterals will be capable of being inscribed in a circle if the first three are so. Shew also that two at least of the opposite sides of $ABCD$ must be equal, and that the two squares upon these sides are together equal to the sum of the squares upon the other two.

XIV.

151. If from any point in the diameter of a semicircle, there be drawn two straight lines to the circumference, one to the bisection of the circumference, the other at right angles to the diameter, the squares upon these two lines are together double of the square upon the semi-diameter.

152. If from any point in the diameter of a circle, straight lines be drawn to the extremities of a parallel chord, the squares on these lines are together equal to the squares on the segments into which the diameter is divided.

153. From a given point without a circle, at a distance from the circumference of the circle not greater than its diameter, draw a straight line to the concave circumference which shall be bisected by the convex circumference.

154. If any two chords be drawn in a circle perpendicular to each other, the sum of their squares is equal to twice the square of the diameter diminished by four times the square of the line joining the center with their point of intersection.

155. Two points are taken in the diameter of a circle at any equal distances from the center, through one of these draw any chord, and join its extremities and the other point. The triangle so formed has the sum of the squares of its sides invariable.

156. If chords drawn from any fixed point in the circumference of a circle, be cut by another chord which is parallel to the tangent at that point, the rectangle contained by each chord, and the part of it intercepted between the given point and the given chord, is constant.

157. If AB be a chord of a circle inclined by half a right angle to the tangent at A, and AC, AD be any two chords equally inclined to AB, $AC^2 + AD^2 = 2 AB^2$

158. A chord POQ cuts the diameter of a circle in Q, in an angle equal to half a right angle; $PO^2 + OQ^2 = 2(\text{rad})^2$.

159. Let $ACDB$ be a semicircle whose diameter is AB, and AD, BC any two chords intersecting in P, prove that
$$AB^2 = DA.AP + CB.BP$$

160. If $ABDC$ be any parallelogram, and if a circle be described passing through the point A, and cutting the sides AB, AC, and the diagonal AD, in the points F, G, H respectively, shew that
$$AB.AF + AC.AG = AD.AH$$

161. Produce a given straight line, so that the rectangle under the given line, and the whole line produced, may equal the square of the part produced.

162. If A be a point within a circle, BC the diameter, and through A, AD be drawn perpendicular to the diameter, and BAE meeting the circumference in E, then $BA.BE = BC.BD$.

163. The diameter ACD of a circle, whose center is C, is produced to P, determine a point F in the line AP such that the rectangle $PF.PC$ may be equal to the rectangle $PD.PA$.

164. To produce a given straight line, so that the rectangle contained by the whole line thus produced, and the part of it produced, shall be equal to a given square.

165. Two straight lines stand at right angles to each other, one of which passes through the center of a given circle, and from any point in the other, tangents are drawn to the circle. Prove that the chord joining the points of contact cuts the first line in the same point, whatever be the point in the second from which the tangents are drawn.

166. A, B, C, D, are four points in order in a straight line, find a point E between B and C, such that $AE.EB = ED.EC$, by a geometrical construction.

167. If any two circles touch each other in the point O, and lines be drawn through O at right angles to each other, the one line cutting the circles in P, P', the other in Q, Q'; and if the line joining the centers of the circles cut them in A, A'; then
$$P'P^2 + Q'Q^2 = A'A^2.$$

BOOK IV.

DEFINITIONS.

I.

A RECTILINEAL figure is said to be inscribed in another rectilineal figure, when all the angular points of the inscribed figure are upon the sides of the figure in which it is inscribed, each upon each.

II.

In like manner, a figure is said to be described about another figure, when all the sides of the circumscribed figure pass through the angular points of the figure about which it is described, each through each.

III.

A rectilineal figure is said to be inscribed in a circle, when all the angular points of the inscribed figure are upon the circumference of the circle.

IV.

A rectilineal figure is said to be described about a circle, when each side of the circumscribed figure touches the circumference of the circle.

V.

In like manner, a circle is said to be inscribed in a rectilineal figure, when the circumference of the circle touches each side of the figure.

VI.

A circle is said to be described about a rectilineal figure, when the circumference of the circle passes through all the angular points of the figure about which it is described.

VII.

A straight line is said to be placed in a circle, when the extremities of it are in the circumference of the circle.

PROPOSITION I. PROBLEM.

In a given circle to place a straight line, equal to a given straight line which is not greater than the diameter of the circle.

Let ABC be the given circle, and D the given straight line, not greater than the diameter of the circle.

It is required to place in the circle ABC a straight line equal to D.

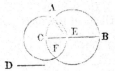

Draw BC the diameter of the circle ABC.
Then, if BC is equal to D, the thing required is done;
for in the circle ABC a straight line BC is placed equal to D.
But, if it is not, BC is greater than D; (hyp.)
make CE equal to D. (I. 3.)
and from the center C, at the distance CE, describe the circle AEF, and join CA.
Then CA shall be equal to D.
Because C is the center of the circle AEF,
therefore CA is equal to CE: (I. def. 15.)
but CE is equal to D; (constr.)
therefore D is equal to CA. (ax. 1.)
Wherefore in the circle ABC, a straight line CA is placed equal to the given straight line D, which is not greater than the diameter of the circle. Q.E.F.

PROPOSITION II. PROBLEM.

In a given circle to inscribe a triangle equiangular to a given triangle.

Let ABC be the given circle, and DEF the given triangle.
It is required to inscribe in the circle ABC a triangle equiangular to the triangle DEF.

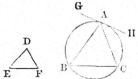

Draw the straight line GAH touching the circle in the point A, (III. 17.)
and at the point A, in the straight line AH,

make the angle *HAC* equal to the angle *DEF*; (I. 23.)
and at the point *A*, in the straight line *AG*,
make the angle *GAB* equal to the angle *DFE*;
and join *BC*; then *ABC* shall be the triangle required.

Because *HAG* touches the circle *ABC*,
and *AC* is drawn from the point of contact,
therefore the angle *HAC* is equal to the angle *ABC* in the alternate segment of the circle: (III. 32.)
but *HAC* is equal to the angle *DEF*; (constr.)
therefore also the angle *ABC* is equal to *DEF*: (ax. 1.)
for the same reason, the angle *ACB* is equal to the angle *DFE*:
therefore the remaining angle *BAC* is equal to the remaining angle *EDF*: (I. 32. and ax. 1.)
wherefore the triangle *ABC* is equiangular to the triangle *DEF*,
and it is inscribed in the circle *ABC*.   Q.E.F.

PROPOSITION III. PROBLEM.

About a given circle to describe a triangle equiangular to a given triangle.

Let *ABC* be the given circle, and *DEF* the given triangle.

It is required to describe a triangle about the circle *ABC* equiangular to the triangle *DEF*.

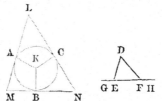

Produce *EF* both ways to the points *G*, *H*;
find the center *K* of the circle *ABC*, (III. 1.)
and from it draw any straight line *KB*;
at the point *K* in the straight line *KB*,
make the angle *BKA* equal to the angle *DEG*, (I. 23.)
and the angle *BKC* equal to the angle *DFH*;
and through the points *A*, *B*, *C*, draw the straight lines *LAM*, *MBN*, *NCL*, touching the circle *ABC*. (III. 17.)

Then *LMN* shall be the triangle required.

Because *LM*, *MN*, *NL* touch the circle *ABC* in the points *A*, *B*, *C*, to which from the center are drawn *KA*, *KB*, *KC*,
therefore the angles at the points *A*, *B*, *C* are right angles: (III. 18.)
and because the four angles of the quadrilateral figure *AMBK* are equal to four right angles,
for it can be divided into two triangles;
and that two of them *KAM*, *KBM* are right angles,
therefore the other two *AKB*, *AMB* are equal to two right angles: (ax. 3.)
but the angles *DEG*, *DEF* are likewise equal to two right angles· (I. 13.)

therefore the angles AKB, AMB are equal to the angles DEG DEF; (ax. 1.)
of which AKB is equal to DEG; (constr.)
wherefore the remaining angle AMB is equal to the remaining angle DEF. (ax. 3.)
In like manner, the angle LNM may be demonstrated to be equal to DFE;
and therefore the remaining angle MLN is equal to the remaining angle EDF; (I. 32. and ax. 3.)
therefore the triangle LMN is equiangular to the triangle DEF:
and it is described about the circle ABC. Q.E.F.

PROPOSITION IV. PROBLEM.
To inscribe a circle in a given triangle.
Let the given triangle be ABC.
It is required to inscribe a circle in ABC.

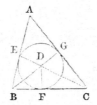

Bisect the angles ABC, BCA by the straight lines BD, CD meeting one another in the point D, (I. 9.)
from which draw DE, DF, DG perpendiculars to AB, BC, CA. (I. 12.)
And because the angle EBD is equal to the angle FBD,
for the angle ABC is bisected by BD,
and that the right angle BED is equal to the right angle BFD; (ax. 11.)
therefore the two triangles EBD, FBD have two angles of the one equal to two angles of the other, each to each;
and the side BD, which is opposite to one of the equal angles in each, is common to both;
therefore their other sides are equal; (I. 26.)
wherefore DE is equal to DF:
for the same reason, DG is equal to DF:
therefore DE is equal to DG: (ax. 1.)
therefore the three straight lines DE, DF, DG are equal to one another;
and the circle described from the center D, at the distance of any of them, will pass through the extremities of the other two, and touch the straight lines AB, BC, CA,
because the angles at the points E, F, G are right angles,
and the straight line which is drawn from the extremity of a diameter at right angles to it, touches the circle: (III. 16.)
therefore the straight lines AB, BC, CA do each of them touch the circle,
and therefore the circle EFG is inscribed in the triangle ABC. Q.E.F.

PROPOSITION V. PROBLEM.

To describe a circle about a given triangle.

Let the given triangle be ABC.
It is required to describe a circle about ABC.

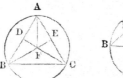

Bisect AB, AC in the points D, E, (I. 10.)
and from these points draw DF, EF at right angles to AB, AC; (I. 11.)
DF, EF produced meet one another:
for, if they do not meet, they are parallel,
wherefore AB, AC, which are at right angles to them, are parallel; which is absurd:
let them meet in F, and join FA;
also, if the point F be not in BC, join BF, CF.
Then, because AD is equal to DB, and DF common, and at right angles to AB,
therefore the base AF is equal to the base FB. (I. 4.)
In like manner, it may be shewn that CF is equal to FA;
and therefore BF is equal to FC; (ax. 1.)
and FA, FB, FC are equal to one another:
wherefore the circle described from the center F, at the distance of one of them, will pass through the extremities of the other two, and be described about the triangle ABC. Q.E.F.

Cor.—And it is manifest, that when the center of the circle falls within the triangle, each of its angles is less than a right angle, (III. 31.) each of them being in a segment greater than a semicircle; but, when the center is in one of the sides of the triangle, the angle opposite to this side, being in a semicircle, (III. 31.) is a right angle; and, if the center falls without the triangle, the angle opposite to the side beyond which it is, being in a segment less than a semicircle, (III. 31.) is greater than a right angle: therefore, conversely, if the given triangle be acute-angled, the center of the circle falls within it; if it be a right-angled triangle, the center is in the side opposite to the right angle; and if it be an obtuse-angled triangle, the center falls without the triangle, beyond the side opposite to the obtuse angle.

PROPOSITION VI. PROBLEM.

To inscribe a square in a given circle.

Let $ABCD$ be the given circle.
It is required to inscribe a square in $ABCD$.

Draw the diameters, AC, BD, at right angles to one another, (III. 1. and I. 11.)
and join AB, BC, CD, DA.
The figure $ABCD$ shall be the square required.
Because BE is equal to ED, for E is the center, and that EA is common, and at right angles to BD;
the base BA is equal to the base AD: (I. 4.)
and, for the same reason, BC, CD are each of them equal to BA, or AD;
therefore the quadrilateral figure $ABCD$ is equilateral.
It is also rectangular;
for the straight line BD being the diameter of the circle $ABCD$, BAD is a semicircle;
wherefore the angle BAD is a right angle: (III. 31.)
for the same reason, each of the angles ABC, BCD, CDA is a right angle:
therefore the quadrilateral figure $ABCD$ is rectangular:
and it has been shewn to be equilateral,
therefore it is a square: (I. def. 30.)
and it is inscribed in the circle $ABCD$. Q.E.F.

PROPOSITION VII. PROBLEM.

To describe a square about a given circle.

Let $ABCD$ be the given circle.
It is required to describe a square about it.

Draw two diameters AC, BD of the circle $ABCD$, at right angles to one another,
and through the points A, B, C, D, draw FG, GH, HK, KF touching the circle. (III. 17.)
The figure $GHKF$ shall be the square required.
Because FG touches the circle $ABCD$, and EA is drawn from the center E to the point of contact A,
therefore the angles at A are right angles: (III. 18.)
for the same reason, the angles at the points B, C, D are right angles;
and because the angle AEB is a right angle, as likewise is EBG,
therefore GH is parallel to AC: (I. 28.)
for the same reason AC is parallel to FK:
and in like manner GF, HK may each of them be demonstrated to be parallel to BED:
therefore the figures GK, GC, AK, FB, BK are parallelograms;
and therefore GF is equal to HK and GH to FK: (I. 34.)
and because AC is equal to BD, and that AC is equal to each of the two GH, FK;

and BD to each of the two GF, HK:
GH, FK are each of them equal to GF, or HK;
therefore the quadrilateral figure $FGHK$ is equilateral.
It is also rectangular;
for $GBEA$ being a parallelogram, and AEB a right angle,
therefore AGB is likewise a right angle: (I. 34.)
and in the same manner it may be shewn that the angles at H, K, F are right angles:
therefore the quadrilateral figure $FGHK$ is rectangular:
and it was demonstrated to be equilateral;
therefore it is a square; (I. def. 30.)
and it is described about the circle $ABCD$.   Q.E.F.

PROPOSITION VIII. PROBLEM.

To inscribe a circle in a given square.

Let $ABCD$ be the given square.
It is required to inscribe a circle in $ABCD$.

Bisect each of the sides AB, AD in the points F, E, (I. 10.)
and through E draw EH parallel to AB or DC, (I. 31.)
and through F draw FK parallel to AD or BC:
therefore each of the figures AK, KB, AH, HD, AG, GC, BG, GD is a right-angled parallelogram;
and their opposite sides are equal: (I. 34.)
and because AD is equal to AB, (I. def. 30.)
and that AE is the half of AD, and AF the half of AB,
therefore AE is equal to AF; (ax. 7.)
wherefore the sides opposite to these are equal, viz. FG to GE:
in the same manner it may be demonstrated that GH, GK are each of them equal to FG or GE:
therefore the four straight lines GE, GF, GH, GK are equal to one another;
and the circle described from the center G at the distance of one of them, will pass through the extremities of the other three, and touch the straight lines AB, BC, CD, DA;
because the angles at the points E, F, H, K, are right angles, (I. 29.)
and that the straight line which is drawn from the extremity of a diameter, at right angles to it, touches the circle: (III. 16. Cor.)
therefore each of the straight lines AB, BC, CD, DA touches the circle, which therefore is inscribed in the square $ABCD$.   Q.E.F.

PROPOSITION IX. PROBLEM.

To describe a circle about a given square.

Let $ABCD$ be the given square.
It is required to describe a circle about $ABCD$.

Join AC, BD, cutting one another in E:
and because DA is equal to AB, and AC common to the triangles $DAC, BAC,$ (I. def. 30.)
the two sides DA, AC are equal to the two BA, AC, each to each;
and the base DC is equal to the base BC;
wherefore the angle DAC is equal to the angle BAC; (I. 8.)
and the angle DAB is bisected by the straight line AC:
in the same manner it may be demonstrated that the angles ABC, BCD, CDA are severally bisected by the straight lines BD, AC:
therefore because the angle DAB is equal to the angle ABC, (I. def. 30.)
and that the angle EAB is the half of DAB, and EBA the half of ABC;
therefore the angle EAB is equal to the angle EBA; (ax. 7.)
wherefore the side EA is equal to the side EB: (I. 6.)
in the same manner it may be demonstrated, that the straight lines EC, ED are each of them equal to EA or EB:
therefore the four straight lines EA, EB, EC, ED are equal to one another;
and the circle described from the center E, at the distance of one of them, will pass through the extremities of the other three, and be described about the square $ABCD$. Q.E.F.

PROPOSITION X. PROBLEM.

To describe an isosceles triangle, having each of the angles at the base double of the third angle.

Take any straight line AB, and divide it in the point C, (II. 11.)
so that the rectangle AB, BC may be equal to the square of CA;
and from the center A, at the distance AB, describe the circle BDE,
in which place the straight line BD equal to AC, which is not greater than the diameter of the circle BDE; (IV. 1.)
and join DA.
Then the triangle ABD shall be such as is required,
that is, each of the angles ABD, ADB shall be double of the angle BAD.
Join DC, and about the triangle ADC describe the circle ACD. (IV. 5.)
And because the rectangle AB, BC is equal to the square on AC,
and that AC is equal to BD, (constr.)
the rectangle AB, BC is equal to the square on BD: (ax. 1.)
and because from the point B, without the circle ACD, two straight lines BCA, BD are drawn to the circumference, one of which cuts, and

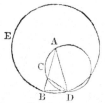

the other meets the circle, and that the rectangle AB, BC, contained by the whole of the cutting line, and the part of it without the circle, is equal to the square on BD which meets it;

therefore the straight line BD touches the circle ACD: (III. 37.)

and because BD touches the circle, and DC is drawn from the point of contact D,

the angle BDC is equal to the angle DAC in the alternate segment of the circle: (III. 32.)

to each of these add the angle CDA;

therefore the whole angle BDA is equal to the two angles CDA, DAC: (ax. 2.)

but the exterior angle BCD is equal to the angles CDA, DAC; (I. 32.)

therefore also BDA is equal to BCD: (ax. 1.)

but BDA is equal to the angle CBD, (I. 5.)

because the side AD is equal to the side AB;

therefore CBD, or DBA, is equal to BCD; (ax. 1.)

and consequently the three angles BDA, DBA, BCD are equal to one another:

and because the angle DBC is equal to the angle BCD

the side BD is equal to the side DC: (I. 6.)

but BD was made equal to CA;

therefore also CA is equal to CD, (ax. 1.)

and the angle CDA equal to the angle DAC; (I. 5.)

therefore the angles CDA, DAC together, are double of the angle DAC:

but BCD is equal to the angles CDA, DAC; (I. 32.)

therefore also BCD is double of DAC:

and BCD was proved to be equal to each of the angles BDA, DBA;

therefore each of the angles BDA, DBA is double of the angle DAB.

Wherefore an isosceles triangle ABD has been described, having each of the angles at the base double of the third angle. Q.E.F.

PROPOSITION XI. PROBLEM.

To inscribe an equilateral and equiangular pentagon in a given circle.

Let $ABCDE$ be the given circle.

It is required to inscribe an equilateral and equiangular pentagon in the circle $ABCDE$.

Describe an isosceles triangle FGH, having each of the angles at G, H double of the angle at F; (IV. 10.)

and in the circle $ABCDE$ inscribe the triangle ACD equiangular to the triangle FGH, (IV. 2.)

so that the angle CAD may be equal to the angle at F,

and each of the angles ACD, CDA equal to the angle at G or H;

wherefore each of the angles ACD, CDA is double of the angle CAD. Bisect the angles ACD, CDA by the straight lines CE, DB; (I. 9.) and join AB, BC, DE, EA.

Then $ABCDE$ shall be the pentagon required.
Because each of the angles ACD, CDA is double of CAD, and that they are bisected by the straight lines CE, DB;
therefore the five angles DAC, ACE, ECD, CDB, BDA are equal to one another:
but equal angles stand upon equal circumferences; (III. 26.)
therefore the five circumferences AB, BC, CD, DE, EA are equal to one another:
and equal circumferences are subtended by equal straight lines; (III. 29.) therefore the five straight lines AB, BC, CD, DE, EA are equal to one another.
Wherefore the pentagon $ABCDE$ is equilateral.
It is also equiangular:
for, because the circumference AB is equal to the circumference DE, if to each be added BCD,
the whole $ABCD$ is equal to the whole $EDCB$: (ax. 2.)
but the angle AED stands on the circumference $ABCD$;
and the angle BAE on the circumference $EDCB$;
therefore the angle BAE is equal to the angle AED: (III. 27.)
for the same reason, each of the angles ABC, BCD, CDE is equal to the angle BAE, or AED:
therefore the pentagon $ABCDE$ is equiangular;
and it has been shewn that it is equilateral:
wherefore, in the given circle, an equilateral and equiangular pentagon has been described. Q.E.F.

PROPOSITION XII. PROBLEM.

To describe an equilateral and equiangular pentagon about a given circle.

Let $ABCDE$ be the given circle.
It is required to describe an equilateral and equiangular pentagon about the circle $ABCDE$.
Let the angular points of a pentagon, inscribed in the circle, by the last proposition, be in the points A, B, C, D, E,
so that the circumferences AB, BC, CD, DE, EA are equal; (IV. 11.)
and through the points A, B, C, D, E draw GH, HK, KL, LM, MG touching the circle; (III. 17.)
the figure $GHKLM$ shall be the pentagon required.
Take the center F, and join FB, FK, FC, FL, FD.
And because the straight line KL touches the circle $ABCDE$ in the point C, to which FC is drawn from the center F,
FC is perpendicular to KL, (III. 18.)

therefore each of the angles at C is a right angle:
for the same reason, the angles at the points B, D are right angles:

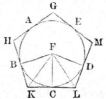

and because FCK is a right angle,
the square on FK is equal to the squares on FC, CK: (I. 47.)
for the same reason, the square on FK is equal to the squares on FB, BK:
therefore the squares on FC, CK are equal to the squares on FB, BK; (ax. 1.)
of which the square on FC is equal to the square on FB;
therefore the remaining square on CK is equal to the remaining square on BK, (ax. 3.) and the straight line CK equal to BK:
and because FB is equal to FC, and FK common to the triangles BFK, CFK,
the two BF, FK are equal to the two CF, FK, each to each:
and the base BK was proved equal to the base KC:
therefore the angle BFK is equal to the angle KFC, (I. 8.)
and the angle BKF to FKC: (I. 4.)
wherefore the angle BFC is double of the angle KFC,
and BKC double of FKC:
for the same reason, the angle CFD is double of the angle CFL,
and CLD double of CLF:
and because the circumference BC is equal to the circumference CD,
the angle BFC is equal to the angle CFD; (III. 27.)
and BFC is double of the angle KFC,
and CFD double of CFL;
therefore the angle KFC is equal to the angle CFL: (ax. 7.)
and the right angle FCK is equal to the right angle FCL;
therefore, in the two triangles FKC, FLC, there are two angles of the one equal to two angles of the other, each to each;
and the side FC which is adjacent to the equal angles in each, is common to both;
therefore the other sides are equal to the other sides, and the third angle to the third angle: (I. 26.)
therefore the straight line KC is equal to CL, and the angle FKC to the angle FLC:
and because KC is equal to CL,
KL is double of KC.
In the same manner it may be shewn that HK is double of BK:
and because BK is equal to KC, as was demonstrated,
and that KL is double of KC, and HK double of BK,
therefore HK is equal to KL: (ax. 6.)
In like manner it may be shewn that GH, GM, ML are each of them equal to HK, or KL:

therefore the pentagon $GHKLM$ is equilateral.
It is also equiangular:
for, since the angle FKC is equal to the angle FLC,
and that the angle HKL is double of the angle FKC,
and KLM double of FLC, as was before demonstrated;
therefore the angle HKL is equal to KLM: (ax. 6.)
and in like manner it may be shewn,
that each of the angles KHG, HGM, GML is equal to the angle HKL or KLM:
therefore the five angles GHK, HKL, KLM, LMG, MGH being equal to one another,
the pentagon $GHKLM$ is equiangular:
and it is equilateral, as was demonstrated;
and it is described about the circle $ABCDE$. Q.E.F.

PROPOSITION XIII. PROBLEM.

To inscribe a circle in a given equilateral and equiangular pentagon.

Let $ABCDE$ be the given equilateral and equiangular pentagon.
It is required to inscribe a circle in the pentagon $ABCDE$.

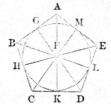

Bisect the angles BCD, CDE by the straight lines CF, DF, (I. 9.)
and from the point F, in which they meet, draw the straight lines FB, FA, FE:
therefore since BC is equal to CD, (hyp.)
and CF common to the triangles BCF, DCF,
the two sides BC, CF are equal to the two DC, CF, each to each;
and the angle BCF is equal to the angle DCF; (constr.)
therefore the base BF is equal to the base FD. (I. 4.)
and the other angles to the other angles, to which the equal sides are opposite:
therefore the angle CBF is equal to the angle CDF:
and because the angle CDE is double of CDF,
and that CDE is equal to CBA, and CDF to CBF;
CBA is also double of the angle CBF;
therefore the angle ABF is equal to the angle CBF;
wherefore the angle ABC is bisected by the straight line BF:
in the same manner it may be demonstrated,
that the angles BAE, AED, are bisected by the straight lines AF, FE.
From the point F, draw FG, FH, FK, FL, FM perpendiculars to the straight lines AB, BC, CD, DE, EA: (I. 12.)
and because the angle HCF is equal to KCF, and the right angle FHC equal to the right angle FKC;

therefore in the triangles *FHC*, *FKC*, there are two angles of the one equal to two angles of the other, each to each;
and the side *FC*, which is opposite to one of the equal angles in each, is common to both;
therefore the other sides are equal, each to each; (I. 26.)
wherefore the perpendicular *FH* is equal to the perpendicular *FK*: in the same manner it may be demonstrated, that *FL*, *FM*, *FG* are each of them equal to *FH*, or *FK*:
therefore the five straight lines *FG*, *FH*, *FK*, *FL*, *FM* are equal to one another:
wherefore the circle described from the center *F*, at the distance of one of these five, will pass through the extremities of the other four, and touch the straight lines *AB*, *BC*, *CD*, *DE*, *EA*,
because the angles at the points, *G*, *H*, *K*, *L*, *M* are right angles,
and that a straight line drawn from the extremity of the diameter of a circle at right angles to it, touches the circle; (III. 16.)
therefore each of the straight lines *AB*, *BC*, *CD*, *DE*, *EA* touches the circle:
wherefore it is inscribed in the pentagon *ABCDE*. Q.E.F.

PROPOSITION XIV. PROBLEM.

To describe a circle about a given equilateral and equiangular pentagon.

Let *ABCDE* be the given equilateral and equiangular pentagon.
It is required to describe a circle about *ABCDE*.

Bisect the angles *BCD*, *CDE* by the straight lines *CF*, *FD*, (I. 9.) and from the point *F*, in which they meet, draw the straight lines *FB*, *FA*, *FE*, to the points *B*, *A*, *E*.
It may be demonstrated, in the same manner as the preceding proposition,
that the angles *CBA*, *BAE*, *AED* are bisected by the straight lines *FB*, *FA*, *FE*.
And because the angle *BCD* is equal to the angle *CDE*, and that *FCD* is the half of the angle *BCD*, and *CDF* the half of *CDE*;
therefore the angle *FCD* is equal to *FDC*; (ax. 7.)
wherefore the side *CF* is equal to the side *FD*: (I. 6.)
In like manner it may be demonstrated,
that *FB*, *FA*, *FE*, are each of them equal to *FC* or *FD*:
therefore the five straight lines *FA*, *FB*, *FC*, *FD*, *FE*, are equal to one another;
and the circle described from the center *F*, at the distance of one of them, will pass through the extremities of the other four, and be described about the equilateral and equiangular pentagon *ABCDE*. Q.E.F.

PROPOSITION XV. PROBLEM.

To inscribe an equilateral and equiangular hexagon in a given circle.

Let $ABCDEF$ be the given circle.
It is required to inscribe an equilateral and equiangular hexagon in it.

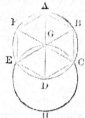

Find the center G of the circle $ABCDEF$,
and draw the diameter AGD; (III. 1.)
and from D, as a center, at the distance DG, describe the circle $EGCH$,
join EG, CG, and produce them to the points B, F;
and join AB, BC, CD, DE, EF, FA:
the hexagon $ABCDEF$ shall be equilateral and equiangular,
because G is the center of the circle $ABCDEF$,
GE is equal to GD:
and because D is the center of the circle $EGCH$,
DE is equal to DG:
wherefore GE is equal to ED, (ax. 1.)
and the triangle EGD is equilateral;
and therefore its three angles EGD, GDE, DEG, are equal to one another: (I. 5. Cor.)
but the three angles of a triangle are equal to two right angles; (I. 32.)
therefore the angle EGD is the third part of two right angles:
in the same manner it may be demonstrated,
that the angle DGC is also the third part of two right angles:
and because the straight line GC makes with EB the adjacent angles EGC, CGB equal to two right angles; (I. 13.)
the remaining angle CGB is the third part of two right angles:
therefore the angles EGD, DGC, CGB are equal to one another:
and to these are equal the vertical opposite angles BGA, AGF, FGE; (I. 15.)
therefore the six angles EGD, DGC, CGB, BGA, AGF, FGE, are equal to one another:
but equal angles stand upon equal circumferences; (III. 26.)
therefore the six circumferences AB, BC, CD, DE, EF, FA, are equal to one another:
and equal circumferences are subtended by equal straight lines: (III. 29.)
therefore the six straight lines are equal to one another,
and the hexagon $ABCDEF$ is equilateral.
It is also equiangular;
for, since the circumference AF is equal to ED,
to each of these equals add the circumference $ABCD$;
therefore the whole circumference $FABCD$ is equal to the whole $EDCBA$:

and the angle *FED* stands upon the circumference *FABCD*,
and the angle *AFE* upon *EDCBA*;
therefore the angle *AFE* is equal to *FED*: (III. 27.)
in the same manner it may be demonstrated,
that the other angles of the hexagon *ABCDEF* are each of them equal to the angle *AFE* or *FED*: therefore the hexagon is equiangular; and it is equilateral, as was shewn;
and it is inscribed in the given circle *ABCDEF*. Q.E.F.

Cor.—From this it is manifest, that the side of the hexagon is equal to the straight line from the center, that is, to the semidiameter of the circle.

And if through the points *A*, *B*, *C*, *D*, *E*, *F* there be drawn straight lines touching the circle, an equilateral and equiangular hexagon will be described about it, which may be demonstrated from what has been said of the pentagon: and likewise a circle may be inscribed in a given equilateral and equiangular hexagon, and circumscribed about it by a method like to that used for the pentagon.

PROPOSITION XVI. PROBLEM.

To inscribe an equilateral and equiangular quindecagon in a given circle.

Let *ABCD* be the given circle.

It is required to inscribe an equilateral and equiangular quindecagon in the circle *ABCD*.

Let *AC* be the side of an equilateral triangle inscribed in the circle, (IV. 2.) and *AB* the side of an equilateral and equiangular pentagon inscribed in the same; (IV. 11.)
therefore, of such equal parts as the whole circumference *ABCDF* contains fifteen,
the circumference *ABC*, being the third part of the whole, contains five;
and the circumference *AB*, which is the fifth part of the whole, contains three;
therefore *BC*, their difference, contains two of the same parts:
bisect *BC* in *E*; (III. 30.)
therefore *BE*, *EC* are, each of them, the fifteenth part of the whole circumference *ABCD*:
therefore if the straight lines *BE*, *EC* be drawn, and straight lines equal to them be placed round in the whole circle, (IV. 1.) an equilateral and equiangular quindecagon will be inscribed in it. Q.E.F.

And in the same manner as was done in the pentagon, if through the points of division made by inscribing the quindecagon, straight lines be drawn touching the circle, an equilateral and equiangular quindecagon will be described about it: and likewise, as in the pentagon, a circle may be inscribed in a given equilateral and equiangular quindecagon, and circumscribed about it.

NOTES TO BOOK IV.

THE Fourth Book of the Elements contains some particular cases of four general problems on the inscription and the circumscription of triangles and regular figures in and about circles. Euclid has not given any instance of the inscription or circumscription of rectilineal figures in and about other rectilineal figures.

Any rectilineal figure, of five sides and angles, is called a pentagon; of seven sides and angles, a heptagon; of eight sides and angles, an octagon; of nine sides and angles, a nonagon; of ten sides and angles, a decagon, of eleven sides and angles, an undecagon, of twelve sides and angles, a duodecagon, of fifteen sides and angles, a quindecagon, &c.

These figures are included under the general name of *polygons*, and are called *equilateral*, when their sides are equal, and *equiangular*, when their angles are equal; also when both their sides and angles are equal, they are called *regular polygons*.

Prop. III. An objection has been raised to the construction of this problem. It is said that in this and other instances of a similar kind, the lines which touch the circle at A, B, and C, should be proved to meet one another. This may be done by joining AB, and then since the angles KAM, KBM are equal to two right angles (III. 18.), therefore the angles BAM, ABM are less than two right angles, and consequently (ax. 12.), AM and BM must meet one another, when produced far enough. Similarly, it may be shewn that AL and CL, as also CN and BN meet one another.

Prop. V. is the same as "To describe a circle passing through three given points, provided that they are not in the same straight line."

The corollary to this proposition appears to have been already demonstrated in Prop. 31. Book III.

It is obvious that the square described about a circle is equal to double the square inscribed in the same circle. Also that the circumscribed square is equal to the square of the diameter, or four times the square of the radius of the circle.

Prop. VII. It is manifest that a square is the only right-angled parallelogram which can be circumscribed about a circle, but that both a rectangle and a square may be inscribed in a circle.

Prop. X. By means of this proposition, a right angle may be divided into five equal parts.

Reference has already been made to the distinction between *analysis* and *synthesis*, and that all Euclid's *direct* demonstrations are *synthetic*, properly so called. There is however a single exception in Prop. 16. Book IV, where the analysis only is given of the Problem. The two methods are so connected in all processes of reasoning, that it is very difficult to separate one from the other, and to assert that *this process* is really *synthetic*, and *that* is really *analytic*. In every operation performed in the construction of a problem, there must be in the mind a knowledge of some properties of the figure which suggest the steps to be taken in the construction of it. Let any Problem be selected from Euclid, and at each step of the operation, let the question be asked, "Why that step is taken?" It will be found that it is *because* of some known property of the required figure. As an example will make the subject more clear to the learner, the Analysis of Euc. IV. 10, is taken from the Appendix, pp. 13, 14, to the larger edition of the Euclid, and to which the learner is referred for more complete information.

In Euc. IV. 10, there are five operations specified in the construction:—
(1) Take *any* straight line AB.

(2) Divide the line AB in C, so that the rectangle AB, BC, may be equal to the square on AC.
(3) Describe the circle BDE with center A and radius AB.
(4) Place the line BD in that circle, equal to the line AC.
(5) Join the points A, D.

Why should either of these operations be performed rather than any others? And what will enable us to foresee that the result of them will be such a triangle as was required? The demonstration affixed to it by Euclid does undoubtedly prove that these operations must, in conjunction, produce such a triangle, but we are furnished in the Elements with no obvious reason for the adoption of these steps, unless we suppose them accidental. To suppose that all the constructions, even the simpler ones, are the result of accident only, would be supposing more than could be shewn to be admissible. No construction of the problem could have been devised without a previous knowledge of some of the properties of the figure. In fact, in directing the figure to be constructed, we assume the possibility of its existence, and we study the properties of such a figure on the hypothesis of its actual existence. It is this study of the properties of the figure *that constitutes the Analysis of the problem*.

Let then the existence of a triangle BAD be admitted, which has each of the angles ABD, ADB double of the angle BAD, in order to ascertain any properties it may possess which would assist in the construction of such a triangle.

Then, since the angle ADB is double of BAD, if we draw a line DC to bisect ADB and meet AB in C, the angle ADC will be equal to CAD, and hence (Euc. I. 6.) the sides AC, CD are equal to one another.

Again, since we have three points A, C, D, not in the same straight line, let us examine the effect of describing a circle through them, that is, describe the circle ACD about the triangle ACD, (Euc. IV. 5.)

Then, since the angle ADB has been bisected by DC, and since ADB is double of DAB, the angle CDB is equal to the angle DAC in the alternate segment of the circle, the line BD therefore coincides with a tangent to the circle at D. (Converse of Euc. III. 32.)

Whence it follows, that the rectangle contained by AB, BC, is equal to the square on BD. (Euc. III. 36.)

But the angle BCD is equal to the two interior opposite angles CAD, CDA, or since these are equal to each other, BCD is the double of CAD, that is, of BAD. And since ABD is also double of BAD, by the conditions of the triangle, the angles BCD, CBD are equal, and BD is equal to DC, that is, to AC.

It has been proved that the rectangle AB, BC, is equal to the square on BD, and hence the point C in AB, found by the intersection of the bisecting line DC, is such, that the rectangle AB, BC is equal to the square on AC. (Euc. II. 11.)

Finally, since the triangle ABD is isosceles, having each of the angles ABD, ADB double of the same angle, the sides AB, AD are equal, and hence the points B, D, are in the circumference of the circle described about A with the radius AB. And since the magnitude of the triangle is not specified, the line AB may be of any length whatever.

From this "Analysis of the problem," which obviously is nothing more than an examination of the properties of such a figure supposed to exist already, it will be at once apparent, *why* those steps which are prescribed by Euclid for its construction, were adopted.

The line AB is taken of any length, *because* the problem does not prescribe any specific magnitude to any of the sides of the triangle.

The circle BDE is described about A with the distance AB, *because* the triangle is to be isosceles, having AB for one side, and therefore the other extremity of the base is in the circumference of that circle.

The line AB is divided in C, so that the rectangle AB, BC shall be equal to the square on AC, *because* the base of the triangle must be equal to the segment AC.

And the line AD is drawn, *because* it completes the triangle, two of whose sides, AB, BD are already drawn.

Whenever we have reduced the construction to depend upon problems which have been already constructed, our analysis may be terminated; as was the case where, in the preceding example, we arrived at the division of the line AB in C, this problem having been already constructed as the eleventh of the second book.

Prop. xvi. The arc subtending a side of the quindecagon, may be found by placing in the circle from the same point, two lines respectively equal to the sides of the regular hexagon and pentagon.

The centers of the inscribed and circumscribed circles of any regular polygon are coincident.

Besides the circumscription and inscription of triangles and regular polygons about and in circles, some very important problems are solved in the constructions respecting the division of the circumferences of circles into equal parts.

By inscribing an equilateral triangle, a square, a pentagon, a hexagon, &c., in a circle, the circumference is divided into three, four, five, six, &c., equal parts. In Prop. 26, Book iii., it has been shewn that equal angles at the centers of equal circles, and therefore at the center of the same circle, subtend equal arcs; by bisecting the angles at the center, the arcs which are subtended by them are also bisected, and hence, a sixth, eighth, tenth, twelfth, &c., part of the circumference of a circle may be found.

If the right angle be considered as divided into 90 degrees, each degree into 60 minutes, and each minute into 60 seconds, and so on, according to the sexagesimal division of a degree; by the aid of the first corollary to Prop. 32, Book i., may be found the numerical magnitude of an interior angle of any regular polygon whatever.

Let θ denote the magnitude of one of the interior angles of a regular polygon of n sides,

then $n\theta$ is the sum of all the interior angles.

But all the interior angles of any rectilineal figure together with four right angles, are equal to twice as many right angles as the figure has sides,

that is, if π be assumed to designate two right angles,

$$n\theta + 2\pi = n\pi,$$

and $n\theta = n\pi - 2\pi = (n-2) \cdot \pi,$

$$\theta = \frac{(n-2)}{n} \pi,$$

the magnitude of an interior angle of a regular polygon of n sides.

By taking $n = 3, 4, 5, 6,$ &c., may be found the magnitude in terms of two right angles, of an interior angle of any regular polygon whatever.

Pythagoras was the first, as Proclus informs us in his commentary, who discovered that a multiple of the angles of three regular figures only, namely, the trigon, the square, and the hexagon, can fill up space round a point in a plane.

It has been shewn that the interior angle of any regular polygon of n

sides in terms of two right angles, is expressed by the equation
$$\theta = \frac{n-2}{n} \cdot \pi.$$

Let θ_3 denote the magnitude of the interior angle of a regular figure of three sides, in which case, $n = 3$.

Then $\theta_3 = \dfrac{3-2}{3} \cdot \pi = \dfrac{\pi}{3}$ = one-third of two right angles

$\therefore 3\theta_3 = \pi,$

and $6\theta_3 = 2\pi,$

that is, six angles, each equal to the interior angle of an equilateral triangle, are equal to four right angles, and therefore six equilateral triangles may be placed so as completely to fill up the space round the point at which they meet in a plane.

In a similar way, it may be shewn that four squares and three hexagons may be placed so as completely to fill up the space round a point.

Also it will appear from the results deduced, that no other regular figures besides these three, can be made to fill up the space round a point; for any multiple of the interior angles of any other regular polygon, will be found to be in excess above, or in defect from four right angles.

The equilateral triangle or trigon, the square or tetragon, the pentagon, and the hexagon, were the only regular polygons known to the Greeks, capable of being inscribed in circles, besides those which may be derived from them.

M. Gauss in his Disquisitiones Arithmeticæ, has extended the number by shewing that in general, a regular polygon of $2^n + 1$ sides is capable of being inscribed in a circle by means of straight lines and circles, in those cases in which $2^n + 1$ is a prime number.

The case in which $n = 4$, in $2^n + 1$, was proposed by Mr Lowry of the Royal Military College, to be answered in the seventeenth number of Leybourn's Mathematical Repository, in the following form —

Required a geometrical demonstration of the following method of constructing a regular polygon of seventeen sides in a circle.

Draw the radius CO at right angles to the diameter AB, on OC and OB, take OQ equal to the half, and OD equal to the eighth part of the radius; make DE and DF each equal to DQ, and EG and FH respectively equal to EQ and FQ; take OK a mean proportional between OH and OQ, and through K, draw KM parallel to AB, meeting the semicircle described on OG in M, draw MN parallel to OC cutting the given circle in N, the arc AN is the seventeenth part of the whole circumference.

A demonstration of the truth of this construction has been given by Mr Lowry himself, and will be found in the fourth volume of Leybourn's Repository. The demonstration including the two lemmas occupies more than eight pages, and is by no means of an elementary character.

QUESTIONS ON BOOK IV.

1. WHAT is the general object of the Fourth Book of Euclid?
2. What consideration renders necessary the first proposition of the Fourth Book of Euclid?
3. When is a circle said to be inscribed within, and circumscribed about a rectilineal figure?

4. When is one rectilineal figure said to be inscribed in, and circumscribed about another rectilineal figure?

5. Modify the construction of Euc. iv. 4, so that the circle may touch one side of the triangle and the other two sides produced.

6. The sides of a triangle are 5, 6, 7 units respectively, find the radii of the inscribed and circumscribed circle.

7. Give the constructions by which the centers of circles described about, and inscribed in triangles are found. In what triangles will they coincide?

8. How is it shewn that the radius of the circle inscribed in an equilateral triangle is half the radius described about the same triangle?

9. The equilateral triangle inscribed in a circle is one-fourth of the equilateral triangle circumscribed about the same circle.

10. What relation subsists between the square inscribed in, and the square circumscribed about the same circle?

11. Enunciate Euc. iii. 22, and extend this property to any inscribed polygon having an even number of sides.

12. Trisect a quadrantal arc of a circle, and shew that every arc which is an $\frac{m}{2^n}$ th part of a quadrantal arc may be trisected geometrically; m and n being whole numbers.

13. If one side of a quadrilateral figure inscribed in a circle be produced, the exterior angle is equal to the interior and opposite angle of the figure. Is this property true of any inscribed polygon having an even number of sides?

14. In what parallelograms can circles be inscribed?

15. Give the analysis and synthesis of the problem—to describe an isosceles triangle, having each of the angles at the base double of the third angle?

16. Shew that in the figure Euc. iv. 10, there are two triangles possessing the required property.

17. How is it made to appear that the line BD is the side of a regular decagon inscribed in the larger circle, and the side of a regular pentagon inscribed in the smaller circle? fig. Euc. iv. 10.

18. In the construction of Euc. iv. 3, Euclid has omitted to shew that the tangents drawn through the points A and B will meet in some point M. How may this be shewn?

19. Shew that if the points of intersection of the circles in Euclid's figure, Book iv. Prop 10, be joined with the vertex of the triangle and with each other, another triangle will be formed equiangular and equal to the former.

20. Divide a right angle into five equal parts. How may an isosceles triangle be described upon a given base, having each angle at the base one-third of the angle at the vertex?

21. What regular figures may be inscribed in a circle by the help of Euc. iv. 10?

22. What is Euclid's definition of a regular pentagon? Would the stellated figure, which is formed by joining the alternate angles of a regular pentagon, as described in the Fourth Book, satisfy this definition?

23. Shew that each of the interior angles of a regular pentagon inscribed in a circle, is equal to three-fifths of two right angles.

24. If two sides not adjacent, of a regular pentagon, be produced to meet: what is the magnitude of the angle contained at the point where they meet?

25. Is there any method more direct than Euclid's for inscribing a regular pentagon in a circle?

QUESTIONS ON BOOK IV.

26. In what sense is a regular hexagon also a parallelogram? Would the same observation apply to all regular figures with an even number of sides?

27. Why has Euclid not shewn how to inscribe an equilateral triangle in a circle, before he requires the use of it in Prop. 16, Book iv?

28. An equilateral triangle is inscribed in a circle by joining the first, third, and fifth angles of the inscribed hexagon.

29. If the sides of a hexagon be produced to meet, the angles formed by these lines will be equal to four right angles.

30. Shew that the area of an equilateral triangle inscribed in a circle is one-half of a regular hexagon inscribed in the same circle.

31. If a side of an equilateral triangle be six inches, what is the radius of the inscribed circle?

32. Find the area of a regular hexagon inscribed in a circle whose diameter is twelve inches. What is the difference between the inscribed and the circumscribed hexagon?

33. Which is the greater, the difference between the side of the square and the side of the regular hexagon inscribed in a circle whose radius is unity, or the difference between the side of the equilateral triangle and the side of the regular pentagon inscribed in the same circle?

34. The regular hexagon inscribed in a circle, is three-fourths of the regular circumscribed hexagon.

35. All the interior angles of an octagon equal to twelve right angles.

36. What figure is formed by the production of the alternate sides of a regular octagon?

37. How many square inches are in the area of a regular octagon whose side is eight inches?

38. If an irregular octagon be capable of having a circle described about it, shew that the sums of the angles taken alternately are equal.

39. Find an algebraical formula for the number of degrees contained by an interior angle of a regular polygon of n sides.

40. What are the three regular figures which can be used in paving a plane area? Shew that no other regular figures but these will fill up the space round a point in a plane.

41. Into what number of equal parts may a right angle be divided geometrically? What connection has the solution of this problem with the possibility of inscribing regular figures in circles?

42. Assuming the demonstrations in Euc iv, shew that any equilateral figure of $3 \cdot 2^n$, $4 \cdot 2^n$, $5 \cdot 2^n$, or $15 \cdot 2^n$ sides may be inscribed in a circle, when n is any of the numbers 0, 1, 2, 3, &c.

43. With a pair of compasses only, shew how to divide the circumference of a given circle into twenty-four equal parts.

44. Shew that if any polygon inscribed in a circle be equilateral, it must also be equiangular. Is the converse true?

45. Shew that if the circumference of a circle pass through three angular points of a regular polygon, it will pass through all of them.

46. Similar polygons are always equiangular is the converse of this proposition true?

47. What are the limits to the *Geometrical* inscription of regular figures in circles? What does *Geometrical* mean when used in this way?

48. What is the difficulty of inscribing geometrically an equilateral and equiangular undecagon in a circle? Why is the solution of this problem said to be beyond the limits of plane geometry? Why is it so difficult to prove that the geometrical solution of such problems is impossible?

GEOMETRICAL EXERCISES ON BOOK IV.

PROPOSITION I. THEOREM.

If an equilateral triangle be inscribed in a circle, the square of the side of the triangle is triple of the square of the radius, or of the side of the regular hexagon inscribed in the same circle.

Let ABD be an equilateral triangle inscribed in the circle ABD, of which the center is C.

Join BC, and produce BC to meet the circumference in E, also join AE.
And because ABD is an equilateral triangle inscribed in the circle;
  therefore AED is one-third of the whole circumference,
    and therefore AE is one-sixth of the circumference,
and consequently, the straight line AE is the side of a regular hexagon
  (IV. 15.), and is equal to EC.
    And because BE is double of EC or AE,
  therefore the square on BE is quadruple of the square on AE,
    but the square on BE is equal to the squares on AB, AE;
therefore the squares on AB, AE are quadruple of the square on AE,
    and taking from these equals the square on AE,
  therefore the square on AB is triple of the square on AE.

PROPOSITION II. PROBLEM.

To describe a circle which shall touch a straight line given in position, and pass through two given points.

Analysis. Let AB be the given straight line, and C, D the two given points.
Suppose the circle required which passes through the points C, D to touch the line AB in the point E.

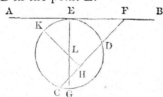

Join C, D, and produce DC to meet AB in F,
  and let the circle be described having the center L,
    join also LE, and draw LH perpendicular to CD.
Then CD is bisected in H, and LE is perpendicular to AB.

Also, since from the point F without the circle, are drawn two straight lines, one of which FE touches the circle, and the other FDC cuts it; the rectangle contained by FC, FD, is equal to the square of FE. (III. 36.)

Synthesis. Join C, D, and produce CD to meet AB in F, take the point E in FB, such that the square on FE, shall be equal to the rectangle FD, FC.

Bisect CD in H, and draw HK perpendicular to CD; then HK passes through the center. (III. 1, Cor. 1.)

At E draw EG perpendicular to FB, then EG passes through the center, (III. 19.) consequently L, the point of intersection of these two lines, is the center of the circle.

It is also manifest, that another circle may be described passing through C, D, and touching the line AB on the other side of the point F; and this circle will be equal to, greater than, or less than the other circle, according as the angle CFB is equal to, greater than, or less than the angle CFA.

PROPOSITION III. PROBLEM.

Inscribe a circle in a given sector of a circle.

Analysis. Let CAB be the given sector, and let the required circle whose center is O, touch the radii in P, Q, and the arc of the sector in D.

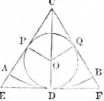

Join OP, OQ, these lines are equal to one another.
Join also CO.

Then in the triangles CPO, CQO, the two sides PC, CO, are equal to QC, CO, and the base OP is equal to the base OQ;
therefore the angle PCO is equal to the angle QCO;
and the angle ACB is bisected by CO:
also CO produced will bisect the arc AB in D. (III. 26.)
If a tangent EDF be drawn to touch the arc AB in D;
and CA, CB be produced to meet it in E, F:
the inscription of the circle in the sector is reduced to the inscription of a circle in a triangle. (IV. 4.)

PROPOSITION IV. PROBLEM.

$ABCD$ *is a rectangular parallelogram. Required to draw* EG, FG *parallel to* AD, DC, *so that the rectangle* EF *may be equal to the figure* EMD, *and* EB *equal to* FD.

Analysis. Let EG, FG be drawn, as required, bisecting the rectangle $ABCD$.

Draw the diagonal *BD* cutting *EG* in *H* and *FG* in *K*.
Then *BD* also bisects the rectangle *ABCD*;
and therefore the area of the triangle *KGH* is equal to that of the two triangles *EHB*, *FKD*.

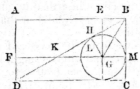

Draw *GL* perpendicular to *BD*, and join *GB*,
also produce *FG* to *M*, and *EG* to *N*.
If the triangle *LGH* be supposed to be equal to the triangle *EHB*, by adding *HGB* to each,
the triangles *LGB*, *GEB* are equal, and they are upon the same base *GB*, and on the same side of it;
therefore they are between the same parallels,
that is, if *L*, *E* were joined, *LE* would be parallel to *GB*;
and if a semicircle were described on *GB* as a diameter, it would pass through the points *E*, *L*; for the angles at *E*, *L* are right angles:
also *LE* would be a chord parallel to the diameter *GB*;
therefore the arcs intercepted between the parallels *LE*, *GB* are equal,
and consequently the chords *EB*, *LG* are also equal;
but *EB* is equal to *GM*, and *GM* to *GN*;
wherefore *LG*, *GM*, *GN*, are equal to one another;
hence *G* is the center of the circle inscribed in the triangle *BDC*.

Synthesis. Draw the diagonal *BD*.
Find *G* the center of the circle inscribed in the triangle *BDC*;
through *G* draw *EGN* parallel to *BC*, and *FKM* parallel to *AB*.
Then *EG* and *FG* bisect the rectangle *ABCD*.
Draw *GL* perpendicular to the diagonal *BD*.
In the triangles *GLH*, *EHB*, the angles *GLH*, *HEB* are equal, each being a right angle, and the vertical angles *LHG*, *EHB*, also the side *LG* is equal to the side *EB*;
therefore the triangle *LHG* is equal to the triangle *EHB*.
Similarly, it may be proved, that the triangle *GLK* is equal to the triangle *KFD*,
therefore the whole triangle *KGH* is equal to the two triangles *EHB*, *KFD*;
and consequently *EG*, *FG* bisect the rectangle *ABCD*.

I.

1. In a given circle, place a straight line equal and parallel to a given straight line not greater than the diameter of the circle.

2. Trisect a given circle by dividing it into three equal sectors.

3. The centers of the circle inscribed in, and circumscribed about an equilateral triangle coincide, and the diameter of one is twice the diameter of the other.

4. If a line be drawn from the vertex of an equilateral triangle, perpendicular to the base, and intersecting a line drawn from either of the angles at the base perpendicular to the opposite side, the distance from the vertex to the point of intersection, shall be equal to the radius of the circumscribing circle.

5. If an equilateral triangle be inscribed in a circle, and a straight line be drawn from the vertical angle to meet the circumference, it will be equal to the sum or difference of the straight lines drawn from the extremities of the base to the point where the line meets the circumference, according as the line does or does not cut the base.

6. The perpendicular from the vertex on the base of an equilateral triangle, is equal to the side of an equilateral triangle inscribed in a circle whose diameter is the base. Required proof.

7. If an equilateral triangle be inscribed in a circle and the adjacent arcs cut off by two of its sides be bisected, the line joining the points of bisection shall be trisected by the sides.

8. If an equilateral triangle be inscribed in a circle, any of its sides will cut off one-fourth part of the diameter drawn through the opposite angle.

9. The perimeter of an equilateral triangle inscribed in a circle is greater than the perimeter of any other isosceles triangle inscribed in the same circle.

10. If any two consecutive sides of a hexagon inscribed in a circle be respectively parallel to their opposite sides, the remaining sides are parallel to each other.

11. Prove that the area of a regular hexagon is greater than that of an equilateral triangle of the same perimeter.

12. If two equilateral triangles be inscribed in a circle so as to have the sides of one parallel to the sides of the other, the figure common to both will be a regular hexagon, whose area and perimeter will be equal to the remainder of the area and perimeter of the two triangles.

13. Determine the distance between the opposite sides of an equilateral and equiangular hexagon inscribed in a circle.

14. Inscribe a regular hexagon in a given equilateral triangle.

15. To inscribe a regular dodecagon in a given circle, and shew that its area is equal to the square of the side of an equilateral triangle inscribed in a circle.

II.

16. Describe a circle touching three straight lines.

17. Any number of triangles having the same base and the same vertical angle, will be circumscribed by one circle.

18. Find a point in a triangle from which two straight lines

drawn to the extremities of the base shall contain an angle equal to twice the vertical angle of the triangle. Within what limitations is this possible?

19. Given the base of a triangle, and the point from which the perpendiculars on its three sides are equal, construct the triangle. To what limitation is the position of this point subject in order that the triangle may lie on the same side of the base?

20. From any point B in the radius CA of a given circle whose center is C, a straight line is drawn at right angles to CA meeting the circumference in D, the circle described round the triangle CBD touches the given circle in D.

21. If a circle be described about a triangle ABC, and perpendiculars be let fall from the angular points A, B, C, on the opposite sides, and produced to meet the circle in D, E, F, respectively, the circumferences EF, FD, DE, are bisected in the points A, B, C.

22. If from the angles of a triangle, lines be drawn to the points where the inscribed circle touches the sides, these lines shall intersect in the same point.

23. The straight line which bisects any angle of a triangle inscribed in a circle, cuts the circumference in a point which is equidistant from the extremities of the side opposite to the bisected angle, and from the center of a circle inscribed in the triangle.

24. Let three perpendiculars from the angles of a triangle ABC on the opposite sides meet in P, a circle described so as to pass through P and any two of the points A, B, C, is equal to the circumscribing circle of the triangle.

25. If perpendiculars Aa, Bb, Cc be drawn from the angular points of a triangle ABC upon the opposite sides, shew that they will bisect the angles of the triangle abc, and thence prove that the perimeter of abc will be less than that of any other triangle which can be inscribed in ABC.

26. Find the least triangle which can be circumscribed about a given circle.

27. If ABC be a plane triangle, GCF its circumscribing circle, and GEF a diameter perpendicular to the base AB, then if CF be joined, the angle GFC is equal to half the difference of the angles at the base of the triangle.

28. The line joining the centers of the inscribed and circumscribed circles of a triangle, subtends at any one of the angular points an angle equal to the semi-difference of the other two angles.

III

29. The locus of the centers of the circles, which are inscribed in all right-angled triangles on the same hypotenuse, is the quadrant described on the hypotenuse.

30. The center of the circle which touches the two semicircles described on the sides of a right-angled triangle is the middle point of the hypotenuse.

31. If a circle be inscribed in a right-angled triangle, the excess of the sides containing the right angle above the hypotenuse is equal to the diameter of the inscribed circle.

32. Having given the hypotenuse of a right-angled triangle, and the radius of the inscribed circle, to construct the triangle.

33. ABC is a triangle inscribed in a circle, the line joining the middle points of the arcs AB, AC, will cut off equal portions of the two contiguous sides measured from the angle A.

IV.

34. Having given the vertical angle of a triangle, and the radii of the inscribed and circumscribed circles, to construct the triangle.

35. Given the base and vertical angle of a triangle, and also the radius of the inscribed circle, required to construct it.

36. Given the three angles of a triangle, and the radius of the inscribed circle, to construct the triangle.

37. If the base and vertical angle of a plane triangle be given, prove that the locus of the centers of the inscribed circle is a circle, and find its position and magnitude.

V.

38. In a given triangle inscribe a parallelogram which shall be equal to one-half the triangle. Is there any limit to the number of such parallelograms?

39. In a given triangle to inscribe a triangle, the sides of which shall be parallel to the sides of a given triangle.

40. If any number of parallelograms be inscribed in a given parallelogram, the diameters of all the figures shall cut one another in the same point.

41. A square is inscribed in another, the difference of the areas is twice the rectangle contained by the segments of the side which are made at the angular point of the inscribed square.

42. Inscribe an equilateral triangle in a square. (1) When the vertex of the triangle is in an angle of the square. (2) When the vertex of the triangle is in the point of bisection of a side of the square.

43. On a given straight line describe an equilateral and equiangular octagon.

VI.

44. Inscribe a circle in a rhombus.

45. Having given the distances of the centers of two equal circles which cut one another, inscribe a square in the space included between the two circumferences.

46. The square inscribed in a circle is equal to half the square described about the same circle.

47. The square is greater than any oblong inscribed in the same circle.

48. A circle having a square inscribed in it being given, to find a circle in which a regular octagon of a perimeter equal to that of the square, may be inscribed.

49. Describe a circle about a figure formed by constructing an equilateral triangle upon the base of an isosceles triangle, the vertical angle of which is four times the angle at the base.

50. A regular octagon inscribed in a circle is equal to the rectangle

contained by the sides of the squares inscribed in, and circumscribed about the circle.

51. If in any circle the side of an inscribed hexagon be produced till it becomes equal to the side of an inscribed square, a tangent drawn from the extremity, without the circle, shall be equal to the side of an inscribed octagon.

VII.

52. To describe a circle which shall touch a given circle in a given point, and also a given straight line.

53. Describe a circle touching a given straight line, and also two given circles.

54. Describe a circle which shall touch a given circle, and each of two given straight lines.

55. Two points are given, one in each of two given circles, describe a circle passing through both points and touching one of the circles.

56. Describe a circle touching a straight line in a given point, and also touching a given circle. When the line cuts the given circle, shew that your construction will enable you to obtain six circles touching the given circle and the given line, but not necessarily in the given point.

57. Describe a circle which shall touch two sides and pass through one angle of a given square.

58. If two circles touch each other externally, describe a circle which shall touch one of them in a given point, and also touch the other. In what case does this become impossible?

59. Describe three circles touching each other and having their centers at three given points. In how many different ways may this be done?

VIII.

60. Let two straight lines be drawn from any point within a circle to the circumference; describe a circle, which shall touch them both, and the arc between them.

61. In a given triangle having inscribed a circle inscribe another circle in the space thus intercepted at one of the angles.

62. Let AB, AC be the bounding radii of a quadrant, complete the square $ABDC$ and draw the diagonal AD, then the part of the diagonal without the quadrant will be equal to the radius of a circle inscribed in the quadrant.

63. If on one of the bounding radii of a quadrant, a semicircle be described, and on the other, another semicircle be described, so as to touch the former and the quadrantal arc; find the center of the circle inscribed in the figure bounded by the three curves.

64. In a given segment of a circle inscribe an isosceles triangle, such that its vertex may be in the middle of the chord, and the base and perpendicular together equal to a given line.

65. Inscribe three circles in an isosceles triangle touching each other, and each of them touching two of the three sides of the triangle.

IX.

66. In the fig. Prop. 10, Book IV., shew that the base BD is the

side of a regular decagon inscribed in the larger circle, and the side of a regular pentagon inscribed in the smaller circle.

67. In the fig. Prop 10, Book IV., produce DC to meet the circle in F, and draw BF, then the angle ABF shall be equal to three times the angle BFD.

68 If the alternate angles of a regular pentagon be joined, the figure formed by the intersection of the joining lines will itself be a regular pentagon

69 If $ABCDE$ be any pentagon inscribed in a circle, and AC, BD, CE, DA, EB be joined, then are the angles ABE, BCA, CDB, DEC, EAD, together equal to two right angles

70. A watch-ribbon is folded up into a flat knot of five edges, shew that the sides of the knot form an equilateral pentagon.

71. If from the extremities of the side of a regular pentagon inscribed in a circle, straight lines be drawn to the middle of the arc subtended by the adjacent side, their difference is equal to the radius; the sum of their squares to three times the square of the radius; and the rectangle contained by them is equal to the square of the radius.

72. Inscribe a regular pentagon in a given square so that four angles of the pentagon may touch respectively the four sides of the square.

73 Inscribe a regular decagon in a given circle.

74 The square described upon the side of a regular pentagon in a circle, is equal to the square of the side of a regular hexagon, together with the square upon the side of a regular decagon in the same circle.

X.

75. In a given circle inscribe three equal circles touching each other and the given circle

76 Shew that if two circles be inscribed in a third to touch one another, the tangents of the points of contact will all meet in the same point.

77. If there be three concentric circles, whose radii are 1, 2, 3; determine how many circles may be described round the interior one, having their centers in the circumference of the circle, whose radius is 2, and touching the interior and exterior circles, and each other.

78. Shew that nine equal circles may be placed in contact, so that a square whose side is three times the diameter of one of them will circumscribe them.

XI.

79. Produce the sides of a given heptagon both ways, till they meet, forming seven triangles; required the sum of their vertical angles.

80 To convert a given regular polygon into another which shall have the same perimeter, but double the number of sides.

81. In any polygon of an even number of sides, inscribed in a circle, the sum of the 1st, 3rd, 5th, &c angles is equal to the sum of the 2nd, 4th, 6th, &c.

82 Of all polygons having equal perimeters, and the same number of sides, the equilateral polygon has the greatest area.

BOOK V.

DEFINITIONS.

I.

A LESS magnitude is said to be *a part* of a greater magnitude, when the less measures the greater, that is 'when the less is contained a certain number of times exactly in the greater.'

II

A greater magnitude is said to be a multiple of a less, when the greater is measured by the less, that is, 'when the greater contains the less a certain number of times exactly'

III

"Ratio is a mutual relation of two magnitudes of the same kind to one another, in respect of quantity"

IV.

Magnitudes are said to have a ratio to one another, when the less can be multiplied so as to exceed the other.

V.

The first of four magnitudes is said to have the same ratio to the second, which the third has to the fourth, when any equimultiples whatsoever of the first and third being taken, and any equimultiples whatsoever of the second and fourth, if the multiple of the first be less than that of the second, the multiple of the third is also less than that of the fourth; or, if the multiple of the first be equal to that of the second, the multiple of the third is also equal to that of the fourth or, if the multiple of the first be greater than that of the second, the multiple of the third is also greater than that of the fourth.

VI

Magnitudes which have the same ratio are called proportionals.

N B 'When four magnitudes are proportionals, it is usually expressed by saying, the first is to the second, as the third to the fourth'

VII.

When of the equimultiples of four magnitudes, (taken as in the fifth definition,) the multiple of the first is greater than that of the second, but the multiple of the third is not greater than the multiple of the fourth, then the first is said to have to the second a greater ratio than the third magnitude has to the fourth; and on the contrary, the third is said to have to the fourth a less ratio than the first has to the second.

VIII.

"Analogy, or proportion, is the similitude of ratios."

IX.

Proportion consists in three terms at least.

X.

When three magnitudes are proportionals, the first is said to have to third, the duplicate ratio of that which it has to the second.

XI.

When four magnitudes are continual proportionals, the first is said to have to the fourth, the triplicate ratio of that which it has to the second, and so on, quadruplicate, &c. increasing the denomination still by unity, in any number of proportionals.

Definition A, to wit, of compound ratio.

When there are any number of magnitudes of the same kind, the first is said to have to the last of them the ratio compounded of the ratio which the first has to the second, and of the ratio which the second has to the third, and of the ratio which the third has to the fourth, and so on unto the last magnitude.

For example, if A, B, C, D be four magnitudes of the same kind, the first A is said to have to the last D, the ratio compounded of the ratio of A to B, and of the ratio of B to C, and of the ratio of C to D; or, the ratio of A to D is said to be compounded of the ratios of A to B, B to C, and C to D.

And if A has to B the same ratio which E has to F; and B to C the same ratio that G has to H; and C to D the same that K has to L; then, by this definition, A is said to have to D the ratio compounded of ratios which are the same with the ratios of E to F, G to H, and K to L. And the same thing is to be understood when it is more briefly expressed by saying, A has to D the ratio compounded of the ratios of E to F, G to H, and K to L.

In like manner, the same things being supposed, if M has to N the same ratio which A has to D; then, for shortness' sake, M is said to have to N the ratio compounded of the ratios of E to F, G to H, and K to L.

XII.

In proportionals, the antecedent terms are called homologous to one another, as also the consequents to one another.

'Geometers make use of the following technical words, to signify certain ways of changing either the order or magnitude of proportionals, so that they continue still to be proportionals.'

XIII.

Permutando, or alternando by permutation, or alternately. This word is used when there are four proportionals, and it is inferred that the first has the same ratio to the third which the second has to the fourth; or that the first is to the third as the second to the fourth: as is shewn in Prop. XVI. of this Fifth Book.

XIV.

Invertendo, by inversion; when there are four proportionals, and it is inferred, that the second is to the first, as the fourth to the third. Prop. B. Book v.

XV

Componendo, by composition; when there are four proportionals, and it is inferred that the first together with the second is to the second as the third together with the fourth, is to the fourth. Prop 18, Book v

XVI

Dividendo, by division, when there are four proportionals, and it is inferred, that the excess of the first above the second, is to the second, as the excess of the third above the fourth, is to the fourth. Prop 17, Book v

XVII

Convertendo, by conversion when there are four proportionals, and it is inferred, that the first is to its excess above the second, as the third to its excess above the fourth. Prop E Book v

XVIII

Ex æquali (sc distantia), or ex æquo, from equality of distance when there is any number of magnitudes more than two, and as many others such that they are proportionals when taken two and two of each rank and it is inferred that the first is to the last of the first rank of magnitudes as the first is to the last of the others 'Of this there are the two following kinds which arise from the different order in which the magnitudes are taken two and two'

XIX

Ex æquali, from equality This term is used simply by itself, when the first magnitude is to the second of the first rank as the first to the second of the other rank and as the second is to the third of the first rank, so is the second to the third of the other, and so on in order and the inference is as mentioned in the preceding definition; whence this is called ordinate proportion. It is demonstrated in Prop 22, Book v.

XX

Ex æquali in proportione perturbata seu inordinata from equality in perturbate or disorderly proportion This term is used when the first magnitude is to the second of the first rank, as the last but one is to the last of the second rank, and as the second is to the third of the first rank so is the last but two to the last but one of the second rank and as the third is to the fourth of the first rank, so is the third from the last to the last but two of the second rank, and so on in a cross order and the inference is as in the 18th definition. It is demonstrated in Prop. 23. Book v

---

AXIOMS

I

EQUIMULTIPLES of the same, or of equal magnitudes, are equal to one another

II

Those magnitudes, of which the same or equal magnitudes are equimultiples, are equal to one another.

* Prop 4. Lib II Archimedis de sphæra et cylindro

III.

A multiple of a greater magnitude is greater than the same multiple of a less.

IV.

That magnitude, of which a multiple is greater than the same multiple of another, is greater than that other magnitude.

PROPOSITION I THEOREM

If any number of magnitudes be equimultiples of as many, each of each; what multiple soever any one of them is of its part, the same multiple shall all the first magnitudes be of all the other.

Let any number of magnitudes AB, CD be equimultiples of as many others E, F, each of each.

Then whatsoever multiple AB is of E, the same multiple shall AB and CD together be of E and F together.

```
A    G    B              C    H    D
|_____|              |_____|

E──                      F─────
```

Because AB is the same multiple of E that CD is of F,
as many magnitudes as there are in AB equal to E, so many are there in CD equal to F.
Divide AB into magnitudes equal to E, viz. AG, GB,
and CD into CH, HD, equal each of them to F;
therefore the number of the magnitudes CH, HD shall be equal to the number of the others AG, GB,
and because AG is equal to E, and CH to F,
therefore AG and CH together are equal to E and F together; (1 ax 2)
for the same reason, because GB is equal to F, and HD to F,
GB and HD together are equal to E and F together;
wherefore as many magnitudes as there are in AB equal to E,
so many are there in AB, CD together, equal to E and F together:
therefore, whatsoever multiple AB is of E,
the same multiple is AB and CD together, of E and F together.

Therefore, if any magnitudes, how many soever, be equimultiples of as many, each of each, whatsoever multiple any one of them is of its part, the same multiple shall all the first magnitudes be of all the others. 'For the same demonstration holds in any number of magnitudes, which was here applied to two.' Q. E. D.

PROPOSITION II. THEOREM

If the first magnitude be the same multiple of the second that the third is of the fourth, and the fifth the same multiple of the second that the sixth is of the fourth, then shall the first together with the fifth be the same multiple of the second, that the third together with the sixth is of the fourth.

Let AB the first be the same multiple of C the second, that DE the third is of F the fourth:

and BG the fifth the same multiple of C the second, that EH the sixth is of F the fourth

Then shall AG, the first together with the fifth, be the same multiple of C the second, that DH, the third together with the sixth, is of F the fourth

```
A      B          G              D    E       H
——————————        ———             ————————    ————
C———                              F———
```

Because AB is the same multiple of C that DE is of F,
there are as many magnitudes in AB equal to C, as there are in DE equal to F.
In like manner, as many as there are in BG equal to C, so many are there in EH equal to F·
therefore as many as there are in the whole AG equal to C,
so many are there in the whole DH equal to F
therefore AG is the same multiple of C that DH is of F,
that is, AG, the first and fifth together, is the same multiple of the second C,
that DH, the third and sixth together, is of the fourth F.
If therefore, the first be the same multiple, &c. Q.E.D.

Cor. From this it is plain, that if any number of magnitudes AB, BG, GH be multiples of another C;
and as many DE, EK, KL be the same multiples of F, each of each,
then the whole of the first, viz AH, is the same multiple of C,
that the whole of the last, viz DL, is of F.

```
A      B      G       H        D     E        K         L
————————————————————————       ——————————————————————
C———                           F———
```

PROPOSITION III THEOREM

If the first be the same multiple of the second, which the third is of the fourth, and if of the first and third there be taken equimultiples; these shall be equimultiples, the one of the second, and the other of the fourth

Let A the first be the same multiple of B the second, that C the third is of D the fourth

and of A, C let equimultiples EF, GH be taken

Then EF shall be the same multiple of B, that GH is of D.

```
E     K       F               G     L      H
————————————————               ——————————————
A———                           C———
B——                            D——
```

Because EF is the same multiple of A, that GH is of C,
there are as many magnitudes in EF equal to A, as there are in GH equal to C·
let EF be divided into the magnitudes EK, KF, each equal to A;
and GH into GL, LH, each equal to C.
therefore the number of the magnitudes EK, KF shall be equal to the number of the others GL, LH.

and because A is the same multiple of B, that C is of D,
and that EK is equal to A, and GL equal to C:
therefore EK is the same multiple of B, that GL is of D:
for the same reason, KF is the same multiple of B, that LH is of D:
and so, if there be more parts in EF, GH, equal to A, C.
therefore, because the first EK is the same multiple of the second B,
which the third GL is of the fourth D,
and that the fifth KF is the same multiple of the second B, which the
sixth LH is of the fourth D;
EF the first, together with the fifth, is the same multiple of the second
B. (v. 2.)
which GH the third, together with the sixth, is of the fourth D.
If, therefore, the first, &c. Q.E.D.

PROPOSITION IV. THEOREM.

If the first of four magnitudes has the same ratio to the second which the third has to the fourth, then any equimultiples whatever of the first and third shall have the same ratio to any equimultiples of the second and fourth, viz 'the equimultiple of the first shall have the same ratio to that of the second, which the equimultiple of the third has to that of the fourth.'

Let A the first have to B the second, the same ratio which the third C has to the fourth D,
and of A and C let there be taken any equimultiples whatever E, F;
and of B and D any equimultiples whatever G, H.
Then E shall have the same ratio to G, which F has to H.

```
K ─────────────        M ─────────────
E ──────────           G ──────────
A ────                 B ────
C ──                   D ──
F ──────               H ──────
L ─────────────        N ─────────────
```

Take of E and F any equimultiples whatever K, L,
and of G, H any equimultiples whatever M, N:
then because E is the same multiple of A, that F is of C;
and of E and F have been taken equimultiples K, L;
therefore K is the same multiple of A, that L is of C. (v. 3.)
for the same reason, M is the same multiple of B, that N is of D.
And because, as A is to B, so is C to D, (hyp.)
and of A and C have been taken certain equimultiples K, L,
and of B and D have been taken certain equimultiples M, N;
therefore if K be greater than M, L is greater than N;
and if equal, equal; if less, less. (v. def. 5.)
but K, L are any equimultiples whatever of E, F, (constr.)
and M, N any whatever of G, H;
therefore as E is to G, so is F to H. (v. def. 5.)
Therefore, if the first, &c. Q.E.D.

Cor. Likewise, if the first has the same ratio to the second, which the third has to the fourth, then also any equimultiples whatever of the first and third shall have the same ratio to the second and fourth; and in like manner, the first and the third shall have the same ratio to any equimultiples whatever of the second and fourth.

Let A the first have to B the second the same ratio which the third C has to the fourth D;

and of A and C let E and F be any equimultiples whatever.

Then E shall be to B as F to D.

Take of E, F any equimultiples whatever, K, L, and of B, D any equimultiples whatever G, H:

then it may be demonstrated, as before, that K is the same multiple of A, that L is of C;

and because A is to B, as C is to D, (hyp.)

and of A and C certain equimultiples have been taken, viz. K and L;

and of B and D certain equimultiples G, H,

therefore, if K be greater than G, L is greater than H;

and if equal, equal; if less, less. (v. def. 5.)

but K, L are any equimultiples whatever of E, F, (constr.)

and G, H any whatever of B, D,

therefore as E is to B, so is F to D. (v. def. 5.)

And in the same way the other case is demonstrated.

PROPOSITION V. THEOREM.

If one magnitude be the same multiple of another, which a magnitude taken from the first is of a magnitude taken from the other, the remainder shall be the same multiple of the remainder, that the whole is of the whole.

Let the magnitude AB be the same multiple of CD, that AE taken from the first, is of CF taken from the other.

The remainder EB shall be the same multiple of the remainder FD, that the whole AB is of the whole CD.

```
G       A       E       B
|-------|-------|-------|
C       F       D
|-------|-------|
```

Take AG the same multiple of FD, that AE is of CF:

therefore AE is the same multiple of CF, that EG is of CD (v. 1.)

but AE, by the hypothesis, is the same multiple of CF, that AB is of CD,

therefore EG is the same multiple of CD that AB is of CL;

wherefore EG is equal to AB (v. ax. 1.)

take from each of them the common magnitude AE,

and the remainder AG is equal to the remainder EB.

Wherefore, since AE is the same multiple of CF, that AG is of FD (constr.)

and that AG has been proved equal to EB,

therefore AE is the same multiple of CF, that EB is of FD:

but AE is the same multiple of CF that AB is of CD (hyp.)

therefore EB is the same multiple of FD, that AB is of CD.

Therefore, if one magnitude, &c. Q.E.D.

PROPOSITION VI. THEOREM.

If two magnitudes be equimultiples of two others, and if equimultiples of these be taken from the first two, the remainders are either equal to these others, or equimultiples of them.

Let the two magnitudes AB, CD be equimultiples of the two E, F, and let AG, CH taken from the first two be equimultiples of the same E, F.

Then the remainders GB, HD shall be either equal to E, F, or equimultiples of them.

```
A    G   B            E——
‾‾‾‾‾‾‾‾‾
K   C   H   D         F——
‾‾‾‾‾‾‾‾‾‾‾‾
```

First, let GB be equal to E:
HD shall be equal to F.
Make CK equal to F:
and because AG is the same multiple of E, that CH is of F (hyp.)
and that GB is equal to E, and CK to F;
therefore AB is the same multiple of E, that KH is of F
but AB, by the hypothesis, is the same multiple of E, that CD is of F;
therefore KH is the same multiple of F, that CD is of F.
wherefore KH is equal to CD. (v. ax. 1.)
take away the common magnitude CH.
then the remainder KC is equal to the remainder HD:
but KC is equal to F (constr.)
therefore HD is equal to F.
Next let GB be a multiple of E.
Then HD shall be the same multiple of F.

```
A    G   B            E——
‾‾‾‾‾‾‾‾‾
K   C   H   D         F——
‾‾‾‾‾‾‾‾‾‾‾‾
```

Make CK the same multiple of F, that GB is of E:
and because AG is the same multiple of E, that CH is of F: (hyp.)
and GB the same multiple of E, that CK is of F;
therefore AB is the same multiple of E, that KH is of F (v. 2.)
but AB is the same multiple of E, that CD is of F, (hyp.)
therefore KH is the same multiple of F, that CD is of F,
wherefore KH is equal to CD. (v. ax. 1.)
take away CH from both;
therefore the remainder KC is equal to the remainder HD:
and because GB is the same multiple of E, that KC is of F, (constr.)
and that KC is equal to HD;
therefore HD is the same multiple of F, that GB is of E.
If, therefore, two magnitudes, &c. Q.E.D.

PROPOSITION A. THEOREM.

If the first of four magnitudes has the same ratio to the second, which the third has to the fourth; then, if the first be greater than the second, the third is also greater than the fourth; and if equal, equal; if less, less.

Take any equimultiples of each of them, as the doubles of each:
then, by def 5th of this book, if the double of the first be greater than the double of the second, the double of the third is greater than the double of the fourth

but if the first be greater than the second,
the double of the first is greater than the double of the second;
wherefore also the double of the third is greater than the double of the fourth;

therefore the third is greater than the fourth:
in like manner if the first be equal to the second, or less than it, the third can be proved to be equal to the fourth, or less than it.
Therefore, if the first, &c. Q.E.D.

PROPOSITION B. THEOREM.

If four magnitudes are proportionals, they are proportionals also when taken inversely.

Let A be to B, as C is to D
Then also inversely, B shall be to A, as D to C.

A———   B———   C———   D———
G———   E———   H———   F———

Take of B and D any equimultiples whatever E and F;
and of A and C any equimultiples whatever G and H.
First, let E be greater than G, then G is less than E:
and because A is to B, as C is to D, (hyp.)
and of A and C, the first and third, G and H are equimultiples;
and of B and D, the second and fourth, E and F are equimultiples
and that G is less than E, therefore H is less than F, (v. def. 5.)
that is, F is greater than H.
if, therefore, E be greater than G,
F is greater than H,
in like manner, if E be equal to G,
F may be shewn to be equal to H;
and if less, less,
but E, F, are any equimultiples whatever of B and D, (constr.)
and G, H any whatever of A and C;
therefore, as B is to A, so is D to C. (v. def 5.)
Therefore, if four magnitudes, &c. Q.E.D.

PROPOSITION C. THEOREM

If the first be the same multiple of the second, or the same part of it, that the third is of the fourth; the first is to the second, as the third is to the fourth.

Let the first A be the same multiple of the second B,
that the third C is of the fourth D,

BOOK V. PROP. D. 213

Then A shall be to B as C is to D.

A—— B——— C——— D———
E———— G————— F———— H—————

Take of A and C any equimultiples whatever E and F;
and of B and D any equimultiples whatever G and H.
Then, because A is the same multiple of B that C is of D; (hyp.)
and that E is the same multiple of A, that F is of C; (constr.)
therefore E is the same multiple of B, that F is of D; (v. 3.)
that is, E and F are equimultiples of B and D.
but G and H are equimultiples of B and D, (constr.)
therefore, if E be a greater multiple of B than G is of B,
F is a greater multiple of D than H is of D;
that is, if E be greater than G,
F is greater than H
in like manner, if E be equal to G, or less than it,
F may be shewn to be equal to H, or less than it,
but E, F are equimultiples, any whatever, of A, C; (constr.)
and G, H any equimultiples whatever of B, D;
therefore A is to B, as C is to D. (v. def 5.)

Next, let the first A be the same part of the second B, that the third C is of the fourth D.

Then A shall be to B, as C is to D.

A—— B——— C——— D———

For since A is the same part of B that C is of D,
therefore B is the same multiple of A, that D is of C:
wherefore, by the preceding case, B is to A, as D is to C;
and therefore inversely, A is to B, as C is to D. (v. B)
Therefore, if the first be the same multiple, &c. Q.E.D.

PROPOSITION D. THEOREM

If the first be to the second as the third to the fourth, and if the first be a multiple, or a part of the second, the third is the same multiple, or the same part of the fourth.

Let A be to B as C is to D:
and first, let A be a multiple of B.
Then C shall be the same multiple of D.

A———— B—— C——— D——
E————— F——

Take E equal to A,
and whatever multiple A or E is of B, make F the same multiple of D.
then, because A is to B, as C is to D; (hyp.)
and of B the second, and D the fourth, equimultiples have been taken, E and F;
therefore A is to E, as C to F (v. 4. Cor.)
but A is equal to E, (constr.)
therefore C is equal to F. (v. A.)

and F is the same multiple of D, that A is of B, (constr.)
therefore C is the same multiple of D, that A is of B.
Next, let A the first be a part of B the second.
Then C the third shall be the same part of D the fourth.
Because A is to B, as C is to D, (hyp.)
then, inversely, B is to A, as D to C (v. b.)

A——— B——— C——— D———

but A is a part of B, therefore B is a multiple of A (hyp.)
therefore, by the preceding case, D is the same multiple of C;
that is, C is the same part of D, that A is of B.
Therefore, if the first, &c. Q E D.

PROPOSITION VII THEOREM

Equal magnitudes have the same ratio to the same magnitude, and the same has the same ratio to equal magnitudes.

Let A and B be equal magnitudes, and C any other.
Then A and B shall each of them have the same ratio to C;
and C shall have the same ratio to each of the magnitudes A and B.

A——— B——— C———
D——— E——— F———

Take of A and B any equimultiples whatever D and E,
and of C any multiple whatever F.
Then, because D is the same multiple of A, that E is of B, (constr.)
and that A is equal to B, (hyp.)
therefore D is equal to E, (v. ax 1)
therefore, if D be greater than F, E is greater than F;
and if equal, equal; if less, less
but D, E are any equimultiples of A, B, (constr.)
and F is any multiple of C,
therefore, as A is to C, so is B to C. (v def 5)
Likewise C shall have the same ratio to A, that it has to B.
For having made the same construction,
D may in like manner be shewn to be equal to E;
therefore, if F be greater than D,
it is likewise greater than E;
and if equal, equal; if less, less;
but F is any multiple whatever of C,
and D, E are any equimultiples whatever of A, B;
therefore, C is to A as C is to B (v. def. 5.)
Therefore, equal magnitudes, &c Q E.D.

PROPOSITION VIII THEOREM.

Of two unequal magnitudes, the greater has a greater ratio to any other magnitude than the less has and the same magnitude has a greater ratio to the less of two other magnitudes, than it has to the greater.

Let AB, BC be two unequal magnitudes, of which AB is the greater,
and let D be any other magnitude,

BOOK V. PROP. VIII. 215

Then AB shall have a greater ratio to D than BC has to D: and D shall have a greater ratio to BC than it has to AB.

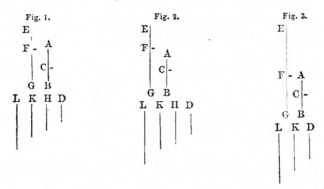

If the magnitude which is not the greater of the two AC, CB, be not less than D,
 take EF, FG, the doubles of AC, CB, (as in fig. 1.)
but if that which is not the greater of the two AC, CB, be less than D, (as in fig. 2 and 3.) this magnitude can be multiplied, so as to become greater than D, whether it be AC, or CB.
 Let it be multiplied until it become greater than D,
  and let the other be multiplied as often;
  and let EF be the multiple thus taken of AC,
  and FG the same multiple of CB:
therefore EF and FG are each of them greater than D:
 and in every one of the cases,
  take H the double of D, K its triple, and so on,
till the multiple of D be that which first becomes greater than FG:
 let L be that multiple of D which is first greater than FG,
  and K the multiple of D which is next less than L.
Then because L is the multiple of D, which is the first that becomes greater than FG,
 the next preceding multiple K is not greater than FG;
  that is, FG is not less than K:
and since EF is the same multiple of AC, that FG is of CB: (constr.)
therefore FG is the same multiple of CB, that EG is of AB; (v. 1.)
 that is, EG and FG are equimultiples of AB and CB;
 and since it was shewn, that FG is not less than K,
 and, by the construction, EF is greater than D;
therefore the whole EG is greater than K and D together:
 but K together with D is equal to L; (constr.)
  therefore EG is greater than L;
  but FG is not greater than L: (constr.)
and EG, FG were proved to be equimultiples of AB, BC;
 and L is a multiple of D; (constr.)
therefore AB has to D a greater ratio than BC has to D. (v. def. 7.)
 Also D shall have to BC a greater ratio than it has to AB.

For having made the same construction,
it may be shewn in like manner, that L is greater than FG,
but that it is not greater than EG,
and L is a multiple of D, (consti.)
and FG, EG were proved to be equimultiples of CB, AB.
therefore D has to CB a greater ratio than it has to AB. (v. def. 7.)
Wherefore, of two unequal magnitudes, &c. Q.E.D.

PROPOSITION IX. THEOREM.

Magnitudes which have the same ratio to the same magnitude are equal to one another; and those to which the same magnitude has the same ratio are equal to one another.

Let A, B have each of them the same ratio to C.
Then A shall be equal to B.

A ———   D ———
         C ———   F ———
B ———   E ———

For, if they are not equal, one of them must be greater than the other:
let A be the greater
then, by what was shewn in the preceding proposition,
there are some equimultiples of A and B, and some multiple of C, such,
that the multiple of A is greater than the multiple of C,
but the multiple of B is not greater than that of C,
let these multiples be taken;
and let D, E be the equimultiples of A, B,
and F the multiple of C,
such that D may be greater than F, but E not greater than F.
Then, because A is to C as B is to C, (hyp.)
and of A, B, are taken equimultiples, D, E.
and of C is taken a multiple F,
and that D is greater than F,
therefore E is also greater than F. (v. def. 5.)
but E is not greater than F, (consti.) which is impossible
therefore A and B are not unequal; that is, they are equal
Next, let C have the same ratio to each of the magnitudes A and B.
Then A shall be equal to B.
For, if they are not equal, one of them must be greater than the other:
let A be the greater
therefore, as was shewn in Prop. VIII.
there is some multiple F of C,
and some equimultiples E and D of B and A such,
that F is greater than E, but not greater than D:
and because C is to B, as C is to A, (hyp.)
and that F the multiple of the first, is greater than E the multiple of the second:
therefore F the multiple of the third, is greater than D the multiple of the fourth. (v. def. 5.)

but F is not greater than D (hyp.); which is impossible:
therefore A is equal to B.
Wherefore, magnitudes which, &c. Q.E.D.

PROPOSITION X. THEOREM.

That magnitude which has a greater ratio than another has unto the same magnitude, is the greater of the two, and that magnitude to which the same has a greater ratio than it has unto another magnitude, is the less of the two.

Let A have to C a greater ratio than B has to C;
then A shall be greater than B.

A——— C——— D——— F———
B——   E——

For, because A has a greater ratio to C, than B has to C,
there are some equimultiples of A and B,
and some multiple of C such, (v. def. 7.)
that the multiple of A is greater than the multiple of C,
but the multiple of B is not greater than it:
let them be taken,
and let D, E be the equimultiples of A, B, and F the multiple of C;
such, that D is greater than F, but E is not greater than F:
therefore D is greater than E:
and, because D and E are equimultiples of A and B,
and that D is greater than E;
therefore A is greater than B. (v. ax. 4.)
Next, let C have a greater ratio to B than it has to A.
Then B shall be less than A.
For there is some multiple F of C, (v. def. 7.)
and some equimultiples E and D of B and A such,
that F is greater than E, but not greater than D:
therefore E is less than D.
and because E and D are equimultiples of B and A,
and that E is less than D,
therefore B is less than A (v. ax. 4.)
Therefore, that magnitude, &c. Q.E.D.

PROPOSITION XI. THEOREM.

Ratios that are the same to the same ratio, are the same to one another.

Let A be to B as C is to D;
and as C to D, so let E be to F.
Then A shall be to B, as E to F.

G——— H——— K———
A——   C——   E——
B—   D—   F—
L——— M——— N———

Take of A, C, E, any equimultiples whatever G, H, K;

and of B, D, F any equimultiples whatever L, M, N.
Therefore, since A is to B as C to D,
and G, H are taken equimultiples of A, C,
and L, M, of B, D,
if G be greater than L, H is greater than M;
and if equal, equal, and if less, less (v. def. 5.)
Again, because C is to D, as E is to F,
and H, K are taken equimultiples of C, E;
and M, N, of D, F;
if H be greater than M, K is greater than N;
and if equal, equal; and if less, less:
but if G be greater than L,
it has been shewn that H is greater than M;
and if equal, equal, and if less, less:
therefore, if G be greater than L,
K is greater than N; and if equal, equal, and if less, less:
and G, K are any equimultiples whatever of A, E,
and L, N any whatever of B, F;
therefore, as A is to B, so is E to F. (v. def. 5.)
Wherefore, ratios that, &c. Q.F.D.

PROPOSITION XII. THEOREM.

If any number of magnitudes be proportionals, as one of the antecedents is to its consequent, so shall all the antecedents taken together be to all the consequents

Let any number of magnitudes A, B, C, D, E, F be proportionals:
that is, as A is to B, so C to D, and E to F.
Then as A is to B, so shall A, C, E together, be to B, D, F together.

```
G————        H————        K————
A———         C———         E———
B——          D——          F—
L—————       M—————       N—————
```

Take of A, C, E any equimultiples whatever G, H, K;
and of B, D, F any equimultiples whatever, L, M, N.
Then, because A is to B, as C is to D, and as E to F;
and that G, H, K are equimultiples of A, C, E,
and L, M, N, equimultiples of B, D, F;
therefore, if G be greater than L,
H is greater than M, and K greater than N;
and if equal, equal, and if less, less (v. def. 5.)
wherefore if G be greater than L,
then G, H, K together, are greater than L, M, N together;
and if equal, equal, and if less, less
but G, and G, H, K together, are any equimultiples of A, and A, C, E together;
because if there be any number of magnitudes equimultiples of as many, each of each, whatever multiple one of them is of its part, the same multiple is the whole of the whole. (v. 1.)

for the same reason L, and L, M, N are any equimultiples of B, and B, D, F:
therefore as A is to B, so are A, C, E together to B, D, F together. (v. def. 5.)

Wherefore, if any number, &c. Q.E.D.

PROPOSITION XIII. THEOREM.

If the first has to the second the same ratio which the third has to the fourth, but the third to the fourth, a greater ratio than the fifth has to the sixth; the first shall also have to the second a greater ratio than the fifth has to the sixth.

Let A the first have the same ratio to B the second, which C the third has to D the fourth, but C the third a greater ratio to D the fourth, than E the fifth has to F the sixth.

Then also the first A shall have to the second B, a greater ratio than the fifth E has to the sixth F.

```
M———      G———      H———
A——       C——       E——
B——       D——       F——
N————     K————     L————
```

Because C has a greater ratio to D, than E to F, there are some equimultiples of C and E, and some of D and F, such that the multiple of C is greater than the multiple of D, but the multiple of E is not greater than the multiple of F: (v. def. 7.)
let these be taken,
and let G, H be equimultiples of C, E,
and K, L equimultiples of D, F, such that G may be greater than K, but H not greater than L·
and whatever multiple G is of C, take M the same multiple of A;
and whatever multiple K is of D, take N the same multiple of B;
then, because A is to B, as C to D, (hyp.)
and of A and C, M and G are equimultiples;
and of B and D, N and K are equimultiples,
therefore, if M be greater than N, G is greater than K;
and if equal, equal; and if less, less. (v. def. 5.)
but G is greater than K; (constr.)
therefore M is greater than N:
but H is not greater than L· (constr.)
and M, H are equimultiples of A, E;
and N, L equimultiples of B, F;
therefore A has a greater ratio to B, than E has to F. (v. def. 7.)
Wherefore, if the first, &c. Q.E.D.

Cor. And if the first have a greater ratio to the second, than the third has to the fourth, but the third the same ratio to the fourth which the fifth has to the sixth; it may be demonstrated, in like manner, that the first has a greater ratio to the second, than the fifth has to the sixth.

PROPOSITION XIV. THEOREM.

If the first has the same ratio to the second which the third has to the fourth, then, if the first be greater than the third, the second shall be greater than the fourth, and if equal, equal, and if less, less.

Let the first A have the same ratio to the second B which the third C has to the fourth D.
If A be greater than C, B shall be greater than D. (fig. 1.)

```
    1              2              3
A ———————       A ————         A ————
B ————          B ————         B ————
C -----         C ————         C ————————
D ————          D ————         D ————
```

Because A is greater than C, and B is any other magnitude,
A has to B a greater ratio than C has to B (v. 8.)
but, as A is to B, so is C to D, (hyp.)
therefore also C has to D a greater ratio than C has to B (v. 13.)
but of two magnitudes, that to which the same has the greater ratio, is the less (v. 10.)
   therefore D is less than B,
   that is, B is greater than D.
Secondly, if A be equal to C, (fig. 2.)
   then B shall be equal to D.
   For A is to B, as C, that is, A to D:
   therefore B is equal to D (v. 9.)
Thirdly, if A be less than C, (fig. 3.)
   then B shall be less than D.
   For C is greater than A;
   and because C is to D, as A is to B,
therefore D is greater than B, by the first case;
   that is, B is less than D.
Therefore, if the first, &c. Q.E.D.

PROPOSITION XV. THEOREM.

Magnitudes have the same ratio to one another which their equimultiples have.

Let AB be the same multiple of C, that DE is of F.
Then C shall be to F, as AB is to DE.

```
A   G   H   B         D   K   L   E
|   |   |             |   |   |
C ————                F ————
```

Because AB is the same multiple of C, that DE is of F;
there are as many magnitudes in AB equal to C, as there are in DE equal to F.
let AB be divided into magnitudes, each equal to C, viz. AG, GH, HB;

and *DE* into magnitudes, each equal to *F*, viz. *DK, KL, LE*:
then the number of the first *AG, GH, HB*, is equal to the number of the last *DK, KL, LE*
and because *AG, GH, HB* are all equal,
and that *DK, KL, LE*, are also equal to one another;
therefore *AG* is to *DK*, as *GH* to *KL*, and as *HB* to *LE* (v. 7.)
but as one of the antecedents is to its consequent, so are all the antecedents together to all the consequents together, (v. 12.)
wherefore as *AG* is to *DK*, so is *AB* to *DE*:
but *AG* is equal to *C* and *DK* to *F*:
therefore, as *C* is to *F*, so is *AB* to *DE*.
Therefore, magnitudes, &c. Q.E.D.

PROPOSITION XVI. THEOREM.

If four magnitudes of the same kind be proportionals, they shall also be proportionals when taken alternately.

Let *A, B, C, D* be four magnitudes of the same kind, which are proportionals, viz. as *A* to *B*, so *C* to *D*
They shall also be proportionals when taken alternately.
that is, *A* shall be to *C*, as *B* to *D*.

```
E ─────        G ─────
A ───          C ───
B ──           D ──
F ──────       H ──────
```

Take of *A* and *B* any equimultiples whatever *E* and *F*:
and of *C* and *D* take any equimultiples whatever *G* and *H*,
and because *E* is the same multiple of *A*, that *F* is of *B*,
and that magnitudes have the same ratio to one another which their equimultiples have, (v. 15.)
therefore *A* is to *B*, as *E* is to *F*:
but as *A* is to *B* so is *C* to *D*; (hyp.)
wherefore as *C* is to *D*, so is *E* to *F*: (v. 11.)
again, because *G, H* are equimultiples of *C, D*,
therefore as *C* is to *D*, so is *G* to *H*. (v. 15.)
but it was proved that as *C* is to *D*, so is *E* to *F*;
therefore, as *E* is to *F*, so is *G* to *H*. (v. 11.)
But when four magnitudes are proportionals, if the first be greater than the third, the second is greater than the fourth;
and if equal, equal; if less, less. (v. 14.)
therefore, if *E* be greater than *G*, *F* likewise is greater than *H*;
and if equal, equal, if less, less:
and *E, F* are any equimultiples whatever of *A, B*; (constr.)
and *G, H* any whatever of *C, D*.
therefore *A* is to *C*, as *B* to *D*. (v. def. 5.)
If then four magnitudes, &c. Q.E.D.

PROPOSITION XVII. THEOREM.

If magnitudes, taken jointly, be proportionals, they shall also be proportionals when taken separately: that is, if two magnitudes together have to one of them, the same ratio which two others have to one of these, the remaining one of the first two shall have to the other, the same ratio which the remaining one of the last two has to the other of these.

Let AB, BE, CD, DF be the magnitudes, taken jointly which are proportionals,
  that is, as AB to BE, so let CD be to DF.
Then they shall also be proportionals taken separately,
  viz. as AE to EB, so shall CF be to FD.

```
G     H   K       X           L     M   N       P
|-----|---|-------|           |-----|---|-------|

A     E B                     C     F D
|-----|-|                     |-----|-|
```

Take of AE, EB, CF, FD any equimultiples whatever GH, HK, LM, MN:
and again, of EB, FD take any equimultiples whatever KX, NP.
Then because GH is the same multiple of AE, that HK is of EB,
therefore GH is the same multiple of AE, that GK is of AB, (v. 1.)
but GH is the same multiple of AE, that LM is of CF:
therefore GK is the same multiple of AB, that LM is of CF.
Again, because LM is the same multiple of CF, that MN is of FD;
therefore LM is the same multiple of CF, that LN is of CD: (v. 1.)
but LM was shewn to be the same multiple of CF, that GK is of AB;
therefore GK is the same multiple of AB, that LN is of CD,
  that is, GK, LN are equimultiples of AB, CD.
Next, because HK is the same multiple of EB, that MN is of FD;
and that KX is also the same multiple of EB, that NP is of FD;
therefore HX is the same multiple of EB, that MP is of FD (v. 2.)
And because AB is to BE, as CD is to DF, (hyp.)
and that of AB and CD, GK and LN are equimultiples,
and of EB and FD, HX and MP are equimultiples;
therefore if GK be greater than HX, then LN is greater than MP;
and if equal, equal; and if less, less. (v. def. 5.)
  but if GH be greater than KX,
then, by adding the common part HK to both,
  GK is greater than HX; (1 ax. 4.)
wherefore also LN is greater than MP;
and by taking away MN from both,
  LM is greater than NP. (1 ax. 5.)
therefore, if GH be greater than KX,
  LM is greater than NP.
In like manner it may be demonstrated,
  that if GH be equal to KX,
LM is equal to NP; and if less, less:
but GH, LM are any equimultiples whatever of AE, CF, (constr.)
and KX, NP are any whatever of EB, FD:
therefore as AE is to EB, so is CF to FD. (v. def. 5.)
  If then magnitudes, &c.   Q.E.D.

PROPOSITION XVIII. THEOREM.

If magnitudes, taken separately, be proportionals, they shall also be proportionals when taken jointly; that is, if the first be to the second, as the third to the fourth, the first and second together shall be to the second, as the third and fourth together to the fourth.

Let AE, EB, CF, FD be proportionals;
that is, as AE to EB, so let CF be to FD.
Then they shall also be proportionals when taken jointly;
that is, as AB to BE, so shall CD be to DF.

```
G       K  O  H          L       N P M
|       |  |  |          |       | | |
A  E B                   C  F D
   |                        |
```

Take of AB, BE, CD, DF any equimultiples whatever GH, HK, LM, MN;
and again, of BE, DF take any equimultiples whatever KO, NP:
and because KO, NP are equimultiples of BE, DF;
and that KH, NM are likewise equimultiples of BE, DF;
therefore, if KO, the multiple of BE, be greater than KH, which is a multiple of the same BE,
then NP, the multiple of DF, is also greater than NM, the multiple of the same DF,
and if KO be equal to KH,
NP is equal to NM; and if less, less.
First, let KO be not greater than KH,
therefore NP is not greater than NM:
and because GH, HK, are equimultiples of AB, BE,
and that AB is greater than BE,
therefore GH is greater than HK; (v. ax. 3.)
but KO is not greater than KH,
therefore GH is greater than KO.
In like manner it may be shewn, that LM is greater than NP.
Therefore, if KO be not greater than KH,
then GH, the multiple of AB, is always greater than KO, the multiple of BE,
and likewise LM, the multiple of CD, is greater than NP, the multiple of DF.
Next, let KO be greater than KH,
therefore, as has been shewn, NP is greater than NM.

```
G       K  H  O          L       N M P
|       |  |  |          |       | | |
A  E B                   C  F D
   |                        |
```

And because the whole GH is the same multiple of the whole AB, that HK is of BE,
therefore the remainder GK is the same multiple of the remainder AE that GH is of AB, (v. 5.)
which is the same that LM is of CD.

In like manner, because LM is the same multiple of CD, that MN is of DE,

therefore the remainder LN is the same multiple of the remainder CF, that the whole LM is of the whole CD: (v. 5.)
but it was shewn that LM is the same multiple of CD, that GK is of AE;
therefore GK is the same multiple of AE, that LN is of CF;
that is, GK, LN are equimultiples of AE, CF.

And because KO, NP are equimultiples of BE, DF,
therefore if from KO, NP there be taken KH, NM, which are likewise equimultiples of BE, DF,
the remainders HO, MP are either equal to BE, DF, or equimultiples of them. (v. 6.)

First, let HO, MP be equal to BE, DF:
then because AE is to EB, as CF to FD, (hyp.)
and that GK, LN are equimultiples of AE, CF;
therefore GK is to EB, as LN to FD: (v. 4. Cor.)
but HO is equal to EB, and MP to FD;
wherefore GK is to HO, as LN to MP;
therefore if GK be greater than HO, LN is greater than MP; (v. A.)
and if equal, equal; and if less, less.

But let HO, MP be equimultiples of EB, FD.
Then because AE is to EB, as CF to FD, (hyp.)

```
G    K   H   O        L    N   M   P
─────────                 ─────────
A  E  B               C   F D
─────                 ─────
```

and that of AE, CF are taken equimultiples GK, LN;
and of EB, FD, the equimultiples HO, MP;
if GK be greater than HO, LN is greater than MP;
and if equal, equal; and if less, less; (v. def. 5.)
which was likewise shewn in the preceding case.

But if GH be greater than KO,
taking KH from both, GK is greater than HO; (I. ax. 5.)
wherefore also LN is greater than MP;
and consequently adding NM to both,
LM is greater than NP: (I. ax. 4.)
therefore, if GH be greater than KO,
LM is greater than NP.

In like manner it may be shewn, that if GH be equal to KO,
LM is equal to NP; and if less, less.

And in the case in which KO is not greater than KH,
it has been shewn that GH is always greater than KO,
and likewise LM greater than NP:
but GH, LM are any equimultiples whatever of AB, CD, (constr.)
and KO, NP are any whatever of BE, DF;
therefore, as AB is to BE, so is CD to DF. (v. def. 5.)

If then magnitudes, &c.   Q.E.D.

PROPOSITION XIX. THEOREM.

If a whole magnitude be to a whole, as a magnitude taken from the first is to a magnitude taken from the other; the remainder shall be to the remainder as the whole to the whole.

Let the whole AB be to the whole CD, as AE a magnitude taken from AB is to CF a magnitude taken from CD.
Then the remainder EB shall be to the remainder FD, as the whole AB to the whole CD.

```
A      E        B
─────────────────
C        F     D
─────────────────
```

Because AB is to CD, as AE to CF:
therefore alternately, BA is to AE, as DC to CF: (v. 16.)
and because if magnitudes taken jointly be proportionals, they are also proportionals, when taken separately; (v. 17.)
therefore, as BE is to EA, so is DF to FC;
and alternately, as BE is to DF, so is EA to FC:
but, as AE to CF, so, by the hypothesis, is AB to CD;
therefore also BE the remainder is to the remainder DF, as the whole AB to the whole CD. (v. 11.)
Wherefore, if the whole, &c. Q.E.D.

COR.—If the whole be to the whole, as a magnitude taken from the first is to a magnitude taken from the other, the remainder shall likewise be to the remainder, as the magnitude taken from the first to that taken from the other. The demonstration is contained in the preceding.

PROPOSITION E. THEOREM.

If four magnitudes be proportionals, they are also proportionals by conversion; that is, the first is to its excess above the second, as the third to its excess above the fourth.

Let AB be to BE, as CD to DF.
Then BA shall be to AE, as DC to CF.

```
A      E        B
─────────────────
C        F     D
─────────────────
```

Because AB is to BE, as CD to DF,
therefore by division, AE is to EB, as CF to FD; (v. 17.)
and by inversion, BE is to EA, as DF is to CF; (v. B.)
wherefore, by composition, BA is to AE, as DC is to CF. (v. 18.)
If therefore four, &c. Q.E.D.

PROPOSITION XX. THEOREM.

If there be three magnitudes, and other three, which, taken two and two, have the same ratio, then if the first be greater than the third, the fourth shall be greater than the sixth, and if equal, equal, and if less, less.

Let A, B, C be three magnitudes, and D, E, F other three, which taken two and two have the same ratio,
viz. as A is to B, so is D to E;
and as B to C, so is E to F.
If A be greater than C, D shall be greater than F;
and if equal, equal; and if less, less.

A——— B——— C———
D——— E——— F———

Because A is greater than C, and B is any other magnitude, and that the greater has to the same magnitude a greater ratio than the less has to it; (v. 8.)
therefore A has to B a greater ratio than C has to B:
but as D is to E, so is A to B, (hyp.)
therefore D has to E a greater ratio than C to B: (v. 13.)
and because B is to C, as E to F,
by inversion, C is to B, as F is to E (v. B.)
and D was shewn to have to E a greater ratio than C to B:
therefore D has to E a greater ratio than F to E. (v. 13 Cor.)
but the magnitude which has a greater ratio than another to the same magnitude, is the greater of the two. (v. 10.)
therefore D is greater than F.
Secondly, let A be equal to C.
Then D shall be equal to F.

A——— B——— C———
D——— E——— F———

Because A and C are equal to one another,
A is to B, as C is to B. (v. 7.)
but A is to B, as D to E, (hyp.)
and C is to B, as F to E; (hyp.)
wherefore D is to E, as F to E: (v. 11. and v. B.)
and therefore D is equal to F. (v. 9.)
Next, let A be less than C.
Then D shall be less than F.

A——— B——— C———
D——— E——— F———

For C is greater than A;
and as was shewn in the first case, C is to B, as F to E,
and in like manner, B is to A, as E to D;
therefore F is greater than D, by the first case;
that is, D is less than F.
Therefore, if there be three, &c.   Q.E.D.

PROPOSITION XXI. THEOREM.

If there be three magnitudes, and other three, which have the same ratio taken two and two, but in a cross order, then if the first magnitude be greater than the third, the fourth shall be greater than the sixth, and if equal, equal, and if less, less.

Let A, B, C be three magnitudes, and D, E, F other three, which have the same ratio, taken two and two, but in a cross order,
viz. as A is to B so is E to F,
and as B is to C, so is D to E.
If A be greater than C, D shall be greater than F;
and if equal, equal; and if less, less.

```
A——    B——    C——
D——    E——    F——
```

Because A is greater than C, and B is any other magnitude,
A has to B a greater ratio than C has to B: (v. 8.)
but as E to F, so is A to B, (hyp.)
therefore E has to F a greater ratio than C to B (v. 13.)
and because B is to C, as D to E; (hyp.)
by inversion, C is to B, as E to D:
and E was shewn to have to F a greater ratio than C has to B;
therefore E has to F a greater ratio than E has to D (v. 13. Cor.)
but the magnitude to which the same has a greater ratio than it has to another, is the less of the two. (v. 10.)
therefore F is less than D;
that is, D is greater than F.
Secondly, let A be equal to C,
D shall be equal to F.

```
A——    B——    C——
D——    E——    F——
```

Because A and C are equal,
A is to B, as C is to B. (v. 7.)
but A is to B, as E to F, (hyp.)
and C is to B, as E to D;
wherefore E is to F, as E to D, (v. 11.)
and therefore D is equal to F. (v. 9.)
Next, let A be less than C,
D shall be less than F.

```
A——    B——    C——
D——    E——    F——
```

For C is greater than A,
and as was shewn, C is to B, as E to D,
and in like manner, B is to A, as F to E;
therefore F is greater than D, by case first;
that is, D is less than F.
Therefore, if there be three, &c. Q.E.D.

PROPOSITION XXII. THEOREM.

If there be any number of magnitudes, and as many others which taken two and two in order, have the same ratio, the first shall have to the last of the first magnitudes, the same ratio which the first has to the last of the others. N.B. This is usually cited by the words "ex aequali," or "ex aequo."

First, let there be three magnitudes A, B, C, and as many others D, E, F, which taken two and two in order, have the same ratio
that is, such that A is to B, as D to E;
and as B is to C, so is E to F.
Then A shall be to C, as D to F.

```
G————        K————        M————
A————        B————        C————
D————        E————        Γ————
H————        L————        N————
```

Take of A and D any equimultiples whatever G and H;
and of B and E any equimultiples whatever K and L;
and of C and F any whatever M and N:
then because A is to B, as D to E,
and that G, H are equimultiples of A, D,
and K, L equimultiples of B, E;
therefore as G is to K, so is H to L. (v. 4.)
for the same reason, K is to M as L to N
and because there are three magnitudes G, K, M, and other three H, L, N, which two and two have the same ratio;
therefore if G be greater than M, H is greater than N;
and if equal, equal; and if less, less. (v. 20.)
but G, H are any equimultiples whatever of A, D,
and M, N are any equimultiples whatever of C, F. (constr.)
therefore, as A is to C, so is D to F. (v. def. 5.)
Next, let there be four magnitudes A, B, C, D,
and other four E, F, G, H, which two and two have the same ratio,
viz. as A is to B, so is E to F;
and as B to C, so F to G;
and as C to D, so G to H
Then A shall be to D, as E to H.

```
A . B . C . D
E   F  G . H
```

Because A, B, C are three magnitudes, and E, F, G other three, which taken two and two, have the same ratio;
therefore by the foregoing case, A is to C, as E to G:
but C is to D, as G is to H;
wherefore again, by the first case A is to D, as E to H:
and so on, whatever be the number of magnitudes.
Therefore, if there be any number, &c. Q.E.D.

PROPOSITION XXIII THEOREM.

If there be any number of magnitudes, and as many others, which taken two and two in a cross order, have the same ratio, the first shall have to the last of the first magnitudes the same ratio which the first has to the last of the others. N.B. This is usually cited by the words "ex æquali in proportione perturbatâ;" or "ex æquo perturbato."

First, let there be three magnitudes A, B, C, and other three D, E, F, which taken two and two in a cross order have the same ratio,
that is, such that A is to B, as E to F,
and as B is to C, so is D to E.
Then A shall be to C, as D to F.

```
G ———       H ———       L ———
A ———       B ———       C ———
D ——        E ——        F ——
K ————      M ————      N ————
```

Take of A, B, D any equimultiples whatever G, H, K;
and of C, E, F any equimultiples whatever L, M, N:
and because G, H are equimultiples of A, B,
and that magnitudes have the same ratio which their equimultiples have, (v. 15.)
therefore as A is to B, so is G to H:
and for the same reason, as E is to F, so is M to N:
but as A is to B, so is E to F; (hyp.)
therefore as G is to H, so is M to N: (v. 11.)
and because as B is to C, so is D to E, (hyp.)
and that H, K are equimultiples of B, D, and L, M of C, E;
therefore as H is to L, so is K to M. (v. 4.)
and it has been shewn that G is to H, as M to N:
therefore, because there are three magnitudes G, H, L, and other three K, M, N, which have the same ratio taken two and two in a cross order,
if G be greater than L, K is greater than N:
and if equal, equal, and if less, less: (v. 21.)
but G, K are any equimultiples whatever of A, D; (constr.)
and L, N any whatever of C, F;
therefore as A is to C, so is D to F. (v. def. 5.)

Next, let there be four magnitudes A, B, C, D, and other four E, F, G, H, which taken two and two in a cross order have the same ratio,
viz. A to B, as G to H;
B to C, as F to G,
and C to D, as E to F.
Then A shall be to D, as E to H.

```
| A B C D |
| E F G H |
```

Because A, B, C are three magnitudes, and F, G, H other three, which taken two and two in a cross order, have the same ratio;

by the first case, A is to C, as F to H;
but C is to D, as E is to F,
wherefore again, by the first case, A is to D, as E to H;
and so on, whatever be the number of magnitudes.
Therefore, if there be any number, &c. Q.E.D.

PROPOSITION XXIV. THEOREM.

If the first has to the second the same ratio which the third has to the fourth, and the fifth to the second the same ratio which the sixth has to the fourth, the first and fifth together shall have to the second, the same ratio which the third and sixth together have to the fourth.

Let AB the first have to C the second the same ratio which DE the third has to F the fourth,
and let BG the fifth have to C the second the same ratio which EH the sixth has to F the fourth
Then AG, the first and fifth together, shall have to C the second, the same ratio which DH, the third and sixth together, has to F the fourth.

```
A       B   G       D       E   H
|-------|---|       |-------|---|

C----           F----
```

Because BG is to C, as EH to F;
by inversion, C is to BG, as F to EH: (v. B.)
and because, as AB is to C, so is DE to F; (hyp.)
and as C to BG, so is F to EH,
ex æquali, AB is to BG, as DE to EH: (v. 22.)
and because these magnitudes are proportionals when taken separately, they are likewise proportionals when taken jointly, (v. 18.)
therefore as AG is to GB, so is DH to HE:
but as GB to C, so is HE to F: (hyp.)
therefore, ex æquali, as AG is to C, so is DH to F. (v. 22.)
Wherefore, if the first, &c. Q.E.D.

Cor. 1.—If the same hypothesis be made as in the proposition, the excess of the first and fifth shall be to the second, as the excess of the third and sixth to the fourth The demonstration of this is the same with that of the proposition, if division be used instead of composition.

Cor. 2.—The proposition holds true of two ranks of magnitudes, whatever be their number, of which each of the first rank has to the second magnitude the same ratio that the corresponding one of the second rank has to a fourth magnitude as is manifest.

PROPOSITION XXV. THEOREM.

If four magnitudes of the same kind are proportionals, the greatest and least of them together are greater than the other two together.

Let the four magnitudes AB, CD, E, F be proportionals.
viz. AB to CD, as E to F;
and let AB be the greatest of them, and consequently F the least.
(v. 14. and A.)

Then AB together with F shall be greater than CD together with E.

```
A     G   B        C   H   D
E————              F————
```

Take AG equal to E, and CH equal to F.
Then because as AB is to CD, so is E to F,
and that AG is equal to E, and CH equal to F,
therefore AB is to CD, as AG to CH: (v. 11, and 7.)
and because AB the whole, is to the whole CD, as AG is to CH,
likewise the remainder GB is to the remainder HD, as the whole AB is to the whole CD: (v. 19.)
but AB is greater than CD; (hyp.)
therefore GB is greater than HD: (v. A.)
and because AG is equal to E, and CH to F;
AG and F together are equal to CH and E together (I. ax. 2.)
therefore if to the unequal magnitudes GB, HD, of which GB is the greater, there be added equal magnitudes, viz. to GB the two AG and F, and CH and E to HD;
AB and F together are greater than CD and E. (I. ax. 4.)
Therefore, if four magnitudes, &c. Q. E. D.

PROPOSITION F. THEOREM.

Ratios which are compounded of the same ratios, are the same to one another.

Let A be to B, as D to E, and B to C, as E to F.
Then the ratio which is compounded of the ratios of A to B, and B to C,
which, by the definition of compound ratio, is the ratio of A to C,
shall be the same with the ratio of D to F, which, by the same definition, is compounded of the ratios of D to E, and E to F.

```
A . B . C
D . E . F
```

Because there are three magnitudes A, B, C, and three others D, E, F, which, taken two and two, in order, have the same ratio;
ex æquali, A is to C, as D to F. (v. 22.)
Next, let A be to B, as E to F, and B to C, as D to E:

```
A . B . C
D . E . F
```

therefore, *ex æquali in proportione perturbata*, (v. 23.)
A is to C, as D to F.
that is, the ratio of A to C, which is compounded of the ratios of A to B, and B to C, is the same with the ratio of D to F, which is compounded of the ratios of D to E, and E to F.

And in like manner the proposition may be demonstrated, whatever be the number of ratios in either case.

PROPOSITION G. THEOREM.

If several ratios be the same to several ratios, each to each, the ratio which is compounded of ratios which are the same to the first ratios, each to each, shall be the same to the ratio compounded of ratios which are the same to the other ratios, each to each.

Let A be to B, as E to F; and C to D, as G to H:
and let A be to B, as K to L; and C to D, as L to M.

Then the ratio of K to M,
by the definition of compound ratio, is compounded of the ratios of K to L, and L to M, which are the same with the ratios of A to B and C to D.

Again, as E to F, so let N be to O; and as G to H, so let O be to P.

Then the ratio of N to P is compounded of the ratios of N to O, and O to P, which are the same with the ratios of E to F, and G to H:

and it is to be shewn that the ratio of K to M, is the same with the ratio of N to P;

or that K is to M, as N to P.

```
A B C D K L M
E F G H N O P
```

Because K is to L, as (A to B, that is, as E to F, that is, as) N to O:
and as L to M, so is (C to D, and so is G to H, and so is) O to P:
ex æquali, K is to M, as N to P. (v. 22.)

Therefore, if several ratios, &c. Q.E.D.

PROPOSITION H. THEOREM.

If a ratio which is compounded of several ratios be the same to a ratio which is compounded of several other ratios; and if one of the first ratios, or the ratio which is compounded of several of them, be the same to one of the last ratios, or to the ratio which is compounded of several of them; then the remaining ratio of the first, or, if there be more than one, the ratio compounded of the remaining ratios, shall be the same to the remaining ratio of the last, or, if there be more than one, to the ratio compounded of these remaining ratios.

Let the first ratios be those of A to B, B to C, C to D, D to E, and E to F;
and let the other ratios be those of G to H, H to K, K to L, and L to M:

also, let the ratio of A to F, which is compounded of the first ratios, be the same with the ratio of G to M, which is compounded of the other ratios;

and besides, let the ratio of A to D, which is compounded of the ratios of A to B, B to C, C to D, be the same with the ratio of G to K, which is compounded of the ratios of G to H, and H to K.

Then the ratio compounded of the remaining first ratios, to wit, of the ratios of D to E, and E to F, which compounded ratio is the ratio of D to F, shall be the same with the ratio of K to M, which is compounded of the remaining ratios of K to L, and L to M of the other ratios.

```
A . B . C . D . E . F
G . H . K . L . M
```

Because, by the hypothesis, A is to D, as G to K,
by inversion, D is to A, as K to G; (v. B.)
and as A is to F, so is G to M; (hyp.)
therefore, ex æquali, D is to F, as K to M. (v. 22.)
If, therefore, a ratio which is, &c. Q.E.D.

PROPOSITION K. THEOREM.

If there be any number of ratios, and any number of other ratios, such, that the ratio which is compounded of ratios which are the same to the first ratios, each to each, is the same to the ratio which is compounded of ratios which are the same, each to each, to the last ratios; and if one of the first ratios, or the ratio which is compounded of ratios which are the same to several of the first ratios, each to each, be the same to one of the last ratios, or to the ratio which is compounded of ratios which are the same, each to each, to several of the last ratios; then the remaining ratio of the first, or, if there be more than one, the ratio which is compounded of ratios which are the same each to each to the remaining ratios of the first, shall be the same to the remaining ratio of the last, or, if there be more than one, to the ratio which is compounded of ratios which are the same each to each to these remaining ratios.

Let the ratios of A to B, C to D, E to F, be the first ratios:
and the ratios of G to H, K to L, M to N, O to P, Q to R, be the other ratios:
and let A be to B, as S to T; and C to D, as T to V; and E to F, as V to X:
therefore, by the definition of compound ratio, the ratio of S to X is compounded of the ratios of S to T, T to V, and V to X, which are the same to the ratios of A to B, C to D, E to F: each to each.

Also, as G to H, so let Y be to Z; and K to L, as Z to a;
M to N, as a to b; O to P, as b to c; and Q to R, as c to d:
therefore, by the same definition, the ratio of Y to d is compounded of the ratios of Y to Z, Z to a, a to b, b to c, and c to d, which are the same, each to each, to the ratios of G to H, K to L, M to N, O to P and Q to R:

therefore, by the hypothesis, S is to X, as Y to d.

Also, let the ratio of A to B, that is, the ratio of S to T, which is one of the first ratios, be the same to the ratio of e to g, which is compounded of the ratios of e to f, and f to g, which, by the hypothesis, are the same to the ratios of G to H, and K to L, two of the other ratios;

and let the ratio of h to l be that which is compounded of the ratios of h to k, and k to l, which are the same to the remaining first ratios, viz. of C to D, and E to F;

also, let the ratio of m to p, be that which is compounded of the ratios of m to n, n to o, and o to p, which are the same, each to each, to the remaining other ratios, viz. of M to N, O to P, and Q to R.

Then the ratio of h to l shall be the same to the ratio of m to p; or h shall be to l, as m to p.

```
                h, k, l.
        A, B; C, D; E, F.       S, T, V, X.
 G, H; K, L; M, N; O, P; Q, R.  Y, Z, a, b, c, d.
 e, f, g.       m, n, o, p.
```

Because c is to f, as (G to H, that is, as) Y to Z;
and f is to g, as (K to L, that is, as) Z to a;
therefore, ex æquali, e is to g, as Y to a: (v. 22.)
and by the hypothesis, A is to B, that is, S to T, as e to g;
wherefore S is to T, as Y to a: (v. 11.)
and by inversion, T is to S, as a to Y: (v. B.)
but S is to X, as Y to D; (hyp.)
therefore, ex æquali, T is to X, as a to d:
also, because h is to k, as (C to D, that is, as) T to V; (hyp.)
and k is to l as (E to F, that is, as) V to X;
therefore, ex æquali, h is to l, as T to X;
in like manner, it may be demonstrated, that m is to p, as a to d;
and it has been shewn, that T is to X, as a to d;
therefore h is to l, as m to p. (v. 11.) Q.E.D.

The propositions G and K are usually, for the sake of brevity, expressed in the same terms with propositions F and H: and therefore it was proper to shew the true meaning of them when they are so expressed; especially since they are very frequently made use of by geometers.

NOTES TO BOOK V.

In the first four Books of the Elements are considered, only the absolute equality and inequality of Geometrical magnitudes. The Fifth Book contains an exposition of the principles whereby a more definite comparison may be instituted of the relation of magnitudes, besides their simple equality or inequality.

The doctrine of Proportion is one of the most important in the whole course of mathematical truths, and it appears probable that if the subject were read simultaneously in the Algebraical and Geometrical form, the investigations of the properties, under both aspects, would mutually assist each other, and both become equally comprehensible, also their distinct characters would be more easily perceived.

Def. I, II. In the first Four Books the word *part* is used in the same sense as we find it in the ninth axiom, "The whole is greater than its part." where the word *part* means any portion whatever of any whole magnitude: but in the Fifth Book, the word *part* is restricted to mean that portion of magnitude which is contained an exact number of times in the whole. For instance, if any straight line be taken two, three, four, or any number of times another straight line, by Euc. I. 3, the less line is called a part, or rather a submultiple of the greater line, and the greater, a multiple of the less line. The multiple is composed of a repetition of the same magnitude, and these definitions suppose that the multiple may be divided into its parts, any one of which is a measure of the multiple. And it is also obvious that when there are two magnitudes, one of which is a multiple of the other, the two magnitudes must be of the same kind, that is, they must be two lines, two angles, two surfaces, or two solids thus, a triangle is doubled, trebled, &c., by doubling, trebling, &c., the base, and completing the figure. The same may be said of a parallelogram. Angles, arcs, and sectors of equal circles may be doubled, trebled, or any multiples found by Prop. XXVI.—XXIX, Book III.

Two magnitudes are said to be *commensurable* when a third magnitude of the same kind can be found which will measure both of them, and this third magnitude is called their *common measure* · and when it is the greatest magnitude which will measure both of them, it is called the *greatest common measure* of the two magnitudes; also when two magnitudes of the same kind have no common measure they are said to be *incommensurable*. The same terms are also applied to numbers.

Unity has no magnitude, properly so called, but may represent that portion of every kind of magnitude which is assumed as the measure of all magnitudes of the same kind. The composition of unities cannot produce Geometrical magnitude, three units are more *in number* than one unit, but still as much different from magnitude as unity itself. Numbers may be considered as quantities, for we consider every thing that can be exactly measured, as a quantity.

Unity is a common measure of all rational numbers, and all numerical reasonings proceed upon the hypothesis that the unit is the same throughout the whole of any particular process. Euclid has not fixed the magnitude of any unit of length, nor made reference to any unit of measure of angles, surfaces, or volumes. Hence arises an essential difference between number and magnitude, unity, being invariable, measures all rational numbers, but though any quantity be assumed as the unit of magnitude, it is impossible to assert that this assumed unit will measure all other magnitudes of the same kind.

236   EUCLID'S ELEMENTS.

All whole numbers therefore are commensurable; for unity is their common measure: also all rational fractions, proper or improper, are commensurable; for any such fractions may be reduced to other equivalent fractions having one common denominator, and that fraction whose denominator is the common denominator, and whose numerator is unity, will measure any one of the fractions. Two magnitudes having a common measure can be represented by two numbers which express the number of times the common measure is contained in both the magnitudes.

But two incommensurable magnitudes cannot be exactly represented by any two whole numbers or fractions whatever; as, for instance, the side of a square is incommensurable to the diagonal of the square. For it may be shewn numerically, that if the side of the square contain one unit of length, the diagonal contains more than one, but less than two units of length. If the side be divided into 10 units, the diagonal contains more than 14, but less than 15 such units. Also if the side contains 100 units, the diagonal contains more than 141, but less than 142 such units. It is also obvious, that as the side is successively divided into a greater number of equal parts, the error in the magnitude of the diagonal will be diminished continually, but never can be entirely exhausted; and therefore into whatever number of equal parts the side of a square be divided, the diagonal will never contain an exact number of such parts. Thus the diagonal and side of a square having no common measure, cannot be exactly represented by any two numbers.

The term *equimultiple* in Geometry is to be understood of magnitudes of the same kind, or of different kinds, taken an equal number of times, and implies only a division of the magnitudes into the same number of equal parts. Thus, if two given lines are trebled, the trebles of the lines are *equimultiples* of the two lines: and if a given line and a given triangle be trebled, the trebles of the line and triangle are equimultiples of the line and triangle as (vi. 1 fig.) the straight line HC and the triangle AHC are equimultiples of the line BC and the triangle ABC: and in the same manner, (vi. 33 fig.) the arc EN and the angle EHN are equimultiples of the arc EF and the angle EHF.

Def. III. Λόγος ἐστὶ δύο μεγεθῶν ὁμογενῶν ἡ κατὰ πηλικότητα πρὸς ἄλληλα ποιὰ σχέσις. By this definition of *ratio* is to be understood the conception of the mutual relation of two magnitudes of the same kind, as two straight lines, two angles, two surfaces, or two solids. To prevent any misconception, Def. IV. lays down the criterion, whereby it may be known what kinds of magnitude can have a ratio to one another; namely, Λόγον ἔχειν πρὸς ἄλληλα μεγέθη λέγεται, ἃ δύναται πολλαπλασιαζόμενα ἀλλήλων ὑπερέχειν. "Magnitudes are said to have a ratio to one another, which, when they are multiplied, can exceed one another," in other words, the magnitudes which are capable of mutual comparison must be of the same kind. The former of the two terms is called the *antecedent*, and the latter, the *consequent* of the ratio. If the antecedent and consequent are equal, the ratio is called a ratio of equality, but if the antecedent be greater or less than the consequent, the ratio is called a ratio of greater or of less inequality. Care must be taken not to confound the expressions "ratio of equality" and "equality of ratio:" the former is applied to the terms of a ratio when they the antecedent and consequent, are equal to one another, but the latter, two or more ratios, when they are equal.

Arithmetical ratio has been defined to be the relation which one number bears to another with respect to *quotity*, the comparison being made by considering what multiple, part or parts, one number is of the other.

An arithmetical ratio, therefore, is represented by the quotient which arises from dividing the antecedent by the consequent of the ratio; or by the fraction which has the antecedent for its numerator and the consequent for its denominator. Hence it will at once be obvious that the properties of arithmetical ratios will be made to depend on the properties of fractions.

It must ever be borne in mind that the subject of Geometry is not number, but the magnitude of lines, angles, surfaces, and solids; and its object is to demonstrate their properties by a comparison of their absolute and relative magnitudes.

Also, in Geometry, *multiplication* is only a repeated addition of the same magnitude; and *division* is only a repeated subtraction, or the taking of a less magnitude successively from a greater, until there be either no remainder, or a remainder less than the magnitude which is successively subtracted.

The Geometrical ratio of any two given magnitudes of the same kind will obviously be represented by the magnitudes themselves; thus, the ratio of two lines is represented by the lengths of the lines themselves; and, in the same manner, the ratio of two angles, two surfaces, or two solids, will be properly represented by the magnitudes themselves.

In the definition of ratio as given by Euclid, all reference to a third magnitude of the same geometrical species, by means of which, to compare the two, whose ratio is the subject of conception, has been carefully avoided. The ratio of the two magnitudes is their relation one to the other, without the intervention of any standard unit whatever, and all the propositions demonstrated in the Fifth Book respecting the *equality* or *inequality* of two or more ratios, are demonstrated independently of any knowledge of the exact numerical measures of the ratios; and their generality includes all ratios, whatever distinctions may be made, as to the terms of them being commensurable or incommensurable.

In measuring any magnitude, it is obvious that a magnitude of the same kind must be used; but the ratio of two magnitudes may be measured by every thing which has the property of quantity. Two straight lines will measure the ratio of two triangles, or parallelograms (VI. 1. fig.): and two triangles, or two parallelograms, will measure the ratio of two straight lines. It would manifestly be absurd to speak of the line as measuring the triangle, or the triangle measuring the line. (See notes on Book II.)

The ratio of any two quantities depends on their *relative* and not their *absolute* magnitudes; and it is possible for the *absolute* magnitude of two quantities to be changed, and their *relative* magnitude to continue the same as before; and thus, the *same ratio* may subsist between two given magnitudes, and any other two of the same kind.

In this method of measuring Geometrical ratios, the measures of the ratios are the same in number as the magnitudes themselves. It has, however, two advantages; first, it enables us to pass from one kind of magnitude to another, and thus, independently of any numerical measure, to institute a comparison between such magnitudes as cannot be directly compared with one another: and secondly, the ratio of two magnitudes of the same kind may be measured by two straight lines, which form a simpler measure of ratios than any other kind of magnitude.

But the simplest method of all would be, to express the measure of the *ratio* of *two magnitudes* by *one;* but this cannot be done, unless the two magnitudes are commensurable. If two lines AB, CD, one of which AB contains 12 units of any length, and the other CD contains 4 units of the same length; then the ratio of the line AB to the line CD, is the same as the ratio of the number 12 to 4. Thus, two numbers may represent the ratio of two lines when the lines are commensurable. In the same manner, two numbers may represent the ratio of two angles, two surfaces, or two solids.

Thus, the ratio of any two magnitudes of the same kind may be expressed by two numbers, when the magnitudes are commensurable. By this means, the consideration of the ratio of two magnitudes is changed to the consideration of the ratio of two numbers, and when one number is divided by the other, the quotient will be a *single number or a fraction*, which will be a *measure of the ratio* of the two numbers, and therefore of the two quantities. If 12 be divided by 4, the quotient is 3, which measures the ratio of the two numbers 12 and 4. Again, if besides the ratio of the lines AB and CD which contain 12 and 4 units respectively, we consider two other lines EF and GH which contain 9 and 3 units respectively; it is obvious that the ratio of the line EF to GH is the same as the ratio of the number 9 to the number 3. And the measure of the ratio of 9 to 3 is 3. That is, the numbers 9 and 3 have the same ratio as the numbers 12 and 4.

But this is a numerical measure of ratio, and can only be applied strictly when the antecedent and consequent are to one another as one number to another.

And generally, if the two lines AB, CD contain a and b units respectively, and q be the quotient which indicates the number of times the number b is contained in a, then q is the measure of the ratio of the two numbers a and b. and if EF and GH contain c and d units, and the number d be contained q times in c. the number a has to b the same ratio as the number c has to d.

This is the numerical definition of proportion, which is thus expressed in Euclid's Elements, Book VII, definition 20. "Four numbers are proportionals when the first is the same multiple of the second, or the same part or parts of it, as the third is of the fourth." This definition of the proportion of four numbers, leads at once to an equation

for, since a contains b, q times, $\frac{a}{b} = q$

and since c contains d, q times; $\frac{c}{d} = q$;

therefore $\frac{a}{b} = \frac{c}{d}$ which is the fundamental equation upon which all the reasonings on the proportion of numbers depend.

If four numbers be proportionals, the product of the extremes is equal to the product of the means.

For if a, b, c, d be proportionals, or $a \cdot b :: c : d$.

Then
$$\frac{a}{b} = \frac{c}{d};$$

Multiply these equals by bd,
$$\frac{abd}{b} = \frac{cbd}{d},$$

or $ad = bc$,

that is, the product of the extremes is equal to the product of the means.

And conversely, If the product of the two extremes be equal to the product of the two means, the four numbers are proportionals.

For if a, b, c, d, be four quantities,

such that $ad = bc$,

then dividing these equals by bd, therefore $\dfrac{a}{b} = \dfrac{c}{d}$,

and $a : b :: c : d$,

or the first number has the same ratio to the second, as the third has to the fourth.

If $c = b$, then $ad = b^2$, and conversely if $ad = b^2$, then $\dfrac{a}{b} = \dfrac{b}{d}$

These results are analogous to Props 16 and 17 of the Sixth Book.

Sometimes a proportion is defined to be the *equality* of two ratios

Def VIII declares the meaning of the term analogy or proportion. The ratio of two lines, two angles, two surfaces or two solids, means nothing more than their relative magnitude in contradistinction to their absolute magnitudes; and a similitude or likeness of ratios implies, at least, the two ratios of the four magnitudes which constitute the analogy or proportion.

Def IX states that a proportion consists in three terms at least; the meaning of which is, that the second magnitude is repeated, being made the consequent of the first, and the antecedent of the second ratio It is also obvious that when a proportion consists of three magnitudes, all three are of the same kind Def. VI appears only to be a further explanation of what is implied in Def VIII.

Def. v. Proportion having been defined to be the *similitude of ratios*, or more properly, *the equality or identity of ratios*, the fifth definition lays down a criterion by which two ratios may be known to be equal, or four magnitudes proportionals, without involving any inquiry respecting the four quantities, whether the antecedents of the ratios contain or are contained in their consequents exactly, or whether there are any magnitudes which measure the terms of the two ratios The criterion only requires, that the relation of the equimultiples expressed should hold good, not merely for any particular multiples, as the doubles or trebles, but for any multiples whatever, whether large or small.

This criterion of proportion may be applied to all Geometrical magnitudes which can be *multiplied*, that is, to all which can be doubled, trebled, quadrupled, &c But it must be borne in mind, that this criterion does not exhibit a definite measure for either of the two ratios which constitute the proportion, but only an undetermined measure for the sameness or equality of the two ratios The nature of the proportion of Geometrical magnitudes neither requires nor admits of a numerical measure of either of the two ratios, for this would be to suppose that all magnitudes are commensurable. Though we know not the definite measure of either of the ratios, further than that they are both equal, and one may be taken as the measure of the other, yet particular conclusions may be arrived at by this method for by the test of proportionality here laid down, it can be proved that one magnitude is greater than, equal to, or less than another that a third proportional can be found to two, and a fourth proportional to three straight lines, also that a mean proportional can be found between two straight lines and further, that which is here stated of straight lines may be extended to other Geometrical magnitudes

The fifth definition is that of equal ratios. The definition of ratio itself (defs 3, 4) contains no criterion by which one ratio may be known to be equal to another ratio analogous to that by which one magnitude is known to be equal to another magnitude (Euc I Ax. 8) The preceding definitions

(3, 4) only restrict the conception of ratio within certain limits, but lay down no test for comparison, or the deduction of properties. All Euclid's reasonings were to turn upon this comparison of ratios, and hence it was competent to lay down a criterion of equality and inequality of two ratios between two pairs of magnitudes. In short, his *effective* definition is a definition of proportionals.

The precision with which this definition is expressed, considering the number of conditions involved in it, is remarkable. Like all complete definitions the terms (the subject and predicate) are convertible: that is,

(*a*) If four magnitudes be proportionals, and any equimultiples be taken as prescribed, they shall have the specified relations with respect to "greater, greater," &c.

(*b*) If of four magnitudes, two and two of the same Geometrical Species, it can be shewn that the prescribed equimultiples being taken, the conditions under which those magnitudes exist, *must be* such as to fulfil the criterion "greater, greater, &c", then these four magnitudes shall be proportionals.

It may be remarked, that the cases in which the second part of the criterion ("equal, equal") can be fulfilled, are comparatively few: namely, those in which the given magnitudes, whose ratio is under consideration, are both exact multiples of some third magnitude—or those which are called *commensurable*. When this, however, is fulfilled, the other two will be fulfilled *as a consequence of this*. When this is not the case, or the magnitudes are *incommensurable*, the other two criteria determine the proportionality. However, when no hypothesis respecting commensurability is involved, the contemporaneous existence of the three cases ("greater, greater, equal, equal; less, less") must be deduced from the hypothetical conditions under which the magnitudes exist, to render the criterion valid.

With respect to this test or criterion of the proportionality of four magnitudes, it has been objected, that it is utterly impossible to make trial of *all* the possible equimultiples of the first and third magnitudes, and also of the second and fourth. It may be replied, that the point in question is not determined by making such trials, but by shewing from the nature of the magnitudes, that whatever be the multipliers, if the multiple of the first exceeds the multiple of the second magnitude, the multiple of the third *will* exceed the multiple of the fourth magnitude, and if equal, *will* be equal, and if less, *will* be less, in any case which may be taken.

The Arithmetical definition of proportion in Book VII Def 20, even if it were equally general with the Geometrical definition in Book v Def 5, is by no means universally applicable to the subject of Geometrical magnitudes. The Geometrical criterion is founded on multiplication, which is always possible. When the magnitudes are commensurable, the multiples of the first and second *may* be equal or unequal; but when the magnitudes are incommensurable, any multiples whatever of the first and second *must* be unequal; but the Arithmetical criterion of proportion is founded on division, which is not always possible. Euclid has not shewn in Book v. how to take *any part* of a line or other magnitude, or that the two terms of a ratio have a common measure, and therefore the numerical definition could not be strictly applied, even in the limited way in which it may be applied.

Number and *Magnitude* do not correspond in all their relations; and hence the distinction between Geometrical ratio and Arithmetical ratio; the former is a comparison κατὰ πηλικότητα, according to quantity, but the latter, according to quotity. The former gives an undetermined, though definite measure, in magnitudes; but the latter attempts to give the exact value in numbers.

The fifth book exhibits no method whereby two magnitudes may be determined to be commensurable, and the Geometrical conclusions deduced from the multiples of magnitudes are too general to furnish a numerical measure of ratios, being all independent of the commensurability or incommensurability of the magnitudes themselves.

It is the numerical ratio of two magnitudes which will more certainly discover whether they are commensurable or incommensurable, and hence, recourse must be had to the forms and properties of numbers. All numbers and fractions are either rational or irrational. It has been seen that rational numbers and fractions *can express* the ratios of Geometrical magnitudes, when they are commensurable. Similar relations of incommensurable magnitudes *may be expressed* by irrational numbers, if the Algebraical expressions for such numbers may be assumed and employed in the same manner as rational numbers. The irrational expressions being considered the exact and definite, though undetermined, values of the ratios, to which a series of rational numbers may successively approximate.

Though two incommensurable magnitudes have not an assignable numerical ratio to one another, yet they have a certain definite ratio to one another, and two other magnitudes may have the same ratio as the first two; and it will be found, that, when reference is made to the numerical value of the ratios of four incommensurable magnitudes, the same irrational number appears in the two ratios.

The sides and diagonals of squares can be shewn to be proportionals, and though the ratio of the side to the diagonal is represented Geometrically by the two lines which form the side and the diagonal, there is no rational number or fraction which will measure exactly their ratio.

If the side of a square contain a units, the ratio of the diagonal to the side is numerically as $\sqrt{2}$ to 1, and if the side of another square contain b units, the ratio of the diagonal to the side will be found to be in the ratio of $\sqrt{2}$ to 1. Again, the two parts of any number of lines which may be divided in extreme and mean ratio will be found to be respectively in the ratio of the irrational number $\sqrt{5} - 1$ to $3 - \sqrt{5}$. Also, the ratios of the diagonals of cubes to the diagonals of one of the faces will be found to be in the irrational or incommensurate ratio of $\sqrt{3}$ to $\sqrt{2}$.

Thus it will be found that the ratios of all incommensurable magnitudes which are proportionals do involve the same irrational numbers, and these may be used as the numerical measures of ratios in the same manner as rational numbers and fractions.

It is not however to such enquiries, nor to the ratios of magnitudes when expressed as rational or irrational numbers, that Euclid's doctrine of proportion is legitimately directed. There is no enquiry into what a ratio is in *numbers*, but whether in diagrams formed according to assigned conditions, the ratios between certain parts of the one are the same as the ratios between corresponding parts of the other. Thus, with respect to any two squares, the question that properly belongs to pure Geometry is:—whether the diagonals of two squares have *the same ratio* as the sides of the squares? Or whether the side of one square has to its diagonal, *the same ratio* as the side of the other square has to its diagonal? Or again, whether in Euc. vi. 2, when BC and DE are parallel, the line BD has to the line DA, *the same ratio* that the line CE has to the line AE? There is no purpose on the part of Euclid, to assign either of these ratios in *numbers*; but only to prove that their universal sameness is inevitably a consequence of the original conditions according to which the diagrams were constituted. There is, consequently, no introduction of the idea of incommensurables; and indeed, with such an object as Euclid had in view, the simple mention of them would have been at least irrelevant and superfluous. If, however, it be attempted to apply numerical considerations to pure geometrical investigations, incommensurables will soon be apparent, and difficulties will arise which were not foreseen. Euclid, however, effects his demonstrations without creating this artificial difficulty, or even recognising its existence. Had he assumed a standard unit of length, he would have involved the subject in numerical considerations; and entailed upon the subject of Geometry the almost insuperable difficulties which attach to all such methods.

It cannot, however, be too strongly or too frequently impressed upon the learner's mind, that all Euclid's reasonings are independent of the numerical expositions of the magnitudes concerned. That the enquiry as to what numerical function any magnitude is of another, belongs not to pure Geometry, but to another Science. The consideration of any intermediate standard unit does not enter into pure Geometry; into Algebraic Geometry it essentially enters, and indeed constitutes the fundamental idea. The former is wholly free from numerical considerations; the latter is entirely dependent upon them.

Def. vii is analogous to Def v, and lays down the criterion whereby the ratio of two magnitudes of the same kind may be known to be *greater* or *less* than the ratio of two other magnitudes of the same kind.

Def xi includes Def x as three magnitudes may be continued proportionals, as well as four or more than four. In continued proportionals, all the terms except the first and last, are made successively the consequent of one ratio, and the antecedent of the next; whereas in other proportionals this is not the case.

A series of numbers or Algebraical quantities in continued proportion, is called a *Geometrical progression*, from the analogy they bear to a series of Geometrical magnitudes in continued proportion.

Def A. The term *compound ratio* was devised for the purpose of avoiding circumlocution, and no difficulty can arise in the use of it, if its exact meaning be strictly attended to.

With respect to the Geometrical measures of compound ratios, three straight lines may measure the ratio of four, as in Prop 23, Book vi. For K to L measures the ratio of BC to CG, and L to M measures the ratio of DC to CE, and the ratio of K to M is that which is said to be compounded of the ratios of K to L, and L to M, which is the same as the ratio which is compounded of the ratios of the sides of the parallelograms.

Both duplicate and triplicate ratio are species of compound ratio.

Duplicate ratio is a ratio compounded of two equal ratios; and in the case of three magnitudes which are continued proportionals, means the ratio of the first to a third proportional to the first and second.

Triplicate ratio, in the same manner, is a ratio compounded of three equal ratios; and in the case of four magnitudes which are continued proportionals, the triplicate ratio of the first to the second means the ratio of the first to a fourth proportional to the first, second, and third magnitudes. Instances of the composition of three ratios, and of triplicate ratio, will be found in the eleventh and twelfth books.

The product of the fractions which represent or measure the ratios of numbers, corresponds to the composition of Geometrical ratios of magnitudes.

It has been shewn that the ratio of two numbers is represented by a fraction whereof the numerator is the antecedent, and the denominator the consequent of the ratio; and if the antecedents of two ratios be multiplied together, as also the consequents, the new ratio thus formed is said to be compounded of these two ratios, and in the same manner, if there be more than two. It is also obvious, that the ratio compounded of two equal ratios is equal to the ratio of the squares of one of the antecedents to its consequent; also when there are three equal ratios, the ratio compounded of the three ratios is equal to the ratio of the cubes of any one of the antecedents to its consequent. And further, it may be observed, that when several numbers are continued proportionals, the ratio of the first to the last is equal to the ratio of the product of all the antecedents to the product of all the consequents.

It may be here remarked, that, though the constructions of the propositions in Book v are exhibited by straight lines, the enunciations are expressed of magnitude in general, and are equally true of angles, triangles, parallelograms, arcs, sectors, &c.

The two following *axioms* may be added to the four Euclid has given

Ax. 5 A part of a greater magnitude is greater than the same part of a less magnitude.

Ax 6 That magnitude of which any part is greater than the same part of another, is greater than that other magnitude.

The learner must not forget that the *capital letters*, used generally by Euclid in the demonstrations of the fifth Book, represent *the magnitudes*, not any numerical or Algebraical measures of them · sometimes, however, the magnitude of a line is represented in the usual way by two letters which are placed at the extremities of the line.

Prop I Algebraically

Let each of the magnitudes A, B, C, &c, be equimultiples of as many a, b, c, &c,

that is, let $A = m$ times $a = ma$,

$B = m$ times $b = mb$,

$C = m$ times $c = mc$, &c.

First, if there be two magnitudes equimultiples of two others,

then $A + B = ma + mb = m(a + b) = m$ times $(a + b)$.

Hence $A + B$ is the same multiple of $(a + b)$, as A is of a, or B of b.

Secondly, if there be three magnitudes equimultiples of three others,

then $A + B + C = ma + mb + mc = m(a + b + c)$

$= m$ times $(a + b + c)$

Hence $A + B + C$ is the same multiple of $(a + b + c)$;

as A is of a, B of b, and C of c

Similarly, if there were four, or any number of magnitudes.

Therefore, if any number of magnitudes be equimultiples of as many, each of each; what multiple soever, any one is of its part, the same multiple shall the first magnitudes be of all the other.

Prop. II Algebraically.

Let A_1 the first magnitude, be the same multiple of a_2 the second, as A_3 the third, is of a_4 the fourth, and A_5 the fifth the same multiple of a_2 the second, as A_6 the sixth, is of a_4 the fourth

That is, let $A_1 = m$ times $a_2 = ma_2$,
$A_3 = m$ times $a_4 = ma_4$,
$A_5 = n$ times $a_2 = na_2$,
$A_6 = n$ times $a_4 = na_4$.

Then by addition, $A_1 + A_5 = ma_2 + na_2 = (m+n) a_2 = (m+n)$ times a_2,
and $A_3 + A_6 = ma_4 + na_4 = (m+n) a_4 = (m+n)$ times a_4

Therefore $A_1 + A_5$ is the same multiple of a_2, as $A_3 + A_6$ is of a_4

That is, if the first magnitude be the same multiple of the second, as the third is of the fourth, &c.

Cor If there be any number of magnitudes A_1, A_2, A_3, &c. multiples of another a, such that $A_1 = ma$, $A_2 = na$, $A_3 = pa$, &c.

And as many others B_1, B_2, B_3, &c the same multiples of another b, such that $B_1 = mb$, $B_2 = nb$, $B_3 = pb$, &c.

Then by addition, $A_1 + A_2 + A_3 + \&c = ma + na + pa + \&c$
$= (m + n + p + \&c) a = (m + n + p + \&c)$ times a
and $B_1 + B_2 + B_3 + \&c. = mb + nb + pb + \&c. = (m + n + p + \&c) b$
$= (m + n + p + \&c)$ times b.

that is $A_1 + A_2 + A_3 + \&c$ is the same multiple of a, that
$B_1 + B_2 + B_3 + \&c.$ is of b.

Prop III. Algebraically
Let A_1 the first magnitude, be the same multiple of a_2 the second,
as A_3 the third, is of a_4 the fourth,
that is, let $A_1 = m$ times $a_2 = ma_2$,
and $A_3 = m$ times $a_4 = ma_4$.

If these equals be each taken n times,
then $nA_1 = mna_2 = mn$ times a_2,
and $nA_3 = mna_4 = mn$ times a_4,
or nA_1, nA_3 each contain a_2, a_4 respectively mn times.

Wherefore nA_1, nA_3 the equimultiples of the first and third, are respectively equimultiples of a_2 and a_4, the second and fourth.

Prop IV. Algebraically.
Let A_1, a_2, A_3, a_4, be proportionals according to the Algebraical definition:
that is, let $A_1 : a_2 :: A_3 : a_4$,
then $\dfrac{A_1}{a_2} = \dfrac{A_3}{a_4}$,

multiply these equals by $\dfrac{m}{n}$, m and n being any integers,

$\therefore \dfrac{mA_1}{na_2} = \dfrac{mA_3}{na_4}$,

or $mA_1 : na_2 :: mA_3 : na_4$.

That is, if the first of four magnitudes has the same ratio to the second which the third has to the fourth, then any equimultiples whatever of the first and third shall have the same ratio to any equimultiples of the second and fourth.

The Corollary is contained in the proposition itself:
for if n be unity, then $mA_1 : a_2 :: mA_3 : a_4$:
and if m be unity, also $A_1 : na_2 :: A_3 : na_4$.

Prop. v. Algebraically.

Let A_1 be the same multiple of a_1,
that A_2 a part of A_1, is of a_2, a part of a_1.
Then $A_1 - A_2$ is the same multiple of $a_1 - a_2$ as A_1 is of a_1
For let $A_1 = m$ times $a_1 = ma_1$,
and $A_2 = m$ times $a_2 = ma_2$,
then $A_1 - A_2 = ma_1 - ma_2 = m(a_1 - a_2) = m$ times $(a_1 - a_2)$,
that is $A_1 - A_2$ is the same multiple of $(a_1 - a_2)$ as A_1 is of a_1.

Prop. vi. Algebraically.

Let A_1, A_2 be equimultiples respectively of a_1, a_2 two others,
that is, let $A_1 = m$ times $a_1 = ma_1$,
$A_2 = m$ times $a_2 = ma_2$.
Also if B_1 a part of $A_1 = n$ times $a_1 = na_1$,
and B_2 a part of $A_2 = n$ times $a_2 = na_2$.
Then by taking equals from equals,
$\therefore A_1 - B_1 = ma_1 - na_1 = (m-n)a_1 = (m-n)$ times a_1,
$A_2 - B_2 = ma_2 - na_2 = (m-n)a_2 = (m-n)$ times a_2,
that is, the remainders $A_1 - B_1, A_2 - B_2$ are equimultiples of a_1, a_2 respectively.
And if $m - n = 1$, then $A_1 - B_1 = a_1$, and $A_2 - B_2 = a_2$:
or the remainders are equal to a_1, a_2 respectively.

Prop. A. Algebraically.

Let A_1, a_2, A_3, a_4 be proportionals,
or $A_1 : a_2 :: A_3 : a_4$,
then $\dfrac{A_1}{a_2} = \dfrac{A_3}{a_4}$.

And since the fraction $\dfrac{A_1}{a_2}$ is equal to $\dfrac{A_3}{a_4}$, the following relations only can subsist between A_1 and a_2; and between A_3 and a_4.

First, if A_1 be greater than a_2, then A_3 is also greater than a_4:
Secondly, if A_1 be equal to a_2; then A_3 is also equal to a_4:
Thirdly, if A_1 be less than a_2, then A_3 is also less than a_4:
Otherwise, the fraction $\dfrac{A_1}{a_2}$ could not be equal to the fraction $\dfrac{A_3}{a_4}$.

Prop. B. Algebraically.

Let A_1, a_2, A_3, a_4 be proportionals,
or $A_1 : a_2 :: A_3 : a_4$.
Then shall $a_2 : A_1 :: a_4 : A_3$.
For since $A_1 : a_2 :: A_3 : a_4$,
$\therefore \dfrac{A_1}{a_2} = \dfrac{A_3}{a_4}$,

and if 1 be divided by each of these equals,

$$1 \div \frac{A_1}{a_1} = 1 \div \frac{A_3}{a_4}$$

or $\dfrac{a_2}{A_1} = \dfrac{a_4}{A_3}$,

and therefore $a_2 : A_1 :: a_4 : A_3$.

Prop c. "This is frequently made use of by geometers, and is necessary to the 5th and 6th Propositions of the 10th Book. Clavius, in his notes subjoined to the 8th def of Book 5, demonstrates it only in numbers, by help of some of the propositions of the 7th Book, in order to demonstrate the property contained in the 5th definition of the 5th book, when applied to numbers, from the property of proportionals contained in the 20th def of the 7th Book: and most of the commentators judge it difficult to prove that four magnitudes which are proportionals according to the 20th def of the 7th Book, are also proportionals according to the 5th def of the 5th Book. But this is easily made out as follows:

First, if A, B, C, D, be four magnitudes, such that A is the same multiple, or the same part of B, which C is of D:

Then A, B, C, D, are proportionals; this is demonstrated in proposition (c)

Secondly, if AB contain the same parts of CD that EF does of GH; in this case likewise AB is to CD, as EF to GH.

```
A      B            E         F
C  K   D            G    L    H
```

Let CK be a part of CD, and GL the same part of GH, and let AB be the same multiple of CK, that EF is of GL: therefore, by Prop c, of Book v, AB is to CK, as EF to GL: and CD, GH, are equimultiples of CK, GL, the second and fourth; wherefore, by Cor Prop 4, Book v, AB is to CD, as EF to GH

And if four magnitudes be proportionals according to the 5th def of Book v, they are also proportionals according to the 20th Def of Book vii.

First, if A be to B, as C to D; then if A be any multiple or part of B, C is the same multiple or part of D, by Prop d, Book v

Next, if AB be to CD, as EF to GH then if AB contain any part of CD, EF contains the same part of GH:

```
A      B           E         F
C  K   D           G    L    H      M
```

for let CK be a part of CD, and GL the same part of GH, and let AB be a multiple of CK: EF is the same multiple of GL: take M the same multiple of GL that AB is of CK, therefore, by Prop c, Book v, AB is to CK, as M to GL: and CD, GH, are equimultiples of CK, GL, wherefore, by Cor Prop 4, Book v, AB is to CD, as M to GH. And, by the hypothesis, AB is to CD, as EF to GH; therefore M is equal to EF by Prop 9, Book v, and consequently, EF is the same multiple of GL that AB is of CK."

This is the method by which Simson shews that the Geometrical definition of proportion is a consequence of the Arithmetical definition, and conversely.

It may however be shewn by employing the equation $\frac{a}{b} = \frac{c}{d}$, and taking ma, mc any equimultiples of a and c the first and third, and nb, nd any equimultiples of b and d the second and fourth.

And conversely, it may be shewn *ex absurdo*, that if four quantities are proportionals according to the fifth definition of the fifth book of Euclid, they are also proportionals according to the Algebraical definition.

The student must however bear in mind, that the Algebraical definition is not equally applicable to the Geometrical demonstrations contained in the sixth, eleventh, and twelfth Books of Euclid, where the Geometrical definition is employed. It has been before remarked, that Geometry is the science of *magnitude* and not of *number*, and though a sum and a difference of two magnitudes can be represented Geometrically, as well as a multiple of any given magnitude, there is no method in Geometry whereby the quotient of two magnitudes of the same kind can be expressed. The idea of a quotient is entirely foreign to the principles of the Fifth Book, as are also any distinctions of magnitudes as being commensurable or incommensurable. As Euclid in Books VII-X has treated of the properties of proportion according to the Arithmetical definition and of their application to Geometrical magnitudes, there can be no doubt that his intention was to exclude all reference to numerical measures and quotients in his treatment of the doctrine of proportion in the Fifth Book; and in his applications of that doctrine in the sixth, eleventh and twelfth books of the Elements.

Prop. C. Algebraically

Let A_1, a_2, A_3, a_4 be four magnitudes.

First let $A_1 = ma_2$ and $A_3 = ma_4$.

Then $A_1 : a_2 :: A_3 : a_4$.

For since $A_1 = ma_2$, $\therefore m = \frac{A_1}{a_2}$;

and $A_3 = ma_4$, $\therefore m = \frac{A_3}{a_4}$.

Hence $\frac{A_1}{a_2} = \frac{A_3}{a_4}$,

and $A_1 : a_2 :: A_3 : a_4$.

Secondly. Let $A_1 = \frac{1}{m} a_2$, and $A_3 = \frac{1}{m} a_4$:

Then, as before, $\frac{A_1}{a_2} = \frac{1}{m}$, and $\frac{A_3}{a_4} = \frac{m}{1}$.

Hence $\frac{A_1}{a_2} = \frac{A_3}{a_4}$,

and $A_1 : a_2 :: A_3 : a_4$.

Prop. D. Algebraically.

Let A_1, a_2, A_3, a_4 be proportionals,

or $A_1 : a_2 :: A_3 : a_4$.

First let A_1 be a multiple of a_2, or $A_1 = m$ times $a_2 = ma_2$.
Then shall $A_3 = ma_4$.
For since $A_1 : a_2 :: A_3 : a_4$,
$$\therefore \frac{A_1}{a_2} = \frac{A_3}{a_4}$$
but since $A_1 = ma_2$,
$$\therefore \frac{ma_2}{a_2} = \frac{A_3}{a_4}, \text{ or } m = \frac{A_3}{a_4},$$
and $A_3 = ma_4$.

Therefore the third A_3 is the same multiple of a_4 the fourth.

Secondly. If $A_1 = \frac{1}{m} a_2$, then shall $A_3 = \frac{1}{m} a_4$.

For since $\frac{A_1}{a_2} = \frac{A_3}{a_4}$,

and $A_1 = \frac{1}{m} a_2$, $\therefore \frac{A_1}{a_2} = \frac{1}{m}$,

$\therefore \frac{A_3}{a_4} = \frac{1}{m}$, and $A_3 = \frac{1}{m} a_4$:

wherefore, the third A_3 is the same part of the fourth a_4.

Prop. VII is so obvious that it may be considered axiomatic. Also Prop VIII. and Prop. IX. are so simple and obvious, as not to require algebraical proof.

Prop x. Algebraically.

Let A_1 have a greater ratio to a, than A_3 has to a.

Then $A_1 > A_3$

For the ratio of A_1 to a is represented by $\frac{A_1}{a}$,

and the ratio of A_3 to a is represented by $\frac{A_3}{a}$,

and since $\frac{A_1}{a} > \frac{A_3}{a}$;

it follows that $A_1 > A_3$.

Secondly. Let a have to A_3 a greater ratio than a has to A_1.

Then $A_3 < A_1$.

For the ratio of $a : A_3$ is represented by $\frac{a}{A_3}$,

and the ratio of $a . A_1$ is represented by $\frac{a}{A_1}$,

and since $\frac{a}{A_3} > \frac{a}{A_1}$,

dividing these unequals by a,

$$\therefore \frac{1}{A_3} > \frac{1}{A_1};$$

and multiplying these unequals by $A_1 . A_3$,

$\therefore A_1 > A_3$,

or $A_3 < A_1$.

NOTES TO BOOK V.

Prop. XI. Algebraically.

Let the ratio of $A_1 : a_2$ be the same as the ratio of $A_3 : a_4$, and the ratio of $A_3 : a_4$ be the same as the ratio of $A_5 : a_6$.

Then the ratio of $A_1 : a_2$ shall be the same as the ratio of $A_5 : a_6$.

For since $A_1 : a_2 :: A_3 : a_4$,

$$\therefore \frac{A_1}{a_2} = \frac{A_3}{a_4},$$

and since $A_3 : a_4 :: A_5 : a_6$,

$$\therefore \frac{A_3}{a_4} = \frac{A_5}{a_6}.$$

Hence $\frac{A_1}{a_2} = \frac{A_5}{a_6}$,

and $A_1 : a_2 :: A_5 : a_6$.

Prop. XII. Algebraically.

Let $A_1, a_2, A_3, a_4, A_5, a_6$ be proportionals, so that $A_1 : a_2 :: A_3 : a_4 :: A_5 : a_6$

Then shall $A_1 : a_2 :: A_1 + A_3 + A_5 : a_2 + a_4 + a_6$.

For since $A_1 : a_2 :: A_3 : a_4 :: A_5 : a_6$,

$$\therefore \frac{A_1}{a_2} = \frac{A_3}{a_4} = \frac{A_5}{a_6}.$$

And $\because \frac{A_1}{a_2} = \frac{A_3}{a_4}, \therefore A_1 a_4 = a_2 A_3$,

$\frac{A_1}{a_2} = \frac{A_5}{a_6}, \therefore A_1 a_6 = a_2 A_5$,

also $A_1 a_2 = a_2 A_1$.

Hence $A_1 (a_2 + a_4 + a_6) = a_2 (A_1 + A_3 + A_5)$, by addition, and dividing these equals by $a_2 (a_2 + a_4 + a_6)$,

$$\therefore \frac{A_1}{a_2} = \frac{A_1 + A_3 + A_5}{a_2 + a_4 + a_6};$$

and $A_1 : a_2 :: A_1 + A_3 + A_5 : a_2 + a_4 + a_6$.

Prop. XIII. Algebraically.

Let $A_1, a_2, A_3, a_4, A_5, a_6$, be six magnitudes, such that $A_1 : a_2 :: A_3 : a_4$, but that the ratio of $A_3 : a_4$ is greater than the ratio of $A_5 : a_6$.

Then the ratio of $A_1 : a_2$ shall be greater than the ratio of $A_5 : a_6$.

For since $A_1 : a_2 :: A_3 : a_4 \therefore \frac{A_1}{a_2} = \frac{A_3}{a_4}$;

but since $A_3 : a_4 > A_5 : a_6 \therefore \frac{A_3}{a_4} > \frac{A_5}{a_6}$.

Hence $\frac{A_1}{a_2} > \frac{A_5}{a_6}$.

That is, the ratio of $A_1 : a_2$ is greater than the ratio of $A_5 : a_6$.

Prop. XIV. Algebraically.

Let A_1, a_2, A_3, a_4 be proportionals.

Then if $A_1 > A_3$, then $a_2 > a_4$, and if equal, equal; and if less, less.

For since $A_1 : a_2 :: A_3 : a_4$,

$$\therefore \frac{A_1}{a_2} = \frac{A_3}{a_4}.$$

11*

Multiply these equals by $\dfrac{a_2}{A_3}$;

$$\therefore \frac{A_1}{A_3} = \frac{a_2}{a_4}:$$

and because these fractions are always equal,
if A_1 be $> A_3$, then a_2 must be greater than a_4,
for if a_2 were not greater than a_4,
the fraction $\dfrac{a_2}{a_4}$ could not be equal to $\dfrac{A_1}{A_3}$;
which would be contrary to the hypothesis.
In the same manner,
if A_1 be $= A_3$, then a_2 must be equal to a_4,
and if A_1 be $< A_3$, a_2 must be less than a_4.
Hence, therefore, if &c.

Prop. xv. Algebraically.
Let A_1, a_2 be any magnitudes of the same kind.
Then $A_1 \cdot a_2 :: mA_1 \cdot ma_2$,
mA_1 and ma_2 being any equimultiples of A_1 and a_2.

For $\dfrac{A_1}{a_2} = \dfrac{A_1}{a_2}$,

and since the numerator and denominator of a fraction may be multiplied by the same number without altering the value of the fraction,

$$\therefore \frac{A_1}{a_2} = \frac{mA_1}{ma_2},$$

and $A_1 \cdot a_2 :: mA_1 \cdot ma_2$.

Prop. xvi. Algebraically.
Let A_1, a_2, A_3, a_4 be four magnitudes of the same kind, which are proportionals,

$$A_1 \cdot a_2 :: A_3 \cdot a_4$$

Then these shall be proportionals when taken alternately, that is,
$A_1 \cdot A_3 :: a_2 \cdot a_4$.

For since $A_1 \cdot a_2 :: A_3 \cdot a_4$,

then $\dfrac{A_1}{a_2} = \dfrac{A_3}{a_4}$

Multiply these equals by $\dfrac{a_2}{A_3}$,

$$\therefore \frac{A_1}{A_3} = \frac{a_2}{a_4},$$

and $A_1 \cdot A_3 :: a_2 \cdot a_4$.

Prop. xvii. Algebraically
Let $A_1 + a_2$, a_2, $A_3 + a_4$, a_4 be proportionals,
then A_1, a_2, A_3, a_4 shall be proportionals.
For since $A_1 + a_2 \cdot a_2 :: A_3 + a_4 \cdot a_4$,

$$\therefore \frac{A_1 + a_2}{a_2} = \frac{A_3 + a_4}{a_4};$$

or $\dfrac{A_1}{a_2} + 1 = \dfrac{A_3}{a_4} + 1$,

and taking 1 from each of these equals,
$$\therefore \frac{A_1}{a_2} = \frac{A_3}{a_4},$$
and $A_1 : a_2 :: A_3 : a_4$.

Prop. XVIII. is the converse of Prop. XVII.
The following is Euclid's indirect demonstration
Let AE, EB, CF, FD be proportionals,
that is, as AE to EB, so let CF be to FD.
then these shall be proportionals also when taken jointly;
that is, as AB to BE, so shall CD be to DF.

```
A      E    B
─────────────
C   Q  F    D
```

For if the ratio of AB to BE be not the same as the ratio of CD to DF;
the ratio of AB to BE is either greater than, or less than the ratio of CD to DF.

First, let AB have to BE a less ratio than CD has to DF;
and let DQ be taken so that AB has to BE the same ratio as CD to DQ:
and since magnitudes when taken jointly are proportionals,
they are also proportionals when taken separately, (v 17)
therefore AE has to EB the same ratio as CQ to QD;
but, by the hypothesis, AE has to EB the same ratio as CF to FD;
therefore the ratio of CQ to QD is the same as the ratio of CF to FD. (v. 11)
And when four magnitudes are proportionals, if the first be greater than the second, the third is greater than the fourth; and if equal, equal; and if less, less, (v 14) but CQ is less than CF,
therefore QD is less than FD; which is absurd.
Wherefore the ratio of AB to BE is not less than the ratio of CD to DF;
that is, AB has the same ratio to BE as CD has to DF.

Secondly By a similar mode of reasoning, it may likewise be shewn, that AB has the same ratio to BE as CD has to DF, if AB be assumed to have to BE a greater ratio than CD has to DF.

Prop. XVIII. Algebraically.
Let $A_1 : a_2 :: A_3 : a_4$.
Then $A_1 + a_2 : a_2 :: A_3 + a_4 : a_4$.
For since $A_1 : a_2 :: A_3 : a_4$,
$$\therefore \frac{A_1}{a_2} = \frac{A_3}{a_4},$$
and adding 1 to each of these equals;
$$\therefore \frac{A_1}{a_2} + 1 = \frac{A_3}{a_4} + 1,$$
$$\text{or,} \quad \frac{A_1 + a_2}{a_2} = \frac{A_3 + a_4}{a_4},$$
and $A_1 + a_2 : a_2 :: A_3 + a_4 : a_4$.

Prop. XIX. Algebraically.
Let the whole A_1 have the same ratio to the whole A_2,
as a_1 taken from the first, is to a_2 taken from the second,
that is, let $A_1 : A_2 :: a_1 : a_2$.
Then $A_1 - a_1 : A_2 - a_2 :: A_1 : A_2$.

For since $A_1 : A_2 :: a_1 : a_2$,

$$\therefore \frac{A_1}{A_2} = \frac{a_1}{a_2}.$$

Multiplying these equals by $\frac{A_2}{a_1}$,

$$\therefore \frac{A_1}{A_2} \times \frac{A_2}{a_1} = \frac{a_1}{a_2} + \frac{A_2}{a_1};$$

$$\text{or,} \quad \frac{A_1}{a_1} = \frac{A_2}{a_2},$$

and subtracting 1 from each of these equals,

$$\therefore \frac{A_1}{a_1} - 1 = \frac{A_2}{a_2} - 1,$$

$$\text{or,} \quad \frac{A_1 - a_1}{a_1} = \frac{A_2 - a_2}{a_2},$$

and multiplying these equals by $\frac{a_1}{A_2 - a_2}$,

$$\therefore \frac{A_1 - a_1}{A_2 - a_2} = \frac{a_1}{a_2},$$

but $\frac{A_1}{A_2} = \frac{a_1}{a_2}$,

$$\therefore \frac{A_1 - a_1}{A_2 - a_2} = \frac{A_1}{A_2},$$

and $A_1 - a_1 : A_2 - a_2 :: A_1 : A_2$.

Cor. If $A_1 : A_2 :: a_1 : a_2$,
Then $A_1 - a_1 : A_2 - a_2 :: a_1 : a_2$, is found proved in the preceding process

Prop. E. Algebraically.

Let $A_1 : a_2 :: A_3 : a_4$,
Then shall $A_1 : A_1 - a_2 :: A_3 : A_3 - a_4$.
For since $A_1 : a_2 :: A_3 : a_4$,

$$\therefore \frac{A_1}{a_2} = \frac{A_3}{a_4},$$

subtracting 1 from each of these equals,

$$\therefore \frac{A_1}{a_2} - 1 = \frac{A_3}{a_4} - 1,$$

$$\text{or,} \quad \frac{A_1 - a_2}{a_2} = \frac{A_3 - a_4}{a_4},$$

but $\frac{A_1}{a_2} = \frac{A_3}{a_4}$.

Dividing the latter by the former of these equals,

$$\therefore \frac{A_1}{a_2} \div \frac{A_1 - a_2}{a_2} = \frac{A_3}{a_4} \div \frac{A_3 - a_4}{a_4};$$

$$\text{or,} \quad \frac{A_1}{a_2} \times \frac{a_2}{A_1 - a_2} = \frac{A_3}{a_4} \times \frac{a_4}{A_3 - a_4},$$

NOTES TO BOOK V.

or $\dfrac{A_1}{A_1-a_2} = \dfrac{A_3}{A_3-a_4}$;

and $A_1 : A_1-a_2 :: A_3 : A_3-a_4$.

Prop. xx. Algebraically.

Let A_1, A_2, A_3 be three magnitudes, and a_1, a_2, a_3, other three such that $A_1 \cdot A_2 :: a_1 \cdot a_2$,
and $A_2 \cdot A_3 :: a_2 : a_3$:
if $A_1 > A_3$, then shall $a_1 > a_3$,
and if equal, equal; and if less, less.

Since $A_1 \cdot A_2 :: a_1 \cdot a_2$, $\therefore \dfrac{A_1}{A_2} = \dfrac{a_1}{a_2}$,

also since $A_2 \cdot A_3 :: a_2 \cdot a_3$, $\therefore \dfrac{A_2}{A_3} = \dfrac{a_2}{a_3}$,

and multiplying these equals,

$\therefore \dfrac{A_1}{A_2} \times \dfrac{A_2}{A_3} = \dfrac{a_1}{a_2} \times \dfrac{a_2}{a_3}$,

or $\dfrac{A_1}{A_3} = \dfrac{a_1}{a_3}$,

and since the fraction $\dfrac{A_1}{A_3}$ is equal to $\dfrac{a_1}{a_3}$;

and that $A_1 > A_3$:

It follows that a_1 is $> a_3$.

In the same way it may be shewn
that if $A_1 = A_3$, then $a_1 = a_3$, and if A_1 be $< A_3$, then $a_1 < a_3$.

Prop. xxi Algebraically.

Let A_1, A_2, A_3, be three magnitudes,
and a_1, a_2, a_4 three others,
such that $A_1 \cdot A_2 : a_2 \; a_3$,
and $A_2 \; A_3 :: a_1 \cdot a_2$.

If $A_1 > A_3$, then shall $a_1 > a_3$, and if equal, equal; and if less, less.

For since $A_1 \cdot A_2 :: a_2 \; a_3$, $\therefore \dfrac{A_1}{A_2} = \dfrac{a_2}{a_3}$,

and since $A_2 \cdot A_3 :: a_1 \cdot a_2$, $\therefore \dfrac{A_2}{A_3} = \dfrac{a_1}{a_2}$.

Multiplying these equals,

$\therefore \dfrac{A_1}{A_2} \times \dfrac{A_2}{A_3} = \dfrac{a_2}{a_3} \times \dfrac{a_1}{a_2}$,

or $\dfrac{A_1}{A_3} = \dfrac{a_1}{a_3}$;

and since the fraction $\dfrac{A_1}{A_3}$ is equal to $\dfrac{a_1}{a_3}$,

and that $A_1 > A_3$.

It follows that also $a_1 > a_3$.

Similarly, it may be shewn, that if $A_1 = A_3$, then $a_1 = a_3$;
and if $A_1 < A_3$, also $a_1 < a_3$.

Prop. XXII. Algebraically.

Let A_1, A_2, A_3 be three magnitudes,
and a_1, a_2, a_3 other three,
such that $A_1 : A_2 :: a_1 : a_2$,
and $A_2 : A_3 :: a_2 : a_3$
Then shall $A_1 : A_3 :: a_1 : a_3$.

For since $A_1 : A_2 :: a_1 : a_2$, $\therefore \dfrac{A_1}{A_2} = \dfrac{a_1}{a_2}$,

and since $A_2 : A_3 :: a_3 : a_4$, $\therefore \dfrac{A_2}{A_3} = \dfrac{a_3}{a_4}$.

Multiply these equals,

$$\therefore \dfrac{A_1}{A_2} \times \dfrac{A_2}{A_3} = \dfrac{a_1}{a_2} \times \dfrac{a_2}{a_3},$$

or $\dfrac{A_1}{A_3} = \dfrac{a_1}{a_3}$,

and $A_1 : A_3 :: a_1 : a_3$

Next if there be four magnitudes, and other four such that

$A_1 : A_2 :: a_1 : a_2$.
$A_2 : A_3 :: a_2 : a_3$,
$A_3 : A_4 :: a_3 : a_4$
Then shall $A_1 : A_4 :: a_1 : a_4$.

For since $A_1 : A_2 :: a_1 : a_2$, $\therefore \dfrac{A_1}{A_2} = \dfrac{a_1}{a_2}$,

$A_2 : A_3 :: a_2 : a_3$, $\therefore \dfrac{A_2}{A_3} = \dfrac{a_2}{a_3}$,

$A_3 : A_4 :: a_3 : a_4$, $\therefore \dfrac{A_3}{A_4} = \dfrac{a_3}{a_4}$.

Multiplying these equals,

$$\therefore \dfrac{A_1}{A_2} \times \dfrac{A_2}{A_3} \times \dfrac{A_3}{A_4} = \dfrac{a_1}{a_2} \times \dfrac{a_2}{a_3} \times \dfrac{a_3}{a_4},$$

or $\dfrac{A_1}{A_4} = \dfrac{a_1}{a_4}$,

and $A_1 : A_4 :: a_1 : a_4$,

and similarly, if there were more than four magnitudes.

Prop. XXIII. Algebraically.

Let A_1, A_2, A_3 be three magnitudes,
and a_1, a_2, a_3 other three,
such that $A_1 : A_2 :: a_2 : a_3$,
and $A_2 : A_3 :: a_1 : a_2$.
Then shall $A_1 : A_3 :: a_1 : a_3$.

For since $A_1 : A_2 :: a_2 : a_3$, $\therefore \dfrac{A_1}{A_2} = \dfrac{a_2}{a_3}$,

and since $A_2 : A_3 :: a_1 : a_2$, $\therefore \dfrac{A_2}{A_3} = \dfrac{a_1}{a_2}$.

Multiplying these equals,

$$\therefore \frac{A_1}{A_2} \times \frac{A_2}{A_3} = \frac{a_2}{a_3} \times \frac{a_1}{a_2},$$

or $\dfrac{A_1}{A_3} = \dfrac{a_1}{a_3}$,

and $A_1 : A_3 :: a_1 : a_3$.

If there were four magnitudes, and other four, such that $A_1 : A_2 :: a_3 : a_4$,

$$A_2 : A_3 .: a_2 : a_3.$$
$$A_3 : A_4 .: a_1 : a_2,$$

Then shall also $A_1 : A_4 :: a_1 : a_4$.

For since $A_1 : A_2 :: a_3 : a_4$, $\therefore \dfrac{A_1}{A_2} = \dfrac{a_3}{a_4}$,

$A_2 : A_3 :: a_2 : a_3$, $\therefore \dfrac{A_2}{A_3} = \dfrac{a_2}{a_3}$,

$A_3 . A_4 . a_1 : a_2$, $\therefore \dfrac{A_3}{A_4} = \dfrac{a_1}{a_2}$.

Multiplying these equals,

$$\therefore \frac{A_1}{A_2} \times \frac{A_2}{A_3} \times \frac{A_3}{A_4} = \frac{a_3}{a_4} \times \frac{a_2}{a_3} \times \frac{a_1}{a_2},$$

or $\dfrac{A_1}{A_4} = \dfrac{a_1}{a_4}$,

$\therefore A_1 . A_4 .. a_1 . a_4$,

and similarly, if there be more than four magnitudes.

Prop. XXIV. Algebraically.

Let $A_1 . a_2 :: A_3 . a_4$,

and $A_5 . a_2 :: A_6 . a_4$,

Then shall $A_1 + A_5 : a_2 .. A_3 + A_6 . a_4$.

For since $A_1 : a_2 :: A_3 : a_4$, $\therefore \dfrac{A_1}{a_2} = \dfrac{A_3}{a_4}$,

and since $A_5 . a_2 .. A_6 . a_4$, $\dfrac{A_5}{a_2} = \dfrac{A_6}{a_4}$.

Divide the former by the latter of these equals,

$$\therefore \frac{A_1}{a_2} \div \frac{A_5}{a_2} = \frac{A_3}{a_4} \div \frac{A_6}{a_4},$$

or $\dfrac{A_1}{a_2} \times \dfrac{a_2}{A_5} = \dfrac{A_3}{a_4} \times \dfrac{a_4}{A_6}$,

$\therefore \dfrac{A_1}{A_5} = \dfrac{A_3}{A_6}$,

adding 1 to each of these equals;

$\therefore \dfrac{A_1}{A_5} + 1 = \dfrac{A_3}{A_6} + 1$,

or $\dfrac{A_1 + A_5}{A_5} = \dfrac{A_3 + A_6}{A_6}$,

and $\dfrac{A_5}{a_2} = \dfrac{A_6}{a_4}$.

Multiply these equals together,

$$\therefore \dfrac{A_1 + A_5}{A_5} \times \dfrac{A_5}{a_2} = \dfrac{A_3 + A_6}{A_6} \times \dfrac{A_6}{a_4},$$

or $\dfrac{A_1 + A_5}{a_2} = \dfrac{A_3 + A_6}{a_4}$,

and $\therefore A_1 + A_5 \; a_2 : A_3 + A_6 : a_4$.

Cor. 1. Similarly may be shewn, that
$$A_1 - A_5 \cdot a_2 : A_3 - A_6 \cdot a_4.$$

Prop. xxv. Algebraically.

Let $A_1 \; a_2 : . \; A_3 \cdot a_4$,

and let A_1 be the greatest, and consequently a_4 the least.

Then shall $A_1 + a_4 > a_2 + A_3$.

Since $A_1 : a_2 . \; A_3 . \; a_4$,

$$\therefore \dfrac{A_1}{a_2} = \dfrac{A_3}{a_4}.$$

Multiply these equals by $\dfrac{a_2}{A_3}$,

$$\therefore \dfrac{A_1}{A_3} = \dfrac{a_2}{a_4},$$

subtract 1 from each of these equals,

$$\therefore \dfrac{A_1}{A_3} - 1 = \dfrac{a_2}{a_4} - 1,$$

or $\dfrac{A_1 - A_3}{A_3} = \dfrac{a_2 - a_4}{a_4}$.

Multiplying these equals by $\dfrac{A_3}{a_2 - a_4}$,

$$\therefore \dfrac{A_1 - A_3}{a_2 - a_4} = \dfrac{A_3}{a_4},$$

but $\dfrac{A_1}{a_2} = \dfrac{A_3}{a_4}$,

$$\therefore \dfrac{A_1 - A_3}{a_2 - a_4} = \dfrac{A_1}{a_2},$$

but $A_1 > a_2$, $\therefore A_1$ is the greatest of the four magnitudes,

$\therefore$ also $A_1 - A_3 > a_2 - a_4$,

add $A_3 + a_4$ to each of these equals,

$A_1 + a_4 > a_2 + A_3$.

"The whole of the process in the Fifth Book is purely logical, that is, the whole of the results are virtually contained in the definitions, in the manner and sense in which metaphysicians (certain of them) imagine all the results of mathematics to be contained in their definitions and hypotheses. No assumption is made to determine the truth of any consequence of this definition, which takes for granted more about number or magnitude than is necessary to understand the definition itself. The latter being once understood, its results are deduced by inspection—of itself only, without the necessity of looking at any thing else. Hence, a great distinction between the fifth and the preceding books presents itself. The first four are a series of propositions, resting on different fundamental assumptions, that is, about different kinds of magnitudes. The fifth is a definition and its development; and if the analogy by which names have been given in the preceding Books had been attended to, the propositions of that Book would have been called *corollaries of the definition.*"—*Connexion of Number and Magnitude,* by Professor De Morgan, p 56

The Fifth Book of the Elements as a portion of Euclid's System of Geometry ought to be retained, as the doctrine contains some of the most important characteristics of an effective instrument of intellectual education. This opinion is favoured by Dr. Barrow in the following expressive terms "There is nothing in the whole body of the Elements of a more subtile invention, nothing more solidly established, or more accurately handled, than the doctrine of proportionals."

QUESTIONS ON BOOK V.

1. EXPLAIN and exemplify the meaning of the terms, *multiple, submultiple, equimultiple*

2. What operations in Geometry and Arithmetic are analogous?

3. What are the different meanings of the term *measure* in Geometry? When are Geometrical magnitudes said to have *a common measure?*

4. When are magnitudes said to have, and not to have, a ratio to one another? What restriction does this impose upon the magnitudes in regard to their *species?*

5. When are magnitudes said to be commensurable or incommensurable to each other? Do the definitions and theorems of Book v include incommensurable quantities?

6. What is meant by the term *geometrical ratio?* How is it represented?

7. Why does Euclid give no independent definition of ratio?

8. What sort of quantities are excluded from Euclid's idea of ratio, and how does his idea of ratio differ from the Algebraic definition?

9. How is *a ratio* represented *Algebraically?* Is there any distinction between the terms, *a ratio of equality,* and *equality of ratio?*

10. In what manner are ratios, in Geometry, distinguished from each other as equal, greater, or less than one another? What objection is there to the use of an independent definition (properly so called) of ratio in a system of Geometry?

11. Point out the distinction between the geometrical and algebraical methods of treating the subject of proportion.

12. What is the geometrical definition of proportion? Whence arises the necessity of such a definition as this?

13. Shew the necessity of the qualification "*any whatever*" in Euclid's definition of proportion.

14. Must magnitudes that are proportional be all of the same kind?

15. To what objection has Euc. v. def. 5, been considered liable?

16. Point out the connexion between the more obvious definition of proportion and that given by Euclid, and illustrate clearly the nature of the advantage obtained by which he was induced to adopt it.

17. Why may not Euclid's definition of proportion be superseded in a system of Geometry by the following: "Four quantities are proportionals,

when the first is the same multiple of the second, or the same part of it, that the third is to the fourth"?

18 Point out the defect of the following definition "Four magnitudes are proportional when equimultiples may be taken of the first and the third, and also of the second and fourth, such that the multiples of the first and second are equal, and also those of the third and fourth"

19 Apply Euclid's definition of proportion, to shew that if four quantities be proportional, and if the first and the third be divided into the same arbitrary number of equal parts, then the second and fourth will either be equimultiples of those parts, or will lie between the same two successive multiples of them

20 The Geometrical definition of proportion is a consequence of the Algebraical definition, and conversely

21. What Geometrical test has Euclid given to ascertain that four quantities are *not* proportionals? What is the Algebraical test?

22 Show in the manner of Euclid, that the ratio of 15 to 17 is greater than that of 11 to 13.

23 How far may the fifth definition of the fifth Book be regarded as an axiom? Is it convertible?

24 Def 9, Book v "Proportion consists of three terms at least" How is this to be understood?

25 Define *duplicate ratio*. How does it appear from Euclid that the duplicate ratio of two magnitudes is the same as that of their squares?

26 When is a ratio compounded of any number of ratios? What is the ratio which is compounded of the ratios of 2 to 5, 3 to 4, and 5 to 6?

27 By what process is a ratio found equal to the composition of two or more given ratios? Give an example, where straight lines are the magnitudes which express the given ratios.

28 What limitation is there to the alternation of a *Geometrical* proportion?

29 Explain the construction and sense of the phrases, *ex æquali*, and *ex æquali in proportione perturbata*, used in proportions

30 Exemplify the meaning of the word *homologous* as it is used in the Fifth Book of the Elements

31 Why, in Euclid v 11, is it necessary to prove that ratios which are the same with the same ratio, are the same with one another?

32. Apply the Geometrical criterion to ascertain whether the four lines of 3, 5, 6, 10 units are proportionals

33 Prove by taking equimultiples according to Euclid's definition, that the magnitudes 4, 5, 7, 9, are not proportionals.

34 Give the Algebraical proofs of Props 17 and 18, of the Fifth Book.

35 What is necessary to constitute an exact definition? In the demonstration of Euc v 18, is it legitimate to assume the converse of the fifth definition of that Book? Does a mathematical definition admit of proof on the principles of the science to which it relates?

36 Explain why the properties proved in Book v. by means of *straight lines*, are true *of any concrete magnitudes*.

37 Enunciate Euc. v 8, and illustrate it by numerical examples

38 Prove Algebraically Euc v 25

39 Shew that when four magnitudes are proportionals, they cannot, when equally increased or equally diminished by any other magnitude, continue to be proportionals

40 What grounds are there for the opinion that Euclid intended to *exclude* the idea of numerical measures of ratios in his Fifth Book?

41. What is the object of the Fifth Book of Euclid's Elements?

BOOK VI.

DEFINITIONS.

I.

SIMILAR rectilineal figures are those which have their several angles equal, each to each, and the sides about the equal angles proportionals.

II.

"Reciprocal figures, viz. triangles and parallelograms, are such as have their sides about two of their angles proportionals in such a manner, that a side of the first figure is to a side of the other, as the remaining side of the other is to the remaining side of the first."

III.

A straight line is said to be cut in extreme and mean ratio, when the whole is to the greater segment, as the greater segment is to the less.

IV.

The altitude of any figure is the straight line drawn from its vertex perpendicular to the base.

PROPOSITION I. THEOREM.

Triangles and parallelograms of the same altitude are one to the other as their bases.

Let the triangles ABC, ACD, and the parallelograms EC, CF, have the same altitude,
  viz. the perpendicular drawn from the point A to BD or BD produced.

As the base BC is to the base CD, so shall the triangle ABC be to the triangle ACD,
  and the parallelogram EC to the parallelogram CF.

Produce BD both ways to the points H, L,
and take any number of straight lines BG, GH, each equal to the base BC; (I. 3.)
and DK, KL, any number of them, each equal to the base CD;
and join AG, AH, AK, AL.

Then, because CB, BG, GH, are all equal,
the triangles AHG, AGB, ABC, are all equal: (I. 38.)
therefore, whatever multiple the base HC is of the base BC,
the same multiple is the triangle AHC of the triangle ABC:
for the same reason whatever multiple the base LC is of the base CD,
the same multiple is the triangle ALC of the triangle ADC:
and if the base HC be equal to the base CL,
the triangle AHC is also equal to the triangle ALC: (I. 38.)
and if the base HC be greater than the base CL,
likewise the triangle AHC is greater than the triangle ALC;
and if less, less;
therefore since there are four magnitudes,
viz. the two bases BC, CD, and the two triangles ABC, ACD;
and of the base BC, and the triangle ABC, the first and third, any equimultiples whatever have been taken,
viz. the base HC and the triangle AHC;
and of the base CD and the triangle ACD, the second and fourth, have been taken any equimultiples whatever,
viz. the base CL and the triangle ALC;
and since it has been shewn, that, if the base HC be greater than the base CL,
the triangle AHC is greater than the triangle ALC;
and if equal, equal; and if less, less;
therefore, as the base BC is to the base CD, so is the triangle ABC to the triangle ACD. (v. def. 5.)
And because the parallelogram CE is double of the triangle ABC, (I. 41.)
and the parallelogram CF double of the triangle ACD,
and that magnitudes have the same ratio which their equimultiples have; (v. 15.)
as the triangle ABC is to the triangle ACD, so is the parallelogram EC to the parallelogram CF;
and because it has been shewn, that, as the base BC is to the base CD, so is the triangle ABC to the triangle ACD;
and as the triangle ABC is to the triangle ACD, so is the parallelogram EC to the parallelogram CF;
therefore, as the base BC is to the base CD, so is the parallelogram EC to the parallelogram CF. (v. 11.)

Wherefore, triangles, &c. Q.E.D.

Cor. From this it is plain, that triangles and parallelograms that have equal altitudes, are to one another as their bases.

Let the figures be placed so as to have their bases in the same straight line; and having drawn perpendiculars from the vertices of the triangles to the bases, the straight line which joins the vertices is parallel to that in which their bases are, (I. 33.) because the perpendiculars are both equal and parallel to one another. (I. 28.) Then, if the same construction be made as in the proposition, the demonstration will be the same.

PROPOSITION II. THEOREM.

If a straight line be drawn parallel to one of the sides of a triangle it shall cut the other sides, or these produced, proportionally: and conversely, if the sides, or the sides produced, be cut proportionally, the straight line which joins the points of section shall be parallel to the remaining side of the triangle.

Let DE be drawn parallel to BC, one of the sides of the triangle ABC. Then BD shall be to DA, as CE to EA.

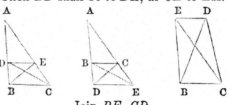

Join BE, CD.

Then the triangle BDE is equal to the triangle CDE, (I. 37.) because they are on the same base DE, and between the same parallels DE, BC;

but ADE is another triangle;

and equal magnitudes have the same ratio to the same magnitude; (V. 7.)

therefore, as the triangle BDE is to the triangle ADE, so is the triangle CDE to the triangle ADE:

but as the triangle BDE to the triangle ADE, so is BD to DA, (VI. 1.) because, having the same altitude, viz. the perpendicular drawn from the point E to AB, they are to one another as their bases;

and for the same reason, as the triangle CDE to the triangle ADE, so is CE to EA:

therefore, as BD to DA, so is CE to EA. (V. 11.)

Next, let the sides AB, AC of the triangle ABC, or these sides produced, be cut proportionally in the points D, E, that is, so that BD may be to DA as CE to EA, and join DE.

Then DE shall be parallel to BC.

The same construction being made,

because as BD to DA, so is CE to EA;

and as BD to DA, so is the triangle BDE to the triangle ADE; (VI. 1.)

and as CE to EA, so is the triangle CDE to the triangle ADE;

therefore the triangle BDE is to the triangle ADE, as the triangle CDE to the triangle ADE; (V. 11.)

that is, the triangles *BDE*, *CDE* have the same ratio to the triangle *ADE*:
therefore the triangle *BDE* is equal to the triangle *CDE*: (v. 9.)
and they are on the same base *DE*:
but equal triangles on the same base and on the same side of it, are between the same parallels; (i. 39.)
therefore *DE* is parallel to *BC*.
Wherefore, if a straight line, &c. Q.E.D.

PROPOSITION III. THEOREM.

If the angle of a triangle be divided into two equal angles, by a straight line which also cuts the base; the segments of the base shall have the same ratio which the other sides of the triangle have to one another: and conversely, if the segments of the base have the same ratio which the other sides of the triangle have to one another; the straight line drawn from the vertex to the point of section, divides the vertical angle into two equal angles.

Let *ABC* be a triangle, and let the angle *BAC* be divided into two equal angles by the straight line *AD*.
Then *BD* shall be to *DC*, as *BA* to *AC*.

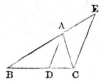

Through the point *C* draw *CE* parallel to *DA*, (i. 31.)
and let *BA* produced meet *CE* in *E*.
Because the straight line *AC* meets the parallels *AD*, *EC*, the angle *ACE* is equal to the alternate angle *CAD*: (i. 29.)
but *CAD*, by the hypothesis, is equal to the angle *BAD*;
wherefore *BAD* is equal to the angle *ACE*. (ax. 1.)
Again, because the straight line *BAE* meets the parallels *AD*, *EC*, the outward angle *BAD* is equal to the inward and opposite angle *AEC*: (i. 29.)
but the angle *ACE* has been proved equal to the angle *BAD*;
therefore also *ACE* is equal to the angle *AEC*, (ax. 1.)
and consequently, the side *AE* is equal to the side *AC*: (i. 6.)
and because *AD* is drawn parallel to *EC*, one of the sides of the triangle *BCE*,
therefore *BD* is to *DC*, as *BA* to *AE*: (vi. 2.)
but *AE* is equal to *AC*;
therefore, as *BD* to *DC*, so is *BA* to *AC*. (v. 7.)
Next, let *BD* be to *DC*, as *BA* to *AC*, and join *AD*.
Then the angle *BAC* shall be divided into two equal angles by the straight line *AD*.
The same construction being made;
because, as *BD* to *DC*, so is *BA* to *AC*;

and as BD to DC, so is BA to AE, because AD is parallel to EC; (VI. 2.)
therefore BA is to AC, as BA to AE: (V. 11.)
consequently AC is equal to AE, (V. 9.)
and therefore the angle AEC is equal to the angle ACE: (I. 5.)
but the angle AEC is equal to the outward and opposite angle BAD,
and the angle ACE is equal to the alternate angle CAD: (I. 29.)
wherefore also the angle BAD is equal to the angle CAD; (ax. 1.)
that is, the angle BAC is cut into two equal angles by the straight line AD.

Therefore, if the angle, &c. Q.E.D.

PROPOSITION A. THEOREM.

If the outward angle of a triangle made by producing one of its sides, be divided into two equal angles, by a straight line, which also cuts the base produced; the segments between the dividing line and the extremities of the base, have the same ratio which the other sides of the triangle have to one another: and conversely, if the segments of the base produced have the same ratio which the other sides of the triangle have; the straight line drawn from the vertex to the point of section divides the outward angle of the triangle into two equal angles.

Let ABC be a triangle, and let one of its sides BA be produced to E; and let the outward angle CAE be divided into two equal angles by the straight line AD which meets the base produced in D.
Then BD shall be to DC, as BA to AC.

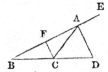

Through C draw CF parallel to AD: (I. 31.)
and because the straight line AC meets the parallels AD, FC, the angle ACF is equal to the alternate angle CAD: (I. 29.)
but CAD is equal to the angle DAE; (hyp.)
therefore also DAE is equal to the angle ACF. (ax. 1.)
Again, because the straight line FAE meets the parallels AD, FC, the outward angle DAE is equal to the inward and opposite angle CFA: (I. 29.)
but the angle ACF has been proved equal to the angle DAE;
therefore also the angle ACF is equal to the angle CFA; (ax. 1.)
and consequently the side AF is equal to the side AC: (I. 6.)
and because AD is parallel to FC, a side of the triangle BCF,
therefore, BD is to DC, as BA to AF: (VI. 2.)
but AF is equal to AC;
therefore as BD is to DC, so is BA to AC. (V. 7.)
Next, let BD be to DC, as BA to AC, and join AD.
The angle CAD, shall be equal to the angle DAE.
The same construction being made,
because BD is to DC, as BA to AC;

and that BD is also to DC, as BA to AF; (VI. 2.)
therefore BA is to AC, as BA to AF: (V. 11.)
wherefore AC is equal to AF, (V. 9.)
and the angle AFC equal to the angle ACF: (I. 5.)
but the angle AFC is equal to the outward angle EAD, (I. 29.)
and the angle ACF to the alternate angle CAD;
therefore also EAD is equal to the angle CAD. (ax. 1.)
Wherefore, if the outward, &c. Q.E.D.

PROPOSITION IV. THEOREM.

The sides about the equal angles of equiangular triangles are proportionals; and those which are opposite to the equal angles are homologous sides, that is, are the antecedents or consequents of the ratios.

Let ABC, DCE be equiangular triangles, having the angle ABC equal to the angle DCE, and the angle ACB to the angle DEC; and consequently the angle BAC equal to the angle CDE. (I. 32.)

The sides about the equal angles of the triangles ABC, DCE shall be proportionals;

and those shall be the homologous sides which are opposite to the equal angles.

Let the triangle DCE be placed, so that its side CE may be contiguous to BC, and in the same straight line with it. (I. 22.)

Then, because the angle BCA is equal to the angle CED, (hyp.)
add to each the angle ABC;

therefore the two angles ABC, BCA are equal to the two angles ABC, CED: (ax. 2.)

but the angles ABC, BCA are together less than two right angles; (I. 17.)

therefore the angles ABC, CED are also less than two right angles:
wherefore BA, ED, if produced will meet: (I. ax. 12.)
let them be produced and meet in the point F:
then because the angle ABC is equal to the angle DCE, (hyp.)
BF is parallel to CD; (I. 28.)
and because the angle ACB is equal to the angle DEC,
AC is parallel to FE: (I. 28.)
therefore $FACD$ is a parallelogram;
and consequently AF is equal to CD, and AC to FD: (I. 34.)
and because AC is parallel to FE, one of the sides of the triangle FBE,
BA is to AF, as BC to CE: (VI. 2.)
but AF is equal to CD;
therefore, as BA to CD, so is BC to CE: (V. 7.)
and alternately, as AB to BC, so is DC to CE; (V. 16.)

again, because CD is parallel to BF,
as BC to CE, so is FD to DE: (VI. 2.)
but FD is equal to AC;
therefore, as BC to CE, so is AC to DE; (V. 7.)
and alternately, as BC to CA, so CE to ED: (V. 16.)
therefore, because it has been proved that AB is to BC, as DC to CE,
and as BC to CA, so CE to ED,
ex æquali, BA is to AC, as CD to DE. (V. 22.)
Therefore the sides, &c. Q.E.D.

PROPOSITION V. THEOREM.

If the sides of two triangles, about each of their angles, be proportionals, the triangles shall be equiangular; and the equal angles shall be those which are opposite to the homologous sides.

Let the triangles ABC, DEF have their sides proportionals,
so that AB is to BC, as DE to EF;
and BC to CA, as EF to FD;
and consequently, ex æquali, BA to AC, as ED to DF.
Then the triangle ABC shall be equiangular to the triangle DEF, and the angles which are opposite to the homologous sides shall be equal, viz. the angle ABC equal to the angle DEF, and BCA to EFD, and also BAC to EDF.

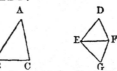

At the points E, F, in the straight line EF, make the angle FEG equal to the angle ABC, and the angle EFG equal to BCA; (I. 23.)
wherefore the remaining angle EGF, is equal to the remaining angle BAC, (I. 32.)
and the triangle GEF is therefore equiangular to the triangle ABC:
consequently they have their sides opposite to the equal angles proportional: (VI. 4.)
wherefore, as AB to BC, so is GE to EF;
but as AB to BC, so is DE to EF; (hyp.)
therefore as DE to EF, so GE to EF; (V. 11.)
that is, DE and GE have the same ratio to EF,
and consequently are equal. (V. 9.)
For the same reason, DF is equal to FG:
and because, in the triangles DEF, GEF, DE is equal to EG, and EF is common,
the two sides DE, EF are equal to the two GE, EF, each to each;
and the base DF is equal to the base GF;
therefore the angle DEF is equal to the angle GEF, (I. 8.)
and the other angles to the other angles which are subtended by the equal sides; (I. 4.)
therefore the angle DFE is equal to the angle GFE, and EDF to EGF.

and because the angle *DEF* is equal to the angle *GEF*,
and *GEF* equal to the angle *ABC*; (constr.)
therefore the angle *ABC* is equal to the angle *DEF*: (ax. 1.)
for the same reason, the angle *ACB* is equal to the angle *DFE*,
and the angle at *A* equal to the angle at *D*:
therefore the triangle *ABC* is equiangular to the triangle *DEF*.
Wherefore, if the sides, &c. Q.E.D.

PROPOSITION VI. THEOREM.

If two triangles have one angle of the one equal to one angle of the other, and the sides about the equal angles proportionals, the triangles shall be equiangular, and shall have those angles equal which are opposite to the homologous sides.

Let the triangles *ABC*, *DEF* have the angle *BAC* in the one equal to the angle *EDF* in the other, and the sides about those angles proportionals; that is, *BA* to *AC*, as *ED* to *DF*.

Then the triangles *ABC*, *DEF* shall be equiangular, and shall have the angle *ABC* equal to the angle *DEF*, and *ACB* to *DFE*.

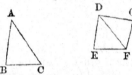

At the points *D*, *F*, in the straight line *DF*, make the angle *FDG* equal to either of the angles *BAC*, *EDF*; (I. 23.)
and the angle *DFG* equal to the angle *ACB*:
wherefore the remaining angle at *B* is equal to the remaining angle at *G* : (I. 32.)
and consequently the triangle *DGF* is equiangular to the triangle *ABC*;
therefore as *BA* to *AC*, so is *GD* to *DF*: (VI. 4.)
but, by the hypothesis, as *BA* to *AC*, so is *ED* to *DF*;
therefore as *ED* to *DF*, so is *GD* to *DF*; (v. 11.)
wherefore *ED* is equal to *DG*; (v. 9.)
and *DF* is common to the two triangles *EDF*, *GDF*:
therefore the two sides *ED*, *DF* are equal to the two sides *GD*, *DF*, each to each ;
and the angle *EDF* is equal to the angle *GDF*; (constr.)
wherefore the base *EF* is equal to the base *FG*, (I. 4.)
and the triangle *EDF* to the triangle *GDF*,
and the remaining angles to the remaining angles, each to each, which are subtended by the equal sides;
therefore the angle *DFG* is equal to the angle *DFE*,
and the angle at *G* to the angle at *E*;
but the angle *DFG* is equal to the angle *ACB*; (constr.)
therefore the angle *ACB* is equal to the angle *DFE*; (ax. 1.)
and the angle *BAC* is equal to the angle *EDF*: (hyp.)
wherefore also the remaining angle at *B* is equal to the remaining angle at *E*; (I. 32.)
therefore the triangle *ABC* is equiangular to the triangle *DEF*.
Wherefore, if two triangles, &c. Q.E.D.

PROPOSITION VII. THEOREM.

If two triangles have one angle of the one equal to one angle of the other, and the sides about two other angles proportionals, then, if each of the remaining angles be either less, or not less, than a right angle, or if one of them be a right angle; the triangles shall be equiangular, and shall have those angles equal about which the sides are proportionals.

Let the two triangles ABC, DEF have one angle in the one equal to one angle in the other,
viz. the angle BAC to the angle EDF, and the sides about two other angles ABC, DEF proportionals,
so that AB is to BC, as DE to EF;
and in the first case, let each of the remaining angles at C, F be less than a right angle.
The triangle ABC shall be equiangular to the triangle DEF,
viz. the angle ABC shall be equal to the angle DEF,
and the remaining angle at C equal to the remaining angle at F.

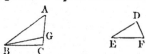

For if the angles ABC, DEF be not equal,
one of them must be greater than the other:
let ABC be the greater,
and at the point B, in the straight line AB,
make the angle ABG equal to the angle DEF; (I. 23)
and because the angle at A is equal to the angle at D, (hyp.)
and the angle ABG to the angle DEF;
the remaining angle AGB is equal to the remaining angle DFE: (I. 32.)
therefore the triangle ABG is equiangular to the triangle DEF·
wherefore as AB is to BG, so is DE to EF; (VI. 4)
but as DE to EF, so, by hypothesis, is AB to BC;
therefore as AB to BC, so is AB to BG· (V. 11)
and because AB has the same ratio to each of the lines BC, BG,
BC is equal to BG; (V. 9)
and therefore the angle BGC is equal to the angle BCG· (I. 5.)
but the angle BCG is, by hypothesis, less than a right angle;
therefore also the angle BGC is less than a right angle,
and therefore the adjacent angle AGB must be greater than a right angle; (I. 13.)
but it was proved that the angle AGB is equal to the angle at F;
therefore the angle at F is greater than a right angle;
but, by the hypothesis, it is less than a right angle; which is absurd.
Therefore the angles ABC, DEF are not unequal,
that is, they are equal
and the angle at A is equal to the angle at D: (hyp.)
wherefore the remaining angle at C is equal to the remaining angle at F: (I. 32)
therefore the triangle ABC is equiangular to the triangle DEF.

Next, let each of the angles at *C*, *F* be not less than a right angle. Then the triangle *ABC* shall also in this case be equiangular to the triangle *DEF*.

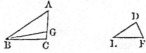

The same construction being made,
it may be proved in like manner that *BC* is equal to *BG*,
and therefore the angle at *C* equal to the angle *BGC*.
but the angle at *C* is not less than a right angle, (hyp.)
therefore the angle *BGC* is not less than a right angle
wherefore two angles of the triangle *BGC* are together not less than two right angles;
which is impossible; (I. 17.)
and therefore the triangle *ABC* may be proved to be equiangular to the triangle *DEF*, as in the first case.
Lastly, let one of the angles at *C*, *F*, viz. the angle at *C*, be a right angle: in this case likewise the triangle *ABC* shall be equiangular to the triangle *DEF*.

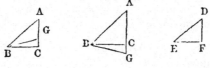

For, if they be not equiangular,
at the point *B* in the straight line *AB* make the angle *ABG* equal to the angle *DEF*;
then it may be proved, as in the first case, that *BG* is equal to *BC*.
and therefore the angle *BCG* equal to the angle *BGC*: (I. 5.)
but the angle *BCG* is a right angle, (hyp.)
therefore the angle *BGC* is also a right angle, (ax. 1.)
whence two of the angles of the triangle *BGC* are together not less than two right angles;
which is impossible (I. 17.)
therefore the triangle *ABC* is equiangular to the triangle *DEF*.
Wherefore, if two triangles, &c. Q.E.D.

PROPOSITION VIII. THEOREM.

In a right-angled triangle, if a perpendicular be drawn from the right-angle to the base, the triangles on each side of it are similar to the whole triangle, and to one another.

Let *ABC* be a right-angled triangle, having the right angle *BAC*; and from the point *A* let *AD* be drawn perpendicular to the base *BC*.

Then the triangles *ABD*, *ADC* shall be similar to the whole triangle *ABC*, and to one another.

Because the angle BAC is equal to the angle ADB, each of them being a right angle, (ax. 11.)
and that the angle at B is common to the two triangles ABC, ABD:
  the remaining angle ACB is equal to the remaining angle BAD; (I. 32.)
  therefore the triangle ABC is equiangular to the triangle ABD, and the sides about their equal angles are proportionals; (VI. 4.)
    wherefore the triangles are similar;' (VI. def. 1.)
  in the like manner it may be demonstrated, that the triangle ADC is equiangular and similar to the triangle ABC.
And the triangles ABD, ACD, being both equiangular and similar to ABC, are equiangular and similar to each other.
  Therefore, in a right-angled, &c. Q.E.D.

Cor. From this it is manifest, that the perpendicular drawn from the right angle of a right-angled triangle to the base, is a mean proportional between the segments of the base; and also that each of the sides is a mean proportional between the base, and the segment of it adjacent to that side: because in the triangles BDA, ADC; BD is to DA, as DA to DC; (VI. 4.)
and in the triangles ABC, DBA; BC is to BA, as BA to BD: (VI. 4.)
and in the triangles ABC, ACD; BC is to CA, as CA to CD. (VI. 4.)

PROPOSITION IX. PROBLEM.

From a given straight line to cut off any part required.

Let AB be the given straight line.
It is required to cut off any part from it.

From the point A draw a straight line AC, making any angle with AB;
  and in AC take any point D,
and take AC the same multiple of AD, that AB is of the part which is to be cut off from it;
  join BC, and draw DE parallel to CB.
  Then AE shall be the part required to be cut off.
Because ED is parallel to BC, one of the sides of the triangle ABC,
  as CD is to DA, so is BE to EA; (VI. 2.)
  and by composition, CA is to AD, as BA to AE: (V. 18.)

but CA is a multiple of AD; (constr.)
therefore BA is of the same multiple AE: (v. D.)
whatever part therefore AD is of AC, AE is the same part of AB:
wherefore, from the straight line AB the part required is cut
off. Q.E.F.

PROPOSITION X. PROBLEM.

To divide a given straight line similarly to a given divided straight line, that is, into parts that shall have the same ratios to one another which the parts of the divided given straight line have.

Let AB be the straight line given to be divided, and AC the divided line.

It is required to divide AB similarly to AC.

Let AC be divided in the points D, E;
and let AB, AC be placed so as to contain any angle, and join BC,
and through the points D, E draw DF, EG parallels to BC. (I. 31.)
Then AB shall be divided in the points F, G, similarly to AC.
Through D draw DHK parallel to AB:
therefore each of the figures, FH, HB is a parallelogram;
wherefore DH is equal to FG, and HK to GB: (I. 34.)
and because HE is parallel to KC, one of the sides of the triangle DKC,
as CE to ED, so is KH to HD: (VI. 2.)
but KH is equal to BG, and HD to GF;
therefore, as CE is to ED, so is BG to GF: (V. 7.)
again, because FD is parallel to GE, one of the sides of the triangle AGE,
as ED is to DA, so is GF to FA; (VI. 2.)
therefore, as has been proved, as CE is to ED, so is BG to GF,
and as ED is to DA, so is GF to FA:
therefore the given straight line AB, is divided similarly to AC. Q.E.F.

PROPOSITION XI. PROBLEM.

To find a third proportional to two given straight lines.

Let AB, AC be the two given straight lines.
It is required to find a third proportional to AB, AC.

Let AB, AC be placed so as to contain any angle:
produce AB, AC to the points D, E;

and make BD equal to AC;
join BC, and through D, draw DE parallel to BC. (I. 31.)
Then CE shall be a third proportional to AB and AC.
Because BC is parallel to DE, a side of the triangle ADE,
AB is to BD, as AC to CE: (VI. 2.)
but BD is equal to AC;
therefore as AB is to AC, so is AC to CE. (V. 7.)
Wherefore, to the two given straight lines AB, AC, a third proportional CE is found. Q.E.F.

PROPOSITION XII. PROBLEM.

To find a fourth proportional to three given straight lines.

Let A, B, C be the three given straight lines.
It is required to find a fourth proportional to A, B, C.
Take two straight lines DE, DF, containing any angle EDF: and upon these make DG equal to A, GE equal to B, and DH equal to C; (I. 3.)

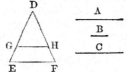

join GH, and through E draw EF parallel to it. (I. 31.)
Then HF shall be the fourth proportional to A, B, C.
Because GH is parallel to EF, one of the sides of the triangle DEF,
DG is to GE, as DH to HF; (VI. 2.)
but DG is equal to A, GE to B, and DH to C;
therefore, as A is to B, so is C to HF. (V. 7.)
Wherefore to the three given straight lines A, B, C, a fourth proportional HF is found. Q.E.F.

PROPOSITION XIII. PROBLEM.

To find a mean proportional between two given straight lines.

Let AB, BC be the two given straight lines.
It is required to find a mean proportional between them.

Place AB, BC in a straight line, and upon AC describe the semicircle ADC,
and from the point B draw BD at right angles to AC. (I. 11.)
Then BD shall be a mean proportional between AB and BC.
Join AD, DC.

And because the angle ADC in a semicircle is a right angle, (III. 31.) and because in the right-angled triangle ADC, BD is drawn from the right angle perpendicular to the base,

DB is a mean proportional between AB, BC the segments of the base: (VI. 8. Cor.)

therefore between the two given straight lines AB, BC, a mean proportional DB is found. Q.E.F.

PROPOSITION XIV. THEOREM.

Equal parallelograms, which have one angle of the one equal to one angle of the other, have their sides about the equal angles reciprocally proportional: and conversely, parallelograms that have one angle of the one equal to one angle of the other, and their sides about the equal angles reciprocally proportional, are equal to one another.

Let AB, BC be equal parallelograms, which have the angles at B equal.

The sides of the parallelograms AB, BC about the equal angles, shall be reciprocally proportional;

that is, DB shall be to BE, as GB to BF.

Let the sides DB, BE be placed in the same straight line; wherefore also FB, BG are in one straight line: (I. 14.)

complete the parallelogram FE.

And because the parallelogram AB is equal to BC, and that FE is another parallelogram,

AB is to FE, as BC to FE: (V. 7.)

but as AB to FE so is the base DB to BE, (VI. 1.)

and as BC to FE, so is the base GB to BF;

therefore, as DB to BE, so is GB to BF. (V. 11.)

Wherefore, the sides of the parallelograms AB, BC about their equal angles are reciprocally proportional.

Next, let the sides about the equal angles be reciprocally proportional, viz. as DB to BE, so GB to BF:

the parallelogram AB shall be equal to the parallelogram BC.

Because, as DB to BE, so is GB to BF;

and as DB to BE, so is the parallelogram AB to the parallelogram FE; (VI. 1.)

and as GB to BF, so is the parallelogram BC to the parallelogram FE;

therefore as AB to FE, so BC to FE: (V. 11.)

therefore the parallelogram AB is equal to the parallelogram BC. (V. 9.)

Therefore equal parallelograms, &c. Q.E.D.

PROPOSITION XV. THEOREM.

Equal triangles which have one angle of the one equal to one angle of the other, have their sides about the equal angles reciprocally proportional. and conversely, triangles which have one angle in the one equal to one angle in the other, and their sides about the equal angles reciprocally proportional, are equal to one another.

Let ABC, ADE be equal triangles, which have the angle BAC equal to the angle DAE.

Then the sides about the equal angles of the triangles shall be reciprocally proportional;

that is, CA shall be to AD, as EA to AB.

Let the triangles be placed so that their sides CA, AD be in one straight line;

wherefore also EA and AB are in one straight line; (I. 14.)
and join BD.

Because the triangle ABC is equal to the triangle ADE,
and that ABD is another triangle;

therefore as the triangle CAB, is to the triangle BAD, so is the triangle AED to the triangle DAB; (V. 7.)

but as the triangle CAB to the triangle BAD, so is the base CA to the base AD, (VI. 1.)

and as the triangle EAD to the triangle DAB, so is the base EA to the base AB; (VI. 1.)

therefore as CA to AD, so is EA to AB: (V. 11.)

wherefore the sides of the triangles ABC, ADE, about the equal angles are reciprocally proportional.

Next, let the sides of the triangles ABC, ADE about the equal angles be reciprocally proportional,

viz. CA to AD as EA to AB.

Then the triangle ABC shall be equal to the triangle ADE.

Join BD as before.

Then because, as CA to AD, so is EA to AB; (hyp.)

and as CA to AD, so is the triangle ABC to the triangle BAD: (VI. 1.)

and as EA to AB, so is the triangle EAD to the triangle BAD; (VI. 1.)

therefore as the triangle BAC to the triangle BAD, so is the triangle EAD to the triangle BAD; (V. 11.)

that is, the triangles BAC, EAD have the same ratio to the triangle BAD:

wherefore the triangle ABC is equal to the triangle ADE. (V. 9.)

Therefore, equal triangles, &c. Q.E.D.

PROPOSITION XVI. THEOREM.

If four straight lines be proportionals, the rectangle contained by the extremes is equal to the rectangle contained by the means: and conversely, if the rectangle contained by the extremes be equal to the rectangle contained by the means, the four straight lines are proportionals.

Let the four straight lines AB, CD, E, F be proportionals, viz. as AB to CD, so E to F.

The rectangle contained by AB, F, shall be equal to the rectangle contained by CD, E.

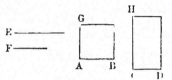

From the points A, C draw AG, CH at right angles to AB, CD: (I. 11.)
and make AG equal to F, and CH equal to E; (I. 3.)
and complete the parallelograms BG, DH. (I. 31.)

Because, as AB to CD, so is E to F;
and that E is equal to CH, and F to AG,
AB is to CD as CH to AG (v. 7.)
therefore the sides of the parallelograms BG, DH about the equal angles are reciprocally proportional.
but parallelograms which have their sides about equal angles reciprocally proportional, are equal to one another: (vi. 14.)
therefore the parallelogram BG is equal to the parallelogram DH:
but the parallelogram BG is contained by the straight lines AB, F;
because AG is equal to F,
and the parallelogram DH is contained by CD and E;
because CH is equal to E,
therefore the rectangle contained by the straight lines AB, F, is equal to that which is contained by CD and E.

And if the rectangle contained by the straight lines AB, F, be equal to that which is contained by CD, E;
these four lines shall be proportional,
viz. AB shall be to CD, as E to F.

The same construction being made,
because the rectangle contained by the straight lines AB, F, is equal to that which is contained by CD, E,
and that the rectangle BG is contained by AB, F;
because AG is equal to F,
and the rectangle DH by CD, E, because CH is equal to E;
therefore the parallelogram BG is equal to the parallelogram DH; (ax. 1.)
and they are equiangular:
but the sides about the equal angles of equal parallelograms are reciprocally proportional. (vi. 14.)
wherefore, as AB to CD, so is CH to AG.

But CH is equal to E, and AG to F;
therefore as AB is to CD, so is E to F. (v. 7.)
Wherefore, if four, &c. Q.E.D.

PROPOSITION XVII. THEOREM.

If three straight lines be proportionals, the rectangle contained by the extremes is equal to the square on the mean, and conversely, if the rectangle contained by the extremes be equal to the square on the mean, the three straight lines are proportionals.

Let the three straight lines A, B, C be proportionals,
viz. as A to B, so B to C.
The rectangle contained by A, C shall be equal to the square on B.

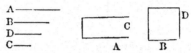

Take D equal to B.
And because as A to B, so B to C, and that B is equal to D;
A is to B, as D to C (v. 7)
but if four straight lines be proportionals, the rectangle contained by the extremes is equal to that which is contained by the means: (VI. 16.)
therefore the rectangle contained by A, C is equal to that contained by B, D:
but the rectangle contained by B, D, is the square on B,
because B is equal to D.
therefore the rectangle contained by A, C, is equal to the square on B.
And if the rectangle contained by A, C, be equal to the square on B, then A shall be to B, as B to C.
The same construction being made,
because the rectangle contained by A, C is equal to the square on B, and the square on B is equal to the rectangle contained by B, D,
because B is equal to D;
therefore the rectangle contained by A, C, is equal to that contained by B, D:
but if the rectangle contained by the extremes be equal to that contained by the means, the four straight lines are proportionals. (VI. 16.)
therefore A is to B, as D to C:
but B is equal to D,
wherefore, as A to B, so B to C.
Therefore, if three straight lines, &c. Q.E.D.

PROPOSITION XVIII. PROBLEM.

Upon a given straight line to describe a rectilineal figure similar, and similarly situated, to a given rectilineal figure.

Let AB be the given straight line, and $CDEF$ the given rectilineal figure of four sides.

It is required upon the given straight line AB to describe a rectilineal figure similar, and similarly situated, to $CDEF$.

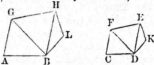

Join DF, and at the points A, B in the straight line AB, make the angle BAG equal to the angle at C, (I. 23.)
and the angle ABG equal to the angle CDF;
therefore the remaining angle AGB is equal to the remaining angle CFD: (I. 32 and ax. 3.)
therefore the triangle FCD is equiangular to the triangle GAB.
Again, at the points G, B, in the straight line GB, make the angle
BGH equal to the angle DFE, (I. 23)
and the angle GBH equal to FDE;
therefore the remaining angle GHB is equal to the remaining angle FED,
and the triangle FDE equiangular to the triangle GBH:
then, because the angle AGB is equal to the angle CFD, and BGH to DFE,
the whole angle AGH is equal to the whole angle CFE; (ax. 2.)
for the same reason, the angle ABH is equal to the angle CDE:
also the angle at A is equal to the angle at C, (constr.)
and the angle GHB to FED:
therefore the rectilineal figure $ABHG$ is equiangular to $CDEF$:
likewise these figures have their sides about the equal angles proportionals;
because the triangles GAB, FCD being equiangular,
BA is to AG, as CD to CF; (VI. 4.)
and because AG is to GB, as CF to FD;
and as GB is to GH, so is FD to FE,
by reason of the equiangular triangles BGH, DFE,
therefore, ex æquali, AG is to GH, as CF to FE. (V. 22.)
In the same manner it may be proved that AB is to BH, as CD to DE:
and GH is to HB, as FE to ED. (VI. 4.)
Wherefore, because the rectilineal figures $ABHG$, $CDEF$ are equiangular.
and have their sides about the equal angles proportionals,
they are similar to one another. (VI. def. 1.)

Next, let it be required to describe upon a given straight line AB, a rectilineal figure similar, and similarly situated, to the rectilineal figure $DKEF$ of five sides.
Join DE, and upon the given straight line AB describe the rectilineal figure $ABHG$ similar, and similarly situated, to the quadrilateral figure $CDEF$, by the former case:
and at the points B, H, in the straight line BH, make the angle
HBL equal to the angle EDK,
and the angle BHL equal to the angle DEK;

therefore the remaining angle at L is equal to the remaining angle at K. (I. 32, and ax. 3.)
And because the figures $ABHG$, $CDEF$ are similar,
the angle GHB is equal to the angle FED; (VI. def. 1.)
and BHL is equal to DEK;
wherefore the whole angle GHL is equal to the whole angle FEK:
for the same reason the angle ABL is equal to the angle CDK:
therefore the five-sided figures $AGHLB$, $CFEKD$ are equiangular:
and because the figures $AGHB$, $CFED$ are similar,
GH is to HB, as FE to ED; (VI. def. 1.)
but as HB to HL, so is ED to EK; (VI. 4.)
therefore, ex æquali, GH is to HL, as FE to EK: (V. 22.)
for the same reason, AB is to BL, as CD to DK:
and BL is to LH, as DK to KE, (VI. 4.)
because the triangles BLH, DKE are equiangular:
therefore because the five-sided figures $AGHLB$, $CFEKD$ are equiangular,
and have their sides about the equal angles proportionals,
they are similar to one another.
In the same manner a rectilineal figure of six sides may be described upon a given straight line similar to one given, and so on.
Q.E.F.

PROPOSITION XIX. THEOREM.

Similar triangles are to one another in the duplicate ratio of their homologous sides.

Let ABC, DEF be similar triangles, having the angle B equal to the angle E,
and let AB be to BC, as DE to EF,
so that the side BC may be homologous to EF. (V. def. 12.)
Then the triangle ABC shall have to the triangle DEF the duplicate ratio of that which BC has to EF.

Take BG a third proportional to BC, EF, (VI. 11.)
so that BC may be to EF, as EF to BG, and join GA.
Then, because as AB to BC, so DE to EF;
alternately, AB is to DE, as BC to EF: (V. 16.)
but as BC to EF, so is EF to BG; (constr.)
therefore, as AB to DE, so is EF to BG: (V. 11.)
therefore the sides of the triangles ABG, DEF, which are about the equal angles, are reciprocally proportional:
but triangles, which have the sides about two equal angles reciprocally proportional, are equal to one another: (VI. 15.)
therefore the triangle ABG is equal to the triangle DEF:
and because as BC is to EF, so EF to BG;

and that if three straight lines be proportionals, the first is said to have to the third, the duplicate ratio of that which it has to the second: (v. def. 10.)
therefore BC has to BG the duplicate ratio of that which BC has to EF:
but as BC is to BG, so is the triangle ABC to the triangle ABG; (vi. 1.)
    therefore the triangle ABC has to the triangle ABG, the duplicate ratio of that which BC has to EF:
        but the triangle ABG is equal to the triangle DEF;
therefore also the triangle ABC has to the triangle DEF, the duplicate ratio of that which BC has to EF.
        Therefore similar triangles, &c.   Q.E.D.

Cor. From this it is manifest, that if three straight lines be proportionals, as the first is to the third, so is any triangle upon the first, to a similar and similarly described triangle upon the second.

PROPOSITION XX. THEOREM.

Similar polygons may be divided into the same number of similar triangles, having the same ratio to one another that the polygons have; and the polygons have to one another the duplicate ratio of that which their homologous sides have.

Let $ABCDE$, $FGHKL$ be similar polygons, and let AB be the side homologous to FG:
    the polygons $ABCDE$, $FGHKL$ may be divided into the same number of similar triangles, whereof each shall have to each the same ratio which the polygons have;
    and the polygon $ABCDE$ shall have to the polygon $FGHKL$ the duplicate ratio of that which the side AB has to the side FG.

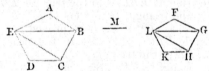

Join BE, EC, GL, LH.
And because the polygon $ABCDE$ is similar to the polygon $FGHKL$, the angle BAE is equal to the angle GFL. (vi. def. 1.)
    and BA is to AE, as GF to FL: (vi. def. 1.)
therefore, because the triangles ABE, FGL have an angle in one, equal to an angle in the other, and their sides about these equal angles proportionals,
    the triangle ABE is equiangular to the triangle FGL: (vi. 6.)
        and therefore similar to it; (vi. 4.)
    wherefore the angle ABE is equal to the angle FGL:
        and, because the polygons are similar,
the whole angle ABC is equal to the whole angle FGH; (vi. def. 1.)
    therefore the remaining angle EBC is equal to the remaining angle LGH: (i. 32. and ax. 3.)
        and because the triangles ABE, FGL are similar,
            EB is to BA, as LG to GF; (vi. 4.)

and also, because the polygons are similar,
AB is to BC, as FG to GH; (VI. def. 1.)
therefore, ex æquali, EB is to BC, as LG to GH; (V. 22.)
that is, the sides about the equal angles EBC, LGH are proportionals;
therefore, the triangle EBC is equiangular to the triangle LGH, (VI. 6.) and similar to it; (VI. 4.)
for the same reason, the triangle ECD likewise is similar to the triangle LHK.
therefore the similar polygons $ABCDE$, $FGHKL$ are divided into the same number of similar triangles.

Also these triangles shall have, each to each, the same ratio which the polygons have to one another,
the antecedents being ABE, EBC, ECD, and the consequents FGL, LGH, LHK:
and the polygon $ABCDE$ shall have to the polygon $FGHKL$ the duplicate ratio of that which the side AB has to the homologous side FG. Because the triangle ABE is similar to the triangle FGL, ABE has to FGL, the duplicate ratio of that which the side BE has to the side GL: (VI. 19.)
for the same reason, the triangle BEC has to GLH the duplicate ratio of that which BE has to GL
therefore, as the triangle ABE is to the triangle FGL, so is the triangle BEC to the triangle GLH (V. 11.)
Again, because the triangle EBC is similar to the triangle LGH, EBC has to LGH, the duplicate ratio of that which the side EC has to the side LH:
for the same reason, the triangle ECD has to the triangle LHK, the duplicate ratio of that which EC has to LH
therefore, as the triangle EBC is to the triangle LGH, so is the triangle ECD to the triangle LHK (V. 11.)
but it has been proved,
that the triangle EBC is likewise to the triangle LGH, as the triangle ABE to the triangle FGL;
therefore, as the triangle ABE to the triangle FGL, so is the triangle EBC to the triangle LGH, and the triangle ECD to the triangle LHK:
and therefore, as one of the antecedents is to one of the consequents, so are all the antecedents to all the consequents: (V. 12.)
that is, as the triangle ABE to the triangle FGL, so is the polygon $ABCDE$ to the polygon $FGHKL$:
but the triangle ABE has to the triangle FGL, the duplicate ratio of that which the side AB has to the homologous side FG, (VI. 19.)
therefore also the polygon $ABCDE$ has to the polygon $FGHKL$ the duplicate ratio of that which AB has to the homologous side FG.
Wherefore, similar polygons, &c. Q.E.D.

Cor. 1. In like manner it may be proved, that similar four-sided figures, or of any number of sides, are one to another in the duplicate ratio of their homologous sides. and it has already been proved in triangles: (VI. 19.) therefore, universally, similar rectilineal figures are to one another in the duplicate ratio of their homologous sides.

Cor. 2. And if to AB, FG, two of the homologous sides, a third proportional M be taken, (VI. 11.)

AB has to M the duplicate ratio of that which AB has to FG: (v. def. 10.)

but the four-sided figure or polygon upon AB, has to the four-sided figure or polygon upon FG likewise the duplicate ratio of that which AB has to FG (vi. 20. Cor 1.)

therefore, as AB is to M, so is the figure upon AB to the figure upon FG: (v. 11.)

which was also proved in triangles: (vi. 19. Cor.)

therefore, universally, it is manifest, that if three straight lines be proportionals, as the first is to the third, so is any rectilineal figure upon the first, to a similar and similarly described rectilineal figure upon the second.

PROPOSITION XXI. THEOREM.

Rectilineal figures which are similar to the same rectilineal figure, are also similar to one another.

Let each of the rectilineal figures A, B be similar to the rectilineal figure C.

The figure A shall be similar to the figure B.

Because A is similar to C,
they are equiangular, and also have their sides about the equal angles proportional (vi def. 1.)

again, because B is similar to C,
they are equiangular, and have their sides about the equal angles proportionals: (vi. def. 1.)

therefore the figures A, B are each of them equiangular to C, and have the sides about the equal angles of each of them and of C proportionals.

Wherefore the rectilineal figures A and B are equiangular, (i. ax. 1.) and have their sides about the equal angles proportionals; (v. 11.)

therefore A is similar to B (vi. def. 1.)

Therefore, rectilineal figures, &c. Q.E.D.

PROPOSITION XXII. THEOREM.

If four straight lines be proportionals, the similar rectilineal figures similarly described upon them shall also be proportionals; and conversely, if the similar rectilineal figures similarly described upon four straight lines be proportionals, those straight lines shall be proportionals.

Let the four straight lines AB, CD, EF, GH be proportionals, viz. AB to CD, as EF to GH;

and upon AB, CD let the similar rectilineal figures KAB, LCD be similarly described;

and upon EF, GH the similar rectilineal figures MF, NH, in like manner:

the rectilineal figure KAB shall be to LCD, as MF to NH.

BOOK VI. PROP. XXII., XXIII.   281

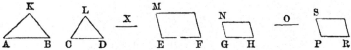

To AB, CD take a third proportional X; (VI. 11.)
and to EF, GH a third proportional O:
and because AB is to CD as EF to GH,
therefore CD is to X, as GH to O; (V. 11.)
wherefore, ex æquali, as AB to X, so EF to O: (V. 22.)
but as AB to X, so is the rectilineal figure KAB to the rectilineal figure LCD,
and as EF to O, so is the rectilineal figure MF to the rectilineal figure NH: (VI. 20. Cor. 2.)
therefore, as KAB to LCD, so is MF to NH. (V. 11.)
And if the rectilineal figure KAB be to LCD, as MF to NH;
the straight line AB shall be to CD, as EF to GH.
Make as AB to CD, so EF to PR, (VI. 12.)
and upon PR describe the rectilineal figure SR similar and similarly situated to either of the figures MF, NH: (VI. 18.)
then, because as AB to CD, so is EF to PR,
and that upon AB, CD are described the similar and similarly situated rectilineals KAB, LCD,
and upon EF, PR, in like manner, the similar rectilineals MF, SR;
therefore KAB is to LCD, as MF to SR:
but by the hypothesis KAB is to LCD, as MF to NH;
and therefore the rectilineal MF having the same ratio to each of the two NH, SR,
these are equal to one another; (V. 9.)
they are also similar, and similarly situated;
therefore GH is equal to PR:
and because as AB to CD, so is EF to PR,
and that PR is equal GH;
AB is to CD, as EF to GH. (V. 7.)
If therefore, four straight lines, &c.   Q.E.D.

PROPOSITION XXIII. THEOREM.

Equiangular parallelograms have to one another the ratio which is compounded of the ratios of their sides.

Let AC, CF be equiangular parallelograms, having the angle BCD equal to the angle ECG.
Then the ratio of the parallelogram AC to the parallelogram CF, shall be the same with the ratio which is compounded of the ratios of their sides.

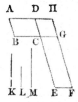

Let BC, CG be placed in a straight line;
therefore DC and CE are also in a straight line; (I. 14.)
and complete the parallelogram DG;
and taking any straight line K,
make as BC to CG, so K to L; (VI. 12.)
and as DC to CE, so make L to M; (VI. 12.)
therefore, the ratios of K to L, and L to M, are the same with the ratios of the sides,
viz. of BC to CG, and DC to CE:
but the ratio of K to M is that which is said to be compounded of the ratios of K to L, and L to M; (V. def. A.)
therefore K has to M the ratio compounded of the ratios of the sides:
and because as BC to CG, so is the parallelogram AC to the parallelogram CH; (VI. 1.)
but as BC to CG, so is K to L;
therefore K is to L, as the parallelogram AC to the parallelogram CH: (V. 11.)
again, because as DC to CE, so is the parallelogram CH to the parallelogram CF;
but as DC to CE, so is L to M;
wherefore L is to M, as the parallelogram CH to the parallelogram CF; (V. 11.)
therefore since it has been proved,
that as K to L, so is the parallelogram AC to the parallelogram CH;
and as L to M, so is the parallelogram CH to the parallelogram GF;
ex æquali, K is to M, as the parallelogram AC to the parallelogram CF: (V. 22.)
but K has to M the ratio which is compounded of the ratios of the sides;
therefore also the parallelogram AC has to the parallelogram CF, the ratio which is compounded of the ratios of the sides.
Wherefore, equiangular parallelograms, &c. Q.E.D.

PROPOSITION XXIV. THEOREM.

Parallelograms about the diameter of any parallelogram, are similar to the whole, and to one another.

Let $ABCD$ be a parallelogram, of which the diameter is AC;
and EG, HK parallelograms about the diameter.
The parallelograms EG, HK shall be similar both to the whole parallelogram $ABCD$, and to one another.

Because DC, GF are parallels,
the angle ADC is equal to the angle AGF: (I. 29.)
for the same reason, because BC, EF are parallels,
the angle ABC is equal to the angle AEF:

and each of the angles BCD, EFG is equal to the opposite angle DAB, (I. 34.)
and therefore they are equal to one another:
wherefore the parallelograms $ABCD$, $AEFG$, are equiangular:
and because the angle ABC is equal to the angle AEF,
and the angle BAC common to the two triangles BAC, EAF,
they are equiangular to one another;
therefore as AB to BC, so is AE to EF: (VI. 4.)
and because the opposite sides of parallelograms are equal to one another, (I. 34.)
AB is to AD as AE to AG; (V. 7.)
and DC to CB, as GF to FE;
and also CD to DA, as FG to GA:
therefore the sides of the parallelograms $ABCD$, $AEFG$ about the equal angles are proportionals;
and they are therefore similar to one another: (VI. def. 1.)
for the same reason, the parallelogram $ABCD$ is similar to the parallelogram $FHCK$:
wherefore each of the parallelograms GE, KH is similar to DB:
but rectilineal figures which are similar to the same rectilineal figure, are also similar to one another: (VI. 21.)
therefore the parallelogram GE is similar to KH.
Wherefore, parallelograms, &c. Q.E.D.

PROPOSITION XXV. PROBLEM.

To describe a rectilineal figure which shall be similar to one, and equal to another given rectilineal figure.

Let ABC be the given rectilineal figure, to which the figure to be described is required to be similar, and D that to which it must be equal.
It is required to describe a rectilineal figure similar to ABC, and equal to D.

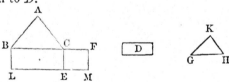

Upon the straight line BC describe the parallelogram BE equal to the figure ABC; (I. 45. Cor.)
also upon CE describe the parallelogram CM equal to D, (I. 45. Cor.)
and having the angle FCE equal to the angle CBL:
therefore BC and CF are in a straight line, as also LE and EM: (I. 29. and I. 14.)
between BC and CF find a mean proportional GH, (VI. 13.)
and upon GH describe the rectilineal figure KGH similar and similarly situated to the figure ABC. (VI. 18.)
Because BC is to GH as GH to CF,

and that if three straight lines be proportionals, as the first is to the third, so is the figure upon the first to the similar and similarly described figure upon the second; (VI. 20. Cor. 2.)

therefore, as BC to CF, so is the rectilineal figure ABC to KGH:
but as BC to CF, so is the parallelogram BE to the parallelogram EF; (VI. 1.)
therefore as the rectilineal figure ABC is to KGH, so is the parallelogram BE to the parallelogram EF: (V. 11.)
and the rectilineal figure ABC is equal to the parallelogram BE; (constr.)
therefore the rectilineal figure KGH is equal to the parallelogram EF: (V. 14.)
but EF is equal to the figure D; (constr.)
wherefore also KGH is equal to D: and it is similar to ABC.

Therefore the rectilineal figure KGH has been described similar to the figure ABC, and equal to D. Q.E.F.

PROPOSITION XXVI. THEOREM.

If two similar parallelograms have a common angle, and be similarly situated; they are about the same diameter.

Let the parallelograms $ABCD$, $AEFG$ be similar and similarly situated, and have the angle DAB common.

$ABCD$ and $AEFG$ shall be about the same diameter.

For if not, let, if possible, the parallelogram BD have its diameter AHC in a different straight line from AF, the diameter of the parallelogram EG,
and let GF meet AHC in H;
and through H draw HK parallel to AD or BC;
therefore the parallelograms $ABCD$, $AKHG$ being about the same diameter, they are similar to one another; (VI. 24.)
wherefore as DA to AB, so is GA to AK: (VI. def. 1.)
but because $ABCD$ and $AEFG$ are similar parallelograms, (hyp.)
as DA is to AB, so is GA to AE;
therefore as GA to AE, so GA to AK; (V. 11.)
that is, GA has the same ratio to each of the straight lines AE, AK;
and consequently AK is equal to AE, (V. 9.)
the less equal to the greater, which is impossible:
therefore $ABCD$ and $AKHG$ are not about the same diameter:
wherefore $ABCD$ and $AEFG$ must be about the same diameter.

Therefore, if two similar, &c. Q.E.D.

PROPOSITION XXVII. THEOREM.

Of all parallelograms applied to the same straight line, and deficient by parallelograms, similar and similarly situated to that which is described upon the half of the line; that which is applied to the half, and is similar to its defect, is the greatest.

Let AB be a straight line divided into two equal parts in C;

and let the parallelogram AD be applied to the half AC, which is therefore deficient from the parallelogram upon the whole line AB by the parallelogram CE upon the other half CB:

of all the parallelograms applied to any other parts of AB, and deficient by parallelograms that are similar and similarly situated to CE, AD shall be the greatest.

Let AF be any parallelogram applied to AK, any other part of AB than the half, so as to be deficient from the parallelogram upon the whole line AB by the parallelogram KH similar and similarly situated to CE:

AD shall be greater than AF.

First, let AK the base of AF, be greater than AC the half of AB:

and because CE is similar to the parallelogram HK, (hyp.)

they are about the same diameter: (vi. 26.)

draw their diameter DB, and complete the scheme:

then, because the parallelogram CF is equal to FE, (i. 43.)

add KH to both:

therefore the whole CH is equal to the whole KE:

but CH is equal to CG, (i. 36.)

because the base AC is equal to the base CB;

therefore CG is equal to KE: (ax. 1.)

to each of these equals add CF;

then the whole AF is equal to the gnomon CHL: (ax. 2.)

therefore CE, or the parallelogram AD is greater than the parallelogram AF.

Next, let AK the base of AF be less than AC:

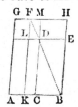

then, the same construction being made, because BC is equal to CA, therefore HM is equal to MG; (i. 34.)

therefore the parallelogram DH is equal to the parallelogram DG; (I. 36.)
wherefore DH is greater than LG:
but DH is equal to DK; (I. 43.)
therefore DK is greater than LG:
to each of these add AL;
then the whole AD is greater than the whole AF.
Therefore, of all parallelograms applied, &c. Q.E.D.

PROPOSITION XXVIII. PROBLEM.

To a given straight line to apply a parallelogram equal to a given rectilineal figure, and deficient by a parallelogram similar to a given parallelogram: but the given rectilineal figure to which the parallelogram to be applied is to be equal, must not be greater than the parallelogram applied to half of the given line, having its defect similar to the defect of that which is to be applied; that is, to the given parallelogram.

Let AB be the given straight line, and C the given rectilineal figure to which the parallelogram to be applied is required to be equal, which figure must not be greater (VI. 27.) than the parallelogram applied to the half of the line, having its defect from that upon the whole line similar to the defect of that which is to be applied;

and let D be the parallelogram to which this defect is required to be similar.

It is required to apply a parallelogram to the straight line AB, which shall be equal to the figure C, and be deficient from the parallelogram upon the whole line by a parallelogram similar to D.

Divide AB into two equal parts in the point E, (I. 10.)
and upon EB describe the parallelogram $EBFG$ similar and similarly situated to D, (VI. 18.)
and complete the parallelogram AG, which must either be equal to C, or greater than it, by the determination.
If AG be equal to C, then what was required is already done:

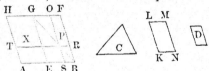

for, upon the straight line AB, the parallelogram AG is applied equal to the figure C, and deficient by the parallelogram EF similar to D.
But, if AG be not equal to C, it is greater than it:
and EF is equal to AG; (I. 36.)
therefore EF also is greater than C.
Make the parallelogram $KLMN$ equal to the excess of EF above C, and similar and similarly situated to D: (VI. 25.)
then, since D is similar to EF, (constr.)
therefore also KM is similar to EF, (VI. 21.)
let KL be the homologous side to EG, and LM to GF:
and because EF is equal to C and KM together,

EF is greater than KM;
therefore the straight line EG is greater than KL, and GF than LM: make GN equal to LK, and GO equal to LM, (I. 3.)
and complete the parallelogram $NGOP$: (I. 31.)
therefore XO is equal and similar to KM:
but KM is similar to EF;
wherefore also XO is similar to EF;
and therefore XO and EF are about the same diameter: (VI. 26.)
let GPB be their diameter and complete the scheme.
Then, because EF is equal to C and KM together,
and XO a part of the one is equal to KM a part of the other,
the remainder, viz. the gnomon ERO, is equal to the remainder C: (ax. 3.)
and because OR is equal to XS, by adding SR to each, (I. 43.)
the whole OB is equal to the whole XB:
but XB is equal to TE, because the base AE is equal to the base EB; (I. 36.)
wherefore also TE is equal to OB: (ax. 1.)
add XS to each, then the whole TS is equal to the whole, viz. to the gnomon ERO:
but it has been proved that the gnomon ERO is equal to C;
and therefore also TS is equal to C.

Wherefore the parallelogram TS, equal to the given rectilineal figure C, is applied to the given straight line AB, deficient by the parallelogram SR, similar to the given one D, because SR is similar to EF. (VI. 24.) Q.E.F.

PROPOSITION XXIX. PROBLEM.

To a given straight line to apply a parallelogram equal to a given rectilineal figure, exceeding by a parallelogram similar to another given.

Let AB be the given straight line, and C the given rectilineal figure to which the parallelogram to be applied is required to be equal, and D the parallelogram to which the excess of the one to be applied above that upon the given line is required to be similar.

It is required to apply a parallelogram to the given straight line AB which shall be equal to the figure C, exceeding by a parallelogram similar to D.

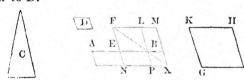

Divide AB into two equal parts in the point E, (I. 10.) and upon EB describe the parallelogram EL similar and similarly situated to D: (VI. 18.)
and make the parallelogram GH equal to EL and C together, and similar and similarly situated to D: (VI. 25.)
wherefore GH is similar to EL: (VI. 21.)

let KH be the side homologous to FL, and KG to FE:
and because the parallelogram GH is greater than EL,
therefore the side KH is greater than FL,
and KG than FE:
produce FL and FE, and make FLM equal to KH, and FEN to KG,
and complete the parallelogram MN:
MN is therefore equal and similar to GH:
but GH is similar to EL;
wherefore MN is similar to EL;
and consequently EL and MN are about the same diameter: (VI. 26.)
draw their diameter FX, and complete the scheme.
Therefore, since GH is equal to EL and C together,
and that GH is equal to MN;
MN is equal to EL and C:
take away the common part EL;
then the remainder, viz. the gnomon NOL, is equal to C.
And because AE is equal to EB,
the parallelogram AN is equal to the parallelogram NB, (I. 36.)
that is, to BM: (I. 43.)
add NO to each;
therefore the whole, viz. the parallelogram AX, is equal to the gnomon NOL:
but the gnomon NOL is equal to C;
therefore also AX is equal to C.
Wherefore to the straight line AB there is applied the parallelogram AX equal to the given rectilineal figure C, exceeding by the parallelogram PO, which is similar to D, because PO is similar to EL. (VI. 24.) Q.E.F.

PROPOSITION XXX. PROBLEM.

To cut a given straight line in extreme and mean ratio.

Let AB be the given straight line.
It is required to cut it in extreme and mean ratio.

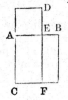

Upon AB describe the square BC, (I. 46.)
and to AC apply the parallelogram CD, equal to BC, exceeding by the figure AD similar to BC: (VI. 29.)
then, since BC is a square,
therefore also AD is a square:
and because BC is equal to CD,
by taking the common part CE from each,
the remainder BF is equal to the remainder AD:
and these figures are equiangular,

therefore their sides about the equal angles are reciprocally proportional: (VI. 14.)
therefore, as *FE* to *ED*, so *AE* to *EB*:
but *FE* is equal to *AC*, (I. 34) that is, to *AB*; (def. 30.)
and *ED* is equal to *AE*;
therefore as *BA* to *AE*, so is *AE* to *EB*:
but *AB* is greater than *AE*;
wherefore *AE* is greater than *EB*: (V. 14.)
therefore the straight line *AB* is cut in extreme and mean ratio in *E*. (VI. def. 3.) Q.E.F.
Otherwise:
Let *AB* be the given straight line.
It is required to cut it in extreme and mean ratio.

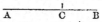

Divide *AB* in the point *C*, so that the rectangle contained by *AB*, *BC*, may be equal to the square on *AC*. (II. 11.)
Then, because the rectangle *AB*, *BC* is equal to the square on *AC*;
as *BA* to *AC*, so is *AC* to *CB*: (VI. 17.)
therefore *AB* is cut in extreme and mean ratio in *C*. (VI. def. 3.) Q.E.F.

PROPOSITION XXXI. THEOREM.

In right-angled triangles, the rectilineal figure described upon the side opposite to the right angle, is equal to the similar and similarly described figures upon the sides containing the right angle.

Let *ABC* be a right-angled triangle, having the right angle *BAC*. The rectilineal figure described upon *BC* shall be equal to the similar and similarly described figures upon *BA*, *AC*.

Draw the perpendicular *AD*: (I. 12.)
therefore, because in the right-angled triangle *ABC*, *AD* is drawn from the right angle at *A* perpendicular to the base *BC*, the triangles *ABD*, *ADC* are similar to the whole triangle *ABC*, and to one another: (VI. 8.)
and because the triangle *ABC* is similar to *ADB*,
as *CB* to *BA*, so is *BA* to *BD*: (VI. 4.)
and because these three straight lines are proportionals,
as the first is to the third, so is the figure upon the first to the similar and similarly described figure upon the second: (VI. 20. Cor. 2.)
therefore as *CB* to *BD*, so is the figure upon *CB* to the similar and similarly described figure upon *BA*;
and inversely, as *DB* to *BC*, so is the figure upon *BA* to that upon *BC*: (V. B.)

for the same reason, as DC to CB, so is the figure upon CA to that upon CB:

therefore as BD and DC together to BC, so are the figures upon BA, AC to that upon BC: (v. 24.)

but BD and DC together are equal to BC;

therefore the figure described on BC is equal to the similar and similarly described figures on BA, AC. (v. A.)

Wherefore, in right-angled triangles, &c. Q.E.D.

PROPOSITION XXXII. THEOREM.

If two triangles which have two sides of the one proportional to two sides of the other, be joined at one angle, so as to have their homologous sides parallel to one another; the remaining sides shall be in a straight line.

Let ABC, DCE be two triangles, which have the two sides BA, AC proportional to the two CD, DE,

viz. BA to AC, as CD to DE;

and let AB be parallel to DC, and AC to DE.

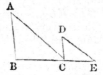

Then BC and CE shall be in a straight line.

Because AB is parallel to DC, and the straight line AC meets them, the alternate angles BAC, ACD are equal; (I. 29.)

for the same reason, the angle CDE is equal to the angle ACD;

wherefore also BAC is equal to CDE: (ax. 1.)

and because the triangles ABC, DCE have one angle at A equal to one at D, and the sides about these angles proportionals,

viz. BA to AC, as CD to DE,

the triangle ABC is equiangular to DCE: (VI. 6.)

therefore the angle ABC is equal to the angle DCE:

and the angle BAC was proved to be equal to ACD;

therefore the whole angle ACE is equal to the two angles ABC, BAC: (ax. 2.)

add to each of these equals the common angle ACB,

then the angles ACE, ACB are equal to the angles ABC, BAC, ACB:

but ABC, BAC, ACB are equal to two right angles: (I. 32.)

therefore also the angles ACE, ACB are equal to two right angles;

and since at the point C, in the straight line AC, the two straight lines BC, CE, which are on the opposite sides of it, make the adjacent angles ACE, ACB equal to two right angles;

therefore BC and CE are in a straight line. (I. 14.)

Wherefore, if two triangles, &c. Q.E.D.

PROPOSITION XXXIII. THEOREM.

In equal circles, angles, whether at the centers or circumferences, have the same ratio which the circumferences on which they stand have to one another: so also have the sectors.

Let ABC, DEF be equal circles; and at their centers the angles BGC, EHF, and the angles BAC, EDF, at their circumferences.

As the circumference BC to the circumference EF, so shall the angle BGC be to the angle EHF, and the angle BAC to the angle EDF;

and also the sector BGC to the sector EHF.

Take any number of circumferences CK, KL, each equal to BC, and any number whatever FM, MN, each equal to EF:

and join GK, GL, HM, HN.

Because the circumferences BC, CK, KL are all equal, the angles BGC, CGK, KGL are also all equal: (III. 27.)

therefore what multiple soever the circumference BL is of the circumference BC, the same multiple is the angle BGL of the angle BGC:

For the same reason, whatever multiple the circumference EN is of the circumference EF, the same multiple is the angle EHN of the angle EHF:

and if the circumference BL be equal to the circumference EN, the angle BGL is also equal to the angle EHN; (III. 27.)

and if the circumference BL be greater than EN,

likewise the angle BGL is greater than EHN; and if less, less:

therefore, since there are four magnitudes, the two circumferences BC, EF, and the two angles BGC, EHF; and that of the circumference BC, and of the angle BGC, have been taken any equimultiples whatever, viz. the circumference BL, and the angle BGL; and of the circumference EF, and of the angle EHF, any equimultiples whatever, viz. the circumference EN, and the angle EHN:

and since it has been proved, that if the circumference BL be greater than EN;

the angle BGL is greater than EHN;

and if equal, equal; and if less, less;

therefore as the circumference BC to the circumference EF, so is the angle BGC to the angle EHF: (v. def. 5.)

but as the angle BGC is to the angle EHF, so is the angle BAC to the angle EDF: (v. 15.)

for each is double of each: (III. 20.)

therefore, as the circumference BC is to EF, so is the angle BGC to the angle EHF, and the angle BAC to the angle EDF.

Also, as the circumference BC to EF, so shall the sector BGC be to the sector EHF.

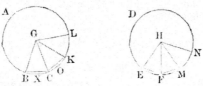

Join BC, CK, and in the circumferences, BC, CK, take any points X, O, and join BX, XC, CO, OK.

Then, because in the triangles GBC, GCK,
the two sides BG, GC are equal to the two CG, GK each to each,
and that they contain equal angles;
the base BC is equal to the base CK, (I. 4.)
and the triangle GBC to the triangle GCK:
and because the circumference BC is equal to the circumference CK,
the remaining part of the whole circumference of the circle ABC, is equal to the remaining part of the whole circumference of the same circle: (ax. 3.)
therefore the angle BXC is equal to the angle COK; (III. 27.)
and the segment BXC is therefore similar to the segment COK; (III. def. 11.)
and they are upon equal straight lines, BC, CK;
but similar segments of circles upon equal straight lines, are equal to one another: (III. 24.)
therefore the segment BXC is equal to the segment COK:
and the triangle BGC was proved to be equal to the triangle CGK;
therefore the whole, the sector BGC, is equal to the whole, the sector CGK:
for the same reason, the sector KGL is equal to each of the sectors BGC, CGK:
in the same manner, the sectors EHF, FHM, MHN, may be proved equal to one another:
therefore, what multiple soever the circumference BL is of the circumference BC, the same multiple is the sector BGL of the sector BGC;
and for the same reason, whatever multiple the circumference EN is of EF, the same multiple is the sector EHN of the sector EHF:
and if the circumference BL be equal to EN, the sector BGL is equal to the sector EHN;
and if the circumference BL be greater than EN, the sector BGL is greater than the sector EHN;
and if less, less;
since, then, there are four magnitudes, the two circumferences BC, EF, and the two sectors BGC, EHF, and that of the circumference BC, and sector BGC, the circumference BL and sector BGL are any equimultiples whatever: and of the circumference EF, and sector EHF, the circumference EN, and sector EHN are any equimultiples whatever;

and since it has been proved, that if the circumference BL be greater than EN, the sector BGL is greater than the sector EHN; and if equal, equal; and if less, less:
therefore, as the circumference BC is to the circumference EF, so is the sector BGC to the sector EHF. (v. def. 5.)
Wherefore, in equal circles, &c.   Q.E.D.

PROPOSITION B. THEOREM.

If an angle of a triangle be bisected by a straight line which likewise cuts the base; the rectangle contained by the sides of the triangle is equal to the rectangle contained by the segments of the base, together with the square on the straight line which bisects the angle.

Let ABC be a triangle, and let the angle BAC be bisected by the straight line AD.

The rectangle BA, AC shall be equal to the rectangle BD, DC, together with the square on AD.

Describe the circle ACB about the triangle, (IV. 5.) and produce AD to the circumference in E, and join EC.
Then because the angle BAD is equal to the angle CAE, (hyp.) and the angle ABD to the angle AEC, (III. 21.)
for they are in the same segment;
the triangles ABD, AEC are equiangular to one another: (I. 32.)
therefore as BA to AD, so is EA to AC; (VI. 4.)
and consequently the rectangle BA, AC is equal to the rectangle EA, AD, (VI. 16.)
that is, to the rectangle ED, DA, together with the square on AD; (II. 3.)
but the rectangle ED, DA is equal to the rectangle BD, DC: (III. 35.)
therefore the rectangle BA, AC is equal to the rectangle BD, DC, together with the square on AD.
Wherefore, if an angle, &c.   Q.E.D.

PROPOSITION C. THEOREM.

If from any angle of a triangle, a straight line be drawn perpendicular to the base; the rectangle contained by the sides of the triangle is equal to the rectangle contained by the perpendicular and the diameter of the circle described about the triangle.

Let ABC be a triangle, and AD the perpendicular from the angle A to the base BC.

The rectangle BA, AC shall be equal to the rectangle contained by AD and the diameter of the circle described about the triangle.

Describe the circle ACB about the triangle, (IV. 5.) and draw its diameter AE, and join EC.

Because the right angle BDA is equal to the angle ECA in a semicircle, (III. 31.)

and the angle ABD equal to the angle AEC in the same segment; (III. 21.) the triangles ABD, AEC are equiangular:

therefore as BA to AD, so is EA to AC; (VI. 4.)

and consequently the rectangle BA, AC is equal to the rectangle EA, AD. (VI. 16.) If therefore from any angle, &c. Q.E.D.

PROPOSITION D. THEOREM.

The rectangle contained by the diagonals of a quadrilateral figure inscribed in a circle, is equal to both the rectangles contained by its opposite sides.

Let $ABCD$ be any quadrilateral figure inscribed in a circle, and join AC, BD.

The rectangle contained by AC, BD shall be equal to the two rectangles contained by AB, CD, and by AD, BC.

Make the angle ABE equal to the angle DBC: (I. 23.)
add to each of these equals the common angle EBD,
then the angle ABD is equal to the angle EBC:
and the angle BDA is equal to the angle BCE, because they are in the same segment: (III. 21.)
therefore the triangle ABD is equiangular to the triangle BCE:
wherefore, as BC is to CE, so is BD to DA; (VI. 4.)

and consequently the rectangle BC, AD is equal to the rectangle BD, CE: (VI. 16.)

again, because the angle ABE is equal to the angle DBC, and the angle BAE to the angle BDC, (III. 21.)
the triangle ABE is equiangular to the triangle BCD:
therefore as BA to AE, so is BD to DC;
wherefore the rectangle BA, DC is equal to the rectangle BD, AE:
but the rectangle BC, AD has been shewn to be equal to the rectangle BD, CE;
therefore the whole rectangle AC, BD is equal to the rectangle AB, DC, together with the rectangle AD, BC. (II. 1.)

Therefore the rectangle, &c. Q.E.D.

This is a Lemma of Cl. Ptolemæus, in page 9 of his Μεγάλη Σύνταξις.

NOTES TO BOOK VI.

In this Book, the theory of proportion exhibited in the Fifth Book, is applied to the comparison of the sides and areas of plane rectilineal figures, both of those which are similar, and of those which are not similar.

Def. I In defining similar triangles, one condition is sufficient, namely, that similar triangles are those which have their three angles respectively equal, as in Prop. 4, Book vi, it is proved that the sides about the equal angles of equiangular triangles are proportionals. But in defining similar figures of more than three sides, both of the conditions stated in Def. I. are requisite, as it is obvious, for instance, in the case of a square and a rectangle, which have their angles respectively equal, but have not their sides about their equal angles proportionals.

The following definition has been proposed: "Similar rectilineal figures of more than three sides, are those which may be divided into the same number of similar triangles." This definition would, if adopted, require the omission of a part of Prop. 20, Book vi.

Def. III. To this definition may be added the following:

A straight line is said to be divided *harmonically*, when it is divided into three parts, such that the whole line is to one of the extreme segments, as the other extreme segment is to the middle part. Three lines are in *harmonical* proportion, when the first is to the third, as the difference between the first and second, is to the difference between the second and third; and the second is called a harmonic mean between the first and third.

The expression 'harmonical proportion' is derived from the following fact in the Science of Acoustics, that three musical strings of the same material, thickness, and tension, when divided in the manner stated in the definition, or numerically, as 6, 4, and 3, produce a certain musical note, its fifth, and its octave.

Def. IV. The term *altitude*, as applied to the same triangles and parallelograms, will be different according to the sides which may be assumed as the base, unless they are equilateral.

Prop. I. In the same manner may be proved, that triangles and parallelograms upon equal bases, are to one another as their altitudes.

Prop. A. When the triangle ABC is isosceles, the line which bisects the exterior angle at the vertex is parallel to the base. In all other cases, if the line which bisects the angle BAC cut the base BC in the point G, then the straight line BD is harmonically divided in the points G, C.

For BG is to GC as BA is to AC, (VI. 3.)

and BD is to DC as BA is to AC, (VI. A.)

therefore BD is to DC as BG is to GC,

but $BG = BD - DG$, and $GC = GD - DC$.

Wherefore BD is to DC as $BD - DG$ is to $GD - DC$.

Hence BD, DG, DC, are in harmonical proportion.

Prop. IV. is the first case of similar triangles, and corresponds to the third case of equal triangles, Prop. 26, Book I.

Sometimes the sides opposite to the equal angles in two equiangular triangles, are called the *corresponding sides*, and these are said to be proportional, which is simply taking the proportion in Euclid alternately.

The term *homologous* (ὁμόλογος), has reference to the places the sides of the triangles have in the ratios, and in one sense homologous sides may be considered as corresponding sides. The homologous sides of any two similar rectilineal figures will be found to be those which are adjacent to two equal angles in each figure.

Prop v, the converse of Prop iv, is the second case of similar triangles, and corresponds to Prop 8, Book i, the second case of equal triangles.

Prop vi is the third case of similar triangles, and corresponds to Prop 4, Book i, the first case of equal triangles.

The property of similar triangles, and that contained in Prop 47, Book i, are the most important theorems in Geometry.

Prop vii is the fourth case of similar triangles, and corresponds to the fourth case of equal triangles demonstrated in the note to Prop 26, Book i.

Prop ix. The learner here must not forget the different meanings of the word *part*, as employed in the Elements. The word here has the same meaning as in Euc i ax 9.

It may be remarked, that this proposition is a more simple case of the next, namely, Prop x.

Prop xi. This proposition is that particular case of Prop xii, in which the second and third terms of the proportion are equal. These two problems exhibit the same results by a Geometrical construction, as are obtained by numerical multiplication and division.

Prop xiii. The difference in the two propositions Euc ii 14, and Euc vi 13, is this in the Second Book, the problem is, to make a rectangular figure or square equal in area to an irregular rectilinear figure, in which the idea of ratio is not introduced. In the Prop in the Sixth Book, the problem relates to ratios only, and it requires to divide a line into two parts, so that the ratio of the whole line to the greater segment may be the same as the ratio of the greater segment to the less.

The result in this proposition obtained by a Geometrical construction, is analogous to that which is obtained by the multiplication of two numbers, and the extraction of the square root of the product.

It may be observed, that half the sum of AB and BC is called the *Arithmetic* mean between these lines, also that BD is called the *Geometric* mean between the same lines.

To find two mean proportionals between two given lines is impossible by the straight line and circle. Pappus has given several solutions of this problem in Book iii of his Mathematical Collections, and Eutocius has given, in his Commentary on the Sphere and Cylinder of Archimedes, ten different methods of solving this problem.

Prop xiv depends on the same principle as Prop xv, and both may easily be demonstrated from one diagram. Join DF, FE, EG in the fig to Prop xiv, and the figure to Prop. xv. is formed. We may add that there does not appear any reason why the properties of the triangle and parallelogram should be here separated, and not in the first proposition of the Sixth Book.

Prop xv holds good when one angle of one triangle is equal to the defect from what the corresponding angle in the other wants of two right angles.

This theorem will perhaps be more distinctly comprehended by the learner, if he will bear in mind, that four magnitudes are reciprocally proportional, when the ratio compounded of these ratios is a ratio of equality

Prop xvii is only a particular case of Prop. xvi, and more properly might appear as a corollary: and both are cases of Prop xiv

Algebraically, Let AB, CD, E, F, contain a, b, c, d units respectively

Then, since a, b, c, d are proportionals, $\therefore \dfrac{a}{b} = \dfrac{c}{d}$

Multiply these equals by bd, $\therefore ad = bc$,

or, the product of the extremes is equal to the product of the means

And conversely, If the product of the extremes be equal to the product of the means,

or $ad = bc$,

then, dividing these equals by bd, $\therefore \dfrac{a}{b} = \dfrac{c}{d}$

or the ratio of the first to the second number, is equal to the ratio of the third to the fourth.

Similarly may be shewn, that if $\dfrac{a}{b} = \dfrac{b}{d}$; then $ad = b^2$.

And conversely, if $ad = b^2$, then $\dfrac{a}{b} = \dfrac{b}{d}$

Prop xviii Similar figures are said to be similarly situated, when their homologous sides are parallel, as when the figures are situated on the same straight line, or on parallel lines, but when similar figures are situated on the sides of a triangle, the similar figures are said to be similarly situated when the homologous sides of each figure have the same relative position with respect to one another; that is, if the bases on which the similar figures stand, were placed parallel to one another, the remaining sides of the figures, if similarly situated, would also be parallel to one another

Prop xx. It may easily be shewn, that the perimeters of similar polygons are proportional to their homologous sides

Prop xxi This proposition must be so understood as to include all rectilineal figures whatsoever, which require for the conditions of similarity another condition than is required for the similarity of triangles See note on Euc vi Def i

Prop xxiii The doctrine of compound ratio, including duplicate and triplicate ratio, in the form in which it was propounded and practised by the ancient Geometers, has been almost wholly superseded However satisfactory for the purposes of exact reasoning the method of expressing the ratio of two surfaces, or of two solids by two straight lines, may be in itself, it has not been found to be the form best suited for the direct application of the results of Geometry Almost all modern writers on Geometry and its applications to every branch of the Mathematical Sciences, have adopted the algebraical notation of a quotient $AB \; BC$; or of a fraction $\dfrac{AB}{BC}$; for expressing the ratio of two lines AB, BC as well as that of a product $AB \times BC$, or $AB \; BC$, for the expression of a rectangle The want of a concise and expressive method of notation to indicate the proportion of Geometrical magnitudes in a form suited for the direct application of the results, has doubtless favoured the introduction of Algebraical symbols into the language of Geometry It must be admitted, however, that such notations in the language of pure Geometry are liable to very serious objections, chiefly on the ground that pure Geometry does not admit the Arithmetical or Algebraical idea of a *product* or a *quotient* into its reasonings. On the other hand, it may be urged, that it is not the employment of symbols which renders a process of reasoning peculiarly Geometrical or Algebraical, but the ideas which are expressed by them. If symbols be employed in Geometrical reasonings, and be understood to express the *magnitudes themselves* and the *conception of their Geometrical ratio*, and not any *measures*, or *numerical values of them*, there would not appear to be any very great objections to their use, provided that the notations employed were such as are not likely to lead to misconception. It is, however, desirable, for the sake of avoiding confusion of ideas in reasoning on the properties of number and of magnitude, that the language and notations employed both in Geometry and Algebra should be rigidly defined and strictly adhered to, in all cases. At the commencement of his Geometrical studies, the student is recommended not to employ the symbols of Algebra in Geometrical demonstrations. How far it may be necessary or advisable to employ them when he fully understands the nature of the subject, is a question on which some difference of opinion exists.

Prop xxv. There does not appear any sufficient reason why this proposition is placed between Prop xxiv and Prop xxvi.

Prop xxvii. To understand this and the three following propositions more easily, it is to be observed

1. "That a parallelogram is said to be applied to a straight line, when it is described upon it as one of its sides. Ex. gr. the parallelogram AC is said to be applied to the straight line AB.

2. But a parallelogram AE is said to be applied to a straight line AB deficient by a parallelogram, when AD the base of AE is less than AB, and therefore AE is less than the parallelogram AC described upon AB in the same angle, and between the same parallels, by the parallelogram DC, and DC is therefore called the defect of AE.

3. And a parallelogram AG is said to be applied to a straight line AB, exceeding by a parallelogram, when AF the base of AG is greater than AB, and therefore AG exceeds AC the parallelogram described upon AB in the same angle, and between the same parallels, by the parallelogram BG."—Simson.

Both among Euclid's Theorems and Problems, cases occur in which the hypotheses of the one, and the data or quæsita of the other, are restricted within certain limits as to *magnitude* and *position*. The determination of these limits constitutes the doctrine of *Maxima and Minima*. Thus —The theorem Euc. vi 27 is a case of the *maximum* value which a figure fulfilling the other conditions can have, and the succeeding proposition is a problem involving this fact among the conditions as a part of the data, in truth, perfectly analogous to Euc. i 20, 22, wherein the limit of possible diminution of the sum of the two sides of a triangle described upon a given base, is the magnitude of the base itself the limit of the side of a square which shall be equal to the rectangle of the two parts into which a given line may be divided, is half the line, as it appears from Euc. ii 5.—*the greatest line* that can be drawn from a given point within a circle to the circumference, Euc. iii 7, is the line which passes through the center of the circle, and *the least line* which can be so drawn from the same point, is the part produced, of the greatest line between the given point and the circumference. Euc. iii 8, also affords another instance of a maximum and a minimum when the given point is outside the given circle.

'Prop. xxxi. This proposition is the general case of Prop. 47, Book i, for any similar rectilineal figure described on the sides of a right-angled triangle. The demonstration, however, here given is wholly independent of Euc. i. 47.

Prop. xxxiii. In the demonstration of this important proposition, angles greater than two right angles are employed, in accordance with the criterion of proportionality laid down in Euc. v. def. 5.

This proposition forms the basis of the assumption of arcs of circles for the measures of angles at their centers. One magnitude may be assumed as the measure of another magnitude of a different kind, when the two are so connected, that any variation in them takes place simultaneously, and in the same direct proportion. This being the case with angles at the center of a circle, and the arcs subtended by them, the arcs of circles can be assumed as the measures of the angles they subtend at the center of the circle.

Prop. B. The converse of this proposition does not hold good when the triangle is isosceles.

QUESTIONS ON BOOK VI.

1. Distinguish between similar figures and equal figures.
2. What is the distinction between *homologous sides*, and *equal sides* in Geometrical figures?
3. What is the number of conditions requisite to determine similarity of figures? Is the number of conditions in Euclid's definition of similar figures greater than what is necessary? Propose a definition of similar figures which includes no superfluous condition.
4. Explain how Euclid makes use of the definition of proportion in Euc. vi. 1.
5. Prove that triangles on the same base are to one another as their altitudes.
6. If two triangles of the same altitude have their bases unequal, and if one of them be divided into m equal parts, and if the other contain n of those parts; prove that the triangles have the same numerical relation as their bases. Why is this Proposition less general than Euc. vi. 1?
7. Are triangles which have one angle of one equal to one angle of another, and the sides about two other angles proportionals, necessarily similar?
8. What are the conditions, considered by Euclid, under which two triangles are similar to each other?
9. Apply Euc. vi. 2, to trisect the diagonal of a parallelogram.
10. When are three lines said to be in harmonical proportion? If both the interior and exterior angles at the vertex of a triangle (Euc. vi. 3, A.) be bisected by lines which meet the base, and the base produced in D, G, the segments BG, GD, GC of the base shall be in Harmonical proportion.
11. If the angles at the base of the triangle in the figure Euc. vi. A, be equal to each other, how is the proposition modified?
12. Under what circumstances will the bisecting line in the fig. Euc. vi. A, meet the base on the side of the angle bisected? Shew that there is an indeterminate case.

13. State some of the uses to which Euc. vi. 4, may be applied.

14. Apply Euc. vi. 4, to prove that the rectangle contained by the segments of any chord passing through a given point within a circle is constant.

15. Point out clearly the difference in the proofs of the two latter cases in Euc. vi. 7.

16. From the corollary of Euc. vi. 8, deduce a proof of Euc. i. 47.

17. Shew how the last two properties stated in Euc. vi. 8. Cor. may be deduced from Euc. i. 47, ii. 2, vi. 17.

18. Given the nth part of a straight line, find by a Geometrical construction, the $(n+1)^{th}$ part.

19. Define what is meant by a mean proportional between two given lines, and find a mean proportional between the lines whose lengths are 4 and 9 units respectively. Is the method you employ suggested by any Propositions in any of the first four books?

20. Determine a third proportional to two lines of 5 and 7 units, and a fourth proportional to three lines of 5, 7, 9, units.

21. Find a straight line which shall have to a given straight line, the ratio of 1 to $\sqrt{5}$.

22. Define reciprocal figures. Enunciate the propositions proved respecting such figures in the Sixth Book.

23. Give the corollary, Euc. vi. 8, and prove thence that the Arithmetic mean is greater than the Geometric between the same extremes.

24. If two equal triangles have two angles together equal to two right angles, the sides about those angles are reciprocally proportional.

25. Give Algebraical proofs of Prop. 16 and 17 of Book vi.

26. Enunciate and prove the converse of Euc. vi. 15.

27. Explain what is meant by saying, that "similar triangles are in the duplicate ratio of their homologous sides."

28. What are the *data* which determine triangles both in species and magnitude? How are those *data* expressed in Geometry?

29. If the ratio of the homologous sides of two triangles be as 1 to 4, what is the ratio of the triangles? And if the ratio of the triangles be as 1 to 4, what is the ratio of the homologous sides?

30. Shew that one of the triangles in the figure, Euc. iv. 10, is a mean proportional between the other two.

31. What is the algebraical interpretation of Euc. vi. 19?

32. From your definition of Proportion, prove that the diagonals of a square are in the same proportion as their sides.

33. What propositions does Euclid prove respecting similar polygons?

34. The parallelograms about the diameter of a parallelogram are similar to the whole and to one another. Shew when they are *equal*.

35. Prove Algebraically, that the areas (1) of similar triangles and (2) of similar parallelograms are proportional to the squares of their homologous sides.

36. How is it shewn that equiangular parallelograms have to one another the ratio which is compounded of the ratios of their bases and altitudes?

37. To find two lines which shall have to each other, the ratio compounded of the ratios of the lines A to B, and C to D.

38. State the force of the condition "similarly described;" and shew that, on a given straight line, there may be described as many polygons of different magnitudes, similar to a given polygon, as there are sides of different lengths in the polygon.

QUESTIONS ON BOOK VI. 301

39. Describe a triangle similar to a given triangle, and having its area double that of the given triangle

40. The three sides of a triangle are 7, 8, 9 units respectively; determine the length of the lines which meeting the base, and the base produced, bisect the interior angle opposite to the greatest side of the triangle, and the adjacent exterior angle

41. The three sides of a triangle are 3, 4, 5 inches respectively, find the lengths of the external segments of the sides determined by the lines which bisect the exterior angles of the triangle

42. What are the segments into which the hypotenuse of a right-angled triangle is divided by a perpendicular drawn from the right angle, if the sides containing it are a and $3a$ units respectively?

43. If the three sides of a triangle be 3, 4, 5 units respectively what are the parts into which they are divided by the lines which bisect the angles opposite to them?

44. If the homologous sides of two triangles be as 3 to 4, and the area of one triangle be known to contain 100 square units, how many square units are contained in the area of the other triangle?

45. Prove that if BD be taken in AB produced (fig Euc vi. 30) equal to the greater segment AC, then AD is divided in extreme and mean ratio in the point B

Shew also, that in the series 1, 1, 2, 3, 5, 8, &c in which each term is the sum of the two preceding terms, the last two terms perpetually approach to the proportion of the segments of a line divided in extreme and mean ratio   Find a general expression (free from surds) for the nth term of this series.

46. The parts of a line divided in extreme and mean ratio are incommensurable with each other

47. Shew that in Euclid's figure (Euc ii. 11) four other lines, besides the given line, are divided in the required manner

48. Enunciate Euc vi 31   What theorem of a previous book is included in this proposition?

49. What is the superior limit, as to magnitude, of the angle at the circumference in Euc vi 33?   Shew that the proof may be extended by withdrawing the usually supposed restriction as to angular magnitude, and then deduce, as a corollary, the proposition respecting the magnitudes of angles in segments greater than, equal to, or less than a semicircle

50. The sides of a triangle inscribed in a circle are a, b, c, units respectively   find by Euc vi c, the radius of the circumscribing circle

51. Enunciate the converse of Euc vi D

52. Shew independently that Euc vi D, is true when the quadrilateral figure is rectangular

53. Shew that the rectangles contained by the opposite sides of a quadrilateral figure which does not admit of having a circle described about it, are together greater than the rectangle contained by the diagonals

54. What different conditions may be stated as essential to the possibility of the inscription and circumscription of a circle in and about a quadrilateral figure?

55. Point out those propositions in the Sixth Book in which Euclid's definition of proportion is directly applied

56. Explain briefly the advantages gained by the application of analysis to the solution of Geometrical Problems

57. In what cases are triangles proved to be *equal* in Euclid, and in what cases are they proved to be *similar*?

GEOMETRICAL EXERCISES ON BOOK VI.

PROPOSITION I. PROBLEM.
To inscribe a square in a given triangle.

Analysis. Let ABC be the given triangle, of which the base BC, and the perpendicular AD are given.

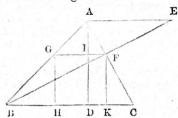

Let $FGHK$ be the required inscribed square.
Then BHG, BDA are similar triangles,
and GH is to GB, as AD is to AB,
but GF is equal to GH;
therefore GF is to GB, as AD is to AB.
Let BF be joined and produced to meet a line drawn from A parallel to the base BC in the point E.
Then the triangles BGF, BAE are similar,
and AE is to AB, as GF is to GB,
but GF is to GB, as AD is to AB;
wherefore AE is to AB, as AD is to AB;
hence AE is equal to AD.
Synthesis. Through the vertex A, draw AE parallel to BC the base of the triangle,
make AE equal to AD,
join EB cutting AC in F,
through F, draw FG parallel to BC, and FK parallel to AD;
also through G draw GH parallel to AD.
Then $GHKF$ is the square required.
The different cases may be considered when the triangle is equilateral, scalene, or isosceles, and when each side is taken as the base.

PROPOSITION II. THEOREM.
If from the extremities of any diameter of a given circle, perpendiculars be drawn to any chord of the circle, they shall meet the chord, or the chord produced in two points which are equidistant from the center.

First, let the chord CD intersect the diameter AB in L, but not at right angles; and from A, B, let AE, BF be drawn perpendicular to CD. Then the points F, E are equidistant from the center of the chord CD.

Join EB, and from I the center of the circle, draw IG perpendicular to CD, and produce it to meet EB in H.

Then IG bisects CD in G; (III. 2.)
and IG, AE being both perpendicular to CD, are parallel. (I. 29.)
Therefore BI is to BH, as IA is to HE; (VI. 2.)
and BH is to FG, as HE is to GE;
therefore BI is to FG, as IA is to GE;
but BI is equal to IA;
therefore FG is equal to GE.
It is also manifest that DE is equal to CF.

When the chord does not intersect the diameter, the perpendiculars intersect the chord produced.

PROPOSITION III. THEOREM.

If two diagonals of a regular pentagon be drawn to cut one another, the greater segments will be equal to the side of the pentagon, and the diagonals will cut one another in extreme and mean ratio.

Let the diagonals AC, BE be drawn from the extremities of the side AB of the regular pentagon $ABCDE$, and intersect each other in the point H.

Then BE and AC are cut in extreme and mean ratio in H, and the greater segment of each is equal to the side of the pentagon.

Let the circle $ABCDE$ be described about the pentagon. (IV. 14.)

Because EA, AB are equal to AB, BC, and they contain equal
    angles;
    therefore the base EB is equal to the base AC, (I. 4.)
    and the triangle EAB is equal to the triangle CBA,
and the remaining angles will be equal to the remaining angles,
    each to each, to which the equal sides are opposite.

Therefore the angle BAC is equal to the angle ABE;
and the angle AHE is double of the angle BAH, (I. 32.)
but the angle EAC is also double of the angle BAC, (VI. 33.)
    therefore the angle HAE is equal to AHE,
and consequently HE is equal to EA, (I. 6.) or to AB.
    And because BA is equal to AE,
    the angle ABE is equal to the angle AEB;

but the angle ABE has been proved equal to BAH:
therefore the angle BEA is equal to the angle BAH:
and ABE is common to the two triangles ABE, ABH;
therefore the remaining angle BAE is equal to the remaining angle AHB;
and consequently the triangles ABE, ABH are equiangular;
therefore EB is to BA, as AB to BH: but BA is equal to EH,
therefore EB is to EH, as EH is to BH,
but BE is greater than EH; therefore EH is greater than HB;
therefore BE has been cut in extreme and mean ratio in H.

Similarly, it may be shewn, that AC has also been cut in extreme and mean ratio in H, and that the greater segment of it CH is equal to the side of the pentagon.

PROPOSITION IV. PROBLEM.

Divide a given arc of a circle into two parts which shall have their chords in a given ratio.

Analysis. Let A, B be the two given points in the circumference of the circle, and C the point required to be found, such that when the chords AC and BC are joined, the lines AC and BC shall have to one another the ratio of E to F.

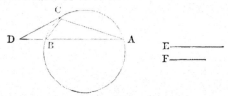

Draw CD touching the circle in C;
join AB and produce it to meet CD in D.
Since the angle BAC is equal to the angle BCD, (III. 32.)
and the angle CDB is common to the two triangles DBC, DAC;
therefore the third angle CBD in one, is equal to the third angle DCA in the other, and the triangles are similar.
therefore AD is to DC, as DC is to DB; (VI. 4.)
hence also the square on AD is to the square on DC as AD is to BD. (VI. 20. Cor.)
But AD is to AC, as DC is to CB, (VI. 4.)
and AD is to DC, as AC to CB, (V. 16.)
also the square on AD is to the square on DC, as the square on AC is to the square on CB;
but the square on AD is to the square on DC, as AD is to DB:
wherefore the square on AC is to the square on CB, as AD is to BD;
but AC is to CB, as E is to F, (constr.)
therefore AD is to DB as the square on E is to the square on F.
Hence the ratio of AD to DB is given,
and AB is given in magnitude, because the points A, B in the circumference of the circle are given.

Wherefore also the ratio of AD to AB is given, and also the magnitude of AD.

Synthesis. Join AB and produce it to D, so that AD shall be to BD, as the square on E to the square on F.

From D draw DC to touch the circle in C, and join CB, CA.

Since AD is to DB, as the square on E is to the square on F, (constr.) and AD is to DB, as the square on AC is to the square on BC;

therefore the square on AC is to the square on BC, as the square on E is to the square on F,

and AC is to BC, as E is to F.

PROPOSITION V. PROBLEM.

A, B, C *are given points. It is required to draw through any other point in the same plane with* A, B, *and* C, *a straight line, such that the sum of its distances from two of the given points, may be equal to its distance from the third.*

Analysis. Suppose F the point required, such that the line XFH being drawn through any other point X, and AD, BE, CH perpendiculars on XFH, the sum of BE and CH is equal to AD.

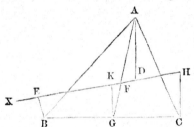

Join AB, BC, CA, then ABC is a triangle.

Draw AG to bisect the base BC in G, and draw GK perpendicular to EF.

Then since BC is bisected in G,

the sum of the perpendiculars CH, BE is double of GK;

but CH and BE are equal to AD, (hyp.)

therefore AD must be double of GK;

but since AD is parallel to GK,

the triangles ADF, GKF are similar,

therefore AD is to AF, as GK is to GF;

but AD is double of GK, therefore AF is double of GF;

and consequently, GF is one-third of AG the line drawn from the vertex of the triangle to the bisection of the base.

But AG is a line given in magnitude and position,

therefore the point F is determined.

Synthesis. Join AB, AC, BC, and bisect the base BC of the triangle ABC in G; join AG and take GF equal to one-third of GA;

the line drawn through X and F will be the line required.

It is also obvious, that while the relative position of the points A, B, C, remains the same, the point F remains the same, wherever the point X may be. The point X may therefore coincide with the point F, and when this is the case, the position of the line FX is left undetermined. Hence the following *porism*.

A triangle being given in position, a point in it may be found, such that any straight line whatever being drawn through that point, the perpendiculars drawn to this straight line from the two angles of the triangle, which are on one side of it, will be together equal to the perpendicular that is drawn to the same line from the angle on the other side of it.

I.

6. TRIANGLES and parallelograms of unequal altitudes are to each other in the ratio compounded of the ratios of their bases and altitudes.

7. If ACB, ADB be two triangles upon the same base AB, and between the same parallels, and if through the point in which two of the sides (or two of the sides produced) intersect two straight lines be drawn parallel to the other two sides so as to meet the base AB (or AB produced) in points E and F. Prove that $AE = BF$.

8. In the base AC of a triangle ABC take any point D; bisect AD, DC, AB, BC, in E, F, G, H respectively: shew that EG is equal to HF.

9. Construct an isosceles triangle equal to a given scalene triangle and having an equal vertical angle with it.

10. If, in similar triangles, from any two equal angles to the opposite sides, two straight lines be drawn making equal angles with the homologous sides, these straight lines will have the same ratio as the sides on which they fall, and will also divide those sides proportionally.

11. Any three lines being drawn making equal angles with the three sides of any triangle towards the same parts, and meeting one another, will form a triangle similar to the original triangle.

12. BD, CD are perpendicular to the sides AB, AC of a triangle ABC, and CE is drawn perpendicular to AD, meeting AB in E: shew that the triangles ABC, ACE are similar.

13. In any triangle, if a perpendicular be let fall upon the base from the vertical angle, the base will be to the sum of the sides, as the difference of the sides to the difference or sum of the segments of the base made by the perpendicular, according as it falls within or without the triangle.

14. If triangles AEF, ABC have a common angle A, triangle ABC : triangle AEF :: $AB.AC$: $AE.AF$.

15. If one side of a triangle be produced, and the other shortened by equal quantities, the line joining the points of section will be divided by the base in the inverse ratio of the sides.

II.

16. Find two arithmetic means between two given straight lines.
17. To divide a given line in harmonical proportion

18. To find, by a geometrical construction, an arithmetic, geometric, and harmonic mean between two given lines.

19. Prove geometrically, that an arithmetic mean between two quantities, is greater than a geometric mean. Also having given the sum of two lines, and the excess of their arithmetic above their geometric mean, find by a construction the lines themselves.

20. If through the point of bisection of the base of a triangle any line be drawn, intersecting one side of the triangle, the other produced, and a line drawn parallel to the base from the vertex, this line shall be cut harmonically.

21. If a given straight line AB be divided into any two parts in the point C, it is required to produce it, so that the whole line produced may be harmonically divided in C and B.

22. If from a point without a circle there be drawn three straight lines, two of which touch the circle, and the other cuts it, the line which cuts the circle will be divided harmonically by the convex circumference, and the chord which joins the points of contact.

III.

23. Shew geometrically that the diagonal and side of a square are incommensurable.

24. If a straight line be divided in two given points, determine a third point, such that its distances from the extremities may be proportional to its distances from the given points.

25. Determine two straight lines, such that the sum of their squares may equal a given square, and their rectangle equal a given rectangle.

26. Draw a straight line such that the perpendiculars let fall from any point in it on two given lines may be in a given ratio.

27. If diverging lines cut a straight line, so that the whole is to one extreme, as the other extreme is to the middle part, they will intersect every other intercepted line in the same ratio.

28. It is required to cut off a part of a given line so that the part cut off may be a mean proportional between the remainder and another given line.

29. It is required to divide a given finite straight line into two parts, the squares of which shall have a given ratio to each other.

IV.

30. From the vertex of a triangle to the base, to draw a straight line which shall be an arithmetic mean between the sides containing the vertical angle.

31. From the obtuse angle of a triangle, it is required to draw a line to the base, which shall be a mean proportional between the segments of the base. How many answers does this question admit of?

32. To draw a line from the vertex of a triangle to the base, which shall be a mean proportional between the whole base and one segment.

33. If the perpendicular in a right-angled triangle divide the hypotenuse in extreme and mean ratio, the less side is equal to the alternate segment.

34. From the vertex of any triangle ABC, draw a straight line meeting the base produced in D, so that the rectangle $BD \cdot DC = AD^2$.

35. To find a point P in the base BC of a triangle produced, so that PD being drawn parallel to AC, and meeting AC produced to D, $AC : CP :: CP : PD$.

36. If the triangle ABC has the angle at C a right angle, and from C a perpendicular be dropped on the opposite side intersecting it in D, then $AD : DB :: AC^2 : CB^2$.

37. In any right-angled triangle, one side is to the other, as the excess of the hypotenuse above the second, to the line cut off from the first between the right angle and the line bisecting the opposite angle.

38. If on the two sides of a right-angled triangle squares be described, the lines joining the acute angles of the triangle and the opposite angles of the squares, will cut off equal segments from the sides, and each of these equal segments will be a mean proportional between the remaining segments.

39. In any right-angled triangle ABC, (whose hypotenuse is AB) bisect the angle A by AD meeting CB in D, and prove that

$$2 AC^2 : AC^2 - CD^2 :: BC : CD$$

40. On two given straight lines similar triangles are described. Required to find a third, on which, if a triangle similar to them be described, its area shall equal the difference of their areas.

41. In the triangle ABC, $AC = 2 BC$. If CD, CE respectively bisect the angle C, and the exterior angle formed by producing AC, prove that the triangles CBD, ACD, ABC, CDE, have their areas as $1, 2, 3, 4$.

V.

42. It is required to bisect any triangle (1) by a line drawn parallel, (2) by a line drawn perpendicular, to the base.

43. To divide a given triangle into two parts, having a given ratio to one another, by a straight line drawn parallel to one of its sides.

44. Find three points in the sides of a triangle, such that, they being joined, the triangle shall be divided into four equal triangles.

45. From a given point in the side of a triangle, to draw lines to the sides which shall divide the triangle into any number of equal parts.

46. Any two triangles being given, to draw a straight line parallel to a side of the greater, which shall cut off a triangle equal to the less.

VI

47. The rectangle contained by two lines is a mean proportional between their squares.

48. Describe a rectangular parallelogram which shall be equal to a given square, and have its sides in a given ratio.

49. If from any two points within or without a parallelogram, straight lines be drawn perpendicular to each of two adjacent sides and intersecting each other, they form a parallelogram similar to the former.

50. It is required to cut off from a rectangle a similar rectangle which shall be any required part of it.

51. If from one angle A of a parallelogram a straight line be drawn cutting the diagonal in E and the sides in P, Q, shew that
$$AE^2 = PE.EQ.$$

52. The diagonals of a trapezium, two of whose sides are parallel, cut one another in the same ratio.

VII.

53. In a given circle place a straight line parallel to a given straight line, and having a given ratio to it, the ratio not being greater than that of the diameter to the given line in the circle.

54. In a given circle place a straight line, cutting two radii which are perpendicular to each other, in such a manner, that the line itself may be trisected.

55. AB is a diameter, and P any point in the circumference of a circle, AP and BP are joined and produced if necessary; if from any point C of AB, a perpendicular be drawn to AB meeting AP and BP in points D and E respectively, and the circumference of the circle in a point F, shew that CD is a third proportional of CE and CF.

56. If from the extremity of a diameter of a circle tangents be drawn, any other tangent to the circle terminated by them is so divided at its point of contact, that the radius of the circle is a mean proportional between its segments.

57. From a given point without a circle, it is required to draw a straight line to the concave circumference, which shall be divided in a given ratio at the point where it intersects the convex circumference.

58. From what point in a circle must a tangent be drawn, so that a perpendicular on it from a given point in the circumference may be cut by the circle in a given ratio?

59. Through a given point within a given circle, to draw a straight line such that the parts of it intercepted between that point and the circumference, may have a given ratio.

60. Let the two diameters AB, CD, of the circle $ADBC$, be at right angles to each other, draw any chord EF, join CE, CF, meeting AB in G and H, prove that the triangles CGH and CEF are similar.

61. A circle, a straight line, and a point being given in position, required a point in the line, such that a line drawn from it to the given point may be equal to a line drawn from it touching the circle. What must be the relation among the data, that the problem may become porismatic, i.e. admit of innumerable solutions?

VIII.

62. Prove that there may be two, but not more than two, similar triangles in the same segment of a circle.

63. If as in Euclid vi. 3, the vertical angle BAC of the triangle BAC be bisected by AD, and BA be produced to meet CE drawn parallel to AD in E; shew that AD will be a tangent to the circle described about the triangle EAC.

64. If a triangle be inscribed in a circle, and from its vertex, lines be drawn parallel to the tangents at the extremities of its base, they will cut off similar triangles.

65. If from any point in the circumference of a circle perpendiculars be drawn to the sides, or sides produced, of an inscribed triangle, shew that the three points of intersection will be in the same straight line.

66. If through the middle point of any chord of a circle, two chords be drawn, the lines joining their extremities shall intersect the first chord at equal distances from its extremities.

67. If a straight line be divided into any two parts, to find the locus of the point in which these parts subtend equal angles.

68. If the line bisecting the vertical angle of a triangle be divided into parts which are to one another as the base to the sum of the sides, the point of division is the center of the inscribed circle.

69. The rectangle contained by the sides of any triangle is to the rectangle by the radii of the inscribed and circumscribed circles, as twice the perimeter is to the base.

70. Shew that the locus of the vertices of all the triangles constructed upon a given base, and having their sides in a given ratio, is a circle.

71. If from the extremities of the base of a triangle, perpendiculars be let fall on the opposite sides, and likewise straight lines drawn to bisect the same, the intersection of the perpendiculars, that of the bisecting lines, and the center of the circumscribing circle, will be in the same straight line.

IX.

72. If a tangent to two circles be drawn cutting the straight line which joins their centers, the chords are parallel which join the points of contact, and the points where the line through the centers cuts the circumferences.

73. If through the vertex, and the extremities of the base of a triangle, two circles be described, intersecting one another in the base or its continuation, their diameters are proportional to the sides of the triangle.

74. If two circles touch each other externally and also touch a straight line, the part of the line between the points of contact is a mean proportional between the diameters of the circles.

75. If from the centers of each of two circles exterior to one another, tangents be drawn to the other circles so as to cut one another, the rectangles of the segments are equal.

76. If a circle be inscribed in a right-angled triangle and another be described touching the side opposite to the right angle and the produced parts of the other sides, shew that the rectangle under the radii is equal to the triangle, and the sum of the radii equal to the sum of the sides which contain the right angle.

77. If a perpendicular be drawn from the right angle to the hypotenuse of a right-angled triangle, and circles be inscribed within the two smaller triangles into which the given triangle is divided, their diameters will be to each other as the sides containing the right angle.

X.

78. Describe a circle passing through two given points and touching a given circle.

79. Describe a circle which shall pass through a given point and touch a given straight line and a given circle.

80. Through a given point draw a circle touching two given circles.

81. Describe a circle to touch two given right lines and such that a tangent drawn to it from a given point, may be equal to a given line.

82. Describe a circle which shall have its center in a given line, and shall touch a circle and a straight line given in position.

XI.

83. Given the perimeter of a right-angled triangle, it is required to construct it, (1) If the sides are in arithmetical progression. (2) If the sides are in geometrical progression.

84. Given the vertical angle, the perpendicular drawn from it to the base, and the ratio of the segments of the base made by it, to construct the triangle.

85. Apply (vi c) to construct a triangle; having given the vertical angle, the radius of the inscribed circle, and the rectangle contained by the straight lines drawn from the center of the circle to the angles at the base.

86. Describe a triangle with a given vertical angle, so that the line which bisects the base shall be equal to a given line, and the angle which the bisecting line makes with the base shall be equal to a given angle.

87. Given the base, the ratio of the sides containing the vertical angle, and the distance of the vertex from a given point in the base; to construct the triangle.

88. Given the vertical angle and the base of a triangle, and also a line drawn from either of the angles, cutting the opposite side in a given ratio, to construct the triangle.

89. Upon the given base AB construct a triangle having its sides in a given ratio and its vertex situated in the given indefinite line CD.

90. Describe an equilateral triangle equal to a given triangle.

91. Given the hypotenuse of a right-angled triangle, and the side of an inscribed square. Required the two sides of the triangle.

92. To make a triangle, which shall be equal to a given triangle, and have two of its sides equal to two given straight lines, and shew that if the rectangle contained by the two straight lines be less than twice the given triangle, the problem is impossible.

XII.

93. Given the sides of a quadrilateral figure inscribed in a circle, to find the ratio of its diagonals.

94. The diagonals AC, BD, of a trapezium inscribed in a circle, cut each other at right angles in the point E;

the rectangle $AB.BC$: the rectangle $AD.DC \cdot BE : ED$.

XIII.

95. In any triangle, inscribe a triangle similar to a given triangle.

96. Of the two squares which can be inscribed in a right-angled triangle, which is the greater?

97. From the vertex of an isosceles triangle two straight lines

drawn to the opposite angles of the square described on the base, cut the diagonals of the square in E and F, prove that the line EF is parallel to the base

98. Inscribe a square in a segment of a circle

99. Inscribe a square in a sector of a circle, so that the angular points shall be one on each radius, and the other two in the circumference.

100. Inscribe a square in a given equilateral and equiangular pentagon

101. Inscribe a parallelogram in a given triangle similar to a given parallelogram.

102 If any rectangle be inscribed in a given triangle, required the locus of the point of intersection of its diagonals.

103. Inscribe the greatest parallelogram in a given semicircle.

104. In a given rectangle inscribe another, whose sides shall bear to each other a given ratio.

105. In a given segment of a circle to inscribe a similar segment.

106. The square inscribed in a circle is to the square inscribed in the semicircle 5 : 2

107 If a square be inscribed in a right-angled triangle of which one side coincides with the hypotenuse of the triangle, the extremities of that side divide the base into three segments that are continued proportionals.

108. The square inscribed in a semicircle is to the square inscribed in a quadrant of the same circle : 8 : 5

109. Shew that if a triangle inscribed in a circle be isosceles, having each of its sides double the base, the squares described upon the radius of the circle and one of the sides of the triangle, shall be to each other in the ratio of 4 : 15

110 APB is a quadrant, SPT a straight line touching it at P, PM perpendicular to CA, prove that triangle SCT : triangle ACB : triangle ACB : triangle CMP.

111. If through any point in the arc of a quadrant whose radius is R, two circles be drawn touching the bounding radii of the quadrant, and r, r' be the radii of these circles shew that $rr' = R^2$

112. If R be the radius of the circle inscribed in a right-angled triangle ABC, right-angled at A, and a perpendicular be let fall from A on the hypotenuse BC, and if r, r' be the radii of the circles inscribed in the triangles ADB, ACD, prove that $r^2 + r'^2 = R^2$.

XIV.

113 If in a given equilateral and equiangular hexagon another be inscribed, to determine its ratio to the given one.

114. A regular hexagon inscribed in a circle is a mean proportional between an inscribed and circumscribed equilateral triangle

115 The area of the inscribed pentagon, is to the area of the circumscribing pentagon, as the square of the radius of the circle inscribed within the greater pentagon, is to the square of the radius of the circle circumscribing it

116 The diameter of a circle is a mean proportional between the sides of an equilateral triangle and hexagon which are described about that circle.

GEOMETRICAL EXERCISES ON BOOK I.

HINTS, &c.

8. This is a particular case of Euc. I. 22. The triangle however may be described by means of Euc. I. 1. Let AB be the given base, produce AB both ways to meet the circles in D, E (fig. Euc I 1); with center A, and radius AE, describe a circle, and with center B and radius BD, describe another circle cutting the former in G. Join GA, GB.

9. Apply Euc. I. 6, 8.

10. This is proved by Euc I. 32, 13, 5.

11. Let fall also a perpendicular from the vertex on the base.

12. Apply Euc. I. 4.

13. Let CAB be the triangle (fig. Euc I. 10), CD the line bisecting the angle ACD and the base AB. Produce CD, and make DE equal to CD, and join AE. Then CB may be proved equal to AE, also AE to AC.

14. Let AB be the given line, and C, D the given points. From C draw CE perpendicular to AB, and produce it making EF equal to CE, join FD, and produce it to meet the given line in G, which will be the point required.

15. Make the construction as the enunciation directs, then by Euc. I. 4, BH is proved equal to CK: and by Euc I. 13, 6, OB is shewn to be equal to OC.

16. This proposition requires for its proof the case of equal triangles omitted in Euclid:—namely, when two sides and one angle are given, but not the angle included by the given sides.

17. The angle BCD may be shewn to be equal to the sum of the angles ABC, ADC.

18. The angles ADE, AED may be each proved to be equal to the complements of the angles at the base of the triangle.

19. The angles CAB, CBA, being equal, the angles CAD, CBE are equal, Euc. I. 13. Then, by Euc. I. 4, CD is proved to be equal to CE. And by Euc I. 5, 32, the angle at the vertex is shewn to be four times either of the angles at the base.

20. Let AB, CD be two straight lines intersecting each other in E, and let P be the given point, within the angle AED. Draw EF bisecting the angle AED, and through P draw PGH parallel to EF, and cutting ED, EB in G, H. Then EG is equal to EH. And by bisecting the angle DEB and drawing through P a line parallel to this line, another solution is obtained. It will be found that the two lines are at right angles to each other.

21. Let the two given straight lines meet in A, and let P be the given point. Let PQR be the line required, meeting the lines AQ, AR in Q and R, so that PQ is equal to QR. Through P draw PS parallel to AR and join RS. Then APSR is a parallelogram and AS, PR the diagonals. Hence the construction.

22. Let the two straight lines AB, AC meet in A. In AB take any point D, and from AC cut off AE equal to AD, and join DE. On DE, or DE produced, take DF equal to the given line, and through F draw FG parallel to AB meeting AC in G, and through G draw GH parallel to DE meeting AB in H. Then GH is the line required.

23 The two given points may be both on the same side, or one point may be on each side of the line. If the point required in the line be supposed to be found, and lines be drawn joining this point and the given points, an isosceles triangle is formed, and if a perpendicular be drawn on the base from the point in the line, the construction is obvious.

24 The problem is simply this—to find a point in one side of a triangle from which the perpendiculars drawn to the other two sides shall be equal. If all the positions of these lines be considered, it will readily be seen in what case the problem is impossible.

25 If the *isosceles triangle* be obtuse-angled, by Euc. 1. 5, 32, the truth will be made evident. If the triangle be acute-angled, the enunciation of the proposition requires some modification.

26 Construct the figure and apply Euc. 1. 5, 32, 15.

If the isosceles triangle have its vertical angle less than two-thirds of a right-angle, the line ED produced, meets AB produced towards the base, and then $3 \cdot AEF = 4$ right angles $+ AFE$. If the vertical angle be greater than two-thirds of a right angle, ED produced meets AB produced towards the vertex, then $3 \cdot AEF = 2$ right angles $+ AFE$.

27. Let ABC be an isosceles triangle, and from any point D in the base BC, and the extremity B, let three lines DE, DF, BG be drawn to the sides and making equal angles with the base. Produce ED and make DH equal to DF and join BH.

28 In the isosceles triangle ABC, let the line DFE which meets the side AC in D and AB produced in E, be bisected by the base in the point E. Then DC may be shewn to be equal to BE.

29 If two equal straight lines be drawn terminated by two lines which meet in a point, they will cut off triangles of equal area. Hence the two triangles have a common vertical angle and their areas and bases equal. By Euc 1. 32 it is shewn that the angle contained by the bisecting lines is equal to the exterior angle at the base.

30 There is an omission in this question. After the words "making equal angles with the sides," add, "and be equal to each other respectively." (1), (3) Apply Euc. 1. 26, 4. (2) The equal lines which bisect the sides may be shewn to make equal angles with the sides.

31 At C make the angle BCD equal to the angle ACB, and produce AB to meet CD in D.

32 By bisecting the hypotenuse, and drawing a line from the vertex to the point of bisection, it may be shewn that this line forms with the shorter side and half the hypotenuse an isosceles triangle.

33 Let ABC be a triangle, having the right angle at A, and the angle at C greater than the angle at B, also let AD be perpendicular to the base, and AE be the line drawn to E the bisection of the base. Then AE may be proved equal to BE or EC independently of Euc. III. 31.

34 Produce EG, FG to meet the perpendiculars CE, BF, produced if necessary. The demonstration is obvious.

35 If the given triangle have both of the angles at the base acute angles, the difference of the angles at the base is at once obvious from Euc. 1. 32. If one of the angles at the base be obtuse, does the property hold good?

36 Let ABC be a triangle having the angle ACB double of the angle ABC, and let the perpendicular AD be drawn to the base BC. Take DE equal to DC and join AE. Then AE may be proved to be equal to EB.

If ACB be an obtuse angle, then AC is equal to the sum of the segments of the base, made by the perpendicular from the vertex A.

37. Let the sides AB, AC of any triangle ABC be produced, the exterior angles bisected by two lines which meet in D, and let AD be joined, then AD bisects the angle BAC. For draw DE perpendicular on BC, also DF, DG perpendiculars on AB, AC produced, if necessary. Then DF may be proved equal to DG, and the squares on DF, DA are equal to the squares on FG, GA, of which the square on FD is equal to the square on DG; hence AF is equal to AG, and Euc. i. 8, the angle BAC is bisected by AD.

38. The line required will be found to be equal to half the sum of the two sides of the triangle.

39. Apply Euc. i. 1, 9.

40. The angle to be trisected is one-fourth of a right angle. If an equilateral triangle be described on one of the sides of a triangle which contains the given angle, and a line be drawn to bisect that angle of the equilateral triangle which is at the given angle, the angle contained between this line and the other side of the triangle will be one-twelfth of a right angle, or equal to one-third of the given angle.

It may be remarked, generally, that any angle which is the half, fourth, eighth, &c., part of a right angle, may be trisected by Plane Geometry.

41. Apply Euc. i. 20.

42. Let ABC, DBC be two equal triangles on the same base, of which ABC is isosceles, fig. Euc. i. 37. By producing AB and making AG equal to AB or AC, and joining GD, the perimeter of the triangle ABC may be shewn to be less than the perimeter of the triangle DBC.

43. Apply Euc. i. 20.

44. For the first case, see Theo. 32, p. 76; for the other two cases, apply Euc. i. 19.

45. This is obvious from Euc. i. 26.

46. By Euc. i. 29, 6, FC may be shewn equal to each of the lines EF, FG.

47. Join GA and AF, and prove GA and AF to be in the same straight line.

48. Let the straight line drawn through D parallel to BC meet the side AB in E, and AC in F. Then in the triangle EBD, EB is equal to ED, by Euc. i. 29, 6. Also, in the triangle EAD, the angle EAD may be shewn equal to the angle EDA, whence EA is equal to ED, and therefore AB is bisected in E. In a similar way it may be shewn, by bisecting the angle C, that AC is bisected in F. Or the bisection of AC in F may be proved when AB is shewn to be bisected in E.

49. The triangle formed will be found to have its sides respectively parallel to the sides of the original triangle.

50. If a line equal to the given line be drawn from the point where the two lines meet, and parallel to the other given line; a parallelogram may be formed, and the construction effected.

51. Let ABC be the triangle; AD perpendicular to BC, AE drawn to the bisection of BC, and AF bisecting the angle BAC. Produce AD and make DA' equal to AD; join FA', EA'.

52. If the point in the base be supposed to be determined, and lines drawn from it parallel to the sides, it will be found to be in the line which bisects the vertical angle of the triangle.

53. Let ABC be the triangle, at C draw CD perpendicular to CB and equal to the sum of the required lines, through D draw DE parallel to CB meeting AC in E, and draw EF parallel to DC, meeting BC in F. Then EF is equal to DC. Next produce CB, making CG equal to CE, and join EG cutting AB in H. From H draw HK perpendicular to EAC, and

HL perpendicular to BC. Then HK and HL together are equal to DC. The proof depends on Theorem 27, p 75

54. Let C' be the intersection of the circles on the other side of the base, and join AC', BC' Then the angles CBA, C'BA being equal, the angles CBP, C BP are also equal, Euc 1 13 next by Euc 1 4, CP, PC' are proved equal, lastly prove CC' to be equal to CP or PC'

55 In the fig Euc 1 1, produce AB both ways to meet the circles in D and E, join CD, CE, then CDE is an isosceles triangle, having each of the angles at the base one-fourth of the angle at the vertex At E draw EG perpendicular to DB and meeting DC produced in G. Then CEG is an equilateral triangle

56 Join CC', and shew that the angles CC'T, CC'G are equal to two right angles, also that the line TC'G is equal to the diameter

57 Construct the figure and by Euc 1 32 If the angle BAC be a right angle, then the angle BDC is half a right angle

58 Let the lines which bisect the three exterior angles of the triangle ABC form a new triangle A'B'C'. Then each of the angles at A, B', C' may be shewn to be equal to half of the angles at A and B, B and C, C and A respectively And it will be found that half the sums of every two of three unequal numbers whose sum is constant, have less differences than the three numbers themselves

59 The first case may be shewn by Euc 1 4 and the second by Euc 1. 32, 6, 15

60 At D any point in a line EF, draw DC perpendicular to EF and equal to the given perpendicular on the hypotenuse With center C and radius equal to the given base describe a circle cutting EF in B At C draw CA perpendicular to CB and meeting EF in A Then ABC is the triangle required

61 Let ABC be the required triangle having the angle ACB a right angle In BC produced, take CE equal to AC, and with center B and radius BA describe a circular arc cutting CE in D, and join AD Then DE is the difference between the sum of the two sides AC, CB and the hypotenuse AB, also one side AC the perpendicular is given Hence the construction. On any line EB take EC equal to the given side, ED equal to the given difference. At C, draw CA perpendicular to CB, and equal to EC, join AD, at A in AD make the angle DAB equal to ADB, and let AB meet EB in B. Then ABC is the triangle required

62 (1) Let ABC be the triangle required, having ACB the right angle Produce AB to D making AD equal to AC or CB then BD is the sum of the sides Join DC then the angle ADC is one-fourth of a right angle, and DBC is one-half of a right angle Hence to construct at B in BD make the angle DBM equal to half a right angle, and at D the angle BDC equal to one fourth of a right angle, and let DC meet BM in C At C draw CA at right angles to BC meeting BD in A and ABC is the triangle required

(2) Let ABC be the triangle, C the right angle from AB cut off AD equal to AC, then BD is the difference of the hypotenuse and one side. Join CD, then the angles ACD, ADC are equal, and each is half the supplement of DAC, which is half a right angle Hence the construction

63 Take any straight line terminated at A Make AB equal to the difference of the sides, and AC equal to the hypotenuse At B make the angle CBD equal to half a right angle, and with center A and radius AC describe a circle cutting BD in D join AD, and draw DE perpendicular to AC. Then ADE is the required triangle.

64. Let BC the given base be bisected in D. At D draw DE at right angles to BC and equal to the sum of one side of the triangle and the perpendicular from the vertex on the base: join DB, and at B in BE make the angle EBA equal to the angle BED, and let BA meet DE in A: join AC, and ABC is the isosceles triangle.

65. This construction may be effected by means of Prob. 4, p. 71.

66. The perpendicular from the vertex on the base of an equilateral triangle bisects the angle at the vertex which is two-thirds of one right angle.

67. Let ABC be the equilateral triangle of which a side is required to be found, having given BD, CD the lines bisecting the angles at B, C. Since the angles DBC, DCB are equal, each being one-third of a right angle, the sides BD, DC are equal, and BDC is an isosceles triangle having the angle at the vertex the supplement of a third of two right angles. Hence the side BC may be found.

68. Let the given angle be taken, (1) as the *included angle* between the given sides; and (2) as the *opposite angle* to one of the given sides. In the latter case, an ambiguity will arise if the angle be an acute angle, and opposite to the less of the two given sides.

69. Let ABC be the required triangle, BC the given base, CD the given difference of the sides AB, AC: join BD, then DBC by Euc. I. 18, can be shewn to be half the difference of the angles at the base, and AB is equal to AD. Hence at B in the given base BC, make the angle CBD equal to half the difference of the angles at the base. On CB take CE equal to the difference of the sides, and with center C and radius CE, describe a circle cutting BD in D: join CD and produce it to A, making DA equal to DB. Then ABC is the triangle required.

70. On the line which is equal to the perimeter of the required triangle describe a triangle having its angles equal to the given angles. Then bisect the angles at the base; and from the point where these lines meet, draw lines parallel to the sides and meeting the base.

71. Let ABC be the required triangle, BC the given base, and the side AB greater than AC. Make AD equal to AC, and draw CD. Then the angle BCD may be shewn to be equal to half the difference, and the angle DCA equal to half the sum of the angles at the base. Hence ABC, ACB the angles at the base of the triangle are known.

72. Let the two given lines meet in A, and let B be the given point.

If BC, BD be supposed to be drawn making equal angles with AC, and if AD and DC be joined, BCD is the triangle required, and the figure ACBD may be shewn to be a parallelogram. Whence the construction.

73. It can be shewn that lines drawn from the angles of a triangle to bisect the opposite sides, intersect each other at a point which is two-thirds of their lengths from the angular points from which they are drawn. Let ABC be the triangle required, AD, BE, CF the given lines from the angles drawn to the bisections of the opposite sides and intersecting in G. Produce GD, making DH equal to DG, and join BH, CH: the figure GBHC is a parallelogram. Hence the construction.

74. Let ABC (fig. to Euc. I. 20.) be the required triangle, having the base BC equal to the given base, the angle ABC equal to the given angle, and the two sides BA, AC together equal to the given line BD. Join DC, then since AD is equal to AC, the triangle ACD is isosceles, and therefore the angle ADC is equal to the angle ACD. Hence the construction.

75. Let ABC be the required triangle (fig. to Euc. I. 18), having the angle ACB equal to the given angle, and the base BC equal to the given

line, also CD equal to the difference of the two sides AB, AC. If BD be joined, then ABD is an isosceles triangle. Hence the synthesis. Does this construction hold good in all cases?

76. Let ABC be the required triangle (fig. Euc. i. 18), of which the side BC is given and the angle BAC, also CD the difference between the sides AB, AC. Join BD; then AB is equal to AD, because CD is their difference, and the triangle ABD is isosceles, whence the angle ABD is equal to the angle ADB; and since BAD and twice the angle ABD are equal to two right angles, it follows that ABD is half the supplement of the given angle BAC. Hence the construction of the triangle.

77. Let AB be the given base; at A draw the line AD to which the line bisecting the vertical angle is to be parallel. At B draw BE parallel to AD; from A draw AE equal to the given sum of the two sides to meet BE in E. At B make the angle EBC equal to the angle BEA, and draw CF parallel to AD. Then ACB is the triangle required.

78. Take any point in the given line, and apply Euc. i. 23, 31.

79. On one of the parallel lines take EF equal to the given line, and with center E and radius EF describe a circle cutting the other in G. Join EG, and through A draw ABC parallel to EG.

80. This will appear from Euc. i. 29, 15, 26.

81. Let AB, AC, AD, be the three lines. Take any point E in AC, and on EC make EF equal to EA, through F draw FG parallel to AB, join GE and produce it to meet AB in H. Then GE is equal to GH.

82. Apply Euc. i. 32, 29.

83. From E draw EG perpendicular on the base of the triangle, then ED and EF may each be proved equal to EG, and the figure shewn to be equilateral. Three of the angles of the figure are right angles.

84. The greatest parallelogram which can be constructed with given sides can be proved to be rectangular.

85. Let AB be one of the diagonals; at A in AB make the angle BAC less than the required angle, and at A in AC make the angle CAD equal to the required angle. Bisect AB in E and with center E and radius equal to half the other diagonal describe a circle cutting AC, AD in F, G. Join FB, BG; then AFBG is the parallelogram required.

86. This problem is the same as the following: having given the base of a triangle, the vertical angle and the sum of the sides, to construct the triangle. This triangle is one half of the required parallelogram.

87. Draw a line AB equal to the given diagonal, and at the point A make an angle BAC equal to the given angle. Bisect AB in D, and through D draw a line parallel to the given line and meeting AC in C. This will be the position of the other diagonal. Through B draw BE parallel to CA, meeting CD produced in E, join AE, and BC. Then ACBE is the parallelogram required.

88. Construct the figures and by Euc. i. 24.

89. By Euc. i. 4, the opposite sides may be proved to be equal.

90. Let ABCD be the given parallelogram; construct the other parallelogram A'B'C'D by drawing the lines required, also the diagonals AC, A'C, and shew that the triangles ABC, A'B'C' are equiangular.

91. AD' and BC' may be proved to be parallel.

92. Apply Euc. i. 29, 32.

93. The points D, D', are the intersections of the diagonals of two rectangles; if the rectangles be completed, and the lines OD, OD' be produced, they will be the other two diagonals.

94. Let the line drawn from A fall without the parallelogram, and

let CC′, BB′, DD′, be the perpendiculars from C, B, D, on the line drawn from A: from B draw BE parallel to AC′, and the truth is manifest. Next, let the line from A be drawn so as to fall within the parallelogram.

95. Let the diagonals intersect in E. In the triangles DCB, CDA, two angles in each are respectively equal and one side DE: wherefore the diagonals DB, AC are equal: also since DE, EC are equal, it follows that EA, EB are equal. Hence DEC, AEB are two isosceles triangles having their vertical angles equal, wherefore the angles at their bases are equal respectively, and therefore the angle CDB is equal to DBA.

96. (1) By supposing the point P found in the side AB of the parallelogram ABCD, such that the angle contained by AP, PC may be bisected by the line PD; CP may be proved equal to CD; hence the solution.

(2) By supposing the point P found in the side AB produced, so that PD may bisect the angle contained by ABP and PC; it may be shewn that the side AB must be produced, so that BP is equal to BD.

97. This may be shewn by Euc. I. 35.

98. Let D, E, F be the bisections of the sides AB, BC, CA of the triangle ABC: draw DE, EF, FD; the triangle DEF is one-fourth of the triangle ABC. The triangles DBE, FBE are equal, each being one-fourth of the triangle ABC: DF is therefore parallel to BE, and DBEF is a parallelogram of which DE is a diagonal.

99. This may be proved by applying Euc. I. 38.

100. Apply Euc. I. 37, 38.

101. On any side BC of the given triangle ABC, take BD equal to the *given base*; join AD, through C draw CE parallel to AD, meeting BA produced if necessary in E, join ED; then BDE is the triangle required. By a process somewhat similar the triangle may be formed when the *altitude* is given.

102. Apply the preceding problem (101) to make a triangle equal to one of the given triangles and of the same altitude as the other given triangle. Then the sum or difference can be readily found.

103. First construct a triangle on the given base equal to the given triangle; next form an isosceles triangle on the same base equal to this triangle.

104. Make an isosceles triangle equal to the given triangle, and then this isosceles triangle into an equal equilateral triangle.

105. Make a triangle equal to the given parallelogram upon the given line, and then a triangle equal to this triangle, having an angle equal to the given angle.

106. If the figure ABCD be one of four sides; join the opposite angles A, C of the figure, through D draw DE parallel to AC meeting BC produced in E, join AE:—the triangle ABE is equal to the four-sided figure ABCD.

If the figure ABCDE be one of five sides, produce the base both ways, and the figure may be transformed into a triangle, by two constructions similar to that employed for a figure of four sides. If the figure consists of six, seven, or any number of sides, the same process must be repeated.

107. Draw two lines from the bisection of the base parallel to the two sides of the triangle.

108. This may be shewn ex absurdo.

109. On the same base AB, and on the same side of it, let two triangles ABC, ABD be constructed, having the side BD equal to BC, the angle ABC a right angle, but the angle ABD not a right angle; then the triangle ABC is greater than ABD, whether the angle ABD be acute or obtuse.

110. Let ABC be a triangle whose vertical angle is A, and whose base

BC is bisected in D; let any line EDG be drawn through D, meeting AC the greater side in G and AB produced in E, and forming a triangle AEG having the same vertical angle A. Draw BH parallel to AC, and the triangles BDH, GDC are equal. Euc. I. 26.

111. Let two triangles be constructed on the same base with equal perimeters, of which one is isosceles. Through the vertex of that which is not isosceles draw a line parallel to the base, and intersecting the perpendicular drawn from the vertex of the isosceles triangle upon the common base. Join this point of intersection and the extremities of the base.

112. (1) DF bisects the triangle ABC (fig. Prop. 6, p. 73.) On each side of the point F in the line BC, take FG, FH, each equal to one-third of BF, the lines DG, DH shall trisect the triangle. Or,

Let ABC be any triangle, D the given point in BC. Trisect BC in E, F. Join AD, and draw EG, FH parallel to AD. Join DG, DH; these lines trisect the triangle. Draw AE, AF and the proof is manifest.

(2) Let ABC be any triangle; trisect the base BC in D, E, and join AD, AE. From D, E, draw DP, EP parallel to AB, AC and meeting in P. Join AP, BP, CP; these three lines trisect the triangle.

(3) Let P be the given point within the triangle ABC. Trisect the base BC in D, E. From the vertex A draw AD, AE, AP. Join PD, draw AG parallel to PD and join PG. Then BGPA is one-third of the triangle. The problem may be solved by trisecting either of the other two sides and making a similar construction.

113. The base may be divided into nine equal parts, and lines may be drawn from the vertex to the points of division. Or, the sides of the triangle may be trisected, and the points of trisection joined.

114. It is proved, Euc. I. 34, that each of the diagonals of a parallelogram bisects the figure, and it may be shewn that they also bisect each other. It is hence manifest that any straight line, whatever may be its position, which bisects a parallelogram, *must* pass through the intersection of the diagonals.

115. See the remark on the preceding problem 114.

116. Trisect the side AB in E, F, and draw EG, FH parallel to AD or BC, meeting DC in G and H. If the given point P be in EF, the two lines drawn from P through the bisections of EG and FH will trisect the parallelogram. If P be in FB, a line from P through the bisection of FH will cut off one-third of the parallelogram, and the remaining trapezium is to be bisected by a line from P, one of its angles. If P coincide with E or F, the solution is obvious.

117. Construct a right-angled parallelogram by Euc. I. 44, equal to the given quadrilateral figure, and from one of the angles, draw a line to meet the opposite side and equal to the base of the rectangle, and a line from the adjacent angle parallel to this line will complete the rhombus.

118. Bisect BC in D, and through the vertex A, draw AE parallel to BC, with center D and radius equal to half the sum of AB, AC, describe a circle cutting AE in E.

119. Produce one side of the square till it becomes equal to the diagonal, the line drawn from the extremity of this produced side and parallel to the adjacent side of the square, and meeting the diagonal produced, determines the point required.

120. Let fall upon the diagonal perpendiculars from the opposite angles of the parallelogram. These perpendiculars are equal, and each pair of triangles is situated on different sides of the same base and has equal altitudes.

121 One case is included in Theo 120. The other case, when the point is in the diagonal produced, is obvious from the same principle

122 The triangles DCF, ABF may be proved to be equal to half of the parallelogram by Euc. I. 41.

123. Apply Euc. I 41, 38

124 If a line be drawn parallel to AD through the point of intersection of the diagonal, and the line drawn through O parallel to AB; then by Euc. I. 43, 41, the truth of the theorem is manifest.

125 It may be remarked that parallelograms are divided into pairs of equal triangles by the diagonals, and therefore by taking the triangle ABD equal to the triangle ABC, the property may be easily shewn.

126 The triangle ABD is one-half of the parallelogram ABCD, Euc. I. 34. And the triangle DKC is one-half of the parallelogram CDHG, Euc. I 41, also for the same reason the triangle AKB is one-half of the parallelogram AHGB therefore the two triangles DKC, AKB are together one-half of the whole parallelogram ABCD. Hence the two triangles DKC, AKB are equal to the triangle ABD · take from these equals the equal parts which are common, therefore the triangle CKF is equal to the triangles AHK, KBD: wherefore also taking AHK from these equals, then the difference of the triangles CKF, AHK is equal to the triangle KBC and the doubles of these are equal, or the difference of the parallelograms CFKG, AHKE is equal to twice the triangle KBD

127 First prove that the perimeter of a square is less than the perimeter of an equal rectangle next, that the perimeter of the rectangle is less than the perimeter of any other equal parallelogram

128 This may be proved by shewing that the area of the isosceles triangle is greater than the area of any other triangle which has the same vertical angle, and the sum of the sides containing that angle is equal to the sum of the equal sides of the isosceles triangle

129 Let ABC be an isosceles triangle (fig. Euc. I 42), AE perpendicular to the base BC, and AECG the equivalent rectangle Then AC is greater than AE, &c

130 Let the diagonal AC bisect the quadrilateral figure ABCD Bisect AC in E, join BE, ED, and prove BE, ED in the same straight line and equal to one another

131 Apply Euc. I 15.

132 Apply Euc. I 20.

133 This may be shewn by Euc. I 20

134 Let AB be the longest and CD the shortest side of the rectangular figure Produce AD, BC to meet in E Then by Euc. I 32

135 Let ABCD be the quadrilateral figure, and E, F, two points in the opposite sides AB, CD, join EF and bisect it in G; and through G draw a straight line HGK terminated by the sides AD, BC, and bisected in the point G Then EF, HK are the diagonals of the required parallelogram

136 After constructing the figure, the proof offers no difficulty

137 If any line be assumed as a diagonal, if the four given lines taken two and two be always greater than this diagonal, a four-sided figure may be constructed having the assumed line as one of its diagonals · and it may be shewn that when the quadrilateral is possible, the sum of every three given sides is greater than the fourth

138 Draw the two diagonals, then four triangles are formed, two on one side of each diagonal Then two of the lines drawn through the points of bisection of two sides may be proved parallel to one diagonal, and two

parallel to the other diagonal, in the same way as Theo. 97, supra. The other property is manifest from the relation of the areas of the triangles made by the lines drawn through the bisections of the sides.

139. It is sufficient to suggest, that triangles on equal bases, and of equal altitudes, are equal.

140. Let the side AB be parallel to CD, and let AB be bisected in E and CD in F, and let EF be drawn. Join AF, BF, then Euc. I. 38.

141. Let BCED be a trapezium of which DC, BE are the diagonals intersecting each other in G. If the triangle DBG be equal to the triangle EGC, the side DE may be proved parallel to the side BC, by Euc. I. 39.

142. Let ABCD be the quadrilateral figure having the sides AB, CD, parallel to one another, and AD, BC equal. Through B draw BE parallel to AD, then ABED is a parallelogram.

143. Let ABCD be the quadrilateral having the side AB parallel to CD. Let E, F be the points of bisection of the diagonals BD, AC, and join EF and produce it to meet the sides AD, BC in G and H. Through H draw LHK parallel to DA meeting DC in L and AB produced in K. Then BK is half the difference of DC and AB.

144. (1) Reduce the trapezium ABCD to a triangle BAE by Prob. 106, supra, and bisect the triangle BAE by a line AF from the vertex. If F fall without BC, through F draw FG parallel to AC or DE, and join AG.

Or thus. Draw the diagonals AC, BD. bisect BD in E, and join AE, EC. Draw FEG parallel to AC the other diagonal, meeting AD in F, and DC in G. AG being joined, bisects the trapezium.

(2) Let E be the given point in the side AD. Join EB. Bisect the quadrilateral EBCD by EF. Make the triangle EFG equal to the triangle EAB, on the same side of EF as the triangle AB. Bisect the triangle EFG by EH. EH bisects the figure.

145. If a straight line be drawn from the given point through the intersection of the diagonals and meeting the opposite side of the square, the problem is then reduced to the bisection of a trapezium by a line drawn from one of its angles.

146. If the four sides of the figure be of different lengths, the truth of the theorem may be shewn. If, however, two adjacent sides of the figure be equal to one another, as also the other two, the lines drawn from the angles to the bisection of the longer diagonal, will be found to divide the trapezium into four triangles which are equal in area to one another. Euc. I. 38.

147. Apply Euc. I. 17, observing that the shortest side is one-half of the longest.

148. Find by Euc. I. 17, a line the square on which shall be seven times the square on the given line. Then the triangle which has these two lines, containing the right angle shall be the triangle required.

149. Apply Euc. I. 47.

150. Let the base BC be bisected in D, and DE be drawn perpendicular to the hypotenuse AC. Join AD. then Euc. I. 47.

151. Construct the figure, and the truth is obvious from Euc. I. 47.

152. See Theo. 32, p. 76, and apply Euc. I. 47.

153. Draw the lines required and apply Euc. I. 47.

154. Apply Euc. I. 47.

155. Apply Euc. I. 47.

156. Apply Euc. I. 47, observing that the square on any line is four times the square on half the line.

157. Apply Euc. I. 47, to express the squares of the three sides in terms of the squares on the perpendiculars and on the segments of AB.

158. By Euc. I. 47, bearing in mind that the square described on any line is four times the square described upon half the line.

159. The former part is at once manifest by Euc. I. 47. Let the diagonals of the square be drawn, and the given point be supposed to coincide with the intersection of the diagonals, the minimum is obvious. Find its value in terms of the side.

160. (a) This is obvious from Euc. I. 13.

(b) Apply Euc. I. 32, 29.

(c) Apply Euc. I. 5, 29.

(d) Let AL meet the base BC in P, and let the perpendiculars from F, K meet BC produced in M and N respectively; then the triangles APB, FMB may be proved to be equal in all respects, as also APC, CKN.

(e) Let fall DQ perpendicular on FB produced. Then the triangle DQB may be proved equal to each of the triangles ABC, DBF; whence the triangle DBF is equal to the triangle ABC.

Perhaps however the better method is to prove at once that the triangles ABC, FBD are equal, by shewing that they have two sides equal in each triangle, and the included angles, one the supplement of the other.

(f) If DQ be drawn perpendicular on FB produced, FQ may be proved to be bisected in the point B, and DQ equal to AC. Then the square on FD is found by the right-angled triangle FQD. Similarly, the square on KE is found, and the sum of the squares on FD, EK, GH will be found to be six times the square on the hypotenuse.

(g) Through A draw PAQ parallel to BC and meeting DB, EC produced in P, Q. Then by the right-angled triangles.

161. Let any parallelograms be described on any two sides AB, AC of a triangle ABC, and the sides parallel to AB, AC be produced to meet in a point P. Join PA. Then on either side of the base BC, let a parallelogram be described having two sides equal and parallel to AP. Produce AP and it will divide the parallelogram on BC into two parts respectively equal to the parallelograms on the sides. Euc. I. 35, 36.

162. Let the equilateral triangles ABD, BCE, CAF be described on AB, BC, CA, the sides of the triangle ABC having the right angle at A.

Join DC, AK. then the triangles DBC, ABE are equal. Next draw DG perpendicular to AB and join CG. then the triangles BDG, DAG, DGC are equal to one another. Also draw AH, EK perpendicular to BC, the triangles EKH, EKA are equal. Whence may be shewn that the triangle ABD is equal to the triangle BUE, and in a similar way may be shewn that CAF is equal to CHE.

The restriction is unnecessary. it only brings AD, AE into the same line.

GEOMETRICAL EXERCISES ON BOOK II.

HINTS, &c.

6. See the figure Euc. II. 5.

7. This Problem is equivalent to the following: construct an isosceles right-angled triangle, having given one of the sides which contains the right angle.

8. In the question for E read D. Construct the square on AB, and the property is obvious.

9. The sum of the squares on the two parts of any lines is least when the two parts are equal

10. A line may be found the square on which is double the square on the given line. The problem is then reduced to:—having given the hypotenuse and the sum of the sides of a right-angled triangle, construct the triangle.

11. This follows from Euc. ii. 5, Cor.

12. This problem is, in other words, Given the sum of two lines and the sum of their squares, to find the lines. Let AB be the given straight line, at B draw BC at right angles to AB, bisect the angle ABC by BD. On AB take AE equal to the side of the given square, and with center A and radius AE describe a circle cutting BD in D, from D draw DF perpendicular to AB, the line AB is divided in F as was required

13. Let AB be the given line. Produce AB to C making BC equal to three times the square on AB. From BA cut off BD equal to BC, then D is the point of section such that the squares on AB and BD are double of the square on AD.

14. In the fig. Euc. ii. 7. Join BF, and draw FL perpendicular on GD. Half the rectangle DB, BG, may be proved equal to the rectangle AB, BC.

Or, join KA, CD, KD, CK. Then CK is perpendicular to BD. And the triangles CBD, KBD are each equal to the triangle ABK. Hence, twice the triangle ABK is equal to the figure CBKD, but twice the triangle ABK is equal to the rectangle AB, BC, and the figure CBKD is equal to half the rectangle DB and CK, the diagonals of the square on AB, BC. Wherefore, &c

15. The difference between the two unequal parts may be shewn to be equal to twice the line between the points of section.

16. This proposition is only another form of stating Euc. ii. 7

17. In the figure, Theo. 7. p. 69, draw PQ, PR, PS perpendiculars on AB, AD, AC respectively: then since the triangle PAC is equal to the two triangles PAB, PAD, it follows that the rectangle contained by PS, AC, is equal to the sum of the rectangles PQ, AB, and PR, AD When is the rectangle PS, AC equal to the *difference* of the other two rectangles?

18. Through E draw EG parallel to AB, and through F, draw FHK parallel to BC and cutting EG in H. Then the area of the rectangle is made up of the areas of four triangles; whence it may be readily shewn that *twice the area* of the triangle AEF, and the figure AGHK is equal to the area ABCD

19. Apply Euc. ii. 11

20. The vertical angles at L may be proved to be equal, and each of them a right angle

21. Apply Euc. ii. 4, 11 i. 47

22. Produce IG, DB to meet in L, and draw the other diagonal LHC, which passes through H, because the complements AG, BK are equal. Then LH may be shewn to be equal to Ff, and to Dd

23. The common intersection of the three lines divides each into two parts, one of which is double of the other, and this point is the vertex of three triangles which have lines drawn from it to the bisection of the bases Apply Euc. ii. 12, 13

24. Apply Theorem 3, p. 104, and Euc. i. 47

25. This will be found to be that particular case of Euc. ii. 12, in which the distance of the obtuse angle from the foot of the perpendicular, is half

of the side subtended by the right angle made by the perpendicular and the base produced.

26 (1) Let the triangle be acute-angled. (Euc. II 13, fig 1.)

Let AC be bisected in E, and BE be joined, also EF be drawn perpendicular to BC. EF is equal to FC. Then the square on BE may be proved to be equal to the square on BC and the rectangle BD, BC.

(2) If the triangle be obtuse-angled, the perpendicular EF falls *within* or without the base according as the bisecting line is drawn from the *obtuse* or the *acute* angle at the base

27. This may be shewn from Theorem 3, p. 114.

28 Let the perpendicular AD be drawn from A on the base BC It may be shewn that the base BC must be produced to a point E, such that CE is equal to the difference of the segments of the base made by the perpendicular

29 Since the base and area are given, the altitude of the triangle is known Hence the problem is reduced to — Given the base and altitude of a triangle, and the line drawn from the vertex to the bisection of the base, construct the triangle

30 This follows immediately from Euc. I. 47

31 Apply Euc II 13

32 The truth of this property depends on the fact that the rectangle contained by AC, CB is equal to that contained by AB, CD

33. Let P the required point in the base AB be supposed to be known Join CP. It may then be shewn that the property stated in the Problem is contained in Theorem 3, p 114

34. This may be shewn from Euc. I 47, II 5 Cor

35. From C let fall CF perpendicular on AB Then ACE is an obtuse-angled, and BEC an acute-angled triangle Apply Euc II 12, 13, and by Euc I 47, the squares on AC and CB are equal to the square on AB

36 Apply Euc I 47, II 4, and the note p 102 on Euc II 4

37 Draw a perpendicular from the vertex to the base, and apply Euc I 47, II 5, Cor Enumerate and prove the proposition when the straight line drawn from the vertex meets the base produced

38. This follows directly from Euc II 13, Case 1

39 The truth of this proposition may be shewn from Euc. I 47, II 4.

40 Let the square on the base of the isosceles triangle be described Draw the diagonals of the square, and the proof is obvious

41. Let ABC be the triangle required, such that the square on AB is three times the square on AC or BC. Produce BC and draw AD perpendicular to BC Then by Euc II 12, CD may be shewn to be equal to one half of BC Hence the construction

42 Apply Euc II 12, and Theorem 38, p 118

43 Draw EF parallel to AB and meeting the base in F; draw also EG perpendicular to the base Then by Euc I 47, II 5, Cor

44 Bisect the angle B by BD meeting the opposite side in D, and draw BE perpendicular to AC Then by Euc I 47, II 5, Cor

45 This follows directly from Theorem 3, p 114

46 Draw the diagonals intersecting each other in P, and join OP By Theo 3, p 114

47 Draw from any two opposite angles, straight lines to meet in the bisection of the diagonal joining the other angles Then by Euc II 12, 13

48. Draw two lines from the point of bisection of either of the bisected sides to the extremities of the opposite side; and three triangles will be formed, two on one of the bisected sides and one on the other, in each of

which is a line drawn from the vertex to the bisection of the base. Then by Theo. 3, p. 114.

49. If the extremities of the two lines which bisect the opposite sides of the trapezium be joined, the figure formed is a parallelogram which has its sides respectively parallel to, and equal to, half the diagonals of the trapezium. The sum of the squares on the two diagonals of the trapezium may be easily shewn to be equal to the sum of the squares on the four sides of the parallelogram.

50. Draw perpendiculars from the extremities of one of the parallel sides, meeting the other side produced, if necessary. Then from the four right-angled triangles thus formed, may be shewn the truth of the proposition.

51. In the problem, for triangle read rectangle. Let ABCD be any trapezium having the side AD parallel to BC. Draw the diagonal AC, then the sum of the triangles ABC, ADC may be shewn to be equal to the rectangle contained by the altitude and half the sum of AD and BC.

52. Let ABCD be the trapezium, having the sides AB, CD, parallel, and AD, BC equal. Join AC and draw AE perpendicular to DC. Then by Euc. II. 13.

53. Let ABC be any triangle; AHKB, AGFC, BDEC, the squares upon their sides; EF, GH, KL the lines joining the angles of the squares. Produce GA, KB, EC, and draw HN, DQ, FR perpendiculars upon them respectively: also draw AP, BM, CS perpendiculars on the sides of the triangle. Then AN may be proved to be equal to AM; CR to CP; and BQ to BS; and by Euc. II. 12, 13.

54. Convert the triangle into a rectangle, then Euc. II. 14.

55. Find a rectangle equal to the two figures, and apply Euc. II. 14.

56. Find the side of a square which shall be equal to the given rectangle See Prob. I. p. 113.

57. On any line PQ take AB equal to the given difference of the sides of the rectangle, at A draw AC at right angles to AB, and equal to the side of the given square; bisect AB in O and join OC; with center O and radius OC describe a semicircle meeting PQ in D and E. Then the lines AD, AE have AB for their difference, and the rectangle contained by them is equal to the square on AC.

58. Apply Euc. II. 14.

GEOMETRICAL EXERCISES ON BOOK III.

HINTS, &c.

7. Euc. III. 3, suggests the construction.

8. The given point may be either within or without the circle. Find the center of the circle, and join the given point and the center, and upon this line describe a semicircle, a line equal to the given distance may be drawn from the given point to meet the arc of the semicircle. When the point is without the circle, the given distance may meet the diameter produced.

9. This may be easily shewn to be a straight line passing through the center of the circle.

10. The two chords form by their intersections the sides of two isosceles triangles, of which the parallel chords in the circle are the bases.

11. The angles in equal segments are equal, and by Euc. I. 29. If the chords are equally distant from the center, the lines intersect the diameter in the center of the circle

12. Construct the figure and the arc BC may be proved equal to the arc B'C'

13. The point determined by the lines drawn from the bisections of the chords and at right angles to them respectively, will be the center of the required circle.

14. Construct the figures the proof offers no difficulty.

15. On any radius construct an isosceles right-angled triangle, and produce the side which meets the circumference.

16. Join the extremities of the chords, then Euc. I. 27, III. 28

17. Take the center O, and join AP, AO, &c and apply Euc. I. 20

18. Draw any straight line intersecting two parallel chords and meeting the circumference

19. Produce the radii to meet the circumference.

20. Join AD, and the first equality follows directly from Euc. III. 20, I. 32 Also by joining AC, the second equality may be proved in a similar way. If however the line AD do not fall on the same side of the center O as E, it will be found that the *difference*, not the *sum* of the two angles, is equal to 2 AED See note to Euc. III. 20, p 155

21. Let DKE, DBO (fig Euc III 8) be two lines equally inclined to DA, then KE may be proved to be equal to BO, and the segments cut off by equal straight lines in the same circle, as well as in equal circles, are equal to one another

22. Apply Euc I 15, and III. 21

23. This is the same as Euc. III. 34, with the condition, that the line must pass through a given point

24. Let the segments AHB, AKC be externally described on the given lines AB, AC, to contain angles equal to BAC Then by the converse to Euc III 32, AB touches the circle AKC, and AC the circle AHB

25. Let ABC be a triangle of which the base or longest side is BC, and let a segment of a circle be described on BC Produce BA, CA to meet the arc of the segment in D, E, and join BD, CE If circles be described about the triangles ABD, ACE, the sides AB, AC shall cut off segments similar to the segment described upon the base BC

26. This is obvious from the note to Euc III 26, p 156

27. The segment must be described on the opposite side of the produced chord By converse of Euc III 32

28. If a circle be described upon the side AC as a diameter, the circumference will pass through the points D, E Then Euc III 21.

29. Let AB, AC be the bounding radii, and D any point in the arc BC, and DE, DF, perpendiculars from D on AB, AC The circle described on AD will always be of the same magnitude, and the angle EAF in it, is constant;—whence the arc EDF is constant, and therefore its chord EF

30. Construct the figure, and let the circle with center O, described on AH as a diameter intersect the given circle in P, Q, join OP, PE, and prove EP at right angles to OP

31. If the tangent be required to be perpendicular to a given line draw the diameter parallel to this line, and the tangent drawn at the extremity of this diameter will be perpendicular to the given line

32. The straight line which joins the center and passes through the intersection of two tangents to a circle, bisects the angle contained by the tangents.

33. Draw two radii containing an angle equal to the supplement of the given angle; the tangents drawn at the extremities of these radii will contain the given angle.

34. Since the circle is to touch two parallel lines drawn from two given points in a third line, the radius of the circle is determined by the distance between the two given points.

35. It is sufficient to suggest that the angle between a chord and a tangent is equal to the angle in the alternate segment of the circle. Euc. iii. 32.

36. Let AB be the given chord of the circle whose center is O. Draw DE touching the circle at any point E and equal to the given line; join DO, and with center O and radius DO describe a circle; produce the chord AB to meet the circumference of this circle in F; then F is the point required.

37. Let D be the point required in the diameter BA produced, such that the tangent DP is half of DB. Join CP, C being the center. Then CPD is a right-angled triangle, having the sum of the base PC and hypotenuse CD double of the perpendicular PD.

38. If BE intersect DF in K (fig Euc iii 37). Join FB, FE, then by means of the triangles, BE is shewn to be bisected in K at right angles.

39. Let AB, CD be any two diameters of a circle, O the center, and let the tangents at their extremities form the quadrilateral figure EFGH. Join EO, OF, then EO and OF may be proved to be in the same straight line; and similarly HO, OK.

Note.—This Proposition is equally true if AB, CD be any two chords whatever. It then becomes equivalent to the following proposition:—The diagonals of the circumscribed and inscribed quadrilaterals, intersect in the same point, the points of contact of the former being the angles of the latter figure.

40. Let C be the point without the circle from which the tangents CA, CB are drawn, and let DE be any diameter, also let AE, BD be joined, intersecting in P, then if CP be joined and produced to meet DE in G, CG is perpendicular to DE. Join DA, EB, and produce them to meet in F.

Then the angles DAE, EBD being angles in a semicircle, are right angles, or DB, EA are drawn perpendicular to the sides of the triangle DEF; whence the line drawn from F through P is perpendicular to the third side DE.

41. Let the chord AB, of which P is its middle point, be produced both ways to C, D, so that AC is equal to BD. From C, D, draw the tangents to the circle forming the tangential quadrilateral CKDR, the points of contact of the sides, being E, H, F, G. Let O be the center of the circle. Join EH, GF, CO, GO, FO, DO. Then EH and GF may be proved each parallel to CD, they are therefore parallel to one another. Whence is proved that both EF and DG bisect AB.

42. This is obvious from Euc. i. 29, and the note to iii. 22 p. 156.

43. From any point A in the circumference, let any chord AB and tangent AC be drawn. Bisect the arc AB in D, and from D draw DE, DC perpendiculars on the chord AB and tangent AC. Join AD, the triangles ADE, ADC may be shewn to be equal.

44. Let A, B, be the given points. Join AB and upon it describe a segment of a circle which shall contain an angle equal to the given angle. If the circle cut the given line, there will be two points, if it only touch the line, there will be one, and if it neither cut nor touch the line, the problem is impossible.

45. It may be shewn that the point required is determined by a perpendicular drawn from the center of the circle on the given line.

46. Let two lines AP, BP be drawn from the given points A, B, making equal angles with the tangent to the circle at the point of contact P, take any other point Q in the convex circumference, and join QA, QB then by Prob 4, p. 71, and Euc i 21.

47. Let C be the center of the circle, and E the point of contact of DF with the circle. Join DC, CE, CF.

48. Let the tangents at E, F meet in a point R. Produce RE, RF to meet the diameter AB produced in S, T Then RST is a triangle, and the quadrilateral RFOE may be circumscribed by a circle, and RPO may be proved to be one of the diagonals.

49. Let C be the middle point of the chord of contact produce AC, BC to meet the circumference in B', A', and join AA', BB

50. Let A be the given point, and B the given point in the given line CD. At B draw BE at right angles to CD, join AB and bisect it in F, and from F draw FE perpendicular to AB and meeting BE in E. E is the center of the required circle.

51. Let O be the center of the given circle Draw OA perpendicular to the given straight line, at O in OA make the angle AOP equal to the given angle, produce PO to meet the circumference again in Q. Then P, Q are two points from which tangents may be drawn fulfilling the required condition

52. Let C be the center of the given circle, B the given point in the circumference, and A the other given point through which the required circle is to be made to pass Join CB, the centre of the circle is a point in CB produced The center itself may be found in three ways.

53. Euc iii 11 suggests the construction

54. Let AB, AC be the two given lines which meet at A, and let D be the given point Bisect the angle BAC by AE, the center of the circle is in AE Through D draw DF perpendicular to AE, and produce DF to G, making FG equal to FD Then DG is a chord of the circle, and the circle which passes through D and touches AB, will also pass through G and touch AC

55. As the center is given, the line joining this point and center of the given circle, is perpendicular to that diameter, through the extremities of which the required circle is to pass

56. Let AB be the given line and D the given point in it, through which the circle is required to pass, and AC the line which the circle is to touch From D draw DE perpendicular to AB and meeting AC in C Suppose O a point in AD to be the center of the required circle Draw OE perpendicular to AC, and join OC, then it may be shewn that CO bisects the angle ACD

57. Let the given circle be described Draw a line through the center and intersection of the two lines Next draw a chord perpendicular to this line, cutting off a segment containing the given angle The circle described passing through one extremity of the chord and touching one of the straight lines, shall also pass through the other extremity of the chord and touch the other line.

58. The line drawn through the point of intersection of the two circles parallel to the line which joins their centers, may be shewn to be double of the line which joins their centers, and greater than any other straight line drawn through the same point and terminated by the circumferences. The greatest line therefore depends on the distance between the centers of the two circles

59. Apply Euc iii 27; i. 6

60. Let two unequal circles cut one another, and let the line ABC drawn through B, one of the points of intersection, be the line required, such that AB is equal to BC. Join O, O' the centers of the circles, and draw OP, O'P' perpendiculars on ABC, then PB is equal to BP', through O' draw O'D parallel to PP', then ODO' is a right-angled triangle, and a semicircle described on OO' as a diameter will pass through the point D. Hence the synthesis. If the line ABC be supposed to move round the point B and its extremities A, C to be in the extremities of the two circles, it is manifest that ABC admits of a maximum.

61. Suppose the thing done, then it will appear that the line joining the points of intersection of the two circles is bisected at right angles by the line joining the centers of the circles. Since the radii are known, the centers of the two circles may be determined.

62. Let the circles intersect in A, B, and let CAD, EBF be any parallels passing through A, B and intercepted by the circles. Join CE, AB, DF. Then the figure CEFD may be proved to be a parallelogram. Whence CAD is equal to EBF.

63. Complete the circle whose segment is ADB, AHB being the other part. Then since the angle ACB is constant, being in a given segment, the sum of the arcs DE and AHB is constant. But AHB is given, hence ED is also given and therefore constant.

64. From A suppose ACD drawn, so that when BD, BC are joined, AD and DB shall together be double of AC and CB together. Then the angles ACD, ADB are supplementary, and hence the angles BCD, BDC are equal, and the triangle BCD is isosceles. Also the angles BCD, BDC are given, hence the triangle BDC is given in species.

Again $AD + DB = 2 AC + 2 BC$, or $CD = AC + BC$.

Whence, make the triangle bdc having its angles at d, c equal to that in the segment BDA; and make $ca = cd - cb$, and join ab. At A make the angle BAD equal to bad, and AD is the line required.

65. The line drawn from the point of intersection of the two lines to the center of the given circle may be shewn to be constant, and the center of the given circle is a fixed point.

66. This is at once obvious from Euc. III. 36.

67. This follows directly from Euc. III. 36.

68. Each of the lines CE, DF may be proved parallel to the common chord AB.

69. By constructing the figure and joining AC and AD, by Euc. III. 27, it may be proved that the line BC falls on BD.

70. By constructing the figure and applying Euc. I. 8, 4, the truth is manifest.

71. The bisecting line is a common chord to the two circles, join the other extremities of the chord and the diameter in each circle, and the angles in the two segments may be proved to be equal.

72. Apply Euc. III. 27, I. 32, 6.

73. Draw a common tangent at C the point of contact of the circles, and prove AC and CB to be in the same straight line.

74. Let A, B, be the centers, and C the point of contact of the two circles, D, E the points of contact of the circles with the common tangent DE, and CF a tangent common to the two circles at C, meeting DF in E. Join DC, CE. Then DF, FC, FE may be shewn to be equal, and FC to be at right angles to AB.

75. The line must be drawn to the extremities of the diameters which are on opposite sides of the line joining the centers.

76. The sum of the distances of the center of the third circle from the centers of the two given circles, is equal to the sum of the radii of the given circles, which is constant.

77. Let the circles touch at C either externally or internally, and their diameters AC, BC through the point of contact will either coincide or be in the same straight line. CDE any line through C will cut off similar segments from the two circles. For joining AD, BE, the angles in the segments DAC, EBC are proved to be equal.

The remaining segments are also similar, since they contain angles which are supplementary to the angles DAC, EBC.

78. Let the line which joins the centers of the two circles be produced to meet the circumferences, and let the extremities of this line and any other line from the point of contact be joined. From the center of the larger circle draw perpendiculars on the sides of the right-angled triangle inscribed within it.

79. In general, the locus of a point in the circumference of a circle which rolls within the circumference of another, is a curve called the *Hypocycloid*; but to this there is one exception, in which the radius of one of the circles is double that of the other. in this case, the locus is a straight line, as may be easily shewn from the figure.

80. Let A, B be the centers of the circles. Draw AB cutting the circumferences in C, D. On AB take CE, DF each equal to the radius of the required circle. the two circles described with centers A, B, and radii AE, BF, respectively, will cut one another, and the point of intersection will be the center of the required circle.

81. Apply Euc. III. 31.

82. Apply Euc. III. 21.

83. (1) When the tangent is on the same side of the two circles. Join C, C' their centers, and on CC' describe a semicircle. With center C' and radius equal to the *difference* of the radii of the two circles, describe another circle cutting the semicircle in D. join DC' and produce it to meet the circumference of the given circle in B. Through C draw CA parallel to DB and join BA, this line touches the two circles.

(2) When the tangent is on the alternate sides. Having joined C, C', on CC' describe a semicircle; with center C, and radius equal to the *sum* of the radii of the two circles describe another circle cutting the semicircle in D, join CD cutting the circumference in A, through C draw CB parallel to CA and join AB.

84. The possibility is obvious. The point of bisection of the segment intercepted between the convex circumferences will be the center of one of the circles, and the center of a second circle will be found to be the point of intersection of two circles described from the centers of the given circles with their radii increased by the radius of the second circle. The line passing through the centers of these two circles will be the locus of the centers of all the circles which touch the two given circles.

85. At any points P, R in the circumferences of the circles, whose centers are A, B, draw PQ, RS, tangents equal to the given lines, and join AQ, BS. These being made the sides of a triangle of which AB is the base, the vertex of the triangle is the point required.

86. In each circle draw a chord of the given length, describe circles concentric with the given circles touching these chords, and then draw a straight line touching these circles.

87. Within one of the circles draw a chord cutting off a segment equal to the given segment, and describe a concentric circle touching the chord:

then draw a straight line touching this latter circle and the other given circle.

88. The tangent may intersect the line joining the centers, or the line produced. Prove that the angle in the segment of one circle is equal to the angle in the corresponding segment of the other circle.

89. Join the centers A, B, at C the point of contact draw a tangent, and at A draw AF cutting the tangent in F, and making with CF an angle equal to one-fourth of the given angle. From F draw tangents to the circles.

90. Let C be the center of the given circle, and D the given point in the given line AB. At D draw any line DE at right angles to AB, then the center of the circle required is in the line AE. Through C draw a diameter FG parallel to DE, the circle described passing through the points E, F, G will be the circle required.

91. Apply Euc. III. 18.

92. Let A, B, be the two given points, and C the center of the given circle. Join AC, and at C draw the diameter DCE perpendicular to AC, and through the points A, D, E describe a circle, and produce AC to meet the circumference in F. Bisect AF in G, and AB in H, and draw GK, HK, perpendiculars to AF, AB respectively, and intersecting in K. Then K is the center of the circle which passes through the points A, B, and bisects the circumference of the circle whose center is C.

93. Let D be the given point and EF the given straight line. (fig. Euc. III. 32.) Draw DB to make the angle DBF equal to that contained in the alternate segment. Draw BA at right angles to EF, and DA at right angles to DB and meeting BA in A. Then AB is the diameter of the circle.

94. Let A, B be the given points, and CD the given line. From E the middle of the line AB, draw EM perpendicular to AB, meeting CD in M, and draw MA. In EM take any point F, draw FH to make the given angle with CD, and draw FG equal to FH, and meeting MA produced in G. Through A draw AP parallel to FG, and CPK parallel to FH. Then P is the center, and C the third defining point of the circle required, and AP may be proved equal to CP by means of the triangles GMF, AMP, and HMF, CMP, Euc. VI. 2. Also CPK the diameter makes with CD the angle KCD equal to FHD, that is, to the given angle.

95. Let A, B be the two given points, join AB and bisect AB in C, and draw CD perpendicular to AB, then the center of the required circle will be in CD. From O the center of the given circle draw CFG parallel to CD, and meeting the circle in F and AB produced in G. At F draw a chord FF' equal to the given chord. Then the circle which passes through the points at B and F, passes also through F'.

96. Let the straight line joining the centers of the two circles be produced both ways to meet the circumference of the exterior circle.

97. Let A be the common center of two circles, and BCDE the chord such that BE is double of CD. From A, B draw AF, BG perpendicular to BE. Join AC, and produce it to meet BG in G. Then AC may be shewn to be equal to CG, and the angle CBG being a right angle, is the angle in the semicircle described on CG as its diameter.

98. The lines joining the common center and the extremities of the chords of the circles, may be shewn to contain unequal angles, and the angles at the centers of the circles are double the angles at the circumferences, it follows that the segments containing these unequal angles are not similar.

99. Let AB, AC be the straight lines drawn from A, a point in the outer

circle to touch the inner circle in the points D, E, and meet the outer circle again at B, C. Join BC, DE. Prove BC double of DE

Let O be the center, and draw the common diameter AOG intersecting BC in F, and join EF. Then the figure DBFE may be proved to be a parallelogram

100. This appears from Euc III 14.

101 The given point may be either within or without the circle. Draw a chord in the circle equal to the given chord, and describe a concentric circle touching the chord, and through the given point draw a line touching this latter circle

102. The diameter of the inner circle must not be less than one-third of the diameter of the exterior circle

103. Suppose AD, DB to be the tangents to the circle AEB containing the given angle   Draw DC to the center C and join CA, CB   Then the triangles ACD, BCD are always equal   DC bisects the given angle at D and the angle ACB   The angles CAB, CBD, being right angles, are constant, and the angles ADC, BDC are constant, as also the angles ACD, BCD, also AC, CB the radii of the given circle.   Hence the locus of D is a circle whose center is C and radius CD.

104 Let C be the center of the inner circle; draw any radius CD, at D draw a tangent CE equal to CD, join CE, and with center C and radius CE describe a circle and produce ED to meet the circle again in F

105 Take C the center of the given circle, and draw any radius CD, at D draw DE perpendicular to DC and equal to the length of the required tangent; with center C and radius CE describe a circle.

106 This is manifest from Euc III 36

107 Let AB, AC be the sides of a triangle ABC. From A draw the perpendicular AD on the opposite side, or opposite side produced. The semicircles described on AB, BC both pass through D.   Euc III 31

108 Let A be the right angle of the triangle ABC, the first property follows from the preceding Theorem 87   Let DE, DF be drawn to E, F the centers of the circles on AB, AC and join EF   Then ED may be proved to be perpendicular to the radius DF of the circle on AC at the point D

109 Let ABC be a triangle, and let the arcs be described on the sides externally containing angles, whose sum is equal to two right angles   It is obvious that the sum of the angles in the remaining segments is equal to four right angles   These arcs may be shewn to intersect each other in one point D   Let a, b, c be the centers of the circles on BC, AC, AB   Join ab, bc, ca, Ab, bC, Ca, aB, Bc, cA, bD, cD, aD)   Then the angle cba may be proved equal to one-half of the angle AbC   Similarly, the other two angles of abc.

110 It may be remarked, that generally, the mode of proof by which, in pure geometry, three lines must, under specified conditions, pass through the same point, is that by reductio ad absurdum   This will for the most part require the converse theorem to be first proved or taken for granted

The converse theorem in this instance is, "If two perpendiculars drawn from two angles of a triangle upon the opposite sides, intersect in a point, the line drawn from the third angle through this point will be perpendicular to the third side"

The proof will be formally thus   Let EHD be the triangle, AC, BD two perpendiculars intersecting in F.   If the third perpendicular EG do not pass through F, let it take some other position as EH, and through F draw EFG to meet AD in G.   Then it has been proved that EG is perpendicular to AD:

whence the two angles EHG, EGH of the triangle EGH are equal to two right angles;—which is absurd.

111. The circle described on AB as a diameter will pass through E and D. Then Euc. III. 36.

112. Since all the triangles are on the same base and have equal vertical angles, these angles are in the same segment of a given circle.

The lines bisecting the vertical angles may be shewn to pass through the extremity of that diameter which bisects the base.

113. Let AC be the common base of the triangles, ABC the isosceles triangle, and ADC any other triangle on the same base AC and between the same parallels AC, BD. Describe a circle about ABC, and let it cut AD in E and join EC. Then, Euc. I. 17; III. 21.

114. Let ABC be the given isosceles triangle having the vertical angle at C, and let FG be any given line. Required to find a point P in FG such that the distance PA shall be double of PC. Divide AC in D so that AD is double of DC, produce AC to E and make AE double of AC. On DE describe a circle cutting FG in P, then PA is double of PC. This is found by shewing that $AP^2 = 4 \cdot PC^2$.

115. On any two sides of the triangle, describe segments of circles each containing an angle equal to two-thirds of a right angle, the point of intersection of the arcs within the triangle will be the point required, such that three lines drawn from it to the angles of the triangle shall contain equal angles. Euc. III. 22.

116. Let A be the base of the tower, AB its altitude, BC the height of the flagstaff, AD a horizontal line drawn from A. If a circle be described passing through the points B, C, and touching the line AD in the point E: E will be the point required. Give the analysis.

117. If the ladder be supposed to be raised in a vertical plane, the locus of the middle point may be shewn to be a quadrantal arc of which the radius is half the length of the ladder.

118. The line drawn perpendicular to the diameter from the other extremity of the tangent is parallel to the tangent drawn at the extremity of the diameter.

119. Apply Euc. III. 21.

120. Let A, B, C, be the centers of the three equal circles, and let them intersect one another in the point D: and let the circles whose centers are A, B intersect each other again in E; the circles whose centers are B, C in F; and the circles whose centers are C, A in G. Then FG is perpendicular to DE; DG to FC; and DF to GE. Since the circles are equal, and all pass through the same point D, the centers A, B, C are in a circle about D whose radius is the same as the radius of the given circles. Join AB, BC, CA; then these will be perpendicular to the chords DE, DF, DG. Again, the figures DAGC, DBFC are equilateral, and hence FG is parallel to AB; that is, perpendicular to DE. Similarly for the other two cases.

121. Let E be the center of the circle which touches the two equal circles whose centers are A, B. Join AE, BE which pass through the points of contact F, G. Whence AE is equal to EB. Also CD the common chord bisects AB at right angles, and therefore the perpendicular from E on AB coincides with CD.

122. Let three circles touch each other at the point A, and from A let a line ABCD be drawn cutting the circumferences in B, C, D. Let O, O', O'' be the centers of the circles, join BO, CO', DO'', these lines are parallel to one another. Euc. I. 5, 28.

123. Proceed as in Theorem 90, supra.

124 The three tangents will be found to be perpendicular to the sides of the triangle formed by joining the centers of the three circles

125 With center A and any radius less than the radius of either of the equal circles, describe the third circle intersecting them in C and D Join BC, CD, and prove BC and CD to be in the same straight line

126. Let ABC be the triangle required, BC the given base, BD the given difference of the sides, and BAC the given vertical angle Join CD and draw AM perpendicular to CD Then MAD is half the vertical angle and AMD a right angle. the angle BDC is therefore given, and hence D is a point in the arc of a given segment on BC Also since BD is given, the point D is given, and therefore the sides BA, AC are given Hence the synthesis.

127 Let ABC be the required triangle, AD the line bisecting the vertical angle and dividing the base BC into the segments BD, DC About the triangle ABC describe a circle and produce AD to meet the circumference in E, then the arcs BE, EC are equal

128 Analysis Let ABC be the triangle, and let the circle ABC be described about it draw AF to bisect the vertical angle BAC and meet the circle in F, make AV equal to AC, and draw CV to meet the circle in T; join TB and TF, cutting AB in D, draw the diameter FS cutting BC in R, DR cutting AF in E, join AS, and draw AK, AH perpendicular to FS and BC. Then shew that AD is half the sum, and DB half the difference of the sides AB, AC Next, that the point F in which AF meets the circumscribing circle is given, also the point E where DE meets AF is given. The points A, K, R, E are in a circle, Euc iii 22

Hence, KF . FR = AF . FE, a given rectangle ; and the segment KR, which is equal to the perpendicular AH, being given, RF itself is given. Whence the construction

129 On AB the given base describe a circle such that the segment AEB shall contain an angle equal to the given vertical angle of the triangle Draw the diameter EMD cutting AB in M at right angles At D in ED, make the angle EDC equal to half the given difference of the angles at the base, and let DC meet the circumference of the circle in C Join CA, CB ; ABC is the triangle required. For, make CF equal to CB, and join FB cutting CD in G

130 Let ABC be the triangle, AD the perpendicular on BC With center A, and AC the less side as radius, describe a circle cutting the base BC in E, and the longer side AB in G, and BA produced in F, and join AE, EG, FC. Then the angle GFC being half the given angle, BAC is given, and the angle BEG equal to GFC is also given Likewise BE the difference of the segments of the base, and BG the difference of the sides, are given by the problem. Wherefore the triangle BEG is given (with two solutions) Again, the angle EGB being given, the angle AGE, and hence its equal AEG is given, and hence the vertex A is given, and likewise the line AE equal to AC the shortest side is given Hence the construction

131 Let ABC be the triangle, D, E the bisections of the sides AC, AB Join CE, BD intersecting in F. Bisect BD in G and join EG Then EF, one-third of EC is given, and BG one-half of BD is also given Now EG is parallel to AC, and the angle BAC being given, its equal opposite angle BEG is also given Whence the segment of the circle containing the angle BEG is also given Hence F is a given point, and FE a given line, whence E is in the circumference of the given circle about F whose radius is FE Wherefore E being in two given circles, it is itself then given intersection.

132. Of all triangles on the same base and having equal vertical angles, that triangle will be the greatest whose perpendicular from the vertex on the base is a maximum, and the greatest perpendicular is that which bisects the base. Whence the triangle is isosceles.

133. Let AB be the given base and ABC the sum of the other two sides; at B draw BD at right angles to AB and equal to the given altitude, produce BD to E making DE equal to BD. With center A and radius AC describe the circle CFG, draw FO at right angles to BE and find in it the center O of the circle which passes through B and E and touches the former circle in the point F. The centers A, O being joined and the line produced, will pass through F. Join OB. Then AOB is the triangle required.

134. Since the area and bases of the triangle are given, the altitude is given. Hence the problem is—given the base, the vertical angle and the altitude, describe the triangle.

135. Apply Euc. III. 27.

136. The fixed point may be proved to be the center of the circle.

137. Let the line which bisects any angle BAD of the quadrilateral, meet the circumference in E, join EC, and prove that the angle made by producing DC is bisected by EC.

138. Draw the diagonals of the quadrilateral, and by Euc. III. 21, I. 29.

139. From the center draw lines to the angles, then Euc. III. 27.

140. The centers of the four circles are determined by the intersections of the lines which bisect the four angles of the given quadrilateral. Join these four points, and the opposite angles of the quadrilateral so formed are respectively equal to two right angles.

141. Let ABCD be the required trapezium inscribed in the given circle (fig. Euc. III. 22.) of which AB is given, also the sum of the remaining three sides and the angle ADC. Since the angle ADC is given, the opposite angle ABC is known, and therefore the point C and the side BC. Produce AD and make DE equal to DC and join EC. Since the sum of AD, DC, CB is given, and DC is known, therefore the sum of AD, DC is given, and likewise AC, and the angle ADC. Also the angle DEC being half of the angle ADC is given. Whence the segment of the circle which contains AEC is given, also AE is given, and hence the point E, and consequently the point D. Whence the construction.

142. Let ADBC be the inscribed quadrilateral; let AC, BD produced meet in O, and AB, CD produced meet in P, also let the tangents from O, P meet the circles in K, H respectively. Join OP, and about the triangle PAC describe a circle cutting PO in G and join AG. Then A, B, G, O may be shewn to be points in the circumference of a circle. Whence the sum of the squares on OH and PK may be found by Euc. III. 36, and shewn to be equal to the square on OP.

143. This will be manifest from the equality of the two tangents drawn to a circle from the same point.

144. Apply Euc. III. 22.

145. A circle can be described about the figure AECBF.

146. Apply Euc. III. 22, 32.

147. Apply Euc. III. 21, 22, 32.

148. Apply Euc. III. 20, and the angle BAD will be found to be equal to BAD and CBD.

149. Let A, B, C, D be the angular points of the inscribed quadrilateral, and E, F, G, H those of the circumscribed one whose points of contact with the circle are at A, B, C, D. Draw the diagonals AC, BD; join EO, OG, O being the center of the circle, and prove EO to be in the same straight line with OG.

ON BOOK III.   337

150. Apply Euc. III. 22.

151. Join the center of the circle with the other extremity of the line perpendicular to the diameter.

152. Let AB be a chord parallel to the diameter FG of the circle, fig. Theo 1, p 160, and H any point in the diameter. Let HA and HB be joined. Bisect FG in O, draw OL perpendicular to FG cutting AB in K, and join HK, HL, OA. Then the square on HA and HF may be proved equal to the squares on FH, HG by Theo 3, p 114; Euc. I. 47; Euc II 9.

153. Let A be the given point (fig. Euc. III. 36, Cor) and suppose AFC meeting the circle in F, C, to be bisected in F, and let AD be a tangent drawn from A. Then $2 AF^2 = AF.AC = AD^2$, but AD is given, hence also AF is given. To construct. Draw the tangent AD On AD describe a semicircle AGD, bisect it in G, with center A and radius AG, describe a circle cutting the given circle in F. Join AF and produce it to meet the circumference again in C.

154. Let the chords AB, CD intersect each other in E at right angles Find F the center, and draw the diameters HEFG, AFK and join AC, CK, BD. Then by Euc II. 4. 5, III. 35.

155. Let E, F be the points in the diameter AB equidistant from the center O; CED any chord; draw OG perpendicular to CED, and join FG, OC The sum of the squares on DF and FC may be shewn to be equal to twice the square on FE and the rectangle contained by AE, EB by Euc. I. 47, II. 5; III 35

156. Let the chords AB, AC be drawn from the point A, and let a chord FG parallel to the tangent at A be drawn intersecting the chords AB, AC in D and E, and join BC. Then the opposite angles of the quadrilateral BDEC are equal to two right angles, and a circle would circumscribe the figure. Hence by Euc I. 36

157. Let the lines be drawn as directed in the enunciation Draw the diameter AE and join CE, DE, BE, then $AC^2 + AD^2$ and $2 AB^2$ may be each shewn to be equal to the square of the diameter.

158. Let QOP cut the diameter AB in O From C the center draw CH perpendicular to QP Then CH is equal to OH, and by Euc II. 9, the squares on PO, OQ are readily shewn to be equal to twice the square on CP

159 From P draw PQ perpendicular on AB meeting it in Q Join AC, CD, DB. Then circles would circumscribe the quadrilaterals ACPQ and BDPQ, and then by Euc III. 36

160 Describe the figure according to the enunciation; draw AE the diameter of the circle, and let P be the intersection of the diagonals of the parallelogram Draw EB, EP, EC, EF, EG, EH. Since AE is a diameter of the circle, the angles at F, G, H, are right angles, and EF, EG, EH are perpendiculars from the vertex upon the bases of the triangles EAB, EAC, EAP. Whence by Euc. II. 13, and theorem 3, page 114, the truth of the property may be shewn

161. If FA be the given line (fig Euc II 11), and if FA be produced to C, AC is the part produced which satisfies the required conditions

162. Let AD meet the circle in G, H, and join BG, GC Then BGC is a right-angled triangle and GD is perpendicular to the hypotenuse, and the rectangles may be each shewn to be equal to the square on BG Euc III. 35; II. 5; I 47. Or, if EC be joined, the quadrilateral figure ADCE may be circumscribed by a circle. Euc III 31, 22, 36, Cor.

163 On PC describe a semicircle cutting the given one in E, and draw EF perpendicular to AD; then F is the point required.

15

164. Let AB be the given straight line. Bisect AB in C and on AB as a diameter describe a circle; and at any point D in the circumference, draw a tangent DE equal to a side of the given square, join DC, EC, and with center C and radius CE describe a circle cutting AB produced in F. From F draw FG to touch the circle whose center is C in the point G

165. Let AD, DF be two lines at right angles to each other, O the center of the circle BFQ, A any point in AD from which tangents AB, AC are drawn, then the chord BC shall always cut FD in the same point P, wherever the point A is taken in AD. Join AP, then BAC is an isosceles triangle,
and $FD \cdot DE + AD^2 = AB^2 = BP \cdot PC + AP^2 = BP \cdot PC + AD^2 + DP^2$,
wherefore $BP \cdot PC = FD \cdot DE - DP^2$.
The point P, therefore, is independent of the position of the point A, and is consequently the same for all positions of A in the line AD

166. The point E will be found to be that point in BC, from which two tangents to the circles described on AB and CD as diameters, are equal, Euc. III 36

167. If AQ, A'P' be produced to meet, these lines with AA' form a right-angled triangle, then Euc. I. 47.

GEOMETRICAL EXERCISES ON BOOK IV.

HINTS, &c.

5 Let AB be the given line. Draw through C the center of the given circle the diameter DCE Bisect AB in F and join FC Through A, B draw AG, BH parallel to FC and meeting the diameter in G, H at G, H draw GK, HL perpendicular to DE and meeting the circumference in the points K, L, join KL; then KL is equal and parallel to AB

6. Trisect the circumference and join the center with the points of trisection

7. See Euc iv 4, 5

8. Let a line be drawn from the third angle to the point of intersection of the two lines, and the three distances of this point from the angles may be shewn to be equal

9. Let the line AD drawn from the vertex A of the equilateral triangle, cut the base BC, and meet the circumference of the circle in D Let DB, DC be joined AD is equal to DB and DC If on DA, DE be taken equal to DB, and BE be joined, BDE may be proved to be an equilateral triangle, also the triangle ABE may be proved equal to the triangle CBD.

The other case is when the line does not cut the base

10 Let a circle be described upon the base of the equilateral triangle, and let an equilateral triangle be inscribed in the circle Draw a diameter from one of the vertices of the inscribed triangle, and join the other extremity of the diameter with one of the other extremities of the sides of the inscribed triangle The side of the inscribed triangle may then be proved to be equal to the perpendicular in the other triangle

11. The line joining the points of bisection, is parallel to the base of the triangle and therefore cuts off an equilateral triangle from the given triangle. By Euc III 21; I 6, the truth of the theorem may be shewn

12. Let a diameter be drawn from any angle of an equilateral tri-

angle inscribed in a circle to meet the circumference. It may be proved that the radius is bisected by the opposite side of the triangle.

13. Let ABC be an equilateral triangle inscribed in a circle, and let AB'C' be an isosceles triangle inscribed in the same circle, having the same vertex A. Draw the diameter AD intersecting BC in E, and BC' in E', and let B'C' fall below BC. Then AB, BE, and AB', B'E', are respectively the semi-perimeters of the triangles. Draw B'F perpendicular to BC, and cut off AH equal to AB, and join BH. If BF can be proved to be greater than B'H, the perimeter of ABC is greater than the perimeter of AB'C'. Next let B'C' fall above BC.

14. The angles contained in the two segments of the circle, may be shewn to be equal, then by joining the extremities of the arcs, the two remaining sides may be shewn to be parallel.

15. It may be shewn that four equal and equilateral triangles will form an equilateral triangle of the same perimeter as the hexagon, which is formed by six equal and equilateral triangles.

16. Let the figure be constructed. By drawing the diagonals of the hexagon, the proof is obvious.

17. By Euc. I. 47, the perpendicular distance from the center of the circle upon the side of the inscribed hexagon may be found.

18. The alternate sides of the hexagon will fall upon the sides of the triangle, and each side will be found to be equal to one-third of the side of the equilateral triangle.

19. A regular duodecagon may be inscribed in a circle by means of the equilateral triangle and square, or by means of the hexagon. The area of the duodecagon is three times the square of the radius of the circle, which is the square of the side of an equilateral triangle inscribed in the same circle. Theorem 1, p. 196.

20. In general, three straight lines when produced will meet and form a triangle, except when all three are parallel or two parallel are intersected by the third. This Problem includes Euc. IV. 5, and all the cases which arise from producing the sides of the triangle. The circles described touching a side of a triangle and the other two sides produced, are called the *escribed* circles.

21. This is manifest from Euc. III. 21.

22. The point required is the center of the circle which circumscribes the triangle. See the notes on Euc. III. 20, p. 155.

23. If the perpendiculars meet the three sides of the triangle, the point is within the triangle, Euc. IV. 4. If the perpendiculars meet the base and the two sides produced, the point is the center of the *escribed* circle.

24. This is manifest from Euc. III. 11, 18.

25. The base BC is intersected by the perpendicular AD, and the side AC is intersected by the perpendicular BE. From Theorem I. p. 160, the arc AF is proved equal to AE, or the arc FE is bisected in A. In the same manner the arcs FD, DE, may be shewn to be bisected in BC.

26. Let ABC be a triangle, and let D, E be the points where the inscribed circle touches the sides AB, AC. Draw BE, CD intersecting each other in O. Join AO, and produce it to meet BC in F. Then F is the point where the inscribed circle touches the third side BC. If F be not the point of contact, let some other point G be the point of contact. Through D draw DH parallel to AC, and DK parallel to BC. By the similar triangles, CG may be proved equal to CF, or G the point of contact coincides with F, the point where the line drawn from A through O meets BC.

27. In the figure, Euc. iv. 5. Let AF bisect the angle at A, and be produced to meet the circumference in G. Join GB, GC and find the center H of the circle inscribed in the triangle ABC. The lines GH, GB, GC are equal to one another.

28. Let ABC be any triangle inscribed in a circle, and let the perpendiculars AD, BE, CF intersect in G. Produce AD to meet the circumference in H, and join BH, CH. Then the triangle BHC may be shewn to be equal in all respects to the triangle BGC, and the circle which circumscribes one of the triangles will also circumscribe the other. Similarly may be shewn by producing BE and CF, &c.

29. First. Prove that the perpendiculars Aa, Bb, Cc pass through the same point O, as Theo. 112, p. 158. Secondly. That the triangles Acb, Bca, Cab are equiangular to ABC. Euc. iii. 21. Thirdly. That the angles of the triangle abc are bisected by the perpendiculars; and lastly, by means of Prob. 4, p. 71, that $ab + bc + ca$ is a minimum.

30. The equilateral triangle can be proved to be the least triangle which can be circumscribed about a circle.

31. Through C draw CH parallel to AB and join AH. Then HAC the difference of the angles at the base is equal to the angle HFC. Euc. iii. 21, and HFC is bisected by FG.

32. Let F, G, (figure, Euc. iv. 5,) be the centers of the circumscribed and inscribed circles, join GF, GA, then the angle GAF which is equal to the difference of the angles GAD, FAD, may be shewn to be equal to half the difference of the angles ABC and ACB.

33. This Theorem may be stated more generally, as follows:

Let AB be the base of a triangle, AEB the locus of the vertex; D the bisection of the remaining arc ADB of the circumscribing circle, then the locus of the center of the inscribed circle is another circle whose center is D and radius DB. For join CD, then P the center of the inscribed circle is in CD. Join AP, PB; then these lines bisect the angles CAB, CBA, and DB, DP, DA may be proved to be equal to one another.

34. Let ABC be a triangle, having C a right angle, and upon AC, BC, let semicircles be described, bisect the hypotenuse in D, and let fall DE, DF perpendiculars on AC, BC respectively, and produce them to meet the circumferences of the semicircles in P, Q, then DP may be proved to be equal to DQ.

35. Let the angle BAC be a right angle, fig. Euc. iv. 4. Join AD. Then Euc. iii. 17, note p. 155.

36. Suppose the triangle constructed, then it may be shewn that the difference between the hypotenuse and the sum of the two sides is equal to the diameter of the inscribed circle.

37. Let P, Q be the middle points of the arcs AB, AC, and let PQ be joined, cutting AB, AC in D E, then AD is equal to AE. Find the center O and join OP, QO.

38. With the given radius of the circumscribed circle, describe a circle. Draw BC cutting off the segment BAC containing an angle equal to the given vertical angle. Bisect BC in D, and draw the diameter EDF. Join FB, and with center F and radius FB describe a circle; this will be the locus of the centers of the inscribed circle (see Theorem 29, supra.) On DE take DG equal to the given radius of the inscribed circle, and through G draw GH parallel to BC, and meeting the locus of the centers in H. H is the center of the inscribed circle.

39. This may readily be effected in almost a similar way to the preceding Problem.

40. With the given radius describe a circle, then by Euc. iii. 34.

41. Let ABC be a triangle on the given base BC and having its vertical angle A equal to the given angle. Then since the angle at A is constant, A is a point in the arc of a segment of a circle described on BC. Let D be the center of the circle inscribed in the triangle ABC. Join DA, DB, DC: then the angles at B, C, A, are bisected. Euc. iv. 4. Also since the angles of each of the triangles ABC, DBC are equal to two right angles, it follows that the angle BDC is equal to the angle A and half the sum of the angles B and C. But the sum of the angles B and C can be found, because A is given. Hence the angle BDC is known, and therefore D is the locus of the vertex of a triangle described on the base BC and having its vertical angle at D double of the angle at A.

42. Suppose the parallelogram to be rectangular and inscribed in the given triangle and to be equal in area to half the triangle; it may be shewn that the parallelogram is equal to half the altitude of the triangle, and that there is a restriction to the magnitude of the angle which two adjacent sides of the parallelogram make with one another.

43. Let ABC be the given triangle, and A'B'C' the other triangle, to the sides of which the inscribed triangle is required to be parallel. Through any point a in AB draw ab parallel to A'B, one side of the given triangle, and through a, b draw ac, bc respectively parallel to AC, BC. Join Ac and produce it to meet BC in D; through D draw DE, DF, parallel to ca, cb, respectively, and join EF. Then DEF is the triangle required.

44. This point will be found to be the intersection of the diagonals of the given parallelogram.

45. The difference of the two squares is obviously the sum of the four triangles at the corners of the exterior square.

46. (1) Let ABCD be the given square: join AC, at A in AC, make the angles CAE, CAF, each equal to one-third of a right angle, and join EF.

(2.) Bisect AB any side in P, and draw PQ parallel to AD or BC, then at P make the angles as in the former case.

47. Each of the interior angles of a regular octagon may be shewn to be equal to three-fourths of two right angles, and the exterior angles made by producing the sides, are each equal to one-fourth of two right angles, or one-half of a right angle.

48. Let the diagonals of the rhombus be drawn; the center of the inscribed circle may be shewn to be the point of their intersection.

49. Let ABCD be the required square. Join O, O the centers of the circles and draw the diagonal AEC cutting OO' in E. Then E is the middle point of OO' and the angle AEO is half a right angle.

50. Let the squares be inscribed in, and circumscribed about a circle, and let the diameters be drawn, the relation of the two squares is manifest.

51. Let one of the diagonals of the square be drawn, then the isosceles right-angled triangle which is half the square, may be proved to be greater than any other right-angled triangle upon the same hypotenuse.

52. Take half of the side of the square inscribed in the given circle, this will be equal to a side of the required octagon. At the extremities on the same side of this line make two angles each equal to three-fourths of two right angles, bisect these angles by two straight lines, the point at which they meet will be the center of the circle which circumscribes the octagon, and either of the bisecting lines is the radius of the circle.

53. First shew the possibility of a circle circumscribing such a figure, and then determine the center of the circle.

54. By constructing the figures and drawing lines from the center of the

circle to the angles of the octagon, the areas of the eight triangles may be easily shown to be equal to eight times the rectangle contained by the radius of the circle, and half the side of the inscribed square.

55. Let AB, AC, AD, be the sides of a square, a regular hexagon and octagon respectively inscribed in the circle whose center is O. Produce AC to E making AE equal to AB; from E draw EF touching the circle in F, and prove EF to be equal to AD.

56. Let the circle required touch the given circle in P, and the given line in Q. Let C be the center of the given circle and C' that of the required circle. Join CC', CQ, QP, and let QP produced meet the given circle in R; join RC and produce it to meet the given line in V. Then RCV is perpendicular to VQ. Hence the construction.

57. Let A, B be the centers of the given circles and CD the given straight line. On the side of CD opposite to that on which the circles are situated, draw a line EF parallel to CD at a distance equal to the radius of the smaller circle. From A the center of the larger circle describe a concentric circle GH with radius equal to the difference of the radii of the two circles. Then the center of the circle touching the circle GH, the line EF, and passing through the center of the smaller circle B, may be shewn to be the center of the circle which touches the circles whose centers are A, B, and the line CD.

58. Let AB, CD be the two lines given in position, and E the center of the given circle. Draw two lines FG, HI parallel to AB, CD respectively and external to them. Describe a circle passing through E and touching FG, HI. Join the centers L, O, and with center O and radius equal to the difference of the radii of these circles describe a circle; this will be the circle required.

59. Let the circle ACP having the center G, be the required circle touching the given circle whose center is B, in the point A, and cutting the other given circle in the point C. Join BG, and through A draw a line perpendicular to BG, then this line is a common tangent to the circles whose centers are B, G. Join AC, GC. Hence the construction.

60. Let C be the given point in the given straight line AB, and D the center of the given circle. Through C draw a line CE perpendicular to AB; on the other side of AB, take CE equal to the radius of the given circle. Draw ED, and at D make the angle EDF equal to the angle DEC, and produce EC to meet DF. This gives the construction for one case, when the given line does not cut or touch the other circle.

61. This is a particular case of the general problem : To describe a circle passing through a given point and touching two straight lines given in position.

Let A be the given point between the two given lines which when produced meet in the point B. Bisect the angle at B by BD, and through A draw AD perpendicular to BD and produce it to meet the two given lines in C, E. Take DF equal to DA, and on CB take CG such that the rectangle contained by CF, CA is equal to the square of CG. The circle described through the points F, A, G, will be the circle required. Deduce the particular case when the given lines are at right angles to one another, and the given point in the line which bisects the angle at B. If the lines are parallel, when is the solution possible ?

62. Let A, B, be the centers of the given circles, which touch externally in E, and let C be the given point in that whose center is B. Make CD equal to AE and draw AD; make the angle DAG equal to the angle ADG: then G is the center of the circle required, and GC its radius.

63. If the three points be such as when joined by straight lines a triangle is formed; the points at which the inscribed circle touches the sides of the triangle, are the points at which the three circles touch one another. Euc. iv. 4. Different cases arise from the relative position of the three points.

64. Bisect the angle contained by the two lines at the point where the bisecting line meets the circumference, draw a tangent to the circle and produce the two straight lines to meet it. In this triangle inscribe a circle.

65. From the given angle draw a line through the center of the circle, and at the point where the line intersects the circumference, draw a tangent to the circle, meeting two sides of the triangle. The circle inscribed within this triangle will be the circle required.

66. Let the diagonal AD cut the arc in P, and let O be the center of the inscribed circle. Draw OQ perpendicular to AB. Draw PE a tangent at P meeting AB produced in E: then BE is equal to PD. Join PQ, PB. Then AB may be proved equal to QE. Hence AQ is equal to BE or DP.

67. Suppose the center of the required circle to be found, let fall two perpendiculars from this point upon the radii of the quadrant, and join the center of the circle with the center of the quadrant and produce the line to meet the arc of the quadrant. If three tangents be drawn at the three points thus determined in the two semicircles and the arc of the quadrant, they form a right-angled triangle which circumscribes the required circle.

68. Let AB be the base of the given segment, C its middle point. Let DCE be the required triangle having the sum of the base DE and perpendicular CF equal to the given line. Produce CF to H, making FH equal to DE. Join HD and produce it, if necessary, to meet AB produced in K. Then CK is double of DF. Draw DL perpendicular to CK.

69. From the vertex of the isosceles triangle let fall a perpendicular on the base. Then, in each of the triangles so formed, inscribe a circle, Euc. iv. 4; next inscribe a circle so as to touch the two circles and the two equal sides of the triangle. This gives one solution: the problem is indeterminate.

70. If BD be shewn to subtend an arc of the larger circle equal to one-tenth of the whole circumference:—Then BD is a side of the decagon in the larger circle. And if the triangle ABD can be shewn to be inscriptible in the smaller circle, BD will be the side of the inscribed pentagon.

71. It may be shewn that the angles ABF, BFD stand on two arcs, one of which is three times as large as the other.

72. It may be proved that the diagonals bisect the angles of the pentagon; and the five-sided figure formed by their intersection, may be shewn to be both equiangular and equilateral.

73. The figure ABCDE is an irregular pentagon inscribed in a circle; it may be shewn that the five angles at the circumference stand upon arcs whose sum is equal to the whole circumference of the circle; Euc. III. 26.

74. If a side CD (figure, Euc. iv. 11) of a regular pentagon be produced to K, the exterior angle ADK of the inscribed quadrilateral figure ABCD is equal to the angle ABC, one of the interior angles of the pentagon. From this a construction may be made for the method of folding the ribbon.

344   GEOMETRICAL EXERCISES ON BOOK IV.

75. In the figure, Euc. IV. 10, let DC be produced to meet the circumference in F, and join FB. Then FB is the side of a regular pentagon inscribed in the larger circle, D is the middle of the arc subtended by the adjacent side of the pentagon. Then the difference of FD and BD is equal to the radius AB. Next, it may be shewn, that FD is divided in the same manner in C as AB, and by Euc. II. 4, 11, the squares on FD and DB are three times the square on AB, and the rectangle of FD and DB is equal to the square on AB.

76. If one of the diagonals be drawn, this line with three sides of the pentagon forms a quadrilateral figure of which three consecutive sides are equal. The problem is reduced to the inscription of a quadrilateral in a square.

77. This may be deduced from Euc. IV. 11.

78. The angle at A the center of the circle (fig. Euc. IV. 10.) is one-tenth of four right angles, the arc BD is therefore one-tenth of the circumference, and the chord BD is the side of a regular decagon inscribed in the larger circle. Produce DC to meet the circumference in F and join BF, then BF is the side of the inscribed pentagon, and AB is the side of the inscribed hexagon. Join FA. Then FCA may be proved to be an isosceles triangle and FB is a line drawn from the vertex meeting the base produced. If a perpendicular be drawn from F on BC, the difference of the squares on FB, FC may be shewn to be equal to the rectangle AB, BC, (Euc. I. 47 ; II. 5, Cor.); or the square on AC.

79. Divide the circle into three equal sectors, and draw tangents to the middle points of the arcs, the problem is then reduced to the inscription of a circle in a triangle.

80. Let the inscribed circles whose centers are A, B touch each other in G, and the circle whose center is C, in the points D, E; join A, D; A, E; at D, draw DF perpendicular to DA, and EF to EB, meeting in F. Let F, G be joined, and FG be proved to touch the two circles in G whose centers are A and B.

81. The problem is the same as to find how many equal circles may be placed round a circle of the same radius, touching this circle and each other. The number is six.

82. This is obvious from Euc. IV. 7, the side of a square circumscribing a circle being equal to the diameter of the circle.

83. Each of the vertical angles of the triangles so formed, may be proved to be equal to the difference between the exterior and interior angle of the heptagon.

84. Every regular polygon can be divided into equal isosceles triangles by drawing lines from the center of the inscribed or circumscribed circle to the angular points of the figure, and the number of triangles will be equal to the number of sides of the polygon. If a perpendicular FG be let fall from F (figure, Euc. IV. 14) the center on the base CD of FCD, one of these triangles, and if GF be produced to H till FH be equal to FG, and HC, HD be joined, an isosceles triangle is formed, such that the angle at H is half the angle at F. Bisect HC, HD in K, L, and join KL; then the triangle HKL may be placed round the vertex H, twice as many times as the triangle CFD round the vertex F.

85. The sum of the arcs on which stand the 1st, 3rd, 5th, &c. angles, is equal to the sum of the arcs on which stand the 2nd, 4th, 6th, &c. angles.

86. The proof of this property depends on the fact, that an isosceles triangle has a greater area than any scalene triangle of the same perimeter.

GEOMETRICAL EXERCISES ON BOOK VI.

HINTS, &c

6. In the figure Euc. vi. 23, let the parallelograms be supposed to be rectangular.
Then the rectangle AC : the rectangle DG :: BC · CG, Euc vi. 1.
and the rectangle DG : the rectangle CF :: CD : EC,
whence the rectangle AC : the rectangle CF :: BC · CD : CG · EC.
In a similar way it may be shewn that the ratio of any two parallelograms is as the ratio compounded of the ratios of their bases and altitudes

7 Let two sides intersect in O, through O draw POQ parallel to the base AB Then by similar triangles, PO may be proved equal to OQ and POFA, QOEB are parallelograms whence AE is equal to FB

8 Apply Euc. vi 4, v 7.

9. Let ABC be a scalene triangle, having the vertical angle A, and suppose ADE an equivalent isosceles triangle, of which the side AD is equal to AE Then Euc vi 15, 16, AC : AB = AD : AE, or AD^2 Hence AD is a mean proportional between AC, AB Euc vi 8.

10. The lines drawn making equal angles with homologous sides, divide the triangles into two corresponding pairs of equiangular triangles; by Euc. vi. 1, the proportions are evident

11 By constructing the figure, the angles of the two triangles may easily be shewn to be respectively equal

12 A circle may be described about the four-sided figure AEDC. By Euc i 13; Euc. iii 21, 22. The triangles ABC, ACE may be shewn to be equiangular.

13 Apply Euc i 48; ii 5. Cor vi. 16

14. This property follows as a corollary to Euc vi 23, for the two triangles are respectively the halves of the parallelograms, and are therefore in the ratio compounded of the ratios of the sides which contain the same or equal angles and this ratio is the same as the ratio of the rectangles by the sides

15 Let ABC be the given triangle, and let the line EGF cut the base BC in G. Join AG Then by Euc vi 1, and the preceding theorem (14,) it may be proved that AC is to AB as GE is to GF.

16 The two means and the two extremes form an arithmetic series of four lines whose successive differences are equal, the difference therefore between the first and the fourth, or the extremes, is treble the difference between the first and the second

17 This may be effected in different ways, one of which is the following At one extremity A of the given line AB draw AC making any acute angle with AB and join BC, at any point D in BC draw DEF parallel to AC cutting AB in E and such that EF is equal to ED, draw FC cutting AB in G. Then AB is harmonically divided in E, G

18 In the figure Euc vi 13 If E be the middle point of AC, then AE or EC is the arithmetic mean, and DB is the geometric mean, between AB and BC. If DE be joined and BF be drawn perpendicular on DE, then DF may be proved to be the harmonic mean between AB and BC

19 In the fig Euc vi 13 DB is the geometric mean between AB and BC, and if AC be bisected in E, AE or EC is the arithmetic mean

The next is the same as—To find the segments of the hypotenuse of a right-angled triangle made by a perpendicular from the right angle, having given the difference between half the hypotenuse and the perpendicular.

20. Let the line DF drawn from D the bisection of the base of the triangle ABC, meet AB in E, and CA produced in F. Also let AG drawn parallel to BC from the vertex A, meet DF in G. Then by means of the similar triangles, DF, FE, FG, may be shewn to be in harmonic progression.

21. If a triangle be constructed on AB so that the vertical angle is bisected by the line drawn to the point C. By Euc. vi. A, the point required may be determined.

22. Let DB, DE, DCA be the three straight lines, fig. Euc. iii. 37, let the points of contact B, E be joined by the straight line BC cutting DA in G. Then BDE is an isosceles triangle, and DG is a line from the vertex to a point G in the base. And two values of the square of BD may be found, one from Theo. 37, p. 118. Euc. iii. 35, ii. 2, and another from Euc. iii. 36, ii. 1. From these may be deduced, that the rectangle DC, GA, is equal to the rectangle AD, CG. Whence the, &c.

23. Let ABCD be a square and AC its diagonal. On AC take AE equal to the side BC or AB; join BE and at E draw EF perpendicular to AC and meeting BC in F. Then EC, the difference between the diagonal AC and the side AB of the square, is less than AB, and CE, EF, FB may be proved to be equal to one another; also CE, EF are the adjacent sides of a square whose diagonal is FC. On FC take FG equal to CE and join EG. Then, as in the first square, the difference CG between the diagonal FC and the side EC or EF, is less than the side EC. Hence EC, the difference between the diagonal and the side of the given square, is contained twice in the side BC with a remainder CG; and CG is the difference between the side CE and the diagonal CF of another square. By proceeding in a similar way, CG, the difference between the diagonal CF and the side CE, is contained twice in the side CE with a remainder; and the same relations may be shewn to exist between the difference of the diagonal and the side of every square of the series which is so constructed. Hence, therefore, as the difference of the side and diagonal of every square of the series is contained twice in the side with a remainder, it follows that there is no line which exactly measures the side and the diagonal of a square.

24. Let the given line AB be divided in C, D. On AD describe a semicircle, and on CB describe another semicircle intersecting the former in P; draw PE perpendicular to AB, then E is the point required.

25. Let AB be equal to a side of the given square. On AB describe a semicircle, at A draw AC perpendicular to AB and equal to a fourth proportional to AB and the two sides of the given rectangle. Draw CD parallel to AB meeting the circumference in D. Join AD, BD, which are the required lines.

26. Let the two given lines meet when produced in A. At A draw AD perpendicular to AB, and AE to AC, and such that AD is to AE in the given ratio. Through D, E, draw DF, EF, respectively parallel to AB, AC and meeting each other in F. Join AF and produce it, and the perpendiculars drawn from any point of this line on the two given lines will always be in the given ratio.

27. The angles made by the four lines at the point of their divergence, remain constant. See Note on Euc. vi. A, p. 295.

28. Let AB be the given line from which it is required to cut off a part BC such that BC shall be a mean proportional between the remainder AC and another given line. Produce AB to D, making BD equal to the other

given line. On AD describe a semicircle, at B draw BE perpendicular to AD. Bisect BD in O and with center O and radius OB describe a semicircle, join OE cutting the semicircle on BD in F, at F draw FC perpendicular to OE and meeting AB in C. C is the point of division, such that BC is a mean proportional between AC and BD.

29. Find two squares in the given ratio, and if BF be the given line (figure, Euc. vi. 4), draw BE at right angles to BF, and take BC, CE respectively equal to the sides of the squares which are in the given ratio. Join EF, and draw CA parallel to EF then BF is divided in A as required.

30. Produce one side of the triangle through the vertex and make the part produced equal to the other side. Bisect this line, and with the vertex of the triangle as center and radius equal to half the sum of the sides, describe a circle cutting the base of the triangle.

31. If a circle be described about the given triangle, and another circle upon the radius drawn from the vertex of the triangle to the center of the circle, as a diameter, this circle will cut the base in two points, and give two solutions of the problem. Give the Analysis.

32. This problem is analogous to the preceding.

33. Apply Euc vi. 8, Cor. 17.

34. Describe a circle about the triangle, and draw the diameter through the vertex A, draw a line touching the circle at A, and meeting the base BC produced in D. Then AD shall be a mean proportional between DC and DB. Euc. iii 36.

35. In BC produced take CE a third proportional to BC and AC; on CE describe a circle, the center being O; draw the tangent EF at E equal to AC, draw FO cutting the circle in T and T', and lastly draw tangents at T, T' meeting BC in P and P'. These points fulfil the conditions of the problem.

By combining the proportion in the construction with that from the similar triangles ABC, DBP, and Euc iii 36, 37 it may be proved that $CA \cdot PD = CP^2$. The demonstration is similar for P D'

36. This property may be immediately deduced from Euc vi 8, Cor.

37. Let ABC be the triangle, right-angled at C, and let AE on AB be equal to AC, also let the line bisecting the angle A, meet BC in D. Join DE. Then the triangles ACD, AED are equal, and the triangles ACB, DEB equiangular.

38. The segments cut off from the sides are to be measured from the right angle, and by similar triangles are proved to be equal, also by similar triangles, either of them is proved to be a mean proportional between the remaining segments of the two sides.

39. First prove $AC^2 \cdot AD^2 \cdot BC \cdot 2 BD$, then $2 . AC^2 \cdot AD^2 \cdot \cdot BC \cdot BD$, whence $2 . AC^2 - AD^2 \cdot AD^2 \quad BC - BD . BD$,
and since $2 \cdot AC^2 - AD^2 = 2 \cdot AC^2 - (AC^2 + DC^2) = AC^2 - CD^2$, the property is immediately deduced.

40. The construction is suggested by Euc i 47, and Euc vi 31.

41. See Note Euc vi. A, p 295. The bases of the triangles CBD, ACD, ABC, CDE may be shewn to be respectively equal to DB, 2 . BD, 3 . BD, 4 . BD.

42. (1) Let ABC be the triangle which is to be bisected by a line drawn parallel to the base BC. Describe a semicircle on AB, from the center D draw DE perpendicular to AB meeting the circumference in E, join EA, and with center A and radius AE describe a circle cutting AB in F, the line drawn from F parallel to BC, bisects the triangle. The proof depends on

Euc. vi. 19, 20, Cor. 2. (2) Let ABC be the triangle, BC being the base. Draw AD at right angles to BA meeting the base produced in D. Bisect BC in E, and on ED describe a semicircle, from B draw BP to touch the semicircle in P. From BA cut off BF equal to BP, and from F draw FG perpendicular to BC. The line FG bisects the triangle. Then it may be proved that BFG : BAD :: BE : BD, and that BAD : BAC :: BD : BC, whence it follows that BFG : BAC :: BE : BC or as 1 : 2.

43. Let ABC be the given triangle which is to be divided into two parts having a given ratio, by a line parallel to BC. Describe a semicircle on AB and divide AB in D in the given ratio; at D draw DE perpendicular to AB and meeting the circumference in E, with center A and radius AE describe a circle cutting AB in F: the line drawn through F parallel to BC is the line required. In the same manner a triangle may be divided into three or more parts having any given ratio to one another by lines drawn parallel to one of the sides of the triangle.

44. Let these points be taken, one on each side, and straight lines be drawn to them; it may then be proved that these points severally bisect the sides of the triangle.

45. Let ABC be any triangle and D be the given point in BC, from which lines are to be drawn which shall divide the triangle into any number (suppose five) equal parts. Divide BC into five equal parts in E, F, G, H, and draw AE, AF, AG, AH, AD, and through E, F, G, H draw FL, FM, GN, HO parallel to AD, and join DL, DM, DN, DO; these lines divide the triangle into five equal parts.

By a similar process, a triangle may be divided into any number of parts which have a given ratio to one another.

46. Let ABC be the larger, abc the smaller triangle, it is required to draw a line DE parallel to AC cutting off the triangle DBE equal to the triangle abc. On BC take BG equal to bc, and on BG describe the triangle BGH equal to the triangle abc. Draw HK parallel to BC, join KG, then the triangle BGK is equal to the triangle abc. On BA, BC take BD to BE in the ratio of BA to BC, and such that the rectangle contained by BD, BE shall be equal to the rectangle contained by BK, BG. Join DE, then DE is parallel to AC, and the triangle BDE is equal to abc.

47. Let ABCD be any rectangle, contained by AB, BC,
Then $AB^2 : AB \cdot BC :: AB : BC$,
and $AB \cdot BC : BC^2 :: AB : BC$,
whence $AB^2 : AB \cdot BC :: AB \cdot BC : BC^2$,
or the rectangle contained by two adjacent sides of a rectangle, is a mean proportional between their squares.

48. In a straight line at any point A, make Ac equal to Ad in the given ratio. At A draw AB perpendicular to cAd, and equal to a side of the given square. On cd describe a semicircle cutting AB in b, and join bc, bd; from B draw BC parallel to bc, and BD parallel to bd, then AC, AD are the adjacent sides of the rectangle. For, CA is to AD as cA to Ad, Euc. vi. 2, and $CA \cdot AD = AB^2$, CBD being a right angled triangle.

49. From one of the given points two straight lines are to be drawn perpendicular, one to each of any two adjacent sides of the parallelogram; and from the other point, two lines perpendicular in the same manner to each of the two remaining sides. When these four lines are drawn to intersect one another, the figure so formed may be shewn to be equiangular to the given parallelogram.

50. It is manifest that this is the general case of Prop 4, p 198

If the rectangle to be cut off be two-thirds of the given rectangle ABCD Produce BC to E so that BE may be equal to a side of that square which is equal to the rectangle required to be cut off, in this case, equal to two-thirds of the rectangle ABCD   On AB take AF equal to AD or BC, bisect FB in G, and with center G and radius GE, describe a semicircle meeting AB, and AB produced, in H and K   On CB take CL equal to AH and draw HM, LM parallel to the sides, and HBLM is two-thirds of the rectangle ABCD

51 Let ABCD be the parallelogram, and CD be cut in P and BC produced in Q. By means of the similar triangles formed, the property may be proved

52 The intersection of the diagonals is the common vertex of two triangles which have the parallel sides of the trapezium for their bases.

53 Let AB be the given straight line, and C the center of the given circle; through C draw the diameter DCE perpendicular to AB   Place in the circle a line FG which has to AB the given ratio, bisect FG in H, join CH, and on the diameter DCE, take CK, CL each equal to CH; either of the lines drawn through K, L, and parallel to AB is the line required.

54. Let C be the center of the circle, CA, CB two radii at right angles to each other; and let DEFG be the line required which is trisected in the points E, F. Draw CG perpendicular to DH and produce it to meet the circumference in K, draw a tangent to the circle at K, draw CG, and produce CB CG to meet the tangent in L, M, then MK may be shewn to be treble of LK

55 The triangles ACD, BCE are similar, and CF is a mean proportional between AC and CB

56 Let any tangent to the circle at E be terminated by AD BC tangents at the extremity of the diameter AB   Take O the center of the circle and join OC, OD, OE, then ODC is a right-angled triangle and OE is the perpendicular from the right angle upon the hypotenuse

57 This problem only differs from problem 56, infra, in having the given point without the given circle

58 Let A be the given point in the circumference of the circle, C its center   Draw the diameter ACB, and produce AB to D, taking AB to BD in the given ratio   from D draw a line to touch the circle in E, which is the point required   From A draw AF perpendicular to DE, and cutting the circle in G

59 Let A be the given point within the circle whose center is C, and let BAD be the line required so that BA is to AD in the given ratio   Join AC and produce it to meet the circumference in E, F   Then EF is a diameter   Draw BG, DH perpendicular on EF· then the triangles BGA, DHA are equiangular   Hence the construction.

60 Through E one extremity of the chord EF, let a line be drawn parallel to one diameter, and intersecting the other   Then the three angles of the two triangles may be shewn to be respectively equal to one another.

61 Let AB be that diameter of the given circle which when produced is perpendicular to the given line CD, and let it meet that line in C, and let P be the given point   it is required to find D in CD, so that DH may be equal to the tangent DF   Make BC CQ   CQ CA, and join PQ, bisect PQ in E, and draw ED perpendicular to PQ meeting CD in D; then D is the point required   Let O be the center of the circle, draw the tangent DF, and join OF, OD, QD, PD   The QD may be shewn

to be equal to DF and to DP. When P coincides with Q, *any* point D in CD fulfils the conditions of the problem, that is, there are innumerable solutions.

62. It may be proved that the vertices of the two triangles which are similar in the same segment of a circle, are in the extremities of a chord parallel to the chord of the given segment.

63. For let the circle be described about the triangle FAC, then by the converse to Euc. III. 32, the truth of the proposition is manifest.

64. Let the figure be constructed, and the similarity of the two triangles will be at once obvious from Euc. III. 32, Euc. I. 29.

65. In the arc AB (fig. Euc. IV. 2) let any point K be taken, and from K let KL, KM, KN be drawn perpendicular to AB, AC, BC respectively, produced if necessary, also let LM, LN be joined, then MLN may be shewn to be a straight line. Draw AK, BK, CK, and by Euc. III. 31, 22, 21. Euc. I. 14.

66. Let AB a chord in a circle be bisected in C, and DE, FG two chords drawn through C, also let their extremities DG, FE be joined intersecting CB in H, and AC in K, then AK is equal to HB. Through H draw MHL parallel to EF meeting FG in M, and DE produced in L. Then by means of the equiangular triangles, HC may be proved to be equal to CK, and hence AK is equal to HB.

67. Let A, B be the two given points, and let P be a point in the locus so that PA, PB being joined, PA is to PB in the given ratio. Join AB and divide it in C in the given ratio, and join PC. Then PC bisects the angle APB. Euc. VI. 3. Again, in AB produced, take AD to AB in the given ratio, join PD and produce AP to E, then PD bisects the angle BPE. Euc. VI. A. Whence CPD is a right angle, and the point P lies in the circumference of a circle whose diameter is CD.

68. Let ABC be a triangle, and let the line AD bisecting the vertical angle A be divided in E, so that BC : BA + AC :: AE : ED. By Euc. VI. 3, may be deduced BC : BA + AC :: AC : AD. Whence may be proved that CE bisects the angle ACD, and by Euc. IV. 4, that E is the center of the inscribed circle.

69. By means of Euc. IV. 4, and Euc. VI. C. this theorem may be shewn to be true.

70. Divide the given base BC in D, so that BD may be to DC in the ratio of the sides. At B, D draw BB', DD' perpendicular to BC and equal to BD, DC respectively. Join BD' and produce it to meet BC produced in O. With center O and radius OD, describe a circle. From A any point in the circumference join AB, AC, AO. Prove that AB is to AC as BD to DC. Or thus. If ABC be one of the triangles. Divide the base BC in D so that BA is to AC as BD to DC. Produce BC and take DO to OC as BA to AC: then O is the center of the circle.

71. Let ABC be any triangle, and from A, B let the perpendiculars AD, BE on the opposite sides intersect in P, and let AF, BG drawn to F, G the bisections of the opposite sides, intersect in Q. Also let FR, GR be drawn perpendicular to BC, AC, and meet in R: then R is the center of the circumscribed circle. Join PQ, QR, these are in the same line.

Join FG, and by the equiangular triangles, GRF, APB, AP is proved double of FR. And AQ is double of QF, and the alternate angles PAQ, QFR are equal. Hence the triangles APQ, RFQ are equiangular.

72. Let C, C' be the centers of the two circles, and let CC' the line joining the centers intersect the common tangent PP' in T. Let the

line joining the centers cut the circles in Q, Q', and let PQ, P'Q' be joined; then PQ is parallel to P'Q'. Join CP, C'P', and then the angle QPT may be proved to be equal to the alternate angle Q'P'T

73. Let ABC be the triangle, and BC its base; let the circles AFB, AFC be described intersecting the base in the point F, and their diameters AD, AE, be drawn; then DA : AE :: BA : AC. For join DB, DF, EF, EC, the triangles DAB, EAC may be proved to be similar.

74 If the extremities of the diameters of the two circles be joined by two straight lines, these lines may be proved to intersect at the point of contact of the two circles, and the two right-angled triangles thus formed may be shewn to be similar by Euc. III. 34

75. This follows directly from the similar triangles

76 Let the figure be constructed as in Theorem 4, p 150, the triangle EAD being right-angled at A, and let the circle inscribed in the triangle ADE touch AD, AE, DE in the points K, L, M respectively. Then AK is equal to AL, each being equal to the radius of the inscribed circle. Also AB is equal to GC, and AB is half the perimeter of the triangle AED

Also if GA be joined, the triangle ADE is obviously equal to the difference of AGDE and the triangle GDE, and this difference may be proved equal to the rectangle contained by the radii of the other two circles

77 From the centers of the two circles let straight lines be drawn to the extremities of the sides which are opposite to the right angles in each triangle, and to the points where the circles touch these sides. Euc vi. 4

78 Let A, B be the two given points, and C a point in the circumference of the given circle. Let a circle be described through the points A, B, C and cutting the circle in another point D. Join CD, AB, and produce them to meet in E. Let EF be drawn touching the given circle in F, the circle described through the points A, B, F, will be the circle required. Joining AD and CB, by Euc. III 21, the triangles CEB, AED are equiangular, and by Euc vi 4, 16, III 36, 37, the given circle and the required circle each touch the line EF in the same point, and therefore touch one another. When does this solution fail?

Various cases will arise according to the relative position of the two points and the circle

79 Let A be the given point, BC the given straight line, and D the center of the given circle. Through D draw CD perpendicular to BC, meeting the circumference in E, F. Join AF, and take FG to the diameter FE, as FC is to FA. The circle described passing through the two points A, G and touching the line BC in B is the circle required. Let H be the center of this circle; join HB, and BF cutting the circumference of the given circle in K, and join EK. Then the triangles FBC, FKE being equiangular, by Euc vi 4, 16, and the construction, K is proved to be a point in the circumference of the circle passing through the points A, G, B. And if DK, KH be joined, DKH may be proved to be a straight line — the straight line which joins the centers of the two circles, and passes through a common point in their circumferences

80 Let A be the given point, B, C the centers of the two given circles. Let a line drawn through B, C meet the circumferences of the circles in G, F, E, D, respectively. In GD produced, take the point H, so that BH is to CH as the radius of the circle whose center

is B to the radius of the circle whose center is C. Join AH, and take KH to DH as GH to AH. Through A, K describe a circle ALK touching the circle whose center is B, in L. Then M may be proved to be a point in the circumference of the circle whose center is C. For by joining HL and producing it to meet the circumference of the circle whose center is B in N; and joining BN, BL, and drawing CO parallel to BL, and CM parallel to BN, the line HN is proved to cut the circumference of the circle whose center is B in M, O, and CO, CM are radii. By joining GL, DM, M may be proved to be a point in the circumference of the circle ALK. And by producing BL, CM to meet in P, P is proved to be the center of ALK, and BP joining the centers of the two circles passes through L the point of contact. Hence also is shewn that PMC passes through M, the point where the circles whose centers are P and C touch each other.

Note. If the given point be in the circumference of one of the circles, the construction may be more simply effected thus:

Let A be in the circumference of the circle whose center is B. Join BA, and in AB produced, if necessary, take AD equal to the radius of the circle whose center is C, join DC, and at C make the angle DCE equal to the angle CDE, the point E determined by the intersection of DA produced and CE, is the center of the circle.

81. Let AB, AC be the given lines and P the given point. Then if O be the center of the required circle touching AB, AC, in R, S, the line AO will bisect the given angle BAC. Let the tangent from P meet the circle in Q, and draw OQ, OS, OP, AP. Then there are given AP and the angle OAP. Also since OQP is a right angle, we have $OP^2 - OQ^2 = OP^2 - OS^2 = PQ^2$ a given magnitude. Moreover the right-angled triangle AOS is given in species, or OS to OA is a given ratio. Whence in the triangle AOP there is given, the angle AOP, the side AP, and the excess of OP^2 above the square of a line having a given ratio to OA, to determine OA. Whence the construction is obvious.

82. Let the two given lines AB, BD meet in B, and let C be the center of the given circle, and let the required circle touch the line AB, and have its center in BD. Draw CFE perpendicular to HB intersecting the circumference of the given circle in F, and produce CE, making EF equal to the radius CF. Through G draw GK parallel to AB, and meeting DB in K. Join CK, and through B, draw BL parallel to KC, meeting the circumference of the circle whose center is C in L, join CL and produce CL to meet BD in O. Then O is the center of the circle required. Draw OM perpendicular to AB, and produce EC to meet BD in N. Then by the similar triangles, OL may be proved equal to OM.

83. (1) In every right-angled triangle when its three sides are in Arithmetical progression, they may be shewn to be as the numbers 5, 4, 3. On the given line AC describe a triangle having its sides AC, AD, DC in this proportion, bisect the angles at A, C by AE, CE meeting in E, and through E draw EF, EG parallel to AD, DC meeting in F and G.

(2) Let AC be the sum of the sides of the triangle, fig Euc vi 13. Upon AC describe a triangle ADC whose sides shall be in continued proportion. Bisect the angles at A and C by two lines meeting in E. From E draw EF, EG parallel to DA, DC respectively.

84. Describe a circle with any radius, and draw within it the straight line MN cutting off a segment containing an angle equal to the given angle, Euc III 34. Divide MN in the given ratio in P, and at P draw PA perpendicular to MN and meeting the circumference in A. Join

AM, AN, and on AP or AP produced, take AD equal to the given perpendicular, and through D draw BC parallel to MN meeting AM, AN, or these lines produced Then ABC shall be the triangle required

85. Let PAQ be the given angle, bisect the angle A by AB, in AB find D the center of the inscribed circle, and draw DC perpendicular to AP. In DB take DE such that the rectangle DE, DC is equal to the given rectangle. Describe a circle on DE as diameter meeting AP in F, G, and AQ in F', G'. Join FG', and AFG' will be the triangle Draw DH perpendicular to FG' and join G'D'. By Euc vi. C, the rectangle FD, DG' is equal to the rectangle ED, DK or CD, DE.

86 On any base BC describe a segment of a circle BAC containing an angle equal to the given angle. From D the middle point of BC draw DA to make the given angle ADC with the base. Produce AD to E so that AE is equal to the given bisecting line, and through E draw FG parallel to BC. Join AB, AC and produce them to meet FG in F and G

87. Employ Theorem 70, p. 310, and the construction becomes obvious.

88. Let AB be the given base, ACB the segment containing the vertical angle; draw the diameter AB of the circle, and divide it in E, in the given ratio, on AE as a diameter, describe a circle AFE, and with center B and a radius equal to the given line, describe a circle cutting AFE in F Then AF being drawn and produced to meet the circumscribing circle in C, and CB being joined, ABC is the triangle required. For AF is to FC in the given ratio.

89. The line CD is not necessarily parallel to AB Divide the base AB in C, so that AC is to CB in the ratio of the sides of the triangle.

Then if a point E in CD can be determined such that when AE, CE, EB, are joined, the angle AEB is bisected by CE, the problem is solved

90 Let ABC be any triangle having the base BC On the same base describe an isosceles triangle DBC equal to the given triangle Bisect BC in E, and join DE, also upon BC describe an equilateral triangle On FD, FB, take EG to EH as EF to FB, also take EK equal to EH and join GH, GK; then GHK is an equilateral triangle equal to the triangle ABC

91. Let ABC be the required triangle, BC the hypotenuse, and FHKG the inscribed square the side HK being on BC Then BC may be proved to be divided in H and K, so that HK is a mean proportional between BH and KC.

92 Let ABC be the given triangle On BC take BD equal to one of the given lines, through A draw AE parallel to BC. From B draw BE to meet AE in E, and such that BE is a fourth proportional to BC, BD, and the other given line Join EC, produce BE to F, making BF equal to the other given line, and join FD then FBD is the triangle required.

93 By means of Euc. vi C, the ratio of the diagonals AC to BD may be found to be as AB AD + BC . CD to AB BE + AD . DC. figure, Euc vi D

94. This property follows directly from Euc vi C.

95. Let ABC be any triangle, and DEF the given triangle to which the inscribed triangle is required to be similar Draw any line de terminated by AB, AC, and on de towards AC describe the triangle def similar to DEF, join Bf, and produce it to meet AC in F' Through F' draw F'D' parallel to fd, F'E' parallel to fe, and join D'E', then the triangle D'E'F' is similar to DEF.

96. The square inscribed in a right-angled triangle which has one of

its sides coinciding with the hypotenuse, may be shewn to be less than that which has two of its sides coinciding with the base and perpendicular

97. Let BCDE be the square on the side BC of the isosceles triangle ABC. Then by Euc. vi. 2, FG is proved parallel to ED or BC.

98. Let AB be the base of the segment ABD, fig. Euc. iii. 30. Bisect AB in C, take any point E in AC and make CF equal to CE upon EF describe a square EFGH: from C draw CG and produce it to meet the arc of the segment in K.

99. Take two points on the radii equidistant from the center, and on the line joining these points, describe a square, the lines drawn from the center through the opposite angles of the square to meet the circular arc, will determine two points of the square inscribed in the sector.

100. Let ABCDE be the given pentagon. On AB, AE take equal distances AF, AG, join FG, and on FG describe a square FGKH. Join AH and produce it to meet a side of the pentagon in L. Draw LM parallel to FH meeting AE in M. Then LM is a side of the inscribed square.

101. Let ABC be the given triangle. Draw AD making with the base BC an angle equal to one of the given angles of the parallelogram. Draw AE parallel to BC and take AD to AE in the given ratio of the sides. Join BE cutting AC in F.

102. The locus of the intersections of the diagonals of all the rectangles inscribed in a scalene triangle, is a straight line drawn from the bisection of the base to the bisection of the shorter side of the triangle.

103. This parallelogram may be proved to be a square.

104. Analysis. Let ABCD be the given rectangle, and EFGH that to be constructed. Then the diagonals of EFGH are equal and bisect each other in P the center of the given rectangle. About EPF describe a circle meeting BD in K, and join KE, KF. Then since the rectangle EFGH is given in species, the angle EPF formed by its diagonals is given: and hence also the opposite angle EKF of the inscribed quadrilateral PEKF is given. Also since KP bisects that angle, the angle PKE is given, and its supplement BKE is given. And in the same way KF is parallel to another given line; and hence EF is parallel to a third given line. Again, the angle EPF of the isosceles triangle EPF is given, and hence the quadrilateral EPFK is given in species.

105. In the figure Euc. iii. 30; from C draw CE, CF making with CD, the angles DCE, DCF each equal to the angle CDA or CDB, and meeting the arc ADB in E and F. Join EF, the segment of the circle described upon EF and which passes through C, will be similar to ADB.

106. The square inscribed in the circle may be shewn to be equal to twice the square on the radius, and five times the square inscribed in the semicircle to four times the square on the radius.

107. The three triangles formed by three sides of the square with segments of the sides of the given triangle, may be proved to be similar. Whence by Euc. vi. 4, the truth of the property.

108. By constructing the figure, it may be shewn that twice the square inscribed in the quadrant is equal to the square on the radius, and that five times the square inscribed in the semicircle is equal to four times the square on the radius. Whence it follows that, &c.

109. By Euc. i. 47, and Euc. vi. 4, it may be shewn, that four times the square on the radius is equal to fifteen times the square of one on the equal sides of the triangle.

110. Constructing the figure, the right-angled triangles SCT, ACB

may be proved to have a certain ratio, and the triangles ACB, CPM in the same way, may be proved to have the same ratio

111. Let BA, AC be the bounding radii, and D a point in the arc of a quadrant. Bisect BAC by AE, and draw through D, the line HDGP perpendicular to AE at G, and meeting AB, AC, produced in H, P. From H draw HM to touch the circle of which BC is a quadrantal arc, produce AH, making HL equal to HM, also on HA, take HK equal to HM. Then K, L, are the points of contact of two circles through D which touch the bounding radii, AB, AC

Join DA. Then, since BAC is a right angle, AK is equal to the radius of the circle which touches BA, BC in K, K', and similarly, AL is the radius of the circle which touches them in L, L'. Also, HAP being an isosceles triangle, and AD drawn to the base, AD^2 is shewn to be equal to AK . KL. Euc III 36, II 5, Cor

112. Let E, F, G be the centers of the circles inscribed in the triangles ABC, ADB, ACD. Draw EH, FK, GL perpendiculars on BC, BA, AC respectively, and join CE, EB, BF, FA, CG, GA. Then the relation between R, r, r', or EH, FK, GL may be found from the similar triangles, and the property of right-angled triangles.

113. The two hexagons consist each of six equilateral triangles, and the ratio of the hexagons is the same as the ratio of their equilateral triangles.

114. The area of the inscribed equilateral triangle may be proved to be equal to half of the inscribed hexagon, and the circumscribed triangle equal to four times the inscribed triangle

115. The pentagons are similar figures, and can be divided into the same number of similar triangles. Euc VI 19.

116. Let the sides AB, BC, CA of the equilateral triangle ABC touch the circle in the points D, E, F, respectively Draw AE cutting the circumference in G, and take O the center of the circle and draw GD draw also HGK touching the circle in G. The property may then be shewn by the similar triangles AHG, AOD.

INDEX

TO THE
PROBLEMS AND THEOREMS
IN THE
GEOMETRICAL EXERCISES.

ABBREVIATIONS.

Senate House Examination for Degrees S H
Smith's Mathematical Prizes S P
Bell's University Scholarships B. S.
St. Peter's College Pet
Clare College Cla
Pembroke College Pem
Gonville and Caius College Cai.
Trinity Hall T H
Corpus Christi College C. C
King's College Ki
Queen's College Qu

St Catharine's College Cath.
Jesus College Jes
Christ's College Chr
St John's College Joh
Magdalene College Mag
Trinity College Trin
Emmanuel College Emm
Sidney Sussex College Sid.
Downing College Down

In the years the centuries are omitted, and the places are supplied by a comma prefixed, thus ,45 means 1845.

EXERCISES ON BOOK I., p. 69, &c

1 Emm ,22 ,35. ,46 Sid ,30. Trin ,37
2 Trin ,40. Cai ,37 Chr. ,58
3 Trin ,32. ,37 ,50. T H. ,52. Joh ,54. S H ,54
4 Sid ,30 ,43 Jes ,50 ,58 Qu ,31 Trin ,40 Cla ,47 Emm ,56.
5 Emm ,21 Qu ,23 ,40 ,42 Trin ,26 ,27 ,29 C C ,30 ,55 Pem ,32, ,38
6 S.H. ,17. Trin ,24 ,37. Qu ,25. Emm ,27 ,48 Cath. ,29. ,48. Pem ,39 ,47 Sid ,40. Chr. ,45 Cla. ,56
7 S. H ,19. Trin ,29. Qu. ,35. Pem ,44 Jes ,49. B S. ,55.
8 Qu ,26. 28 S H ,49. ,50 Pet. ,56 Emm ,30 C C ,57. Cai ,55
9 Mag ,38 Joh. ,58.
10 Emm. ,34.
11 Cai ,40 Joh ,50.
12 S H. ,40. ,51.
13 Cath. ,51. S H ,50
14
15 Pet ,57
16 Cath. ,22. ,33. Trin ,37
17 Cai 57.
18 Chr ,56.
19 Emm. ,56.
20 T H ,51.
21 Jes ,58
22 S H ,50
23 Qu. ,19 T H ,51 Emm ,51. Pem ,57
24 Jes ,58
25 S H. ,44. Cla. ,55
26 Cai ,41.
27 Chr. ,26. ,41. ,52. Jes ,52. Joh. ,51. Pet. ,38 Trin ,39 ,50 Mag ,51.
28 S. H ,58.
29 C C ,53 S H. ,59.
30 C. C ,53 Qu ,54 Chr ,56.
31 Trin. ,31.
32 S. H ,36. ,48 Mag ,47 Chr ,54.
33 Emm ,25
34 Joh ,49. Qu. ,25
35 Chr. ,28. Pem ,42. Jes. ,51.
36 Trin 26. Sid ,43. C C ,57.
37 Pem ,29. B S ,48. Qu. ,52.
38 Qu ,50
39 Qu ,34 Cath ,35. Emm. ,35. Sid ,38. B S. ,40. Trin. ,27.
40 Trin ,34
41 S. H ,55.

INDEX. 357

42 S H. ,04. C. C. ,23. Chr ,29. ,50. Cath ,35. Jes ,52. Pet. ,36. Qu. ,39. Trin ,37. ,49. Cai. ,40. Pem. ,48.
43 Trin. ,54. Emm. ,54.
44 Trin ,58.
45 Cai. ,55
46 Pet ,58.
47 Chr. ,55.
48 Cai. ,49.
49 Jes. ,54.
50 S. H. ,53.
51 Trin. ,39. ,51 Pem. ,51.
52 Trin ,43.
53 Joh. ,26 Pem ,47. Chr. ,52 ,53.
54 Cai ,46. Qu. ,48
55 Cai ,31. Joh. ,30
56
57 Jes ,52. Cai. ,56.
58 Jes. ,55.
59 Pet ,51
60 Chr ,39.
61 Pet ,36.
62 Trin. ,52. ,54. T. H. ,52.
63 Pet. ,51
64 Trin ,51.
65 Jes. ,54.
66 Pet. ,51.
67 S H. ,48.
68
69 T H. ,54.
70 Trin. ,40.
71
72 Cai ,33. Qu. ,33.
73 Trin. ,49.
74 Qu ,31. Chr. ,56 Sid. ,36. Pet. ,53.
75 Qu. ,49
76 Qu ,24.
77 Cla. ,51.
78 Qu ,32. Jes. ,36. S. II ,49. ,50
79 S H. ,49 Mag. ,52.
80 Qu ,37.
81 Trin. ,48.
82 Chr. ,58.
83 Chr. ,52.
84 Trin. ,52.
85 Cath. ,49.

86 Cla. ,57.
87 Pet. ,46
88 C. C. ,50 Cai ,53
89 Mag ,51. ,58.
90 Jes. ,51.
91 Cath ,49. S. H. ,54.
92 Jes ,55.
93 Cai. ,46.
94 Jes. ,49.
95 Chr. ,43.
96 Joh ,31.
97 Cai ,36. Cath. ,55.
98 Emm. ,30. Cath. ,57.
99 Trin ,59.
100 Pet. ,51.
101 Qu ,29 ,35. ,37. B S. ,39
102
103 Mag. ,52.
104 Chr. ,47. Cla. ,48.
105 Pet. ,51.
106 Sid. ,45 Chr. ,47. Emm ,47.
107 S H. ,52.
108 Emm. ,57.
109 S H ,04. Cai. ,34 Emm ,59
110 Qu. ,25 Trin ,25 ,38. Pet ,39. Jes. ,52 Pem ,42
111 S H. ,03. ,18. Trin ,25. ,44. Cla. ,51. ,36.
112 Qu. ,29. ,37. ,26. Trin ,27 ,33 ,36. ,40. ,49. ,50. Chr. ,44 Pem ,45. Cath. ,58 Emm ,54 Jes ,52. S H ,50 C. C. ,58
113 Emm. ,32.
114 Qu ,19. ,37. Emm ,25 ,53. Mag. ,29. ,32. Cai. ,34. Trin. ,37 ,38 Pet. ,41 ,52
115 S H. ,18
116 Qu. ,39 Mag ,54 S. H ,59.
117 Trin. ,29.
118 Emm. ,22. C. C ,58.
119 Pet. ,15.
120 S. H. ,35. ,48. Joh. ,87.

121 Pet. ,38. Chr. ,39.
122 S H. ,53.
123 Joh ,58.
124 C. C. ,46.
125 Pem. ,46.
126 S. H ,54.
127 Emm. ,31. Chr. ,38.
128 Trin ,48 Cath. ,46.
129
130 Pem ,47
131 Cla.
132 Ki. ,18 S H. ,53. Chr. ,55. ,57.
133 Qu ,30. Chr. ,46.
134 Pet. ,58
135 Jes. ,57.
136 Mag. ,57.
137 Cai ,52
138 Trin. ,37 ,50 ,52. Joh. ,47 Emm ,52. ,53. ,56. Chr. ,50. T. H. ,52.
139 Cla ,36
140 Mag. ,49.
141 Cla. ,36.
142 Joh. ,58. Chr ,58.
143 Trin. ,53. ,54
144 Joh. ,16 Qu. ,30. Pem. ,33. ,49 Jes. ,46 Trin. ,47. ,58. C C ,58.
145 Pet ,27
146 S. H. ,36.
147 Chr. ,54
148 Cla ,56.
149 Jes. ,20. Qu. ,32. ,48. Cath. ,35. S H ,59
150 Trin. ,40
151 Pet. ,32, ,35.
152 Pet ,49.
153 S H. ,55.
154 Jes ,53.
155 Chr. ,56.
156 T H ,52.
157 Joh. ,20 Emm. ,26.
158 Sid ,46. Mag. ,58.
159 Cai ,37.
160 Emm. ,32 Qu. ,35. ,50 C C ,36 ,59. Mag ,59. B S ,47.
161 Trin. ,21. ,50.
162 Jes. ,35.

INDEX.

EXERCISES ON BOOK II, p. 113, &c

1 S II. ,14. ,50 Joh ,18 Trin. ,35. Chr. ,55
2 Joh ,17.
3 S II ,16 ,59. Trin. ,27. ,30. ,37. ,47 ,18 Mag ,31. ,43 Pet ,29. ,38. Sid ,34. Emm ,21. ,27. ,37 ,44 Cai. ,43. Qu. ,37. T. H ,55
4 Emm ,34 Pem ,46 Mag ,51.
5 S II. ,03 Joh ,18. Qu ,21. Trin. ,37 Sid. ,42. Chr. ,45. ,46. ,48.
6 Pet. ,52.
7 Pet ,58.
8 Jes ,54.
9 S H ,50.
10 Cai ,58.
11 Jes. ,53.
12 Pet. ,25.
13 Chr ,40.
14 Trin ,42.
15 Pet ,37.
16 T. H. ,40. ,54.
17 Qu. ,37.
18 S H ,38.

19 Chr. ,48 ,51. Jes. ,18. Sid. ,49 Pet ,55. Pem ,58.
20 Emm. ,56
21
22 Qu. ,50
23 Qu. ,24.
24 Chr. ,49.
25 S H ,10. ,04 Trin ,29.
26 Pet ,43.
27 Chr ,49.
28 Qu. ,55.
29 Qu ,57.
30 Qu ,51.
31 Mag ,57.
32 Cai. ,59.
33 Chr. ,57.
34 Cai. ,44
35 Joh ,44.
36 Trin ,19. Cai ,57.
37 Joh ,13 Emm ,25 ,36 Trin ,32 Mag. ,33 ,40 Pet ,52. S H. ,53.
38 Joh. ,21 S. H. ,50 Pet ,54.
39 Joh ,25.
40 Cai ,42.
41 S H ,53.
42 T. H ,58

43 Joh. ,26. Jes. ,37. Mag ,12
44 Pet. ,44
45 Emm. ,23. ,26 ,28 ,43 ,51 Trin ,27. ,41 ,49 ,50. Pet. ,30 Mag ,53 ,43. ,46 ,52 B S ,38. C C. ,51. Chr. ,41. ,47. ,50
46 Emm ,28. Sid. ,33. C C ,39
47 Joh ,19 Qu ,29. ,30. ,48.
48 Chr ,30. Emm ,36. S. H. ,15 Cath. ,52.
49 S H ,07. T H. ,44. Pem ,52 Joh. ,41. Trin ,53 Emm. ,52 S. H. ,59.
50 Emm ,28. ,46. Trin. ,32. Pem. ,47.
51 Chr ,51
52 Pet ,53.
53 Cai. ,28.
54
55
56
57 Jes ,58.
58 S H ,59.

EXERCISES ON BOOK III, p 160, &c

1 Chr. ,28. S. H ,36. ,59 Cai ,44.
2 Qu ,23. T. H. ,54. Mag ,53.
3 Trin ,27.
4 Mag ,53.
5 S H ,04 Sid ,41.
6 Trin ,19 ,23. Qu ,21 ,22 Pem ,30. ,39. Sid. ,36 Pet. ,31. Emm ,34. ,42. ,44. T. H. ,54
7 Emm. ,22. Pem. ,36. Joh. ,57 S. H. ,53
8 Pet. ,29. Cla ,46.
9 Qu. ,56.

10 Mag ,46
11 Mag ,47
12 S H ,43
13 S H. ,18.
14 Cath. ,53.
15
16
17 Joh. ,57
18 Trin ,19. Sid. ,33. Cai ,34 Emm ,34 Qu. ,36 S. H ,53 Chr. ,56 Joh ,57 ,58.
19 Emm. ,24.
20 C C. ,42.
21 Joh ,21
22 Trin ,52. T. H. ,58.

23 Joh. ,17
24 Joh ,21.
25 Chr. ,27.
26 S H ,18.
27 Pet ,47.
28 S H ,49.
29 Trin. ,39.
30 Emm. ,54.
31 S H ,53.
32 S H ,59.
33 Qu ,57
34 Pet ,55.
35 Trin ,30 ,39. C C. ,35. ,45. Emm. ,37. Chr ,39. Pem. ,40.
36 Sid ,35
37 Joh. ,30.

INDEX. 350

38 Joh. ,20. Emm. ,26.
39 Cath. ,31.
40 Qu ,36.
41 Joh. ,28. Qu. ,35.
42 Emm ,56.
43 Trin. ,57.
44
45 Qu. ,58.
46 Pem. ,45.
47 S H. ,14. Qu. ,20 ,32 Joh. ,25. Emm ,32 Chr ,45. Cai. ,44.
48 Pet ,56.
49 Trin. ,57.
50 Trin ,34.
51 Cai ,32. ,41.
52 Emm ,21. Pem. ,32. Cla. ,36. Cai. ,45
53 S H. ,53.
54 Cla ,56
55 S H ,55.
56 Cla. ,56.
57 Emm. ,57.
58 Trin. ,43.
59
60 Trin. ,11.
61 Qu ,36.
62 Cai ,44.
63 Jes. ,33
64 Joh. ,22.
65 S H. ,29.
66 Joh. ,42. Chr. ,53
67 S H ,25
68 Cai ,43 Emm. ,44
69 Joh ,14. Chr. ,26. C C ,55.
70 Trin. ,29. Sid. ,45 S H. ,50.
71 Jes. ,58.
72 Chr ,48. Sid. ,52.
73 Trin. ,39
74 S H ,36 Jes ,57
75 S H. ,02. Pem. ,32. T H ,44.
76 Trin. ,15.
77 S H. ,04. 59.
78 Pet 39 Emm ,56.
79 Joh ,30. Cai. ,36. Cla. ,46
80 Trin ,35.
81 S. H. ,59.
82 Kl ,50.

83 S H. ,03. Qu. ,22. Emm. ,27. Sid. ,30 Cath ,30. ,35. Mag ,34. ,37. ,45. B S ,39 ,43. C. C. ,57.
84 Pet ,37.
85 Qu. ,33.
86 Joh. ,47.
87 Cai. ,48.
88
89 Joh ,19. Qu. ,26.
90 S H ,58
91 Qu ,52.
92 Qu. ,39. Pem. ,43
93 Joh. ,30.
94 Trin. ,24.
95 Qu ,54
96 Joh. ,17.
97 Sid ,35 Pem. ,42
98 Qu ,58.
99 Cai ,31.
100 S H ,48 Qu ,57.
101 S H ,50. Qu ,54. Pem. ,50.
102 Cai ,47
103 Cai ,40.
104 Emm. ,56. ,57
105 T. H. ,58
106 Pet ,52
107 Cai. ,39 Jes ,26 C C ,38.
108 Pet ,39 Pem. ,45.
109 Chr ,40.
110 Trin ,29. ,32. ,38 S H. ,08. Pet ,19 ,20. ,21. Qu. ,20 ,28 Mag ,30. B S ,39 Chr. ,51.
111 S H ,19
112 Joh ,31
113 Emm ,28
114 Joh ,25
115 S. H. ,20 Trin ,22 ,25 Mag ,37. Qu ,39
116 S H. ,03.
117 Trin. ,20.
118 Jes ,54.
119 Cai. ,51.
120 Cai. ,37.
121 Cai. ,42.
122 Cai. ,36
123 Pet. ,48. Joh. ,58.

124 Qu. ,54.
125 Pet. ,52.
126 Trin. ,42.
127
128 S H ,04 Joh. ,16 Qu. ,20 ,55 ,29 Trin. ,22. ,28 Pet. ,31. B. S. ,30. ,34.
129 Pet ,43.
130 Trin ,33.
131 Pem ,44.
132 Trin ,20.
133 Sid ,35
134 T H. ,58
135 Qu ,49.
136 Qu. ,54.
137 Joh. ,58.
138 Emm ,47.
139 Jes. ,19
140 Joh. ,41 ,42. ,49.
141 Qu ,33.
142 Joh ,20.
143 Joh ,25. T H. ,55.
144 T. H ,58.
145 S. H. ,48.
146 Cath ,58.
147 T. H ,54.
148 Cla.
149
150 Jes ,56.
151 Mag. ,19.
152 Joh. ,18 ,19 Qu. ,26. ,39 Mag ,29. Emm ,30. Pem. ,44
153 Mag ,35
154 Cath ,30.
155 Joh ,31
156 Trin ,26 Pem ,34.
157 C C ,46.
158 Joh. ,35
159 Trin. ,38. Joh ,19. Chr ,39 Jes ,43. S H ,42. T H. ,53
160 Jes ,38 C. C. ,38.
161 Jes. ,44
162 C C. ,33
163 Pet ,32
164 C. C ,25 B. S ,28. Mag ,45
165 Cath ,30.
166 Joh ,36.
167 C. C. ,39.

360   INDEX.

EXERCISES ON BOOK IV., p. 196, &c.

1 S. H. ,08. ,12 Chr. ,33 Pet. ,34. ,38. Trin. ,19.
2 Qu ,20. Emm. ,27 Cath ,34 Trin ,44. Jes ,46 Ki. ,37. Joh. ,57.
3 Qu ,20. ,30 ,34. Trin ,29. Emm. ,30. C C. ,35 B S ,36. Pem ,40. ,48. ,52. Jes ,52.
4 Joh. ,16 Pet ,36.
5 Trin ,31.
6 Emm ,24 Qu. ,32.
7 Trin. ,37. Jes. ,47.
8
9 Trin ,23 Sid. ,39. ,47 Qu ,41. C. C ,45.
10 Chr. ,27.
11 S H. ,16 Qu ,20. ,27. C. C ,28. Joh. ,39
12 Joh. ,29.
13 S H. ,13 Trin. ,22.
14 S H ,38.
15 Chr. ,45.
16 Cai. ,38.
17 Cai ,35.
18 Joh ,23
19 Trin ,21. Chr. ,30 ,34.
20 Trin. ,44. ,48.
21 Cai ,42
22 Cai ,32
23 Mag. ,35.
24 Joh. ,22.
25 Trin ,30. S H. ,36.
26 Pem. ,29. C C. ,41
27 Pem ,31.
28 Joh ,42
29 Jes ,33.
30 Trin ,41.
31 Qu ,20.
32 Joh ,30.
33 Joh ,31.
34 Pem ,29 ,35
35 S H ,13. Qu. ,19. Emm. ,21 ,33. B S ,26 Cai. ,35 Pem. ,36.
36 Jes ,31.
37 Trin ,40.
38 Joh. ,18.
39 Joh ,17. Trin. ,36
40 Pet. ,25.
41 Qu ,31.
42 Pet ,43
43 Joh. ,25
44 Trin ,29.
45 Cai. ,37.
46 Trin ,26. Qu. ,32. Chr ,40 Pem ,49.
47 Trin ,23 Emm. ,28. ,32 ,36.
48 Emm. ,21. Trin. ,36. Pem. ,42.
49 Chr. ,26. ,42
50 Emm. ,21 ,25 ,40 ,45 Chr ,39. Pet. ,35 B S ,41.
51 Cai. ,38. Jes ,49.
52 Trin ,21.
53 Emm ,24.
54 Joh. ,18. Jes. ,49.
55 Pet. ,25
56 Trin. ,37.
57 Trin. ,23. Qu. ,37.
58 Qu ,21 ,26. ,36.
59
60 Emm ,25 Mag. ,42.
61 Qu. ,26.
62 Cai ,33 B S ,40.
63 Joh ,14. ,16 ,37. S. H. ,41
64 Sid ,29. Qu ,43.
65 Trin ,31.
66 C. C. ,38
67 Chr. ,32.
68 C. C. ,44
69 Qu ,44.
70 Cath. ,30. Mag ,33. ,37
71 Cai. ,40.
72 Sid. ,38. Trin. ,39.
73 Cu. ,41.
74 Trin ,33.
75 C C. ,24.
76 Trin. ,22 B. S. ,27
77 Pem. ,36.
78 Trin ,36
79 Jes ,19. Trin ,22. ,25 ,27. Qu. ,35. Pem ,37 Mag ,45.
80 Qu ,31. ,40. Trin. ,12
81 Jes ,38.
82 Trin ,27. Mag. ,43.
83 Cai ,38.
84 Trin ,19.
85 Trin ,24.
86 Joh. ,25
87 S H. ,08. Trin. ,24. ,30. Qu. ,31. ,35. Cai ,35

EXERCISES ON BOOK VI., p 302, &c.

1 Qu ,38. Jes ,46
2 C C. ,31
3 Jes ,19 Trin ,32 ,44.
4 Qu. ,23 Sid. ,34. C C ,40
5 Ki. ,45.
6 Pet. ,38
7 Cath ,51.
8 S H ,50
9 Pem ,46 T. H ,46.
10 Joh ,23.
11 Cath. ,30. Emm. ,31. Sid. ,44
12 Trin ,23 Cai. ,35 Mag ,37.
13 Trin ,30 S H. ,04. Mag ,44.
14 Qu ,20 ,26 ,32.
15 Joh. ,26.
16 Cai ,31
17 Trin —
18 Qu ,38 Chr. ,43. Trin. ,33. ,44.
19 Emm ,23. ,30. B S. ,29
20 Chr. ,36

21 Joh. ,20.
22 Joh. ,15.
23 Joh. ,14. Trin. ,27. ,28. ,32. ,34. ,41. ,44. Cath. ,34. Chr. ,44.
24 Joh. ,19.
25 Qu. ,30. C. C. ,40.
26 Joh. ,28.
27 Qu. ,38.
28 Qu. ,34.
29 Qu. ,24.
30 Pem. ,33.
31 Trin. ,11. ,28. ,43. Jes. ,19. Qu. ,21. ,23. ,26. C. C. ,26. Pem. ,32. ,34. ,43. Cai. ,33. Emm. ,21.
32 Joh. ,26.
33 Qu. ,48.
34 Pet. ,28. ,35.
35 Joh. ,19.
36 Cai. ,36.
37 Joh. ,26.
38 Joh. ,15. C. C. ,37.
39 Trin. ,25.
40 Joh. ,17.
41 Joh. ,42.
42 Emm. ,47.
43 Pet. ,25.
44 Trin. ,38.
45 Joh. ,21.
46 Pet. ,32.
47 Joh. ,20.
48 Joh. ,14.
49 Qu. ,36.
50 Qu. ,25.
51 Pet. ,54.
52 Cai. ,44.
53 Joh. ,15.

54 Chr. ,41.
55 S. H. ,50.
56 Mag. ,41.
57 Pet. ,25.
58 Joh. ,17.
59 Qu. ,22.
60 Qu. ,21.
61 Trin. ,26.
62 Pet. ,35.
63 Joh. ,19.
64 Sid. ,30. Emm. ,49.
65 Pem. ,30. S. P. ,42.
66 Qu. ,35. ,36. Pem. ,37.
67 Trin. ,21.
68 Joh. ,35.
69 Pet. ,26.
70 S. H. ,18. Qu. ,20.
71 Joh. ,18. Cath. ,31.
72 Cai. ,45.
73 Trin. ,35.
74 Pem. ,31. ,43. Qu. ,19. ,25. ,43. Trin. ,22. ,37. Cai. ,43. Mag. ,32.
75 Chr. ,48.
76 S. H. ,39. Pem. ,43.
77 Qu. ,41.
78 Trin. ,22. Qu. ,39. Chr. ,42.
79 Qu. ,22. ,38. Trin. ,42. ,44.
80 Qu. ,29. ,35. ,41. S. P. ,43.
81 Qu. ,40.
82 Qu. ,23. ,36. ,38.
83 Joh. ,13. Trin. ,20. Emm. ,24. Chr. ,37. ,45. Qu. ,36. ,22. ,44.

84 Trin. ,44.
85 Trin. ,32.
86 Qu. ,37.
87 Joh. ,29. Qu. ,43.
88 Joh. ,18.
89 Qu. ,21.
90 Trin. ,36.
91 S. H. ,25.
92 Pet. ,33.
93 Joh. ,19.
94 Joh. ,22. Emm. ,26.
95 Pem. ,34. C. C. ,30.
96 Joh. ,38.
97 Cath. ,31.
98 Emm. ,46.
99 Joh. ,13. ,21. Trin. ,29. ,34. Qu. ,43. ,38.
100 C. C. ,28. Pem. ,42.
101 C. C. ,35. S. H. ,11. Pem. ,46. T.H. ,46.
102 Qu. ,41. ,42.
103 S. H. ,09. B. S. ,30. ,31.
104 S. H. ,36.
105 Sid. ,29.
106 Pet. ,36.
107 Cai. ,39.
108 Trin. ,11. ,20. ,32. ,33. Chr. ,35.
109 Pet. ,37.
110 Cai. ,31.
111 Joh. ,31. Qu. ,44.
112 C. C. ,30.
113 Joh. ,20.
114 Emm. ,37.
115 Trin. ,20.
116 Cath. ,48.

THE END.

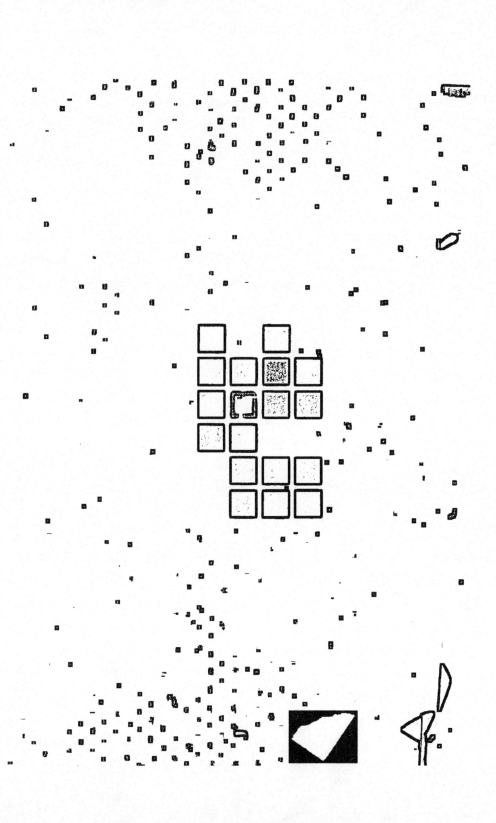